Wilkie C

Andrew Lycett has a degree in history from Oxford University. After several years as a foreign correspondent, he has been a biographer since the early 1990s. His books include highly praised lives of Ian Fleming, Dylan Thomas, Rudyard Kipling and Sir Arthur Conan Doyle. He is a fellow of the Royal Society of Literature and the Royal Geographical Society. He lives in north London.

ALSO BY ANDREW LYCETT

'Clean outlines, crystal clear English, and a clear-eyed picture of his subject, cap-a-pie. [Lycett's] a terrific narrator . . . the Hemingway of biographers . . . Wilkie's early life is told more fully than any other account I've read . . . This is a fine, and pre-eminently useful, biography of the most elusive character in Victorian literature.'

John Sutherland, *Spectator*

'This splendid biography of a 19th-century writer . . . brings to life quite brilliantly this extraordinary man: a career measured by spectacular highs and terrible disappointment and a complicated love life that would not look out of place in a TV soap opera today.'

Andy Plaice, *Daily Express*

'Sensible, thoughtful and never less than scrupulous, Lycett is just the right biographer to assess whether such potentially sensational material should affect our interpretation of Collins's work . . . The connection between Collins's own jaundiced view of marriage and his literary plottings is shrewdly analysed by Lycett in a book that helps to rehabilitate a still under-rated author.'

Miranda Seymour, *Sunday Times*

'Here is the author of *The Moonstone* as a character from one of his "sensation" novels . . . except that this is all true.'

Michael Prodger, *New Statesman*

'[An] admirable biography . . . Lycett is at his best on Collins as a man of his age . . . The friendship between Dickens and Collins . . . is one of the highlights . . . It also gives some wonderful "I never knew that" moments . . . This biography does exactly what a good biography should: returns us to the work.'

Stuart Kelly, *Scotland on Sunday*

'Andrew Lycett, a seasoned and thorough biographer with several other literary lives under his belt . . . is completely at home in Wilkie's world and the topography of mid-Victorian London. He brings out the milieu in which Wilkie moved with practised ease . . . Lycett has sleuthed away into his subject's hidden life with an industry worthy of Collins himself. He can have left few stones unturned in exposing Wilkie's secrets and the result is the most complete portrait that we have of a man increasingly respected as the near equal of his famous friend.'

Nigel Jones, *History Today*

'As delicate as he is thorough, Lycett peels away the layers of deception with which Collins protected himself and shows us the engagingly vulnerable figure beneath.'

John Preston, *Evening Standard*

'[Lycett] is excellent on Collins's friendship with Dickens, which he presents, convincingly, as much more of a relationship of equals than Dickens biographers allow.'

Judith Flanders, *The Times*

'It is hard to fault this generous and scrupulously researched biography.'

Robert Douglas-Fairhurst, *Daily Telegraph*

Wilkie Collins

A Life of Sensation

ANDREW LYCETT

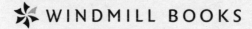 WINDMILL BOOKS

Published by Windmill Books 2014

2 4 6 8 10 9 7 5 3 1

Copyright © Andrew Lycett 2013

Andrew Lycett has asserted his right under the Copyright, Designs and
Patents Act, 1988, to be identified as the author of this work.

First published in Great Britain in 2013 by Hutchinson

Windmill Books
The Random House Group Limited
20 Vauxhall Bridge Road, London SW1V 2SA

Addresses for companies within The Random House Group Limited
can be found at: www.randomhouse.co.uk/offices.htm

The Random House Group Limited Reg. No. 954009

www.randomhouse.co.uk

A CIP catalogue record for this book
is available from the British Library

ISBN 9780099557340

The Random House Group Limited supports the Forest Stewardship
Council® (FSC®), the leading international forest-certification organisation.
Our books carrying the FSC label are printed on FSC®-certified paper.
FSC is the only forest-certification scheme supported by the
leading environmental organisations, including Greenpeace.
Our paper procurement policy can be found at:
www.randomhouse.co.uk/environment

Map by Jamie Whyte

Typeset in Janson MT by Palimpsest Book Production Limited,
Falkirk, Stirlingshire

Printed and bound by CPI Group (UK) Ltd, Croydon, CR0 4YY

To my sisters, Caroline and Charlotte

CONTENTS

LIST OF ILLUSTRATIONS

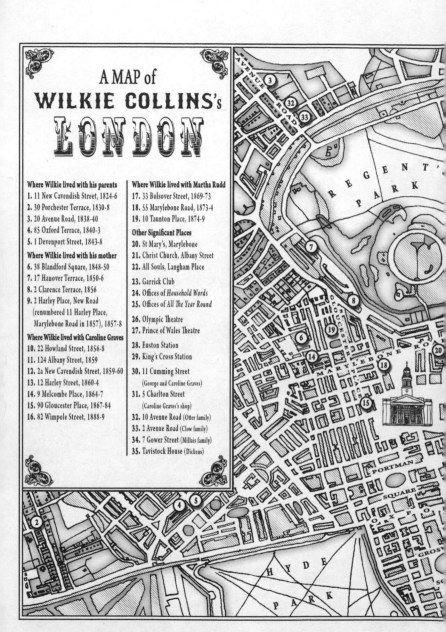

A MAP of WILKIE COLLINS's LONDON

Where Wilkie lived with his parents
1. 11 New Cavendish Street, 1824-6
2. 30 Porchester Terrace, 1830-8
3. 20 Avenue Road, 1838-40
4. 85 Oxford Terrace, 1840-3
5. 1 Devenport Street, 1843-8

Where Wilkie lived with his mother
6. 38 Blandford Square, 1848-50
7. 17 Hanover Terrace, 1850-6
8. 2 Clarence Terrace, 1856
9. 2 Harley Place, New Road
   (renumbered 11 Harley Place,
   Marylebone Road in 1857), 1857-8

Where Wilkie lived with Caroline Graves
10. 22 Howland Street, 1856-8
11. 124 Albany Street, 1859
12. 2a New Cavendish Street, 1859-60
13. 12 Harley Street, 1860-4
14. 9 Melcombe Place, 1864-7
15. 90 Gloucester Place, 1867-84
16. 82 Wimpole Street, 1888-9

Where Wilkie lived with Martha Rudd
17. 33 Bolsover Street, 1869-73
18. 55 Marylebone Road, 1873-4
19. 10 Taunton Place, 1874-9

Other Significant Places
20. St Mary's, Marylebone
21. Christ Church, Albany Street
22. All Souls, Langham Place
23. Garrick Club
24. Offices of *Household Words*
25. Offices of *All The Year Round*
26. Olympic Theatre
27. Prince of Wales Theatre
28. Euston Station
29. King's Cross Station
30. 11 Cumming Street
    (George and Caroline Graves)
31. 5 Charlton Street
    (Caroline Graves's shop)
32. 10 Avenue Road (Otter family)
33. 2 Avenue Road (Clow family)
34. 7 Gower Street (Millais family)
35. Tavistock House (Dickens)

Wilkie Collins Family Tree

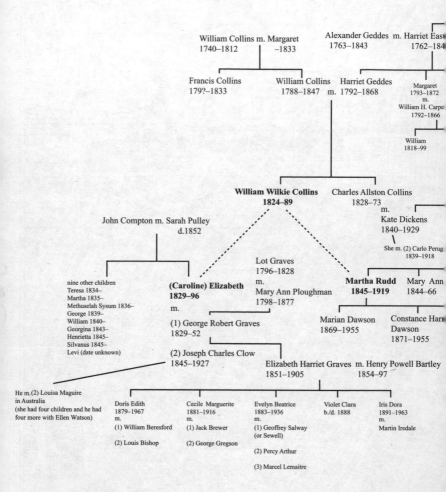

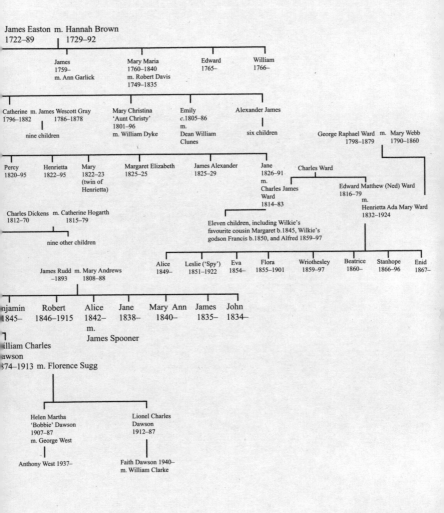

James Easton m. Hannah Brown
1722–89   1729–92

James
1759–
m. Ann Garlick

Mary Maria
1760–1840
m. Robert Davis
1749–1835

Edward
1765–

William
1766–

Catherine m. James Wescott Gray
1796–1882   1786–1878

nine children

Mary Christina
'Aunt Christy'
1801–96
m. William Dyke

Emily
c.1805–86
m.
Dean William
Clunes

Alexander James

six children

George Raphael Ward m. Mary Webb
1798–1879   1790–1860

Percy
1820–95

Henrietta
1822–95

Mary
1822–23
(twin of
Henrietta)

Margaret Elizabeth
1825–25

James Alexander
1825–29

Jane
1826–91
m.
Charles James
Ward
1814–83

Charles Ward

Edward Matthew (Ned) Ward
1816–79
m.
Henrietta Ada Mary Ward
1832–1924

Charles Dickens m. Catherine Hogarth
1812–70   1815–79

nine other children

Eleven children, including Wilkie's
favourite cousin Margaret b.1845, Wilkie's
godson Francis b.1850, and Alfred 1859–97

Alice
1849–

Leslie ('Spy')
1851–1922

Eva
1854–

Flora
1855–1901

Wriothesley
1859–97

Beatrice
1860–

Stanhope
1866–96

Enid
1867–

James Rudd m. Mary Andrews
–1893   1808–88

njamin
1845–

Robert
1846–1915

Alice
1842–
m.
James Spooner

Jane
1838–

Mary Ann
1840–

James
1835–

John
1834–

illiam Charles
awson
874–1913 m. Florence Sugg

Helen Martha
'Bobbie' Dawson
1907–87
m. George West

Lionel Charles
Dawson
1912–87

Anthony West 1937–

Faith Dawson 1940–
m. William Clarke

'Nothing in this world is hidden for ever. The gold which had laid for centuries unsuspected on the ground, reveals itself one day on the surface. Sand turns traitor, and betrays the footstep that has passed over it, water gives back to the tell-tale surface the body that has been drowned. Fire itself leaves the confession, in ashes, of the substance consumed in it. Hate breaks its prison-secrecy in the thoughts, through the doorway of the eyes; and Love finds the Judas who betrays it with a kiss. Look where we will, the inevitable law of revelation is one of the laws of nature: the lasting preservation of a secret is a miracle which the world has never yet seen.'

No Name, first scene, Chapter 4

INTRODUCTION

I N THE SPRING of 1868, Wilkie Collins was living a nightmare that could have come straight out of one of his best-selling sensation novels.

A visitor to his recently acquired five-storey house in Gloucester Place, Marylebone, would have found him propped up in bed, squinting through round spectacles as he desperately tried to dictate the latest chapter of his new book, *The Moonstone*, to the teenage girl he grandly called his amanuensis, but who was actually the daughter of one of his two mistresses.

Visible above the bedclothes would have been Wilkie's large, friendly face, framed by a bushy beard and straggly whiskers, though marred by a slight bump on the right of his forehead. He was an incurable fidget, so, unless it was very cold (and it often was, since he refused to have gas of any kind in the house), he would have been orchestrating his words with expansive gestures from his tiny, delicate hands, which, it was often observed, matched his under-sized feet – another physical quirk that marked him out from the crowd.

When he wrote, he normally kept what he called his 'stock-in-trade' beside him – a japanned box containing a well-thumbed pile of papers on which he scribbled ideas for the extraordinary plots his readers so enjoyed. Nearby in the flickering candlelight stood another vital prop – a bottle of laudanum, his palliative draught of choice when he needed to alleviate his pain, which was now excruciating.

The ostensible reason for his discomfort was gout, a long-standing affliction, which had spread from his limbs to his bloodshot grey eyes and made reading near impossible. But a host of other troubles now bore down on him and added to his malaise. His beloved mother had recently died in Kent and, to his eternal regret, he had been bedridden and unable to attend her funeral. An old friend was going through an ill-tempered divorce that promised to add to Wilkie's financial woes and expose the secrets of the rackety lives he and some of his close friends had led. At the same time, his long-term mistress, Caroline Graves, had decided she had had enough of their curious double life, which required her to hide away in Gloucester Place and share him with another woman, Martha Rudd, who lived nearby. Caroline wanted to marry someone younger, and soon.

These developments threatened not only to upset Wilkie's peace of mind but to tarnish his respectable Victorian image. Despite his reputation as a literary iconoclast, he had worked hard over the years to present himself as a bachelor clubman with impeccable bookish inclinations. Like his friend Charles Dickens, he would have been distraught if any details of his intimate personal relationships had become public knowledge.

Wilkie could do little about these concerns, at least for the time being, since he had a book to finish. As a professional who took pride in his work ethic, he had not developed a name as a sensation novelist over the past decade by missing his deadlines. Now he could only increase his intake of laudanum and focus his energies on the schedules for the monthly serialisation of his work in Dickens's magazine *All the Year Round*.

His current compromised situation was ironic, since his sensation novels were based on exposing the double standards and hypocrisy beneath the surface of Victorian society. This particular genre had emerged in recent years to satisfy a public that had tired of both the formulaic exoticism of gothic tales and the limp, aristocratic 'silver fork' novels that had flourished in the 1830s. As the number of outlets for stories expanded at a time when the harshness of the industrial world crowded in, readers craved more visceral excitement when they opened a book. Authors responded by adopting the approach of the Fat Boy in the *Pickwick Papers*, 'I wants to make your flesh creep.'

Aimed specifically to shock, sensation novels specialised in plots that exposed deep-rooted domestic or family secrets. They took their readers through the experience of uncovering illegitimacy, bigamy and matrimonial irregularity; of unearthing complex wills that authenticated some people and disinherited others; of vicariously observing apparently decent citizens engaged in criminal activity, including murder; and of delving into cases of legalistic deception and financial skulduggery.

Part of their success came from audience participation. Sensation novels encouraged their readers to get in on the act of uncovering these secrets, and to do so in that most personal of environments, the home. Henry James referred respectfully to their unravelling of 'those most mysterious of mysteries, the mysteries which are at our own doors'. A less sympathetic contemporary, Henry Mansel, commented on the excitement, or rather horror, of discovering that a recent casual acquaintance might be a monstrous Count Fosco (from Wilkie's *The Woman in White*) or the woman you found so charming, a bigamous Lady Audley (the heroine of Mary Elizabeth Braddon's *Lady Audley's Secret*).

In *The Moonstone*, Wilkie would take these themes and give them a modern twist in a fully-fledged detective novel, a category of fiction ideally suited to questing, enquiring, scientifically minded Victorians. T.S. Eliot would describe the book as 'the first and greatest English detective novel'. Though there were in fact earlier examples, it is still one of the very best, not least for Wilkie's deft mocking of his contemporaries' demands for exactitude. In this respect it was also an anti-detective novel *avant la lettre*.

One feature of such stories was the gap between appearances and reality – something that Wilkie highlighted in his recurring references to the injustices perpetrated against women as a result of the unthinking hypocrisy of laws and conventions, particularly relating to marriage. The irony was that in 1868 the author was himself living secretly with two women, neither of whom was his wife. His duplicity involved no great crime, but it hinted at a fascinating, wilfully muddied story about the interplay between his own complex domestic arrangements, the racy, topical books he wrote, and the cant-ridden world he inhabited. It was definitely something worth exploring. It was time to become a literary sleuth.

FIRST EPOCH

I

REGENCY PRELUDE

WILKIE COLLINS WAS a Georgian manqué in a world of earnest Victorians. He was born on 8 January 1824, at a time when Britain was beginning to cast off the frothy excesses of the Regency period and knuckle down to the 'long' nineteenth century. Although George IV had been on the throne for almost four years, the playful spirit of his youth survived in London's new buildings as his capital city continued to expand in competition with Paris. In the process, John Nash's Regent Street had pushed through the dank slums of the West End to join up with the Adam brothers' grand Portland Place and open the way to the rural expanses of Marylebone Park, around which a number of elegant stucco terraces bearing Hanoverian names were then being built. (This would soon be called the Regent's Park, while the New Road, just to its south, would become known as the Marylebone Road.)

These developments confirmed the position of the Duke of Portland's land as a prime piece of London real estate. For the best part of a century, successive Dukes had been building town houses in grid-like fashion across his holdings in the wider Marylebone area (west of Portland Place, north of Oxford Street and south of New Road). Wilkie was born in the centre of this urban village, at 11 New Cavendish Street, an east–west thoroughfare that incorporated part of the Portland family name.

He remained close to these roots. Although he later enjoyed visiting France, Italy and other European countries, crossed the Atlantic, and took frequent trips to the English seaside, he always returned to the area in or just outside the bounds of Marylebone. More than most nineteenth-century writers, including Dickens, he was a London man.

This was the part of town where his grandfather, William, had settled when he arrived from County Wicklow forty years earlier. According to family tradition, the Collinses were originally English but had emigrated to Ireland from Sussex in the wake of William III. One of their ancestors is said to have been Samuel Collins, an anatomist who travelled widely in Europe and took his medical degree in Padua, before becoming one of Charles II's doctors and later President of the College of Physicians.

After marrying an Edinburgh woman, William pursued a topsy-turvy career as a writer and picture dealer, working out of a house in Great Titchfield Street (another Portland family name), where the couple had two sons, William and Francis (or Frank), born in 1788 and 1790 respectively.

The elder William was a sociable man with wide-ranging, often radical, enthusiasms. Around the time his sons were born, he still saw a literary future for himself as a writer and editor. In 1787 he put together the *New Vocal Miscellany*, a collection of unpublished verse, whose tone is boisterous and Hogarthian, as in 'The Kept Miss', a song about a courtesan called Sally, which starts:

See the Park throng'd with coaches – the Nobles all run
To view the dear Angel! Her ruin's begun;

Princes, Dukes, Lords, and Bankers are first in her train,
In raptures they ogle – as yet but in vain . . .

After a special admirer tires of her, she throws herself into pleasure: 'Wherever the Ton goes she's sure to resort.' Soon reduced to earning her living on the streets, it is not long before 'worn with disease' she 'crawls' to the Lock Hospital for sufferers of venereal disease.

Six years later, at the height of the French Revolution, William wrote 'The Slave Trade', a pamphlet poem attacking the global trafficking of humans. His brother James would take its message to heart: after becoming a priest, he joined the Society for the Propagation of the Gospel and was posted to the old slaving 'grand emporium' Cape Coast Castle, in modern Ghana. William's son, also called William, described this as a 'lucrative' appointment, but expressed 'great agitation' in a letter to a friend about the 'considerable risk' involved. It was a valid concern, since James died within a couple of years of taking up his post, and his son Francis, who worked as an assistant teacher of native children, suffered the same fate.

However, William Collins Senior was not cut out to be a penitent or a missionary. In his other occupation as a rackety picture dealer, he befriended local artists, including the hard-drinking, debt-ridden George Morland, about whom he wrote some reminiscences which appeared as the second of the three volumes in his *Memoirs of a Picture*, published in 1805.

In the cut-throat Georgian art market there were inevitably charlatans, who faked works and duped their customers. This book, later described by the author's grandson Wilkie as a 'Shandean profusion of . . . digressions and ancecdotes', related the picaresque progress of a painting by the 'immortal Guido' (Guido Reni) as it passed through a succession of dealers and forgers. One of its underlying themes was the changing nature of the artistic profession: no longer was it necessary to have an influential patron. Morland, who specialised in rustic and moralising genre scenes, showed it was possible to make a living by selling his output directly to customers. Dealers such as William Collins Senior helped facilitate this, publishing and selling art at different stages of production, from canvases to engravings and prints.

Morland, the old roué, clearly provided good copy because there were at least three further biographies of him in the next two years. Half a century later Wilkie Collins followed suit, using this same colourful background for an equally opportunistic novella, *A Rogue's Life*. As his vocation as an author would show, he drew his own lessons from this material – creative works, whether painted or written, were commodities that required marketing and protecting from exploitation.

One of William Collins's sons, Frank, saw enough of a future in the family business to follow his father as a print dealer. The other, William Junior, preferred the more high-minded tradition of painting, and was no doubt influenced by the artists he met at the Collins family houses in Great Titchfield Street and then in nearby Great Portland Street. While still in his teens, he decided to enroll at the Royal Academy Schools, whose job of nurturing new artistic talent had been one of the two declared aims of the founders of the Academy in 1768 (the other being the holding of annual exhibitions to promote their own work).

The Schools still emphasised the skills of copying rather than self-expression, preparing their pupils for a market that favoured neo-classical and historical works of art. Young William sat through lessons in anatomy from Sir Anthony Carlisle, a surgeon who would illustrate his talks by bringing in muscular models, including Indian jugglers. William also experienced the eclecticism of the remarkable Swiss-born professor of painting Henry Fuseli, whose love of dramatic effect prefigured the Romantic movement.

Eschewing, as he put it, any desire to rush 'into rivalry with Michel Angelo', William turned his talents to landscapes and other genre pictures, though, in keeping with evolving taste, he often added significant narrative threads to his paintings; in other words, he made them tell a story. In this respect, he drew on his experience as the son of a dealer, investing his carefully crafted paintings with the immediacy of the great English caricatures found in his father's print shop.

His first real success came in 1812, the year of his father's death, when his painting *Disposal of a Favourite Lamb* sold for 140 guineas. Wilkie later described this work as having 'simple yet impressive pathos' (others might describe it as sentimentality). It proved popular: one small engraving went through 15,000 impressions, and so helped keep the now fatherless Collins family solvent.

Two years later William met Harriet Geddes, the woman who would become his wife. Short, dark-haired and pleasant-featured (rather than beautiful), she hailed from a different Regency background, one familiar to readers of Jane Austen. Her family were respectable country folk, borderline gentry, usually pressed for money and constrained by social convention, but nevertheless eager to make their mark in the post-Napoleonic world. She was the eldest of six children of Captain Alexander Geddes, a retired infantry officer of Scottish origin, and another Harriet (née Easton), whose family had been prominent traders in the cathedral city of Salisbury. Born in Worcestershire towards the end of her father's military career, the younger Harriet was brought up in Alderbury, a village six miles outside Salisbury.

As she chronicled in an unpublished memoir, written ostensibly as fiction but following closely the course of her early life, Harriet Geddes looked back on her upbringing in Wiltshire with a mixture of affection and frustration. Her easy-going father rented a cottage and smallholding from the Earl of Radnor,

owner of nearby Longford Castle. Owing to his army background, he was socially acceptable enough to mix with the local
elite, both in country drawing rooms and within 'the Close' (the
secluded world of high-minded clerics associated with
the Cathedral). He survived on a tiny inheritance, but was always
looking forward to gaining a substantial capital sum from a
lawsuit in Edinburgh. When the case finally reached court, he
received considerably less than he had hoped, and this dwindled
to nothing after he entrusted the proceeds to a couple of dubious
stockbrokers. His financial difficulties were exacerbated since
five of his six children were girls, who needed furnishing with
attractive dowries.

Harriet settled into a joyless round of provincial balls at a time
when eligible army officers were notably absent on campaigns
abroad. Always keen on the theatre (her favourite play was Oliver
Goldsmith's *She Stoops to Conquer*), she toyed with becoming an
actress and was offered a position at the Theatre Royal in fashionable Bath. But her mother was opposed to her taking a job that
was at the time equated with loose living and even prostitution,
so Harriet reluctantly agreed to receive training from a family
friend with a view to becoming a governess. This friend converted
her to Evangelicalism, the popular strain of Protestantism that
combined Biblical fundamentalism with aspirations to social
improvement.

Eventually Harriet found a teaching job in London, where
her younger sister Margaret, who had also been forced to earn
a living, was already enjoying considerable success as a painter.
Margaret had shown such talent from an early age that the Earl
of Radnor had allowed her to copy pictures from his excellent
art collection and introduced her to sitters. After deciding to
pursue her studies in the capital, Margaret was initially offered
help by one of her father's less scrupulous stockbrokers, who
promised to present her to the leading portrait painter, Sir Thomas

Lawrence. When that arrangement fell through, the generous Earl again stepped in with an offer to finance a further year in London for her to test the market and find her professional feet.

Margaret duly prospered, exhibiting at both the Royal Academy and the Royal Institution. In the bitterly cold winter of 1814, she was visited in her lodgings in Mortimer Street (at the heart of the Portland estate) by Harriet, who was about to take up employment at a small nearby school run by a Frenchwoman. Margaret introduced her sister to a circle of young painters, including William Collins, who was also starting to make his way in the art world.

In her memoir, Harriet tells how she had heard so much about Collins from Margaret that she was rather disappointed by the pale figure with 'very refined and regular' features when she eventually met him at a ball. Nonetheless, there must have been a powerful mutual attraction because he subsequently invited her to meet his mother and brother, to whom he was close. He also asked her to accompany him to the hay fields of Hendon, a popular day's outing from London. However, William was almost as penniless as Harriet. His father had died encumbered with debts, so William and his family were forced to rent out half their house (thus saving sixty guineas a year) and sell practically everything they owned: at one stage a friend found them eating off a box in place of a table.

William only survived because of the generosity of his first patron, Sir Thomas Freeman-Heathcote. Still responsible for his recently widowed mother, he did not feel financially secure enough to offer Harriet his hand in marriage. When his son Wilkie touched on this matter in his first book, a biography of his father (written with a sense of filial obligation in 1848, when he was twenty-four), he hinted at his own aversion to the social conventions of marriage when he commented that William 'honourably shrunk from the responsibility of fettering a young girl with the anxieties and disappointments of that most weary of social ordeals, "a long engagement"'.

Harriet had little option but to return home to the country and make the most of any positions she might obtain as a governess, while William, having pledged 'to abstain from any compliance with desires calculated to weaken my faculties', set about expanding his professional contacts and his range of subject matter. After being made an Associate of the Royal Academy in late 1814, he teamed up the following year with James Stark, another of the artists whom Harriet had met through her sister in London, for a trip to the Norfolk coast, close to Stark's home in Norwich. As a result, British seascapes became part of William's repertoire (one of them being snapped up by the Prince of Wales for 150 guineas three years later).

The Collins family finances now began to improve and they were able to move into a larger house, 11 New Cavendish Street. In 1817, William visited Paris, where he hoped to hone his skills by studying the masterpieces in the Louvre. He was accompanied by Washington Allston and Charles Leslie, two like-minded American artists, whom he had welcomed into his family. The Harvard-educated Allston, sometimes known as the American Titian, was a more overtly Romantic painter. He was also a deep thinker who liked to engage in philosophical debate with Samuel Taylor Coleridge, whom he had befriended in Rome a decade earlier. After returning to Boston in 1818, Allston wrote regularly to William, praising his talents and telling him how on one occasion he had been dreaming of London and of sitting 'opposite to each other by the fireside, with your good Mother & Frank and Leslie between us'.

By then, William's output was becoming sought after. He had several aristocratic clients, including Lord Liverpool and the Duke of Newcastle, whose country houses he would visit for lengthy periods of artistic endeavour. When not working on coastal or rural genre subjects, he busied himself with money-spinning portraits – to the dismay of some fellow painters, such as Benjamin Haydon, who felt that true art was to be found in grand historical subjects rather than mundane likenesses of individuals. Despite Allston's influence, William's sensitive, painstaking style remained conservative and Academic; he was aware of, but by no means eager to emulate, the searing Romanticism of contemporaries such as J.M.W. Turner.

He was supported in this approach by Sir George Beaumont, a dilettante and collector who preferred no-nonsense naturalists such as Collins over the more innovative Turner, Constable and Blake. In 1818, William accepted Beaumont's invitation to experience the beauty of Cumberland, where he met William Wordsworth and his circle of friends, including Robert Southey. William enjoyed tramping over the Lakeland hills with Wordsworth, hearing the 'poetical associations connected with the scenes'. However, he found himself at the centre of a literary dispute when he painted Coleridge's fifteen-year-old daughter Sara as 'The Highland Girl' of Wordsworth's poem. At that time Wordsworth had fallen out with Coleridge and did not think Sara a suitable model. But Coleridge was delighted: owing to his estrangement from his wife and from Wordsworth, he had not seen his daughter for six years, so when his friend Washington Allston's pupil Charles Leslie brought the canvas to him in Highgate, he was not even certain of the identity of 'the most beautiful Fancy-figure I ever saw'.

When Coleridge discovered who it was, he sent William a letter of thanks for the 'exquisite picture [which] . . . has quite haunted my eye ever since', and which he kept above his desk for the rest of his life. He also enclosed a couple of tickets to one of his forthcoming lectures. It was the start of a warm and productive period of friendship between the philosopher-poet and the artist. The portrait was highly praised when exhibited at the Royal Academy in London, helping William gain election as a full Academician two years later.

For a traditionalist such as William this was recognition indeed. In May 1821, Allston wrote encouragingly to him from the United States, 'Sommerset [*sic*] House [the headquarters of the Royal Academy] I suppose is now in its glory, and you shining away there amongst the stars of the first magnitude: Turner, like the Great Bear, turning the lesser lights around him into utter darkness – and [David] Wilkie, like a Chaldean Magician, conjuring sentiment out of pots and kettles . . . & Leslie winning the hearts of the ladies by his spells of grace and beauty.'

The Academy may have been in its glory, but it was also the battleground of artistic cliques, with some painters, such as Haydon and Constable, feeling a real sense of grievance about the privilege and patronage associated with the place. In this tainted atmosphere William found a soulmate in David Wilkie, a contemporary at the Royal Academy Schools, who mixed psychologically astute portraiture with historical naturalism. Despite Wilkie's diffident manner, which did not always endear him to others, the two men became friends.

At short notice they travelled together to Edinburgh in August 1822 to record George IV's visit to Scotland – the first ever by a reigning British monarch. Determined that his progress through his northern kingdom should be marked with suitable pageantry, the King, who was known for his love of ostentation, took advice from Sir Walter Scott, who suggested that he should wear full Scottish regalia, including a kilt, which for many years in the previous century had been banned as a symbol of Jacobitism. As a strong monarchist with a docile dog called 'Prinny' (the King's nickname), William Collins was ideally suited to record this great event. Although it was long thought that he had failed to complete any substantial work, an oil painting by him, titled *The Landing of George IV at Leith*, emerged as recently as 2004 in an auction at Bonhams.

One reason was that William's mind was elsewhere. Over the years he had seen Harriet Geddes a few more times when she visited her sister Margaret. The latter's career continued to flourish, even after her marriage in 1817 to William Hookham Carpenter, the son of a prosperous Old Bond Street bookseller, print publisher and art dealer, and the birth of four (eventually eight) children.

However, it was not until January 1822 that William and Harriet's romance was rekindled, as a result of a chance meeting in Piccadilly and later a party where she taught him to dance the quadrille. After he invited her to the theatre to see a show by the 'personator' (impressionist) Charles Mathews, said to be the inspiration for Dickens's Alfred Jingle in *The Pickwick Papers*, she became separated from her chaperone – her brother-in-law William Carpenter – and, as she recalled, 'I soon found my hand in his, and when I gently tried to withdraw it, a whisper asked me to let him retain it. From that time I knew nothing of Mathews. In vain he sang, danced, changed into seven people at once etc. etc. I was as one blind and deaf to all but one . . .'

With marriage now on the agenda, Harriet felt compelled to tell William that her prospects, as a governess, were rather different from her successful artist sister's. He did not mind this, but made clear that he too was constrained by domestic problems: his mother, who was still dependent on him, was concerned that her high-flying son should marry such a lowly and inconsequential figure. Harriet brushed any objections aside, declaring she would be happy to live with the Collins family in their house in New Cavendish Street. A tentative date for the wedding was set in August. But when William received notice that he was required in Scotland for the royal visit, they agreed to postpone their nuptials.

Once the King's visit was over, William contacted Harriet, saying he had made arrangements for her to travel to Leith on the steamer *James Watt*. He pointed out that marriage in Scotland was much easier than in England.

Harriet duly followed William's instructions, which led her, after a two-night passage on the North Sea, to the Edinburgh house of his friends, the sculptor Samuel Joseph and his wife. On 16 September 1822 they were married in the English Episcopal Church, a ceremony attended only by the Josephs and one other friend of Harriet's. The minister who officiated was Dr Archibald Allison, a beacon of the Scottish Enlightenment and a celebrated essayist, who refused to accept a fee because William had the same name as the eighteenth-century poet.

After a short honeymoon on an island in the Firth of Forth, the newly-weds were back in London before the month was out. It was all something of a surprise to their friends. Even though David Wilkie had been in Edinburgh with William a few weeks earlier, he had known nothing of the impending marriage. He commented to his sister that the couple had been 'sighing for years, till they could sigh no longer . . . She seems a nice woman, not particularly handsome, but accomplished and intelligent, and I dare say much attracted to him.' She needed to be, because Harriet and her new husband were about to start married life in New Cavendish Street, in the company of old Mrs Collins and her younger son Frank.

2

EARLY YEARS AND TRAVELS

WILKIE COLLINS'S BIRTH in Marylebone on Thursday 8 January 1824 coincided with an event thirty miles away. The previous day, the assizes in Hertford reached a verdict in the trial of John Thurtell, who was accused of the notorious Radlett murder, and Britain's newspapers were determined to record every last gory detail. Little more than two months earlier, an investigation by the Bow Street Runners had led to the arrest of Thurtell, a shady promoter of illegal prizefighting, who was charged with the gruesome killing of a London solicitor in a lane in Radlett, Hertfordshire. Thurtell's trial for this murder over a gambling debt started on 6 January. By the end of the following day it was all over; in sentencing Thurtell to be hanged, the judge declared that he was satisfied with the accused man's guilt 'as if he had seen him commit the crime with his mortal eyes'.

On 8 January, newspapers overflowed with news of the verdict. The *Morning Chronicle* devoted three of its four pages to the trial, and *The Times* three of its eight pages, plus an editorial. Other print media eagerly followed suit; indeed, in many respects they led the way. Since labourers and servant girls could not afford newspapers, whose prices were kept artificially high by swingeing stamp duties, they devoured a range of cheaper, rougher chapbooks, pamphlets and broadsheets. Operating out of the Seven Dials slums in London's Covent Garden and selling through hawkers across the realm, James Catnach, one of the most successful printers of such material, is reported to have sold a quarter of a million copies of a pamphlet relating to the Radlett murder in the weeks before the trial, and a further half million of a sequel in the months following the verdict. Crime stories, particularly murder, attracted readers of all classes, and the more lurid the details, the better.

Thurtell was executed on 9 January, but his name lingered on in people's memories as the personification of evil. After his body was sent to St Bartholomew's Hospital for dissection, the shape of his head was argued over by practitioners of phrenology, who were keen to demonstrate physical evidence of his debased nature. He became a prize exhibit in the Chamber of Horrors when Madame Tussaud's wax museum opened in Baker Street the following decade. When the interest in him refused to die, Thackeray described Thurtell as 'the best friend the penny-a-line men had for many a day'.

Serious writers were just as fascinated with this killer. Walter Scott visited the site of the Radlett murder. Edward Bulwer-Lytton conjured up a version of Thurtell when he needed an assassin in his novel *Pelham*. And when Wilkie Collins and his friend Charles Dickens wrote an account of their visit to the races in Doncaster in 1857, they called on Thurtell and another murderer, William Palmer, the so-called Rugeley poisoner, who had been executed the previous year, for suitable comparisons for the malevolent-looking bookmakers they saw there.

By then, murder, and crime in general, had become as much a part of the fabric of nineteenth-century existence as fog, omnibuses and seaside holidays. Summoning an unwelcome frisson became an art form and an antidote to the monotony of daily life. And when a new genre of writing, sensation literature, was developed to reflect this demand for edgy material, Wilkie Collins would be found in its vanguard.

Since there was no bureaucracy to register births until 1837 (and no statutory requirement before 1875), Wilkie Collins's arrival in the world in early January 1824 went without official record. It was a home delivery in New Cavendish Street and appears to have been a difficult accouchement since the right side of his forehead had a pronounced bump, which might have been caused by the midwife or obstetrician manipulating the forceps.

At his baptism six weeks later at the local St Marylebone church, the infant was marked down in the parish register as William Wilkie Collins, reflecting the family's traditional practice of calling its eldest males William, seemingly in tribute to the Dutch-born Protestant monarch who had quelled the Jacobite rebellion in Ireland. He was given his middle name after his father's great friend, the Scots artist David Wilkie, who was his godfather. Wilkie was the name by which he was later known, but for the first two decades of his life he was known as Willie or Willy.

Built in neo-classical style, with an elegant steeple, the church was an imposing symbol of the neighbourhood's growing significance. Dedicated to St Mary the Virgin, it stood on the New Road looking out over Regent's Park. Nearby was the ancient Tyburn stream, which wound down from Hampstead to the River Thames (thus the conjoined name Mary-le-bourne or burn, later Marylebone). Although there had been a place of worship there for centuries, this latest building dated only from 1817, when it had been refashioned and greatly expanded by the architect Thomas Hardwick to cater for new parishioners from the Portland estate and other nearby areas stretching to St John's Wood.

It had notable artistic connections, represented in the transparency (or picture window), by Benjamin West, President of the Royal Academy, the institution greatly revered by William Collins. It would later become the local, if seldom frequented, church of Wilkie Collins's friend Charles Dickens, when he lived in Devonshire Terrace.

Baby Wilkie appears in his father's drawings as a fat-cheeked infant with dark hair and no hint of his cranial deformity. He had grey eyes and was small for his age, though he would grow to five foot six inches, an average height for a man of his time. When David Wilkie, a lifelong bachelor, first encountered him at his christening, he was so unfamiliar with babies that he did not know what to do. After examining his godson's eyes as if they were a puppy's, he handed him back to his parents, declaring with an air of satisfaction, 'He sees.'

William Collins, now in his mid-thirties, was reaching the peak of his creative and earning powers, which meant he was often away, sketching or visiting aristocratic patrons. A fine-featured man, with warm, searching eyes and thick, well-kempt hair, he was generally liked for his calm, unassuming manner. An art critic described him as no genius, but 'simply a gentleman, mild and pleasing, without foppery, affectation, or even peculiarity of any kind.' Those who knew him better noticed a priggish streak. This was linked to his strong religious faith, based on a personalised form of Evangelicalism, which stressed the importance of hard work, Biblical study and prayer.

Wilkie stayed at home with his mother, who supervised his early education and was responsible, he acknowledged, for 'whatever of poetry and imagination there may be in my composition'.

Harriet Collins was witty and intelligent enough to win the admiration of men such as Coleridge, but she could also be garrulous, which would later irritate Wilkie's friend Charles Dickens.

At New Cavendish Street, Wilkie and his mother had plenty of company. His grandmother and unmarried uncle Frank still lived with them. Wilkie's aunt Christy, his mother's younger sister Christina, often helped with the two boys, while another aunt, Margaret Carpenter, lived nearby, though she was more preoccupied with tending her expanding family and developing her career as a painter.

After being elected a full Academician in 1820, William found himself increasingly (and by no means unwillingly) a member of the artistic establishment – a position that, in an age of competing artistic tendencies, meant he was also in the thick of controversy. He was roundly criticised by the excitable Benjamin Haydon following the death in April 1825 of Henry Fuseli, who had taught them both at the Royal Academy Schools. Haydon was unhappy about what he saw as the development of the Royal Academy into a 'nest of portrait painters'. He called on the government to take action to prevent history painters of his kind being usurped by aspiring portraitists, including Collins, who, he seemed to imply, were adopting a rather lackadaisical approach to their profession.

Haydon overestimated William's influence and misrepresented his output, which that year included rustic scenes such as *Buying Fish on the Beach – Hazy Morning* and *The Cottage Door*, which seemed designed not to ruffle feathers in the politically repressive years following Waterloo. However, such attacks spurred William to perfect his respectable nature scenes rather than waste unnecessary time on portraits.

In the summer of 1825, he removed his wife and baby Wilkie from the heat and bustle of Marylebone to a house in then rural

Hendon, a favourite spot of his. When not sketching *en plein air*, he liked to walk five or six miles to Highgate and discuss matters of philosophy with his friend Coleridge.

William enjoyed looking out over the city from the salubrious heights of north London, for in 1826 he left New Cavendish Street and took a small house in Hampstead. It was there, at 2 Pond Street, a short walk from the Heath, on a site currently occupied by the Royal Free Hospital, that another Collins son, Charles, was born on 25 January 1828. Like his brother Wilkie, Charles was given an artist's middle name, Allston, in homage to his father's American friend Washington Allston.

At this time, David Wilkie was away on a three-year tour of Europe, from where he sent back enthusiastic reports of the works of Michelangelo and other Italian old masters. William reciprocated with his latest news: 'Your godson grows a strapping fellow, and has a little blue-eyed red-haired bonny bairn, as a brother, about three months old.'

Hoping to settle permanently in Hampstead (and also to accommodate his now ailing mother), William looked into buying land and building his own house there, close to other friends, including the artist John Linnell. After David Wilkie returned from the Continent in July 1828, William came under renewed pressure to follow him on a similar career-defining European tour, but, as long as his mother was alive, he felt unable to do so.

As a compromise, while plans for his house in Hampstead were being drawn up, he took his wife, mother and children across the Channel to Boulogne, where in the summer of 1829 he painted *The Mussel Gatherers – Coast of France*, for which his banker client, Sir Thomas Baring, would pay four hundred guineas, one of his highest fees. Always alert for authenticity, William came across a fisherman who had witnessed a shipwreck near Boulogne in which everyone had died except a black man. However, the quarantine laws then in force would not allow anyone to help the half-drowned survivor. When William's son Wilkie later retold the story, he would write, with some passion, 'No one attempted to approach, or succour him, but the fisherman; who, in defiance of all danger and objection, carried the poor wretch to a straw-hut on the beach; and, taking off his own clothes, laid down by him the whole night long, endeavouring to restore the dying negro by the vital warmth of his own body. This sublime act of humanity was, however, unavailing – when morning dawned, the negro was dead!' William Collins recorded this unfortunate incident in a sketch called 'Good Samaritan', which had the kind of narrative immediacy later found in his son's written work.

On his return to England, the paperwork relating to the Hampstead house was still not completed, so the family stayed briefly in Ramsgate, a seaside resort in Kent, which several of William's friends, including the Linnells and Coleridge, had visited and recommended. Still hankering after North London, William took a short lease on a property in Hampstead Square, close to the Heath, then, in mid-1830, moved back into town to 30 Porchester Terrace, a house with a decent-sized room which could be used as a studio, just north of Hyde Park in Bayswater. The surrounding area was still partly rural, but the Collinses felt at home since John Linnell lived at number 38, having made the same journey south from Hampstead two years earlier.

Wilkie had his first experience of politics, sitting at the window of this new house, at the time of the First Reform Act in April 1832. When, after much agitation, this controversial extension of the franchise was finally passed, jubilant crowds roamed the streets threatening to break the windows of any building not lit up in celebration. The Collins boys found themselves caught up in the excitement: Wilkie recalled a mob marching six abreast, smashing the glass of an un-illuminated house on the other side of the street. As the vigilantes surged forward, cheering the passage of the Act, he could not help expressing the same senti-ment. But his spontaneous demonstration of political feeling infuriated his father, a High Tory, who had shown his colours when he told a friend that he equated political reform with cholera as a scourge of the age and evidence of God's wrath.

In William Collins's mind, politics and religion were closely linked, and this would prove significant as Wilkie's opinions began to develop. There was no doubting William's commitment to God; his letters were full of it: 'I could go on for an hour describing our blessings,' he wrote to his wife on one of his trips. 'Your heart is not insensible to the mercies of Providence, and when I return we will thank our heavenly father together.' Reading the Bible was a regular evening feature in the Collins household. However, like many thoughtful Anglicans in an uncertain age, he was still looking to find an appropriate spiritual response to fill the space between direct communication with the Deity, as practised by dissenters, and the elaborate ritual associated with Roman Catholics.

Over the years he moved fitfully from Evangelicalism to a more rigid High Church set of beliefs associated with the Oxford Movement, or Tractarians, in the 1830s. The Reform Bill had played its part in the birth of this latter faction, which was to split the Church of England, because one of its lesser-known provisions (and the one that particularly exercised the conservative-minded William Collins) was a reduction in the number of Irish bishops. Coming so soon after Catholic emancipation in 1829, this additional concession was regarded by reactionary Anglican clerics as yet another attack on the established Church, indicative of the lax liberalism to be found not only in its own affairs but in society as a whole. This was the point made in John Keble's 'national apostasy' sermon, which kick-started the Oxford Movement in July 1833, leading to the first *Tract for the Times* written by the Reverend John Henry Newman of Oriel College, Oxford, later in the year. However, the Movement's conservatism would push it nearer to the Roman Catholic Church, to the extent that some supporters, including Newman, became dissatisfied with the compromises involved and preferred to align themselves completely with Rome.

As an ardent Protestant, William Collins did not follow Newman down that path. His adventures on the fringes of Tractarianism took a different route, buffeted by the many spiritual cross-currents of the time. He had always been interested in philosophical and religious enquiry, from his early discussions with fellow artists such as Allston and Wilkie to his association with Coleridge.

Through a combination of these influences William came into the orbit of Edward Irving, an unorthodox preacher, whose brand of Evangelicalism and social conservatism was popular in his native Scotland. When Irving moved to London as a Church of Scotland minister in 1822, one of his two contacts was David Wilkie (who painted his portrait). Irving was quickly taken up and lionised, becoming a member of Coleridge's philosophical circle in Highgate, where another participant was a retired Royal Artillery doctor called James Thompson, a neighbour of William's in Hampstead. Wilkie Collins later emphasised the significance of this circle to his father: 'Here he first met that original and extraordinary character, Edward Irving, whose preaching was at that time drawing its greatest multitude of hearers . . . From the discussions upon matters of worship constantly occurring between Coleridge and Irving, Mr. Collins, and others of the poet's guests, gathered such fresh information, and acquired such new ideas, as they never afterwards forgot.'

As the decade progressed, Irving was drawn to 'speaking in tongues' as a way of getting in touch with the Holy Spirit. This gained him the support of a rich, Conservative banker, Henry Drummond, who from 1826 held regular conferences on the study of prophecy at his estate in Albury, Surrey. When news came of an outbreak of Pentecostalism in Scotland, these 'Irvingites' sent a small delegation to investigate, among them Dr Thompson who, in 1831, wrote *A Brief Account of a Visit to Some of the Brethren in the West of Scotland*.

A year later, these 'Irvingites' coalesced into the Catholic Apostolic Church, centred at Irving's church in Newman Street, London, and backed by Henry Drummond. However, religious trends were fickle in those turbulent times and, as Irving himself became increasingly obsessed with spontaneous communication with God, he lost his religious and social credibility, leading to his formal removal from the Church of Scotland and to his Catholic Apostolic Church going its own way. In 1835, Dr Thompson put himself forward for election as one of this new Church's apostles. Although defeated, he went on to run its affairs in Southampton.

On the fringes of Drummond's Albury conferences was a Yorkshire-born preacher called William Dodsworth, whose beliefs were more in keeping with William Collins's. In 1829, Drummond arranged for Dodsworth to take over a small chapel in Margaret Street, Marylebone, where William often went to hear him preach. Like many astute clerics, Dodsworth married well – in his case, Elizabeth Buller-Yarde-Buller, the daughter of a rich, well-connected parishioner, Lady Buller, who lived in York Terrace, one of the new Nash developments in the Regent's Park.

Although he had been interested in Irving's charismatic approach, Dodsworth moved away from the increasingly wayward Scottish preacher in the early 1830s. William eagerly followed suit, as shown in the many positive comments about Dodsworth in his correspondence. In October 1831, when his wife Harriet was staying in Brighton with Dr Thompson and his family, William informed her, 'Mr Dodsworth continues his sermons upon the fearful character of the present time.' Underlining his sense of the links between politics and religion, he asked her to seek the opinion of 'our friend Dr Thompson' on 'recent events' relating to the agitation surrounding the Reform Bill. Two years later, when she was again away, he reported going 'to Mr Dodsworth's, heard an excellent sermon & stayed to thank the Lord for all his mercies "for they endure for ever".'

Although William was happy to follow Dodsworth, traces of his old Evangelicalism remained. This was evident in his determination to uphold the sanctity of Sundays. On more than one occasion he upbraided John Linnell, his neighbour in Porchester Terrace, for failing to respect the Sabbath – once for tending his peach and nectarine trees, and another time for daring to paint on the Lord's Day. He even threatened to take Linnell, a Baptist, to court over the matter. Such intransigence could sometimes take a nasty turn. When he accused Linnell of not paying his gardener, he was met with a strong denial, to which William haughtily enquired, 'Of what consequence is it whether you cheated a man out of his wages or not, when you are constantly doing things ten times worse?' Asked if he was still referring to the nectarine incident, William admitted he was, and, according to Linnell's biographer A.T. Story, went on to say 'that a man who would break the Sabbath would do any other bad thing'. Story added a comment that probably echoed his subject's view of William: 'The worthy Academician, though an amiable, was in many respects rather a weak-minded, man. He appeared always to be oppressed by the twin bugbears, propriety and respectability, and found it difficult to forgive anyone who failed in his respect to them.'

This piousness was reflected in the upbringing of the Collins children, who were constantly urged to be good. Writing from the Warwickshire seat of Sir George Phillips, a rich textile magnate, William exhorted his sons, 'Go on praying to God, through Jesus Christ, to enable you, by his holy spirit, to be blessings to your parents; and then you must be happy.' He signed off in an unctuous manner that would come to infuriate Wilkie: 'And now, my dear boys, I must leave you and prepare for going to Church . . . where I shall pray for my two children and their mother as well, as for all the world beside.'

On this occasion Mama was at home, but this was not always the case. Wilkie had to endure long periods when both his mother and father were absent. For several years she had suffered from 'nerves'. As a result, she was often away, convalescing with her parents, visiting friends, or 'taking the waters' in coastal resorts. It seems that, for all her sociability, she had difficulty coping with a life centred on her husband's activities. 'At home very poorly from anxiety and fatigue,' read one of her diary entries in 1835. Her afflictions were not uncommon at the time, particularly among women, who struggled in a male-dominated industrial society. Although Harriet was a spirited woman, who would later write a fine quasi-fictional memoir, there is no evidence of her having any outlet for her creativity.

A branch of medicine sprang up to minister to such complaints. Her husband played along, telling her he hoped that, as a result of a regime of rides and walks, she might 'by the blessing of God have found some benefit for your nerves', and on another occasion, that 'Dr Quin', one of several doctors the family used, 'says you may with much chance of benefit take tepid sea water baths twice or perhaps thrice a week.'

Young Wilkie took note and would later write sympathetically about women with anxiety disorders. His novels would reflect how, as the century progressed, neuroses became more openly discussed and studied. He would try to recreate in his narrative style the experience of nervous agitation, with its highs and lows, its terrors and searing emotions.

Although not always at home, Harriet managed to supervise Wilkie's education. She encouraged him in his early reading, such as Joseph Ritson's edition of the ballads of Robin Hood. Wilkie had developed an enduring love of the sea; so, when he stayed in Ramsgate, his father gave him Isaac Taylor's *The Ship*, part of a popular educative series for the young.

As Wilkie grew older he became a devoted reader of Walter Scott, while other favourite books included *Don Quixote*, *The Vicar of Wakefield*, *The Arabian Nights* and the nautical adventure stories of Captain Marryat – all of which suggested his notably eclectic tastes.

In 1833, the Collins family circumstances changed radically as a result of the deaths in quick succession of Wilkie's good-natured Uncle Frank and his grandmother, old Mrs Collins. Frank's loss from typhus in his early forties proved the last straw for his mother, who had been in poor health for several years. It also hit William hard, since he relied heavily on his brother's encyclopaedic knowledge of the art world.

He followed Harriet into a state of melancholy, which was only mitigated by his religious faith. When he visited Kent the following May, he found relief in the beauty of the countryside and in 'the society of Christians. No other society can comfort me – the society of the world depresses me greatly. I am sadly low in mind at times, and in body weak – apt to be vexed, very impatient, not bearing my afflictions with that patience, which

afflictions were sent to teach.' He tried to improve his low
spirits by taking his family on an extended and rather gruelling tour of Wales in the summer of 1834. This trip was to
prove a dry run for William's postponed Italian grand tour
two years later. However, though change was in the air, he
could not yet tear himself away from his work. So, in January
1835, shortly after his eleventh birthday, Wilkie was despatched
to school for the first time. He attended the Maida Hill
Academy, an undistinguished and short-lived establishment
run by the Reverend James Gall, off the Edgware Road. Aside
from a bout of measles, Wilkie seemed content enough: his
mother's diary recorded how he brought friends home and
accompanied his brother on expeditions to the zoo. The year
ended on a note of triumph when Wilkie won the school prize
– a copy of the *Essays* written by the profoundly conservative
Poet Laureate Robert Southey, whom his father had met in
the Lake District in 1818.

Wilkie's education was cut short or, as he later saw it, enhanced
when, in September 1836, his father decided that the time had
finally come to make the journey to Italy, since he no longer
had the excuse of his mother to detain him. As an artist, he was
convinced – or had had it drummed into him by David Wilkie
– that he was at a stage in his artistic development when he
would benefit from greater knowledge of the Italian masters.
Although his own style tended towards Dutch figurative painting,
William believed that art in Italy could only be properly appreciated by a mature artist.

It was a testament to William's dedication to his profession
that, approaching the age of fifty, he was prepared not only to
devote two years of his life to improving his skills, but to take

his family with him. Travelling to Italy involved long and often uncomfortable journeys by coach and boat; visas were difficult and time-consuming to obtain; and disease, notably cholera, was a hazard at every stage.

In Paris, their first significant stop, the Collinses called on friends, including Miss Thompson, sister of the Irvingite doctor, and saw the sights, including the Louvre, where they happened to meet William's patron Sir Robert Peel and his family. William was impressed by the way the Bonapartist system of patronage ensured that all artists were gainfully employed. He wondered if it might be replicated in Britain, where the Royal Academy was in the process of moving from Somerset House to shared premises with the National Gallery in Trafalgar Square.

Another series of gruelling coach trips took the family south to the Mediterranean, where they were held up in Nice for six weeks because of a deadly cholera outbreak in Italy. While twelve-year-old Wilkie tried to keep up his studies by taking lessons from a young Jewish tutor, William made the most of his letters of introduction to the British Consul. These had been written by Sir William Knighton, keeper of the privy purse and physician in ordinary to George IV, who was a great friend and patron of David Wilkie, and by Sir William's brother-in-law, a well-travelled naval captain called Edward Harker. With his contacts to the royal household, Knighton was one of several men who regularly smoothed the progress of William's career. William regarded him highly, and was saddened, while in Nice, to learn of his death.

After getting the all-clear to travel, the Collinses spent surprisingly little time in Florence, given its artistic treasures. The city was simply inhospitable: nothing was open because of the Christmas and New Year holidays and it was extremely cold, with snow knee-deep. They hurried on to Rome, where William looked forward to finding a studio and resuming his work.

The Collinses settled into a suite of apartments in the via Felice, looking out onto the fashionable Pincian Hill, close to the Villa Borghese. Their house had a niche above the door for a statue of the Madonna, which was much revered, as the neighbours sang to it every evening. Wilkie was impressed when, by chance, he and his father met Wordsworth nearby. He later recalled the Lakeland poet as kindly and mild, but 'quite out of his element' abroad – a man terrified by any suggestion of cholera, counselling William not to proceed to Naples for that very reason, and determined to leave Italy as soon as he could. William ignored this alarmism. Instead, as he told David Wilkie, he 'lost no time in getting to *pictorial head quarters*', meaning the Vatican and the Sistine Chapel, where he marvelled at the paintings and frescos of Raphael and Michelangelo.

He also enjoyed the company of local British artists, particularly Joseph Severn and the portrait painter Thomas Brigstocke, who both allowed him to use their models and studios. Other artists based in Rome, or passing through, included the sculptor Richard James Wyatt, Thomas Uwins, who specialised in portraits and landscapes, and Samuel Palmer, John Linnell's new son-in-law.

While Harriet's diary gives the impression that she and her husband seldom strayed outside the sphere of other expatriates, Wilkie adapted easily to local ways, picking up Italian, enjoying Roman cuisine and developing a taste for opera. He was drawn to the historical aspects of Rome. Stimulated by visits to the Colosseum, the Pincian Hill and other ancient sites, he became fascinated by the city's past – not the Christianised version that captured his parents' imaginations, but the more dramatic struggles of Classical times, as given life in Bulwer-Lytton's hugely successful novel of 1834, *The Last Days of Pompeii*.

Meanwhile, William and Harriet studiously kept up their

Tractarian-style observances, though even such committed Protestants could not completely ignore Catholicism in such a place. They went to Mass at the Vatican over Easter and attended the funeral of Thomas Weld, the first Englishman to be made a cardinal for well over a century. However, their distaste for local practices was clear in Harriet's angry reaction when she witnessed the 'most ridiculous and disgusting ceremony' of animals being baptised. 'The chief drawback to the enjoyment of the beauties and advantages of Italy' was, she felt, 'the dreadful and debasing idolatry they call the Christian religion.' And in true English anti-papist style, she was incensed by the cult of the Virgin: 'Not a trace to be found of the religion revealed in God's word but a few names for instance, Jesu Christo, but how his mother is exalted on every occasion above him.'

Wilkie perked up when a younger painter called Edward (Ned) Ward arrived with his friend John Leech, the future *Punch* illustrator. Feeling stifled by the religiosity of his parents, he looked to Ward, a high-spirited banker's son, studying to be a history artist, to introduce him to the more earthy aspects of the Eternal City. The effusive dark-haired Ward shared Wilkie's interest in the local culture: he 'sang, chiefly in Italian, and danced the Tarantella with the grace and agility of a native'. Ward had tried his hand at banking but, unlike his older brother Charles, had found it 'most uncongenial' and reverted to his first love, painting. In Rome, he enrolled at the prestigious Accademia di San Luca and then, as a protegé of David Wilkie, sought out William Collins, whom he found 'a very sincere kind of man'.

A little more than a decade later, Wilkie would perform the crucial role of giving the bride away when Ward secretly married one of his teenage pupils, against the wishes of her parents. This act of comradeship suggested a history of shared escapades, which almost certainly started in Rome. It is not surprising to find that Wilkie later gave two boastful accounts of his first amorous encounter at around this time. In one description, to the German critic Ernst von Wolzogen, he was not too specific, recalling how he had fallen in love with a woman at least three times his age and how he had been consumed with jealousy whenever her husband was nearby.

In the other, to Charles Dickens when they visited Italy together in 1853, he provided more detail. As Dickens wrote soon after to his sister-in-law Georgina Hogarth, Wilkie 'gave us . . . in a carriage one day, a full account of his first love adventure. It was at Rome it seemed, and proceeded, if I may be allowed the expression, to the utmost extremities – he came out quite a pagan Jupiter in the business.'

Both these reports say that Wilkie was twelve at the time. But that should not be taken too literally. Indeed, by naming Rome, Dickens puts the date at 1837 when Wilkie was thirteen (or perhaps fourteen, since the Collins family returned there the following summer).

However, it is not difficult to imagine Wilkie venturing into the city one night, accompanied by Ward, and meeting a voluptuous Roman lady who helped him lose his viginity. Even if this was a fanciful story that Wilkie span to entertain Dickens, it nevertheless suggests he was a precocious youth who was discovering his sexuality and indicates why he later looked back on Italy as a country of freedom and passion.

In early May, William Collins was ready to move south with his family to Naples, where he again settled into a round of painting and hobnobbing with local artists and celebrities. The domestic emphasis of Neapolitan art was more in keeping with his own style than the rich classicism that prevailed in Rome. But after a leisurely month they began noticing ominous signs of a worsening cholera epidemic. They quickly made their way by boat down the coast to Sorrento, where, as the summer heat intensified, they set up house on a clifftop overlooking the sea, and Wilkie began to take Latin lessons.

This was not how he wanted to spend his time. After his amorous adventures (imagined or otherwise) in Rome, his energies were focused elsewhere. As the pagan Jupiter noted by Dickens, he became restless and obstreperous, causing Harriet to confide to her diary, 'Willy very tiresome all day. His father obliged to punish him at dinner time. Made us all miserable.'

The next day William felt ill. It was the beginning of a long period of confinement to his bed with pains throughout his body, especially in his eyes. He tried various remedies for this rheumatic fever, but they all proved unsuccessful. Eventually his doctor suggested he should take the sulphur baths on the nearby island of Ischia.

To cheer him while he lay ill, his wife read him a recent English best-seller, *Gilbert Gurney*, the fictionalised autobiography of the witty Regency man of letters and serial hoaxer Theodore Hook. If Wilkie listened in, he would have been intrigued by this writer of the 'silver-fork' school, derided as snobbish by William Hazlitt in his 1827 essay 'The Dandy School', but later a formative influence on Wilkie's own 'sensation' novels.

As William's health slowly improved, he started taking donkey rides with his sons. Wilkie enjoyed this, but continued to irritate his convalescing father. His mother recorded that he had 'offended his father' and been forbidden to ride. A few days later the stroppy testosterone-fuelled teenager was 'in disgrace again'. True to form, he had been reading *A Sentimental Journey*, Laurence Sterne's spicy novel about a young man's grand tour, similar to his own. He had been given this by an American in Naples, together with another 'amusing' work, Goethe's *The*

Sorrows of Young Werther, about a sensitive young artist's passion for a married woman.

Back in Naples in early November 1837, William was still weak. Harriet's composure was not helped when, as she and her husband attended church on New Year's Eve for the first time since his illness, Charley fell off a wall and broke his arm while playing with friends near the Villa Reale promenade. The poor boy's pained screams that night did not give the family the happiest of starts to 1838. Harriet admonished herself, 'I take shame to myself for not taking my boys with me to church in the afternoon as I ought to have done.' And she reflected in her diary, 'Many months of this past year have been passed in much anxiety and fatigue caused by the severe affliction of rheumatism etc suffered by my husband. Many times my patience has failed me. Many times my heart has been oppressed with weariness by reason of sin . . . Lord remove these burdens that come from the bondage of Satan.'

Harriet's problems did not prevent her enjoying the local social life. New friends included the respected Russell family, headed by Sir Henry Russell, a former chief justice of Bengal who had recently inherited a baronetcy, together with Swallowfield Park, an estate in Berkshire which would later be familiar to Wilkie through his friendship with Sir Henry's sons, Henry and Charles.

Returning to Rome with Harriet and the two boys in February 1838, William took rooms on the Corso and seemed set to stay for some time. He got to know the latest batch of artists from Britain, including George Richmond, and Sir Henry Knighton, son of the late royal doctor and another protégé of David Wilkie.

William was particularly eager for news about the Royal Academy in its new headquarters in Trafalgar Square. The postal deliveries further south had been sporadic, and he had not received vital letters from his brother-in-law, William Hookham Carpenter, who was looking after the sale of his pictures. Everything he had seen on his journey reinforced his conviction of the importance of having a national centre of artistic excellence. But when he suggested that the Academy, like its French and German rivals, should have a propagandising outpost in Rome, he was rebuffed in London.

This sense of isolation contributed to William's sudden decision to return home. He admitted to David Wilkie that he was tired 'of the rambling, unsettled life a man necessarily leads when in a foreign country, with such a variety of attractions'. He longed 'to be at work in England', but the immediate problem was how to transport the fruits of his Italian labours, an estimated eight hundred sketches and oils. He had been told that the Austrian customs officials were particularly philistine and routinely tore paintings, so he resolved to send half his output back to London by sea.

Eventually, after almost two years away, the family began their return journey. Even at this stage it was a leisurely affair. Passing through Florence, William was delighted to meet a direct descendant of Michelangelo, who showed him the original manuscript of a sonnet by the master. He took time off in Parma to see the Correggios that had so impressed David Wilkie. In Venice he caused consternation when, in his determination to paint a particular scene, he insisted on parking his gondola – and keeping it stationary – in the middle of the crowded Grand Canal on market day.

The Collinses arrived back in London on 15 August 1838, six weeks after the coronation of the nineteen-year-old Queen Victoria. After a short stay with the Carpenters, they moved to 20 Avenue Road, just north of Regent's Park, close to their old stamping ground in Marylebone. They soon got to know a family at number 10 called the Otters, who were related to the

Irvingite Dr James Thompson, and would become good friends. Although the Collinses did not stay there long, Avenue Road made a strong impression on Wilkie. In 1859, when he needed a suitable location for the dramatic opening scene of *The Woman in White*, he set part of it there, with its comfortable detached houses and leafy surroundings.

Four days after returning to London, the family visited the recently knighted Sir David Wilkie in Vicarage Gate, Kensington. The Scottish painter told his sister that they were all 'in the highest spirits, quite delighted with the style of living in Italy. They are, indeed, so satisfied with having seen Italy, that it will be some time before they can get reconciled to the sobriety and darkness of this climate.'

This was certainly true of Wilkie, who would always hanker after the warmth and sensuality of the Mediterranean. Nevertheless, for all his knowledge of Italian food and (he liked to think) women, he remained in many ways a callow, unformed youth. At least, after two years in often stifling proximity to his parents, he was beginning to realise that he had little sympathy for their Tractarian approach. He had also learned a degree of intellectual and emotional self-sufficiency. And that, more than anything, would prove the lasting legacy of his time in Italy.

3

A PLAN OF INSTRUCTION

I F WILKIE THOUGHT that, at the age of fourteen and a half, he had finished his formal education, his father had other ideas. Since fault lines had recently opened up in their relationship, William Collins was more determined than ever to have another, perhaps last-ditch, attempt at turning his potentially wayward son into a devout Christian gentleman. As his chosen instrument, he found a combative cleric, the Reverend Henry Cole, who was so much a creature of his spiritually turbulent times that he might have been a novelist's invention.

In the autumn of 1838, while William busied himself with new paintings based on his Italian study tour, Wilkie was packed off across town to Highbury Place, Islington, where Cole ran a small, eponymous Academy that prepared boys for university and professional careers. The school's prospectus appeared conventional enough, offering a 'plan of instruction [which] embraces the Greek and Latin Classics, English (to which particular attention is paid both in the reading of authors and composition), French, History, the mathematics, use of the globes, Geography and Writing &c.'

But behind an unexceptional public face, it was an unusual institution, whose principal, the Reverend Cole, was a Biblical fundamentalist of extreme opinions, particularly on matters relating to religion and education. Only four years earlier he had been locked in an intemperate dispute with Adam Sedgwick, the respected Professor of Geology at Cambridge. He had attacked Sedgwick's advocacy of the new science of geology, arguing that, by questioning the scriptural account of creation, it threatened the fundamentals of divinely inspired Christianity. As well as writing at length on the subject to *The Times*, Cole published a 136-page pamphlet called (in full) 'Popular Geology Subversive of Divine Revelation! A Letter to the Rev. Adam Sedgwick, Woodwardian Professor of Geology in the University of Cambridge; Being a Scriptural Refutation of the Geological Positions and Doctrines Promulgated in His Lately Published Commencement Sermon'. Although a reviewer in the *Morning Post* praised Cole's 'considerable biblical learning', the *Athenaeum* was not so generous, dismissing him as an intolerant bigot who 'assumes a more than papal infallibility, and pronounces his anathemas with a complacency that would be fearful if it were not ludicrous'.

A graduate of Clare Hall, Cambridge, Cole had travelled an uneven path towards his uncompromising beliefs. A decade earlier he had written an equally scathing attack on the millenarianist, Edward Irving. And although William Collins would not have agreed with him then, he clearly did so now, having himself followed William Dodsworth (but not Dr James Thompson) away from Irving's sect to become a run-of-the-mill Tractarian, or follower of the Oxford Movement, the nearest description of Cole's beliefs.

Indeed, one consequence of (perhaps even a contributory reason for) William's recent move to Avenue Road was that he was closer to Christ Church, Albany Street, a new church on the eastern side of Regent's Park, which the first incumbent, his clerical friend Dodsworth, was developing into a centre for the Oxford Movement in London. The building itself was one of the first tangible results of Bishop Blomfield's great church construction programme in the capital, undertaken partly for demographic reasons – to cater for growing numbers – and partly as an Anglican propagandist exercise – to counter the pincer movement influences of dissent and Roman Catholicism. As a devout member of the congregation, William Collins recommended for the altar a copy of Raphael's *Transfiguration* (originally from the Vatican) which had been painted by Thomas Brigstocke, one of the artists who had helped him in Rome. William further demonstrated his closeness to Dodsworth by making him an executor of his will – a choice which failed to impress his son. When Dodsworth died in 1855, Wilkie sent his mother *The Times* obituary, enquiring if this referred to 'poor old pompous Doddy' – a comment which suggested that she was complicit and thought much the same.

A shared enthusiasm for the reactionary precepts of Tractarianism was an important reason for William Collins to entrust his elder son to Henry Cole. Another was the Academy's reputation in thinking conservative circles. The name of Edmund Southey on the list of pupils in the 1841 census suggests this. He was the nephew of the diehard anti-Catholic Poet Laureate, and son of Dr Henry Herbert Southey, a metropolitan lunacy commissioner who lived in Harley Street in the centre of Marylebone and who had studied with William Collins's friend, the late royal physician, Sir William Knighton.

To reach his new boarding school, Wilkie would have crossed Regent's Park and taken two horse-drawn omnibuses, a journey of some eight miles. A short walk then brought him to 39 Highbury Place, a large double-fronted Georgian house with a fine view across the open spaces of Highbury Fields.

Given Cole's outspoken views, Wilkie was surprisingly reticent about him and the two and a half years he spent under his tutelage. He left no obvious pen portrait of Cole, though he did refer in one of his letters home to his head's wife, Frances, with a mixture of affection and condescension: 'There has been nothing new here except this: the beautiful and amiable wife of the governor of this fortress told me with her own lips that I can tell a <u>lie</u>! beautifully. She is a bit inclined, poor dear to anger.'

Wilkie did indeed regard his school as a prison, where he was cut off from the outside world and from the kind of gossip and excitement he had come to enjoy over the past two years abroad. He once complained, 'In this cursed place one cannot get any news.' Not that he provided much communication in the other direction: he seems to have been so cowed by the school's dismal atmosphere that he clammed up. His eight surviving letters to his parents were dutiful in tone, as if he were trying to impress on them that he was making the most of an establishment that cost them £90 a year (the equivalent of £9,300 in today's money). Two of these letters were devoted to uninspired regurgitations of books in Virgil's *Aeneid*. In another, he rehashed in careful copperplate hand some arguments from Homer on the uselessness of democracy. But then rote learning was one of Cole's much vaunted pedagogic methods: he made his pupils recite back everything they had learned each day, arguing that this helped them to retain what they had studied.

Twice, in show-off manner, Wilkie lapsed into Italian in his letters home, playfully purporting to write from 'Piazza di Highbury'. Otherwise he gave little evidence of enjoying himself, though he did like skating and playing with model boats, as well as a 'delectably luscious' cake his mother had sent him through the post. Health, particularly his father's, seemed to be a regular concern, and, a taste of things to come, he once referred to his own eyes, as if he had been experiencing problems with them.

The subtext of his letters was that he was bored, not

particularly happy, and not much of a scholar. His response was to turn in on himself and inhabit a world of the imagination. Mrs Cole had implied as much in her comment about his ability to 'lie beautifully' – an essential quality for a future novelist, and a talent appreciated by his fellow pupils. Almost half a century later, at the end of his life, he recalled how a martinet dormitory 'captain' forced him to tell stories. 'The oldest of the boys, appointed to preserve order, was placed in authority over us as captain of the room. He was as fond of hearing stories, when he had retired for the night, as the Oriental despot to whose literary tastes we are indebted for "The Arabian Nights"; and I was the unhappy boy chosen to amuse him. It was useless to ask for mercy and beg leave to be allowed to go to sleep. "You will go to sleep, Collins, when you have told me a story." In the event of my consenting to keep awake and to do my best, I was warned beforehand to "be amusing if I wished to come out of it with comfort to myself". If I rebelled, the captain possessed a means of persuasion in the shape of an improved cat-o'-ninetails invented by himself. When I was obstinate, I felt the influence of persuasion. When my better sense prevailed, I learnt to be amusing on a short notice – and have derived benefit from those early lessons at a later period of my life.'

This story is odd, since, when Wilkie entered the school, he was one of the senior boys. However, he was smallish in stature, which might have resulted in his being victimised. In retrospect, his period abroad had proved a mixed blessing: his fluency in French enabled him to rattle off set pieces such as Voltaire's epic poem *La Henriade*, which may have been satisfying for him but which caused resentment among his fellow pupils, who gave him the unendearing nickname, 'French frog'.

Doubtless he was well equipped to keep his vile dormitory head enthralled with racy tales of travels. Even this had its occasional rewards: 'Like other despots, the captain had his intervals of generosity,' and would ply Wilkie with cakes, encouraging him in a 'passion for pastry', which, along with his mother's confections and the French and Italian cuisine he had grown to love, would make him portly in later years.

His account of the captain's autocratic behaviour suggests the school had an uncouth, bullying culture at variance with Cole's claims. This undermined another of the principal's arguments in favour of his Academy's limited numbers: that the larger roll in public schools required senior boys to be appointed as monitors, with dark powers of supervision over their juniors.

Instead, he offered a regime of tight surveillance: 'Whereas with us, this dominion is held by myself and masters over all the pupils, from the moment they rise in the morning till they return to rest. They are never left without a watchful eye, and ear, and guide, either in school or out of school. In all their play-hours, walks &c. a master or masters are ever with them. And I can conscientiously testify that no evil communication passes between my pupils, from half years' end to half years' end; excepting, on an occasion, from new pupils, who have been under a very different system and element of things'. One suspects Wilkie was included in this latter category. Having enjoyed considerable freedom in the warmth of southern Europe, he reacted defiantly to this chilling level of control. As a result, he was, in his own words, 'perpetually getting punished as "a bad boy"'. Cole used him as an example, telling his other pupils if they misbehaved, 'If it had been Collins I should not have felt shocked and surprised. Nobody <u>expects</u> anything of <u>him</u>. But You!! &c &c.'

By the summer of 1840, Wilkie was sixteen and a half and aching to get away from Mr Cole's clutches. He might have left earlier, had it not been for his father's health. In the last couple of years, the inflammation in William's eyes had worsened: it was probably related to what he called rheumatic fever, but was more likely a symptom of advanced gout. Either way, it was a terrible affliction for an artist. At one stage a rumour went round that he had completely lost his sight. So in July he went in search of a cure at a spa in Bad Schwalbach, near Wiesbaden, and Wilkie was condemned to a further few months in Highbury Place.

William was accompanied on his travels by several members of the Otter family, his neighbours in Avenue Road. With their blood ties to his old Irvingite friend, Dr Thompson, they were part of an extended network of a kind that featured regularly throughout Wilkie's life. Living at number 10 were Elizabeth Otter, the widow of a naval officer, who was about seventy and had her main home in the town of Portsmouth, and several of her nephews and nieces, including Charles, a barrister, and his unmarried sister Amelia. Collins family correspondence around this time is full of references to them. The two families were in and out of each other's houses, and the Otter women would frequently look after Charley and Wilkie when home from school. On his trip to Germany William was accompanied by old Mrs Otter and her niece Amelia, as well as by a friend of the latter called Ann Musgrave, a twenty-nine-year-old teacher at a small boarding school for girls in Newark, Nottinghamshire, run by Amelia Thompson, Dr James Thompson's sister, whom the Collinses had met in Paris.

After returning home in better shape, William took a part-time job as librarian at the Royal Academy, which appealed to his sense of loyalty to the institution. However, a doctor impressed on him that the underlying cause of his health problems was the damp clay in Avenue Road, and that he would experience a marked improvement if he lived somewhere with drier soil. William found a handsome, four-storey house, newly built on gravel, at 85 Oxford Terrace in Bayswater. In the autumn of 1840, the family moved across town and again found itself living close to Hyde Park.

This was the catalyst for Wilkie to leave his school. Henry Cole boasted that pupils left him at sixteen or seventeen, trained for the world and 'soundly educated as gentlemen, both classically and mathematically, so as to sit at ease by the side of any university educated man, and possessing solid and dignified moral sentiments and principles.'

Although this may have been broadly true of Wilkie, it was irrelevant since he lacked conventional ambition and had other ideas about his future. In *Hide and Seek*, one of his most autobiographical novels, a young man spoke of wanting a life of adventure – on board a merchant ship, prospecting in Australia or exploring in the Arctic. But these were the fantasies of an adolescent; Wilkie's real preoccupation was already fiction. He had lapped up the novels the American lent him in Naples. Now, when not spinning stories, he was reading and contemplating how to improve on them.

That October he begged his mother to send him a book called *Tales for an Idler*, in which he mentioned four stories with particular enthusiasm – all by women, one by the Irish writer Mrs S.C. Hall and three by the Honourable Mrs Caroline Norton. This was an unusual request for a schoolboy, but a timely enquiry since the high-born dandy found in the silver-fork style of fiction of the previous decade was already being reclothed in more democratic garb as the urban flâneur or idler, and given an English makeover as a quirky observer of humanity by Dickens in *Sketches by Boz* and *The Pickwick Papers*, both published in 1836. The latter book included the famous account of the breach of (matrimonial) promise case, Bardell v. Pickwick. This was based in part on the real-life law suit involving the same Caroline Norton, in which her abusive husband unsuccessfully sued the Prime Minister, Lord Melbourne, on the grounds of adultery with her. (Dickens himself wrote about the court case in his daytime role as a reporter for the *Morning Chronicle*.)

Already a prolific polemicist, fiction writer and editor, Caroline Norton would go on to campaign for many causes, particularly the rights of women, beset by inequitable matrimonial laws which, in her case, allowed her husband to keep custody of their children, even after he had regularly beaten her. Her activism led to the passage of the 1839 Custody of Infants Act, which mitigated the existing situation and gave women, albeit limited, rights of access to their children. This early piece of feminist legislation opened the way later in the century for further changes in the law that would confirm women's property rights and make marriage a more equal relationship.

It was a theme Wilkie would feature sympathetically in his novels. However, at this stage his interest in Caroline Norton reflected his general inquisitiveness, coupled with a canny sixth sense that women were an emerging force in the world of letters.

Liberation from Henry Cole's Academy came from an unexpected quarter. Until recently, William Collins had entertained hopes that his elder son might go up to Oxford University and prepare to become a clergyman. To this end, Wilkie was confirmed at Dodsworth's Christ Church, Albany Street, in early 1841.

But William's dream of a clerical career for his son proved short-lived. Instead, he arranged for him to join a firm of London tea merchants, run by a youngish businessman called Edmund Antrobus.

Wilkie's new employer was something of an art connoisseur and would commission William to paint a study of his three children. While there is no evidence of him as a Tractarian, he was also a conservative polemicist in the same, if rather more secular, style as Henry Cole. He became a magistrate with a particular interest in female drunkenness and juvenile delinquency. When, in 1848, London was threatened by Chartist unrest, Antrobus penned two alarmist pamphlets, whose main call was for an increase in the police force. He followed these up in 1853 with a work entitled *The Prison and the School* – all suggesting that Wilkie was in for a disciplined time, which was exactly what his father intended.

'My son requires the most unremitting parental discipline and control,' remarked the father of Wilkie's alter ego, Zack Thorpe, in his 1854 novel *Hide and Seek*, adding, 'When he is not under my own eye at home, he must be under the eyes of devout friends, in whom I can place unlimited confidence. One of these devout friends is ready to receive him into his counting-house; to keep him industriously occupied from nine in the morning till six in the evening; to surround him with estimable examples; and, in short, to share with me the solemn responsibility of managing his moral and religious training.'

Wilkie remonstrated with his father in the manner of Zack, who argued that 'he had no head for arithmetic . . . and felt perfect horror at the bare idea of entering a tea-broker's office . . . It was all very well for mother to say "hush" when his father was breaking his heart. Yes, breaking his heart! Make him anything but a tea-broker. He didn't care what.'

But William refused to be swayed. In January 1841, around the time of his seventeenth birthday, Wilkie reluctantly made his way from Bayswater to Antrobus's offices at 446 Strand (West), where he would spend the next five years. In his efforts to maximise passing trade, Antrobus had situated his premises in the busiest part (close to Trafalgar Square) of one of the liveliest streets in London. The surrounding area buzzed with theatres, offices, hostelries and booksellers. At night it was given over to prostitutes. Just across the Strand, past what is now Charing Cross station, were the Hungerford Steps, where young Charles Dickens had worked in Warren's blacking factory a decade and a half earlier. At the other end of the street, close to the Aldwych, was Coutts Bank, where Sir Edmund Antrobus, a cousin of Wilkie's boss, was a director, and Charles Ward, father of the artist Ned, was a senior manager.

Edmund Antrobus himself had been in the tea business since 1823, though his firm had been trading for a century and held a royal warrant. A few years earlier he demonstrated his professional expertise in evidence to a House of Commons enquiry into tea duties, where he expounded on the differences between congou and bohea varieties of tea, revealing that the average Englishman had a clear preference for the former, and it was no use trying to change his taste as he would not buy any alternative.

Wilkie's duties were not particularly onerous, allowing him plenty of time for his 'tale-writing'. When Antrobus found his young apprentice distracted in this way, he would reprimand him and give him extra tasks. But Wilkie was still able to find 'an hour or two in the day for my favourite pursuit'.

In the summer of 1841, William and Harriet Collins spent time apart, as had become their habit. She and her son Charley stayed for most of July and August at old Mrs Otter's other house in Southsea, a Portsmouth suburb favoured by genteel service families. William, who had been mourning the death in June of Sir David Wilkie, was left holding the fort at Oxford Terrace with Wilkie.

Living together in these circumstances, the complexities of

their relationship became more apparent. Beneath the stern disciplinarian was a loving father longing to reveal his feelings. In a letter to his absent wife, William showed parental pride in referring to a poem Wilkie had written: 'Don't say a word to him however about it, I should never be allowed to see another, the most remarkable thing about it is supposing that Berger is in love with Miss R.b.rts.' It seems Wilkie was already taking an interest in the thriving book trade around his workplace and was referring to G. Berger, a fiercely Protestant bookseller-cum-publisher in Holywell Street off the Strand.

In September, William departed on his own vacation, leaving Wilkie 'Master at the great house', as he described Oxford Terrace to his wife, while he spent three weeks at Seaford in Sussex, where he was joined by Wilkie's boss, Edmund Antrobus. William had now exhausted his Italian repertoire and, after a period of markedly religious works, reverted to his old mixture of seaside paintings and portraiture.

From Seaford William wrote in unusually brusque terms to Harriet, accusing her of sending him an 'unsatisfactory letter' which contained no information about their children. As a result, he had thought of returning the next day, 'but as I find I shall not be a welcome guest, I must I suppose remain a little longer.'

Almost a year later, not much had changed in Wilkie's life. He was still going through the motions in the tea business, and still seizing any opportunity to write his own stories. Despairing slightly, his father approached his old patron Sir Robert Peel in May 1842, hoping he might find Wilkie a job in the Civil Service. Peel was again Prime Minister, but even he had nothing to offer.

Three months earlier William's deteriorating health forced him reluctantly to give up his part-time job as librarian at the Royal Academy. It was a responsibility he had always taken seriously, remonstrating with Benjamin Haydon, in modern trade union style, 'If it were not for the Academy, depend on it, Artists would be treated like Carpenters.' Even Haydon, an entrenched opponent of this official institution, was won over by his manner, if not by his arguments, observing, 'Collins is one of the most amiable of men. He is a submissive Conservative, without servility, and an Academician without hypocrisy. He is an academical limbeck or retort – whatever comes into his mind, comes out Academical paste – you cannot help loving the fellow.'

At a loose end, William accepted a commission from the Edinburgh publisher Robert Cadell to illustrate the Abbotsford edition of Sir Walter Scott's novel *The Pirate*. This coincided with an invitation to visit Captain Henry Otter, one of the younger generation of that family, who was involved in surveying off the west coast of Scotland for the Royal Navy. Since *The Pirate* was set in the Orkney and Shetland Islands, and Wilkie was still interested enough in ships not totally to dismiss talk of a possible naval career, it seemed a good opportunity for father and son to journey north together.

After a choppy voyage up the east coast, Wilkie felt an almost forgotten sense of excitement at being in a strange place. He loved Edinburgh (or at least the lively, dirty Old Town as opposed to the melancholy, well-ordered New Town, where he and his father visited his mother's old friends, the Smiths). He rushed around, clambering up Arthur's Seat, and casting his inquisitive youthful eye over 'Rizzio's blood, Queen Mary's work basket, the Calton Hill, dirty children, filthy fish wives', and much more besides, until, as he told his mother, 'I'm out of breath and so will you be if you read this description through once.' He and William paid a pilgrimage to Abbotsford, Walter Scott's former home in Melrose on the Borders, and he even managed to visit Lasswade, where his maternal grandmother once lived in the Midlothian countryside.

Henry Otter was temporarily quartered in the very north, at Thurso in Caithness, which suited William as it was close to the islands he wanted to visit. The Collinses boarded the weekly steamer to Wick, where they were met by Otter, who took them on his tandem to Thurso. As it was mid-June, Wilkie was fascinated to experience the effects of the midnight sun and be able to read in the open air at all hours. He probably also noted a nearby town called Armadale, a name he later used as the title of a novel.

After a visit to John O'Groats (which involved a gruelling thirty-six-mile ride), Wilkie and his father returned to Wick, before embarking to their ultimate destination, Lerwick in Shetland, where William, impervious to the elements, pushed himself to complete his commission for *The Pirate*. His son wrote a comical portrait of him 'with one knee on the ground, steadying himself against the wind; his companion holding a tattering umbrella over him, to keep the rain off his sketch-book.' There were no suggestions of conflict between the two on this occasion. Wilkie enjoyed the quirkiness and sociability of Scottish inns, which he would recall in novels such as *Man and Wife*. However, he preferred the more varied terrain around Thurso, which he described in a manner that betrayed his artistic background, as he noted his surroundings with a painterly eye and described the colour of the sea, 'as deeply and brilliantly blue, on sunny days, as the Mediterranean itself – and the extraordinary northern clearness of the atmosphere, lighted to a late hour of the night by a small dull glow of sunlight lingering in the western hemisphere.'

The combination of dramatic Scottish stories and sparkling light effects stimulated Wilkie's imagination, for, back in London in August, he alarmed his aunt Catherine Gray with his animated renderings of 'the most terrible portions' of two early nineteenth-century novels that epitomised the lurid Gothic genre: *The Monk* by Matthew Gregory Lewis and *Frankenstein* by Mary Shelley. He reported to his mother, who was visiting the Otter 'clan' in Southsea, 'Every sentence that fell from my lips, was followed in rapid succession by – "Lor!" – "Oh"! "Ah!" "He! He!" "Good Gracious"! &c &c.,' adding that he did not think his 'country relations [had] ever encountered . . . such a hash of diablerie, demonology, & massacre with their Souchong and bread and butter.' Not content with making their hair stand on end, he intended serving up another course of fantastical interpretations of 'the Ancient Mariner, Jack the Giant Killer, The Mysteries of Udolpho and an enquiry into the life and actions (when they were little girls) of the witches in Macbeth'. He was enjoying himself as he began to find a voice as a narrator of creepy tales.

Aunt Catherine was one of Harriet's younger sisters who had married a local Wiltshire artist, John Westcott Gray, and spawned a large family. Like her sibling Margaret Carpenter, she was an accomplished portrait painter who would exhibit *Portrait of Two Sisters*, said to be two of her daughters, at the Royal Academy in 1844. She had recently moved to London and was living in straitened circumstances at various addresses in Marylebone, not far from her sisters.

Wilkie's depiction of the Grays as 'country relations' betrayed some snobbery on Harriet's side of the family. He regarded Aunt Catherine with amusement, once imagining a French farce in which she was in one drawing room and his mother in another. Over the next couple of years she and her children featured regularly in Wilkie's life, before fading from the picture.

One of his Gray cousins came to the rescue, when, left in charge of the 'great house', Wilkie agreed to accommodate three unexpected female visitors from the Clarkson family, another of the High Church clans the Collinses collected around them. They were Sarah Clarkson, widow of a Cambridgeshire vicar, who, together with her two daughters, had been living with her son, George Clarkson, vicar of Amberley. Wilkie fussed over whether he had done the right thing in enlisting Marion Gray's assistance, enquiring of his absent mother, 'A woman is wanted in the house isn't she?' Rather belying his vaunted experience of the opposite sex in Italy, he seemed particularly worried about the more intimate duties of housekeeping: 'Good God, suppose they should want a change of chemises!'

Getting back to work after giving up his honorary post at the Royal Academy meant that William could again concentrate on his painting. He moved around the corner from Oxford Terrace to 1 Devonport Street, where he found a house with the proper studio he had always wanted. Until then, he had made do with a room with a high ceiling or a skylight.

Despite his change of address, he remained close to the Bullars, his next-door neighbours in Oxford Terrace, who adhered to the general pattern of high-minded churchiness found in friends of the Collinses. Living there in Bayswater were John Bullar and his brother Henry, both barristers, as well as John's bright, independent-minded wife, Rosa, who became a good friend of Harriet.

The Bullar boys were sons of John Bullar, a philanthropic schoolteacher in Southampton who, among his many roles, was local secretary for the British and Foreign Bible Society. He combined political radicalism (being a profound opponent of slavery) with social conservatism (writing, as the *Oxford Dictionary of National Biography* puts it, 'a collection of edifying poetry with which he sought to counter the anti-religious tide of popular culture epitomised by the poetry of Lord Byron'). Two more of his sons, Joseph and William, were distinguished doctors in Southampton, where they would help found the Royal South Hampshire Infirmary (later Hospital). In 1841 Joseph published a book about his recent winter travels in the Azores with his brother Henry. This was illustrated with his own sketches, which were engraved, according to his preface, by Mr Thompson and 'his clever daughters', suggesting that the connection between the Bullars and Collinses also involved James Thompson, the Irvingite Apostle in Southampton. In an anonymously published book of philosophical essays entitled *Evening Thoughts, by a Physician*, Joseph Bullar later presented William Collins ('our own Collins') in the unusual guise of a religious painter, whose depictions of nature were, like those of Claude and Ruysdael, 'the outward and visible image of an internal and Divine power'. As a forward-looking doctor, Joseph would correspond with Darwin and go on to publish papers on subjects such as lunacy, epilepsy and the medical uses of chloroform and opium – studies which, given the closeness between their families, were almost certainly significant in educating Wilkie Collins in these subjects.

Now in his mid-fifties and increasingly frail, William asked John and Henry Bullar to act as witnesses to his will in May 1843. John was also appointed one of his executors, along with two clergymen, the Reverends William Dodsworth and Francis Thomas New, the vicar and curate of Christ Church, Albany Street.

Still fondly imagining his son might be suited for a naval career, William approached Charles Ward Senior at Coutts Bank in June 1843 to see if his connections might find an opening for Wilkie in the Admiralty, but again he was rebuffed. William took the news stoically, telling Harriet that if Wilkie 'does justice to the abilities the Almighty has given him and takes care of his soul & body, all must be well.'

Wilkie did come good, but not necessarily in the way his father wanted. In the summer, his perseverance with 'tale-writing' at last brought dividends as his vivid stories began to find markets. His first known success was 'Volpurno', a well-turned vignette about the ill-fated marriage of an English beauty and a moody student of astronomy with a history of derangement. It was set in Venice, with a palpable sense of the muggy splendour of the city Wilkie had visited five years earlier. Its initial appearance was in the New York magazine the *Albion, or British, Colonial and Foreign Weekly Gazette* on 8 July 1843, which suggests there was an earlier version published in Britain, but where is unknown. This was followed the next month by 'The Last Stage Coachman' in the *Illuminated Magazine*, edited by the prolific playwright and man of letters, Douglas Jerrold. A lament for an earlier mode of transport in an age when the railway was beginning to encroach, it provided a convincing portrait of an old-style coachman and his working environment, though Wilkie was keen not to appear too realistic, for he concluded his short story with a description of a magnificent phantom coach of a now disappearing kind.

For all his aspirations to fairness, William Collins could not help regarding his younger son as less of a liability than Wilkie. Although weak in physique and timid by nature, Charley had shown a considerable talent for painting, and in January 1844 won a coveted place at the Royal Academy Schools. Unlike his brother, Charley was devout and was confirmed a few months later by the Bishop of London, Charles James Blomfield, at Christ Church, Albany Street. This time the event was noted in William's diary. In the official church record, Charley's name appeared a couple of pages ahead of Christina Rossetti, from another artistic family living in Charlotte Street, who was confirmed in 1845, aged fourteen.

Charley's acceptance as a student at the Schools came a few days after his brother's twentieth birthday, which Wilkie celebrated with a series of drunken parties. In a letter to his mother, which is notable for his calling himself 'Wilkie Collins' for the first time, he claimed to have got home from one of these sprees at ten past four in the morning. Until this moment the name 'William' had always comprised part of his signature, and he had been known as 'Willy' or 'Willie'. But now the time had come to assert his identity and, in a gesture of Oedipal significance, he discarded his father's moniker. Henceforth, he was to be simply Wilkie Collins.

Strangely, his ebullience and apparent independence did not stop him attending a reunion at Henry Cole's Academy later that month. His former headmaster's wife seemed to have a lingering erotic charge. As he told his mother, one item on the timetable was, 'Mrs C to be embraced by the scholars at ½ past six precisely', suggesting a prim woman who demanded attention from her former charges.

In April, William went to stay with Dr James Norris, President of Corpus Christi College in Oxford, where he observed with relish the latest developments in the controversy involving the Oxford Movement. The battle lines were now drawn between the Anglican establishment and the Tractarians, who attacked moral and theological laxity and advocated traditional religious practices which, for some, were uncomfortably close to the Roman Catholic Church. The previous May, the leading Tractarian Edward Pusey had been suspended from preaching in Oxford for two years after voicing unorthodox ideas about the Holy Eucharist. William showed his colours when he described Pusey's treatment as 'persecution' by 'the steady-going jog-trots of this learned and powerful University'. He also arranged for his host to read some of Wilkie's writings. Norris was impressed and expressed the wish that the young man had had the advantage of a university education. But William realised it was too late, feeling also that, having now briefly experienced college life himself, he was not sure if it would have been right for his son.

It was indeed too late. In August, Wilkie was due to leave for Paris with Charles Ward, his friend Ned's elder brother. At the time the Ward family lived in Russell Place, Fitzroy Square, next door to the artist Daniel Maclise, who had enjoyed his first break when he sketched Sir Walter Scott in his native city of Cork in Ireland. After moving to London he had gained a reputation as a painter of portraits and history subjects (like Ned Ward), and as a magazine and book illustrator who mixed easily with authors such as Dickens. With his good looks and flowing dark hair, Maclise was a womaniser, who had enjoyed an affair with Benjamin Disraeli's former mistress, Lady Henrietta Sykes. This had led to an abortive divorce case, not unlike the one involving Caroline Norton. With Dickens and their mutual friend, the actor W.C. Macready, Maclise was also deeply involved in the London theatre.

The Wards were not only neighbours of Maclise but also good friends: in 1846 Ned Ward would paint the portrait of the Irishman that now hangs in the National Portrait Gallery. Whenever Wilkie visited the Ward brothers, he would have been spurred by the air of artistic endeavour, both there and next door.

Wilkie had not recently spent much time at Russell Place, however. In July he complained that he had only seen 'Romeo Ward' once in the previous fortnight. This was a reference to Charles, who was romancing Wilkie's sweet seventeen-year-old cousin Jane Carpenter. However, since Charles was thirty and working with his father at Coutts, this caused consternation to both families.

The trip to Paris promised to be an extended stag party, with Charles Ward enjoying his last months as a bachelor, and Wilkie re-enacting the excitements of earlier Continental escapades in Rome with his companion's younger brother Ned. The two men established themselves in the central Hotel de Tours, from where Wilkie sent back curious (and, one imagines, carefully edited) accounts of his exploits, in the manner of disaffected youth through the ages. He visited Versailles and the

Louvre, but was only impressed by a couple of history paintings in the latter. *Otello* at the Opéra was 'monotonously dismal', the Théâtre-Français a bore. Even a wedding proved tedious: '[I] don't take much interest in Matrimony,' he wrote to his mother, 'so can't tell you anything more about the ceremony of marriage here than that the bridegrooms looked foolish and wore ill-cut coats and that the Priests looked sulky and had generally speaking red noses.' He would remain unconvinced about matrimony and would never himself take a bride. However, he was fascinated with the institution, which he observed and regularly commented on in his novels.

He was happy to admit to 'dissipating fearfully – gardens, theatres and Cafés', but avoided any reference to encounters with the opposite sex, and his letters give little sense of the vitality of street life during the latter years of the July Monarchy, when new ideas were circulating, writers such as Balzac were surfacing, and the cancan was flourishing in boulevard cafés. His enjoyment of this side of Paris was doubtless enhanced when they met Charles's louche neighbour, the artist Daniel Maclise.

Wilkie's apparent indifference to mainstream Parisian culture did not stop him asking his parents if they could wring some extra holiday for him from his boss. References such as this, together with records of William Collins's bank accounts, which show him paying sums regularly to his son as well as occasionally to Antrobus, suggest that Wilkie was never more than an apprentice, possibly unsalaried and subsidised by his father.

After returning home via Southampton, and visiting his mother at the Otters' in Southsea, Wilkie once more assumed his perch in the Strand. His surreptitious writing now became more ambitious as he began a novel called (in full) *Iolani; or, Tahiti as it was; A Romance*, which told the thrilling if improbable story of Iolani, the villainous high priest and brother of the king, his involvement in sorcery, revenge and bloody inter-tribal conflict, and his cruelty after his concubine Idia seeks to prevent their daughter being sacrificed, according to traditional custom.

Wilkie drew heavily on his copy of *Polynesian Researches*, a travelogue by the missionary William Ellis, published in four volumes in 1832–4. This was an account of Ellis's efforts to introduce Christianity into a corrupt, primitive society where practices such as infanticide and polygamy existed. Despite his own family's links with muscular Christianity (epitomised by the death of his great uncle in the Gold Coast), Wilkie did not adopt the civilising narrative of Ellis's story, using only its detail, including the names of his main protagonists, various tribal customs and aspects of the island's history.

Iolani was notable for introducing several themes that would become staples in Wilkie's later fiction – notably, his vivid portrayal of an evil villain (reprised in Count Fosco in *The Woman in White*) and his sympathetic treatment of strong, independent women. His splitting of the book into three separate parts gave it the sense of a drama, divided into acts – another idea he used in later novels. Its full title was significant because, in labelling it a romance, Wilkie sought to place himself in the tradition of Walter Scott, who in his 1824 'Essay on Romance' had defined the genre as 'a fictitious narrative in prose or verse; the interest of which turns upon marvellous and uncommon incidents'. Wilkie was happy to describe several of his other books as romances, including his next work *Antonina* (1850) and his great mystery story *The Moonstone* (1868).

Wilkie used his father's contacts to send his manuscript to the established publishers Longman. Although it was accepted by the firm's reader, negotiations for its publication broke down after they failed to agree terms (despite William offering to cover a third of the costs). Wilkie then sent it to Chapman and Hall, until recently Dickens's publishers. However, he heard nothing from them during the summer of 1845, by which time he was itching to get back to Paris. His travelling companion of the previous year was now, at least temporarily, indisposed: on 4 February, Charles Ward had married his sweetheart Jane Carpenter and was occupied with family affairs.

So in early September 1845, Wilkie journeyed back to Paris on his own. He again showed a strange mix of enthusiasm and disdain, extravagantly comparing a history painting exhibited at Versailles, Horace Vernet's *The Capture of Abd-el-Kader's Camp at Taguim*, to Michelangelo's *Last Judgement*, while concluding that two shows of up-and-coming landscape and history painters were dire – 'the worst Suffolk street landscape is superior to the best picture' in the former, while the standards in the latter were 'ineffably below those of the Royal Academy students'.

By chance he met William Hookham Carpenter, his uncle by marriage and Charles Ward's new father-in-law, who was in Paris 'on government business' linked to his recent appointment as Keeper of Prints and Drawings at the British Museum. When his father scolded him for failing to answer his letters, Wilkie responded indignantly, poking fun at the old man's religious convictions: 'Considering that he is a lamb of Mr Dodsworth's flock, Mr Collins evinces a most unchurchmanlike disposition to scandalise other people.' His scripturally-minded mother saw Paris as a Babylon where Satan more or less walked the streets. This caused Wilkie to remonstrate with her too: '"The Evil One" (whom you mention with somewhat unladylike want of courtesy at the close of your letter) is such an exceedingly gentlemanlike dog in this city, with his theatres and his kitchens, that I find it rather difficult to "cut his commission".'

Again there was no mention of women. But he did ask for an advance of £100, later cut to £10, arguing cheekily that he had been given money for the trip to Paris, but not for his return. He threatened that, without the cash, he would have to remain in situ, 'the actual difference between imprisonment at Paris and imprisonment at the Strand being too inconsequential to be worth ascertaining to a nicety.'

When he did get back to his office, he must have learnt that Chapman and Hall, like Longman, was not interested in *Iolani*. No letter specifically states this, but nothing more was heard of the manuscript until it was sold in an auction in 1900, and it was not published until 1999. Feeling this rejection, Wilkie began contemplating another novel, *Antonina*, a grand historical saga about the fall of Rome, a subject he had been mulling over since visiting the city almost a decade earlier. He had read Bulwer-Lytton's *The Last Days of Pompeii* and Gibbon's *Decline and Fall of the Roman Empire*, but he wanted to do further research and with the help of the Librarian at the British Museum, Sir Henry Ellis, he obtained a reader's ticket there in March 1846.

Six months earlier, in September, his mother had been holi-daying as usual on the south coast and had stayed with the Antrobuses in Torquay, but soon afterwards relations between the two families broke down. A letter from Wilkie to a friend (perhaps a colleague in his Strand office or even Charles Ward) referred to 'old tea-bags' (Antrobus) reneging on a promise to pay Wilkie £200 a year, after declaring 'that he could have had plenty of young men in his office, my equals in birth and educa-tion'. As a result there was 'a mighty feud "henceforth and forever" between the "houses twain" of Collins and Antrobus.' Wilkie asked his correspondent to furnish him with any relevant details he came across, promising 'whatever you tell me shall be kept "as secret as the grave", or one of your domestic epistles'. He ended with the request, 'Burn this immediately'.

The records are sparse during this period. The manuscript for *Antonina* shows that Wilkie started it on 23 April 1846, less than a month after receiving his British Museum ticket. On 18 May he was admitted to train as a barrister at Lincoln's Inn. He almost certainly left Antrobus several weeks or even months earlier. But, as long as his father was alive, there was no question of his being allowed to concentrate on writing. He had to make another attempt at an accepted profession. Luckily, several close family friends, including Charles Otter and John and Henry Bullar, his neighbours in Oxford Terrace, were connected to Lincoln's Inn. So it was like paying an entry subscription to a conservative Tractarian clan when Wilkie handed over his initial fees and began to go through the motions of a legal career.

The Inn's terms were hardly taxing and so, by July, he was able to take a short holiday in Belgium with Charles Ward, who left his young wife and their seven-month-old daughter in London. Wilkie was also turning his back on responsibilities. His father's health had deteriorated, and his parents spent some time in the countryside at Iver in Buckinghamshire. Despite resorting to Battley's Drops, a tincture of opium, to give him respite from pain, William was wasting away, and in November he reluctantly called a halt to all involvement with the Royal Academy. He struggled on a little longer, and died on 17 February 1847. After a small private funeral six days later, he was buried in the same cemetery as his mother and brother, in St Mary's Church, Paddington Green. Aside from legacies to his cousin, Mrs Elizabeth Jones in Dublin, and four of Harriet's sisters, he bequeathed the remainder of his estate in trust to provide an income to his wife during her lifetime, and then to be shared equally by his sons and their heirs after her death. His main asset was £11,548 in government securities, known as consols, but this amount increased with the sale of various paintings and his estate was eventually worth over £16,000 – at least £1 million today. This was a notable achievement for an early Victorian who had grown up in relative poverty and made his living as an artist. And it would provide a welcome and rather essential financial cushion as Wilkie set out into adulthood.

4

GETTING INTO PRINT

ONE WARM SPRING morning in May 1848, Wilkie had a date he could not ignore. Despite its proximity to the street where he was born, All Souls, Langham Place, John Nash's elegant church at the top of Regent Street, was not a place he had often visited. But his friend Ned Ward was getting married there on 4 May, and Wilkie had an important role to perform. Thirty-one-year-old Ned's intended bride was his neighbour Henrietta Ward (no relation). But, at fifteen, she did not have her parents' permission to marry. Thus the whole process of arranging the wedding, in which Wilkie was intimately involved, had to be done carefully and secretly.

The two Wards' passion for each other had been clear for over four years – more or less since the day Henrietta's artist father George Raphael Ward, who lived in Fitzroy Square, walked around the corner to Ned's family house in Russell Place after the coincidence of their surnames led to one too many mix-ups in the delivery of his post. George Raphael had liked young Ned and engaged him to teach his precocious dark-haired daughter.

Benefiting from Ned's tuition, Henrietta had her first painting accepted at the Royal Academy in 1846. She was still only fourteen when, soon afterwards, she accepted his proposal of marriage. But her parents objected, and asked them to wait a couple of years. This did not stop Ned celebrating their engagement with a magnificent ball in his studio. Henrietta wore a dazzling yellow tarlatan dress, with a double skirt, tied with satin ribbons and looped at the side with a white rose.

Despite the happy occasion, Henrietta was taken aback when the celebrated baritone Henry Russell, who was providing the evening's entertainment, sang 'The Madman' (or 'The Maniac'). This melodramatic song told of a prisoner who, haunted by visions of his lover, protests his sanity in deranged fashion. It 'made us all shiver', Henrietta later recalled, and it was meant to, for Russell regarded himself as a musical Charles Dickens, using songs to educate his audience about social problems. In this one, he was exposing the evils of the private lunatic asylum, where individuals could be confined and forgotten, a theme Wilkie later took up in his novels.

Henrietta put aside any presentiments as she struggled with her mother who, she said, was 'jealous at my affection being given so fully to my future husband'. Her parents insisted she should be chaperoned wherever she went. But when she found that Ned's letters to her had been opened, she was incensed and, being a wilful young woman, planned her secret marriage in the Royal Academy's Octagon Room, where the paintings for that year's Summer Exhibition were being displayed.

Wilkie, who had been asked to give the bride away, also acted as Cupid, using his legal training to help obtain a special marriage licence. 'He impressed great caution and secrecy, as he planned out the whole affair with zest and enjoyment', Henrietta recalled. The plan was that on the morning of the wedding she would tell her parents she was spending the day with Jane Ward, the wife of Ned's brother Charles, in St Johns Wood. Once there, she would make her way to All Souls in Langham Place.

Having gone through this diversionary procedure, she arrived at the church to find Ned standing brazenly outside in a brilliant white waistcoat with a matching gardenia in his lapel. As usual, he had been carried away by his own enthusiasm and she feared that his casual ostentation might have alerted her parents. But the service went without incident. Wilkie 'gave me away to the best of men, with a hearty good will', she recalled.

After the ceremony there was a surreal moment when Wilkie hailed a cab. Before the newly-weds could pull away, their party was accosted by a crowd of revellers dressed in tree-like foliage, who were acting out parts of the traditional pagan ritual of Jack in the Green in belated celebration of May Day. Any suggestion of mob rule was alarming since, only the previous month, the Chartists had marched on London in protest against living and working conditions – the British equivalent of the revolutions then taking place in France and across Europe. The threat of the Chartists was taken seriously in both Ward families, with Ned and his new father-in-law serving as volunteer special constables.

The couple returned to Charles and Jane Ward's house in Grove End Road, St Johns Wood, where they were joined for dinner by Henrietta's unwitting mother and father, and by Wilkie and Charley Collins. After the meal she and Ned walked back to Fitzroy Square, accompanied by her parents. She later described how her heart was racing as she imagined 'how furious they would be when they found out that I had disobeyed'.

Three months later, her parents still, extraordinarily, gave no indication of knowing about the marriage. However, the tension of enforced secrecy was making Henrietta ill. On 1 June she reached the age of sixteen and Ned could no longer be accused of abducting her if they ran away together, which was their plan, with Wilkie again making the arrangements. He booked for them to stay initially in Iver, Buckinghamshire – possibly at the place his father had visited on his final holiday the previous year. From there Henrietta and Ned proceeded on a more leisurely honey-moon in Holland and Belgium, taking care to avoid Paris, which was still in the throes of insurrection. Wilkie would mull over the experience and return to the issue of marriage to a young girl without her parents' consent in his novel *Basil* (1852) and his later extended short story *Miss or Mrs?* (1872).

Since studying in Rome a decade earlier, Ned Ward had associated with a group of painters known as the Clique, most of whom had been at the Royal Academy Schools in the mid-1830s. Other members included William Powell Frith, Augustus Egg and Richard Dadd, though the latter's involvement was curtailed after he was committed to the Bethlem (or Bedlam) mental hospital for murdering his father in 1843. The Clique met regularly to sketch, but had no particular agenda, aside from maintaining the unholy fusion of Academic traditionalism and Hogarthian populism that had been the hallmark of both David Wilkie and William Collins. Frith, a friend of Dickens, specialised in literary themes, though he would later find fame with large narrative paintings, such as *Life at the Seaside* (1854) and *The Derby Day* (1856–8). Egg, the sharp-featured son of a gunmaker from Alsace, was noted for his hospitality, particularly after moving to Bayswater in 1847.

Influenced by his friend Thomas Babington Macaulay, Ward specialised in historical subjects. He was promoted professionally by Samuel Carter Hall, a prolific Irish-born journalist who edited the *Art Journal*, the first periodical to report on the art market. A prim character (often said to be the model for Mr Pecksniff in Dickens's *Martin Chuzzlewit*), he was married to Anna (Mrs S.C. Hall), one of the writers whose work Wilkie had asked his mother to send him at school, and together they had a wide circle of literary and artistic friends.

Wilkie was surrounded by such talented people as he strove to make his mark on the world in the wake of his father's death.

He temporarily stopped work on his novel *Antonina*, and turned to writing William Collins's biography. It says something about Wilkie's easy-going nature that he was prepared, out of a sense of filial duty, to put his own career on hold, forget differences of opinion and carry out this task.

Wilkie set about asking his father's friends – mainly artists, authors and actors – for accounts of his life. He was still studying for the Bar, but that summer he allowed himself a few weeks in Normandy and Paris with Charles Ward. Then he returned to work. After unsuccessfully sounding out John Murray, he reached an agreement with Longman to publish *Memoirs of the Life of William Collins* on the old-fashioned subscription basis, which meant asking William's former patrons and friends to pay one guinea in advance. This was too much for the rigid Tory, John Wilson Croker, who said he would prefer to wait until the book appeared. But others were happy to put up the money, including Sir Robert Peel, who was now in opposition after failing to carry his party over the Repeal of the Corn Laws and who, crucially for the success of the exercise, consented to have the *Memoirs* dedicated to him. Potential subscribers were relieved to learn that the veteran man of letters Alaric A. Watts would help the inexperienced Wilkie edit the book.

In the spring of 1848, Wilkie's attention was temporarily distracted by Ned Ward's marriage to Henrietta. However, with Watts's help, the *Memoirs* proceeded smoothly and proofs were available in August. Forgoing his usual holiday, Wilkie helped his mother move – together with her sons, a couple of servants and the family cat, Snooks – to a smaller, more manageable house at 38 Blandford Square. This was an up-and-coming area just north of the Marylebone Road and favoured by several of Wilkie's friends, including the newly married Wards.

By December that year, the *Memoirs* were ready for publication. Although favourably reviewed in the *Observer*, the book did not win universal plaudits. After reading it on a Boxing Day train journey, the diarist Henry Crabb Robinson declared it 'an ordinary work, which to one unacquainted with the art could give no pleasure'. He recalled meeting William in Rome, while travelling with Wordsworth a decade earlier. As a practising Unitarian, he had decided not to follow up the acquaintance after a friend told him of William's withering comment, 'I would not shake hands with a Unitarian knowingly.'

This pronouncement displayed the worst of William's Tractarian prejudices against Nonconformism. The last few years of his life had seen an intensification of the dispute between a laissez-faire Anglican Church establishment and Tractarian fundamentalists pushing for a return to more traditional rites. In 1845, John Newman, one of the latter, had taken the argument to its logical conclusion and embraced Roman Catholicism, where he was followed by others, including both Dodsworth and New, the vicar and curate at Christ Church, Albany Street.

Having completed the *Memoirs*, Wilkie was free to return to *Antonina*. However, he was determined not to ignore his other interests: in January 1849 he informed Washington Allston's nephew, Richard Dana Jr, in Boston, that although he did not 'follow my father's profession', he did dabble in 'painting in leisure moments, in humble amateur-fashion, for my own amuse-ment'. (Dana, a lawyer by training, had enjoyed great success a few years earlier with his sea-faring memoir, *Two Years Before the Mast*. However, he had sold the rights to Harper Brothers for $250: the book is reputed to have made the company $50,000.)

As a result it was not unexpected when in May a painting of his called *The Smuggler's Retreat* appeared at the Royal Academy Summer Exhibition. Wilkie had been working up to this moment, as three drawings now held in the Morgan Library in New York demonstrate. The first is a sketch of a castle by a river, signed 'W. Wilkie Collins' and dated April 1841. Given the date, it may have been a doodle from his early days at

Antrobus. The second drawing shows an Italianate group of buildings, and the third, a rural scene reminiscent of his father's work, carries an 1844 watermark.

As he intimated to Dana, his artistic endeavours were never particularly serious. In this spirit, he had taken his 'cherished painting box' to France on his trip with Charles Ward almost two years earlier, and produced three works, two of which he admitted were failures (including one executed at the abbey of St Georges de Boscherville, outside Rouen, on an outing he wrote up for *Bentley's Miscellany*), but the third he described as 'exceedingly good, and a most elaborate undertaking – for it occupied three days of my time'. This may well have been the canvas he submitted to the Summer Exhibition. Unfortunately, its current whereabouts is unknown and no image has survived.

Charley Collins, who had shown a portrait of Rosa, John Bullar's wife, there two years earlier, was also represented on the walls of the Royal Academy in 1849. However, the most interesting and controversial works in the exhibition came from two of Charley's friends, John Everett Millais and William Holman Hunt, whose paintings *Lorenzo and Isabella* and *Rienzi Vowing to Obtain Justice for the Death of his Young Brother* were the first to carry the initials PRB, designating a new artistic group, the Pre-Raphaelite Brotherhood.

Unlike the Clique, the Brotherhood had a manifesto. Its members were tired of the dull formalism of most Academic art, with its obeisance to the old masters. (A bête noire was Sir Joshua Reynolds, the first president of the Royal Academy, who was dubbed Sir Sloshua for his slapdash brushwork.) Instead, they returned to the simple naturalism of painters before Raphael. They would not fully establish themselves for a couple more years. However, their ideas were now on the agenda, an artistic reflection of the yearning for traditionalism which had also spawned Pusey and Newman.

The atmosphere at the new Collins family house in Blandford Square reflected this intellectual diversity, with Wilkie associating with the Clique through Ned Ward, and Charley affiliating himself with the Pre-Raphaelites. As Wilkie had told Dana, 'I live very much in the society of artists'. And it was a way of life his mother encouraged. As a reaction against the travails of her husband's final years, Harriet had begun to relax and enjoy herself. Just shy of sixty, she could still be staid, advising Henrietta Ward against combining a career as an artist with bringing up a family, which was surprising for someone whose sister had undertaken both roles so successfully. But she loved the company of her sons' artistic friends – not only the Wards, but Charley's Pre-Raphaelite colleagues, particularly Millais and Holman Hunt, who flirted outrageously with her.

One way of merging literary and artistic interests was amateur dramatics. After an early dinner at 5pm, Wilkie and his friends would stage their own plays in the 'Theatre Royal, Back Drawing Room'. One of their first productions, on 19 June 1849, was *The Good Natur'd Man* by Oliver Goldsmith, which featured Wilkie as producer, actor and author of a new prologue. The combined role was not easy: 'The disappointments we have met with in getting up the Play would fill a three volume novel,' he told one of the Clarkson girls. But he managed to corral Ned Ward (who also designed the costumes) and another Clique member, William Powell Frith, as actors. Charley also played a part, as did John Millais. Harriet, who had once hoped to be an actress, could not fail to have been thrilled.

Irish-born Goldsmith was a cult figure among Wilkie and his friends. A few years earlier Ned had painted the scene (recounted in Boswell's *Life of Johnson*) where Dr Johnson appears just as Goldsmith is about to be evicted by his landlady for non-payment of his rent. The good doctor finds the manuscript of *The Vicar of Wakefield* and promptly sells it for £60. Wilkie no doubt enjoyed this insight into the writing profession (together with the detail that Goldsmith had spent his last money on a bottle of Madeira). Wilkie would have empathised with Goldsmith's physical deformities, particularly his protuberant brow, though he himself was never described as 'monkey face'. A substantial biography of Goldsmith had recently been published by Dickens's friend John Forster, so, if Wilkie did not know before, he would have learned how Goldsmith had been appointed historian of the Royal Academy by his friend Sir Joshua Reynolds.

Now Frith painted a scene directly from *The Good Natur'd Man*. His *Mr Honeywood Introduces the Bailiffs to Mrs Richland as his Friends* would be exhibited at the Royal Academy the following year. Although he does not specifically state so, he was clearly working from a Blandford Square production. So it is interesting to speculate which actor in the work was Wilkie. Since he was reported to have given the main parts in this production to his friends and to have concentrated on his role as stage manager, he probably took a smaller part – perhaps one of the bailiffs in Frith's painting.

By the middle of 1849 Wilkie's novel *Antonina* was nearing completion. Set in the early fifth century, with Rome under siege from the Goths, it told the story of a young Roman girl – the title's namesake – caught between two cultures after she falls in love with the chieftain of the invading forces. In highlighting the contrasts between Christianity and paganism within Rome and between Classical civilisation and barbarism in Europe, Wilkie suggested something of the cultural tensions in late 1840s Britain (where another example of backward-looking traditionalism could be found in the cult of Gothic architecture). Inspired by his research, he worked hard to conjure up ancient Rome, backing his factual references with notes and geographical detail, with the result that *Antonina* sometimes reads like a guidebook, interspersed with Wilkie's own recollections of places such as the Pincian Hill.

Wilkie was still finding his feet as a novelist and not yet confident enough to give full rein to his imagination. He remained self-conscious about his technique, drawing on his familiarity with art for ways of creating and heightening interest, so that, 'in the painter's phrase, the "effects" might thus be best "massed," and the "lights and shadows" most harmoniously "balanced" and "discriminated"', as he put it in his first preface to this book.

There was also evidence of his maturing ideas. He commented incisively on the role of women among the Goths, emphasizing the wilfulness of the chieftain's sister, who was bent on revenge on anything or anyone Roman (including Antonina) because the city had been responsible for the deaths of her children. However, his strongest attack was reserved for intolerance and bullying, either by parents or religious families. There was more than a hint of a personal agenda in his portrayal of Antonina's father, Numerian, who breaks her lute, her favourite means of self-expression, describing it as 'the invention of libertines'.

Still needing a publisher, he approached Richard Bentley, who had made his name in the 1830s with cheapish editions of novels. In 1837, Bentley hired the up-and-coming Charles Dickens to edit his new monthly magazine *Bentley's Miscellany*. But the two men fell out, leading Dickens to decamp to Chapman and Hall and rail against the 'Burlington Street Brigand'. By 1849, Bentley was suffering financial difficulties, though this might not have been known to Wilkie, who showed astute bargaining skills in his dealings with the publisher, emphasising not only the success of the biography of his father, but also the topicality of Rome as a subject in the aftermath of the 1848 Revolution that had forced Pope Pius IX to flee the city. Despite a last-minute hitch, when Wilkie fretted that Antonina was not a suitable name as it recalled the dissolute wife of the Byzantine general Belisarius, he was rewarded with a deal that gave him £100 on publication and £100 after five hundred copies were sold.

Before the book appeared, Wilkie returned to the stage – this time in public – at Miss Kelly's Theatre, situated at the back of the actress Miss Fanny Kelly's house in Dean Street, Soho. The sweet, round-faced Miss Kelly had been helped financially in the building of the theatre, which doubled as an acting school, by the art-loving 'Bachelor Duke', the sixth Duke of Devonshire. Dickens had used the place since the mid-1840s for performances by his occasional theatrical company, the Amateurs. Having translated *A Court Duel*, a French melodrama set in the early eighteenth century, Wilkie arranged a performance on 26 February 1850 on behalf of the Female Emigration Fund, recently established by the MP Sidney Herbert to help destitute seamstresses find a new life in the colonies. It was a fashionable cause: the lure of the city undermined family life, putting unemployed women onto the streets and into the grip of prostitution. It complemented another of Dickens's initiatives – Urania Cottage, a refuge for fallen women, which he had established in Shepherds Bush with financial help from Angela Burdett-Coutts (of the banking family).

In *A Court Duel*, Charley Collins took the lead, while Wilkie acted a comic courtier. There was also a part for Henry Brandling, who had entered the Royal Academy Schools at the same time as Charley. To lend credibility, since the performance was a public one, a professional actress was recruited, Jane Mordaunt, whose most recent appearance had been in the royal theatricals at Windsor Castle. As nieces of Lady Cranstoun, she and her more successful elder sister Louisa (in real life, Lady Boothby, wife of a baronet) were often hired to play high-society roles.

However, there was another side to Jane, as is clear from her entry in a contemporary publication *The Swell's Night Guide*, which detailed the various bawdy houses, drinking dens and gambling joints that might be patronised by a hedonistic young gentleman, as well as listing the names of several of the more superior *demi-mondaines* they might encounter. This sounds exactly the sort of reading matter that a bored law student with a taste for the nightlife might have picked up from one of the cheap booksellers around the Strand. Listed among the actresses was Jane Mordaunt: 'Her hair is dark, long and luxuriant; her eyes large, dark, soft, and melting; while her smile has fascination in it that . . . [would] have tempted even the moral St Anthony.'

The day after the performance at Miss Kelly's Theatre, *Antonina* was published in a three-volume edition (the industry standard for novels), with a dedication to Lady Chantrey, widow of his father's colleague, the sculptor Sir Francis Chantrey, who had amassed a fortune from his busts of the great and the good. She did not know Wilkie, but one thing he had learned from his father was the value of such contacts. When Mrs Hunter, David Wilkie's sister, went to Bentley's offices to pick up her reserved copy, she was (erroneously) told it was a gift from the author. As soon as the cost-conscious Wilkie heard about this, he quickly moved to inform Bentley that the people on a list he had given the publisher were expected to pay for their copies. Among them was his father's old friend Dr James Thompson, who had moved from Southampton and was living near Henry Drummond, the wealthy leading figure in the Catholic Apostolic Church in the Surrey village of Albury.

Perhaps Wilkie wanted to understand more about his father's spiritual life, for he went to stay with Thompson in March but disliked the countryside, with its 'cursed confused chirping of birds – an unnecessarily large supply of fresh air – and a d—d absence of cabs, omnibuses, circulating libraries, public houses, newspaper offices, pastry cooks shops, and other articles of civilisation'. He was more interested in the progress of his book and asked Charles Ward to send him copies of any review he saw – and apply to 'Mamma Collins for payment of your charges'.

These notices were generally favourable, led by the respected Henry Chorley in the *Athenaeum*, who welcomed 'a richly-coloured impassioned story, busy with life, importunately strong in its appeals to our sympathy', though he warned Wilkie against 'the vices of the French school . . . against catering for prurient tastes', and, an augury of his criticism of Wilkie's later sensation works, he became unnecessarily personal when he asked, 'Need we remind a painter's son how much Terror and Power are enhanced by Beauty?'

The anonymous reviewer in the *Spectator* took a similar approach, accusing Wilkie of being too rhetorical ('Everything is pitched in too high a key') and of describing scenes with 'too much of the glare and mannerism of the scene-painter'. In other words, Wilkie had failed to move far enough from the artificial theatricality of Ned Ward's canvases. Nevertheless, the reviewer acknowledged that Wilkie had 'a painter's eye for description, much eloquence of a florid kind, clever "treatment" and invention in the incidents, with some tenderness if not pathos'.

Wilkie would draw on his artistic background and his understanding of technique throughout his working life, but he had made up his mind where his future lay, and it was not in painting. His cousin Alexander Gray later described how Wilkie 'showed me a picture which he had just finished and said it would be the last he intended painting. He then showed me his first book, Antonina, or The Fall of Rome, of which he made me a present, saying his future would be devoted to writing books.'

As the summer of 1850 drew on, the atmosphere in the Collins house in Blandford Square was unsettled. Like others in the vicinity, Harriet regarded the area as a staging post, but she had still not yet decided where she wanted to live permanently. With this matter still in the air in July, Wilkie took a working holiday in Cornwall, where he wanted to write an upbeat travel journal. This was an established, indeed hackneyed, genre: many people had produced accounts of treks to the Lakes or the Highlands, but Wilkie thought he could interest readers by making a point of exploring a part of the country not yet touched by the railways. As he was hoping for publication, he needed someone to illustrate his words. Since his brother was otherwise occupied with the Pre-Raphaelites, he

teamed up with Charley's friend Henry Brandling, an interesting
choice since he came from a distinguished Northumbrian family,
which, after making money in coal, had helped bring the railways
to the north-east. The two industries were closely linked, since
the first railways had been developed to carry coal. Indeed, the
first working railway was at the Middleton Colliery in Yorkshire,
owned by one of Henry's ancestors in the mid-eighteenth century.
Subsequently Henry's father Robert had raised money for his
friend, the engineer and railway pioneer George Stephenson, in
gratitude for inventing the miners' safety lamp. After his father's
death in 1848, Henry had followed Wilkie on a drawing tour of
northern France. This resulted later that year in a book of litho-
graphs, printed by M. and N. Hanhart from an address in Fitzroy
Square, where Henry lived with his sister Emma, a beauty whose
looks had stirred the local artistic community.

Since Cornwall was beyond the reach of the railway line, there
had been no reason to build a bridge over the river Tamar, which
divides the county from Devon. So the two men began their
journey by boat, from Plymouth to St Germans. From there they
travelled along the south coast, through Looe, 'a snug cosy primitive old place', and Liskeard, which was rather different, with an
inn so unwelcoming that Wilkie wanted to rename it the Sackcloth
and Ashes. This was an exception, however: generally speaking he
loved the locals' company and lapped up their stories of Druid
history and Celtic legends. He also delighted in the variations in
the landscape, particularly the dramatic rocks and cliffs by the sea.

Before reaching Lands End, he dipped down to the Lizard,
the southernmost point of England, where he was entranced by
Kynance Cove with its natural amphitheatre of rocks. When
Tennyson, the new poet laureate, had been there a couple of
years earlier, he had noted its 'glorious grass green monsters
of waves'. Wilkie strove to improve on this in telling his mother
about the colours of the rocks – 'deep red and rich brown and
green and yellow and silver grey – as bright as polished marble',

with the sea 'a <u>Mediterranean blue</u> and the sky covered with minute driving, fleecy clouds'.

On his way back, passing northwards via Newquay, he visited a strict Carmelite convent at Lanherne House, formerly owned by the landed Arundell family, in the village of St Mawgan. Setting aside his innate anti-Catholicism, he was impressed by the commitment of the nuns, with their capacity for good works and their 'generous sympathy for those weaknesses of impatience and irresolution in others'. He was interested how 'that vigilant and indestructible papal religion, which defies alike hidden conspiracy and open persecution,' has maintained its hold in this cut-off place.

At one stage Wilkie had hoped that Charles Ward would again steal away from his family and meet him in Penzance. But Ward was unable to make it and, when he looked to France instead, Wilkie mocked him, saying that no scenery there could compare with Cornwall, where even the food was superb. He declared that he had only eaten red meat once and instead had feasted on a diet of duck, geese, pickled pilchards, curried lobster, clotted cream, jam tarts 'and fifty other succulent dishes'.

Predictably, Wilkie ran out of money and had to ask his mother to bail him out. By then, she had decided to move to Hanover Terrace on the edge of Regent's Park – a desirable property which she had probably had her eye on for some time. Wilkie tried to dissuade her, arguing that she would let herself in for additional financial dues associated with living in the Park. But she was a determined woman and, though both her sons were away, she pressed ahead. Charley was involved with his Pre-Raphaelite friends – or, as Charles Ward disparagingly put it to Wilkie, 'busily engaged in painting a fly's eye with lashes to match'. Wilkie had to beg her to look after his papers and to inform him of the number of her chosen house, otherwise he would not know where to return to.

Once ensconced at 17 Hanover Terrace, a generously sized house where he commandeered a study and Charley a studio,

Wilkie offered the manuscript of his Cornish trip to Richard Bentley, who agreed on 18 November to publish it on a shared profits basis. By a separate agreement, Brandling was engaged to provide twelve drawings (to be lithographed by Wilkie's old family friend John Linnell). Although Wilkie saw fit to complain about the delays before the work 'rambled into print', everything moved forward with alacrity. He may not have got the book into the shops by Christmas as he had hoped, but he was poring over the proofs before the end of the year and *Rambles Beyond Railways* was published on 30 January 1851 to general acclaim.

Now that Bentley had been responsible for two of his books, Wilkie regarded him as his regular publisher and offered him a story for *Bentley's Miscellany*. This was 'The Twin Sisters', a well-observed piece which combined two of his favourite themes – the power of love at first sight and the disturbing effects of the double or doppelgänger. It tells of a man who falls instantly in love with a girl he sees on a balcony. After pursuing her and discovering she is called Jane Langley, he becomes engaged to her. When he visits her parents' house, he discovers she has a twin sister, Clara, who, he is now adamant, is the girl he saw on the balcony and the only person he can ever marry. Although this causes great consternation in the Langley family, he defends himself to the girls' father, saying he has remained true to his conscience and his 'first sensations'. Clara is initially unwilling to countenance any wedding. But Jane, who has developed an almost mystical stoicism, encourages her to change her mind. The narrator is duly married to the girl he first saw on the balcony and passes into familial obscurity. The story is really about the dignity of Jane, the sister who has been passed over. Wilkie shows his empathy for such women when he concludes, 'Reader, when you are told, that what is impressive and pathetic in the Drama of Human Life has passed with a past age of Chivalry and Romance, remember Jane Langley, and quote in contradiction the story of the twin sisters!'

No sooner had this story been published than Wilkie received an approach that was to alter his life radically. Charles Dickens was now at the height of his powers, a celebrated novelist and the owner and editor of a weekly magazine, *Household Words*, with offices in Wellington Street, close to where Wilkie had worked in the Strand. The location gave the phenomenally energetic Dickens access to one of his great loves, the stage. He frequently attended West End productions and promoted the theatre whenever he could. When he established the grand-sounding Guild of Literature and Art, it was natural that he should put on a play to raise funds.

The Guild's more mundane aim was to provide assistance to writers and artists who had fallen on hard times. Dickens was supported in this by his friend, Sir Edward Bulwer-Lytton, novelist and playwright and owner of a substantial recently Gothicised seat at Knebworth in Hertfordshire. With the specific intention of raising money for the construction of cottages for these deserving toilers on land he had donated at Knebworth, Bulwer-Lytton had written a five-act comedy called *Not So Bad As We Seem*, which Dickens arranged to be staged at Devonshire House in Piccadilly, the London home of the Duke of Devonshire.

As usual, Dickens rallied his friends to take part in the production. However, William Wills, the sub-editor who did the day-to-day work at *Household Words*, suddenly decided that he did not fancy amateur theatricals and pulled out. Left with a gap in his cast list, Dickens wrote to another of his actors, Augustus Egg, who was also a member of the Guild, 'I think *you* told *me* that Mr. Wilkie Collins would be glad to play any part in Bulwer's Comedy, and I think *I* told *you* that I considered him a very desirable recruit. There is a Valet, called (as I remember) Smart – a small part, but, what there is of it, decidedly good; he opens the play – which I should be delighted to assign to him . . . Will you undertake to ask him if I shall cast him in this part?'

SECOND EPOCH

5

DICKENS AND A NOVEL

LITTLE MORE THAN two months later, Wilkie donned a valet's costume and appeared before the Queen in the gilded library at Devonshire House. It was not a great part, but it would transform his life by bringing him into the orbit of Dickens, the greatest writer in Britain, who would become his firm friend.

Wilkie's role in *Not So Bad As We Seem* reflected the two men's current unequal standings. In this eighteenth-century pastiche, he played a lowly servant whose job was to announce visitors to his master, Lord Wilmot, portrayed by the domineering Dickens. In real life, twenty-seven-year-old Wilkie was merely a student – both in matters of law and in the ways of the world – while Dickens was a hugely successful author with a large family and vast experience.

Wilkie had the innocence and potential of youth. His recent portrait by Millais showed an agreeable man tapping his fingers thoughtfully as if aware of domestic responsibilities (the shield in the top left-hand corner symbolised his attachment to home), yet alert to opportunities. Meanwhile Dickens was showing signs of middle age. At thirty-nine, he was tiring of domestic responsibilities and concerned that his wife, Catherine, was suffering from chronic depression.

With the first performance of the play due at the end of April, there was little time for familiarisation. Wilkie met Dickens over dinner on 12 March, followed that same evening by a reading of the text in John Forster's rooms in Lincoln's Inn Fields. There was another run-through a few days later at Miss Kelly's Theatre, and then several rehearsals. Wilkie's fellow actors were literary and artistic associates of Dickens, including Forster, Douglas Jerrold and Mark Lemon, the editor of *Punch*. The only member of the cast Wilkie really knew was Augustus Egg.

Dickens oversaw all aspects of the production. Eager to construct a portable stage for use at different venues, he liaised with carpenters, tailors and musicians, as well as briefing the artists Clarkson Stanfield and David Roberts, who were painting the backdrops. Dickens also had to deal with the possibility of Rosina – Bulwer-Lytton's estranged and unstable wife – turning up, as she threatened, in the costume of an orange girl and handing out copies of a libellous memoir about her husband. To ensure no unwanted intrusion, Dickens arranged for his friend Inspector Charles Field, head of the Metropolitan Police detective department to patrol the venue and, if necessary, prevent her entry. Dickens was fascinated by the recent phenomenon of the detective, whose investigative and surveillance powers he felt brought a sense of order to London's teeming streets. The department had only been in existence for less than a decade, but already Dickens had written several pieces celebrating its activities for *Household Words*. Even in the middle of the frenzied preparations for *Not So Bad As We Seem*, he found time to write a report with Wills on the workings of Bow Street police station, which appeared in his paper on 26 April.

Rehearsals suffered a setback when Dickens experienced two family bereavements in quick succession. On 31 March 1851 his father died, and a fortnight later, when he was presiding at a meeting of the General Theatrical Fund and his wife was taking a rest cure in Malvern for her depression, his daughter Dora was snatched from him, aged only eight months. He might have coped with the first loss, but the second floored him. In calling Catherine back to London, he could not bring himself to tell her that their daughter was dead (he couched his letter to say that Dora was very ill and that Catherine should brace herself for the possibility that she might be dead before she returned to the capital). This could be interpreted as an act of cowardice, but it was actually a gesture of kindness to a woman who was already emotionally vulnerable. Dickens was forced to ask the Duke to postpone the play's first night – a delicate task, since Queen Victoria was scheduled to attend.

Not So Bad As We Seem was finally ready for its dress rehearsal at Devonshire House on 14 May. This performance was reserved for the families and friends of the participants, including Harriet Collins, her son Charley, and Ned Ward, who had designed the invitation, and his wife Henrietta.

Although the Guild had been set up partly in protest against the alleged inefficiency of the Royal Literary Fund, the Queen took no offence and rearranged her calendar so that she, Prince Albert and their guests, the Crown Prince and Princess of Prussia, could attend the postponed first night on 16 May. In all, some two hundred people, paying £5 a head, crammed into the gallery of the library at Devonshire House. The venture was a financial success, even if the critical consensus was mixed, suggesting that the five-act play lacked plot and was too long, ending at half past twelve (the Duke of Wellington voted with his feet and left after the second act).

Dickens was soon planning further performances, which necessitated making cuts to the play and adding a short farce called *Mr Nightingale's Diary*, which he had written with Mark

Lemon. Based on the 'personator' Charles Mathews, who had featured in Harriet Collins's courtship, this was little more than a showcase for Dickens's wide-ranging talents as an actor, and, in its subject matter, a forerunner of his speaking tours. Wilkie's performances were also recognised since, in a reduced cast, he was asked to play the landlord of an inn – still a menial role, but indicative of his acting abilities.

This was all good fun, but hardly cutting edge. Nor did it do much to dispel the idea that, for all their charitable aims, Dickens's theatrical exploits were acts of shameless self-promotion. Before his family losses, he had intended his play to provide a curtain raiser to the main spectacle of the summer, the Great Exhibition, a display of the best of Britain's industry, which was inaugurated by the Queen in Hyde Park on 1 May.

Dickens may also have hoped to piggy-back on another event, the regular Summer Exhibition at the Royal Academy, which opened its doors a few days later. The main body of work that year comprised a conventional mix of historical and literary paintings, some by members of Dickens's cast, including Egg's saucy study of Pepys being introduced to Nell Gwyn, and Frank Stone's rather safer scene from *The Merchant of Venice*. Ned Ward also contributed a powerful historical tableau of the French royal family.

These works could not disguise the stir caused by the latest offerings of the Pre-Raphaelite Brotherhood. Since their first appearance in 1849, the reaction to this group had not only intensified but become dangerously personalised, with Frank Stone using his position as art correspondent of the *Athenaeum* to vilify them, and William Rossetti striking back with a vituperative attack on Stone in a piece in the *Critic*, written with his brother Dante Gabriel Rossetti, a member of the Brotherhood.

At the 1850 Summer Exhibition Dickens leaped instinctively to the support of his friend Stone, using *Household Words* to mock the backward-looking tendencies of the Brotherhood (the progressive ethos of the Great Exhibition was more to his taste). He particularly took against Millais's *Christ in the House of His Parents*, mocking its hyperrealism and describing the whole as 'mean, odious, repulsive, and revolting'. His criticism was puzzling, since, in his own writing, he was attempting much the same as the Pre-Raphaelites – to show the reality of the human condition, using whatever uncompromising hues and perspectives were required.

In 1851, Millais was back at the Royal Academy, together with Holman Hunt and Charley Collins who, although not formally a member of their group, worked closely with them. *Convent Thoughts*, Charley's painting for the exhibition, showed a novice nun in a walled garden full of exquisitely detailed flowers, and was as Pre-Raphaelite as anything by Millais, Hunt or Rossetti. It also indicated how different a character he was from his brother. For while Wilkie had rejected his father's religion (and in particular its institutionalised side), Charley still followed it. The traditional practices of Tractarianism were the guiding principles of his art, and he shared them with the high-minded Rossetti family, his fellow parishioners at Christ Church in Albany Street, who lived in Charlotte Street (later Hallam Street) in the heart of the Portland estate. Gabriele, the Rossetti paterfamilias, had been forced to flee his native Italy because of his involvement with the Carbonari secret society. After coming to England and marrying, he taught Italian at the new Anglican King's College, London, and had four children of roughly Charley's age – Maria, Dante Gabriel, William Michael and Christina. The atmosphere in the Rossetti household was noisy, emotional and conspiratorial, as noted by Holman Hunt when he chanced on a gathering of 'all escaped revolutionists'.

Charley was closer to the Rossettis than Wilkie, partly through the church, and partly because he was infatuated with Maria Rossetti, the most devout of the four children and said to be the model for *Convent Thoughts*. Although the painting was executed in the Oxford garden of Thomas Combe, a Tractarian printer who had prospered as owner of the Oxford University Press, Charley also had in mind the new 'Puseyite Nunnery', or Sisterhood of the Holy Cross, in Park Village West, off Regent's Park, where he now lived. Linked to Christ Church, Albany Street, this community, formed in 1845, was the first Anglican convent of modern times, an attempt by the Tractarians to revert to traditional Church practices.

Such places were not obvious outposts of feminism. Nevertheless, like Charley's painting, the convent raised pertinent questions about women in Victorian society. Should they remain traditional 'angels in the house', committed to child rearing and domesticity? Or should they be allowed to make their own way in the world? And what if this meant rejecting the male sex, like the members of the Park Village Sisterhood? As Maria's sister Christina would write in her poem 'The Convent Threshold', such communities offered refuge to victims of violence and even love. They also gave succour and hope to fallen women, which provided a new twist to the traditional male problem of differentiating between angels and whores.

These questions had a particular resonance for Charley, since Maria Rossetti had recently rejected him as a lover (she later joined a different nunnery), and at much the same time, after an indecisive vote, the Pre-Raphaelite Brotherhood declined to admit him as a member. These two setbacks were to scar him for life.

At the 1851 Summer Exhibition the attack on the Brotherhood

was joined by *The Times*, which accused the Academicians of 'disgrac(ing) their walls' by showing the works of Millais, Hunt and Collins – 'a class of juvenile artists who style themselves "P.R.B." . . . Their faith seems to consist in an absolute contempt for perspective and the known laws of light and shade, an aversion to beauty in every shape, and a singular devotion to the minute accidents of their subjects, including . . . every excess of sharpness and deformity.' Charley was still identified in the art world as a member of the Brotherhood.

This stimulated a robust riposte from the art critic John Ruskin, who had so far been lukewarm towards a group he suspected of dangerously Roman Catholic tendencies. He now leaped to their defence in a letter to *The Times*, praising the 'honesty' of their work and forecasting they could 'rise to very real greatness'.

Dickens on this occasion was too taken up with family and thespian matters to re-enter the fray. Instead, Wilkie had his say in *Bentley's Miscellany*. With his background, he was well placed to comment on the art world. However, his report was strangely oblique, suggesting he felt compromised at having to review an exhibition in which his brother was represented. After summarising the other paintings on show, he commented grumpily on the Pre-Raphaelites, echoing the near universal complaint about their unusual use of perspective, though he did manage to strike a positive note in his conclusion that 'Mr Collins was the superior in refinement, Mr Millais in brilliancy, and Mr Hunt in dramatic power.'

Wilkie's critique reflected his ambivalent response to the Brotherhood. His attitude was coloured by worries about Charley, who he felt was becoming too constrained by 'extreme Church discipline and rigorous self-denial in matters of fasting and calendar observances' at a time when he himself was trying to throw off all vestiges of his father's beliefs. So, like Dickens, he tended to ignore the PRB's claim to be realists and to look on them as a retrogressive force.

As a result of his concerns about his brother, Wilkie paid a fraternal visit during the summer to the Surrey farm where Charley was painting with two of his closest Pre-Raphaelite friends, 'Johnny' Millais and 'Maniac' Hunt. Millais had successfully sweetened the blow of Charley's rejection by the group by prevailing on Thomas Combe's wife to purchase *Convent Thoughts*, which was appropriate since it was painted in her Oxford garden.

Wilkie was reaching the end of his five-year apprenticeship for the Bar. His letters give a sense of his lifestyle: aside from a few additional performances with Dickens's Guild of Literature and Art, he amused himself by gambling (though his stakes were small) and by frequenting risqué French plays at the St James's Theatre, in the company of Joseph Cridland, a Lincoln's Inn solicitor, who was a friend of Wilkie's fellow law student Edward Smyth Pigott.

Wilkie also continued to write for *Bentley's Miscellany*, where his pieces that summer included a series on Britain's picture galleries. However, he was happier in the autumn when he expanded his range of outlets and began writing for the *Leader*, a weekly radical newspaper nominally edited by George Henry Lewes and Thornton Leigh Hunt. This was the obvious home for his essay 'A Plea for Sunday Reform', a direct refutation of his father's Sabbatarianism, in which he argued that museums and galleries should be allowed to open their doors on Sundays, thus helping to expand the minds of the people and keep them out of gin palaces.

By then, Thornton Leigh Hunt had had a child with his colleague Lewes's wife and another was on the way. Lewes's response was an affair with Marian Evans, a radical, agnostic writer, later known under the pen name George Eliot. So intense was the sexual energy that it was not unexpected when the *Leader* fell into financial difficulties, from which it was rescued by Wilkie's friend Edward Smyth Pigott, the son of a wealthy West Country landowner.

In early November 1851 Wilkie was staying with Pigott at Grove House in Weston-super-Mare. This was one of two large estates (the other was Brockley Hall in North Somerset) owned by the Smyth Pigotts, a dynamic and often spectacularly dysfunctional family, which, in one way or another, would provide plenty of copy for Wilkie over the years.

Both young men were about to be called to the Bar and needed to consider their futures. For Pigott, matters were simple enough. Although a younger son, he had plenty of money to indulge his interests, which currently included running the *Leader*. For Wilkie the future was not so clear cut. Having no desire to continue with the law, he was determined to make his living as a writer. But, as his father had warned, it was a precarious existence. He stood to inherit some money when his mother died, and for the time being he had a generous allowance, but his prospects were by no means assured though, for now, he was happy to write the occasional piece for the *Leader*.

From Weston-super-Mare, Wilkie joined Dickens's Guild company for its next performances of *Not So Bad As We Seem* in Bath and Bristol. The audience in the Assembly Rooms in Bath was large but remarkably po-faced. Dickens, who liked to enjoy himself, insisted that his cast hold a party at their hotel in Bristol, where everyone, including Wilkie, ended up playing his favourite game of leapfrog.

In November, Wilkie and Pigott celebrated after being called to the Bar. Wilkie invited several friends, including Sir Thomas Henry, a respected Bow Street magistrate. He ended up getting pickled. 'What a night!' he told Pigott the following day. 'What speeches! What songs! I carried away much clarets (*sic*) and am rather a seedy barrister this morning.'

For the time being Wilkie was content to put the finishing touches to a Christmas story. Since this was the sort of thing Dickens specialised in, Wilkie was positioning himself directly in the steps of the master. *Mr Wray's Cash-Box* was a neatly turned, if seasonally sentimental, tale about the theft of a prized statue of Shakespeare from a retired actor. In the preface he stressed that it was based on a true story, a conceit he often repeated in his later fiction. He sold the piece to Bentley as a stand-alone Christmas special, hoping it would be illustrated by Charley and his Pre-Raphaelite friends. As he explained to Bentley, 'One of these "Brothers" happens to be <u>my</u> brother as well.' In the event, only one sketch, by Millais, appeared with the story, which was published in the nick of time on 23 December. Wilkie's confidence in Bentley faltered when an advertisement appeared in *The Times* referring to the artist as Willais and himself as the author of a work called *Antonini*.

As a result of this effort, along with concerns about his future and Charley's, Wilkie was suffering from nervous exhaustion. This was not exactly a breakdown, but the first of the anxiety attacks that would blight him in years to come. For rest and recuperation over Christmas he accepted an invitation to visit Joseph Stringfield, a doctor in Weston-super-Mare, to whom he had been introduced by Pigott. He even turned down further work for the *Leader*, telling Pigott that he would have done this with pleasure, but his own doctor forbade him from using his '<u>brains</u> just yet; and I feel that the doctor is right'.

Stringfield had recently lost his wife, Jane, following the death of a premature son. The *Bristol Mercury* considered Wilkie important enough to announce from Weston-super-Mare on 27 December: 'Wilkie Collins Esq., author of 'Antonina',

'Rambles Beyond Railways', the new Christmas work entitled 'Mr Wray's Cash-Box and other literature, is spending a few days with J. Stringfield Esq. at Verandah-house in this town.'

Still in Somerset, after dinner on New Year's Day 1852, Wilkie was taken to visit a foreign Count who lived nearby with his British wife. The object of the evening was to test the claims of animal magnetism, the then fashionable idea that the body contained a vital fluid that allowed subjects to be put in a trance, or mesmerised (the word 'hypnotism' was not yet familiar). Over the previous decade the practice had been given scientific credence by the physician Dr John Elliotson, of University College, London, whose friend Dickens had investigated and written sympathetically about it. There were now serious hopes that it could be used for therapeutic purposes. In search of enlightenment, Wilkie attended several further evenings of experiments in animal magnetism and wrote them up for the *Leader*, where he stated that he wanted to confine himself 'as strictly as possible to simple narrative – or, in other words, to be the reporter, rather than the judge'.

In one of his six pieces for the newspaper he told how Mademoiselle V., a French associate of the Count's wife, was made sleepy after contact with magnetised objects, such as a thimble and a mirror. Initially, the trials aimed to show how suggestible she had become. Some worked and others did not. On one occasion she was given a glass of water and Wilkie was asked to imagine that it contained a non-lethal dose of poison. While he was thinking of strychnine, she went into convulsions and appeared to be in agony. When she requested some milk to take away the taste, she lapped up the contents of another glass of water, which the Count had 'magnetised'.

At another house, a larger crowd became agitated when a 'patient', this time a novice at the game, began to laugh hysterically after being magnetised. When Mademoiselle V. turned her talents to clairvoyance, Wilkie was astonished when she gave him an accurate description of the person he was imagining – his brother Charley.

In his articles for the *Leader*, Wilkie called for further investigation into mesmerism, stressing its practicality (though his main example – that it would allow life models at the Royal Academy to maintain static positions – was esoteric). G.H. Lewes, who was still involved with the paper, published a counter-blast, 'The Fallacy of Clairvoyance', which argued that these apparently objective happenings resulted from the suggestibility (he did not quite say gullibility) of the audience, who unwittingly provided the information for the medium's work. (He was referring to what, in modern parlance, is called 'cold reading'.) Wilkie objected to this insinuation and fired off a measured response. It was the start of a lifelong interest in the powers of the mind, the significance of different ways of seeing and experiencing reality, and the potential of alternative states of consciousness.

Whether it was this new intellectual diversion, or simply the opportunity for rest, Wilkie's short stay in Somerset seems to have worked. He returned to London in improved spirits; having hired a local upholsterer to refurbish his study, he was soon working hard on new projects. First, he penned further thoughts on the *Leader*'s future, which had been discussed with Pigott in Weston-super-Mare. Addressing the paper's content and layout, Wilkie suggested it should print more law reports – perhaps in the hope that they might provide background material for his fiction. He was also concerned that religion had crept into the *Leader*'s pages in a manner he considered profane. 'I am neither a Protestant, a Catholic – or a Dissenter,' he noted in an unusually clear statement of his beliefs. 'I do not desire to discuss this or that particular creed; but I believe Jesus Christ to be the son of God; and believing that, I think it a blasphemy to use his name' in the manner of a couple of recent pieces. This was surprising, as was the vehemence of his opinions, which led him to declare he did not want his name appended to any future contributions. However, it was a statement of his beliefs that remained fairly consistent throughout his life.

Turning his hand back to fiction, he wrote 'A Passage in the Life of Mr Perugino Potts' which he sent to *Bentley's Miscellany*. It was an entertaining vignette that mixed autobiography and invention to tell of a painter who, after exhausting his career possibilities in London, goes in some desperation to Rome to learn to paint in the style of Raphael and Michelangelo. After several misadventures Potts finds a protectress in the form of a stout Marchesina who, as her price, wants to marry him. When he flees in terror, she follows him to England, causing him to exclaim, 'Marriage and murder – murder and marriage, will alternately threaten me for the remainder of my life! Art, farewell! henceforth the rest of my existence is dedicated to perpetual flight!' With its sardonic tone and clear sense of place and time, this story shows Wilkie's emerging authorial voice, as well as his invention of a fictional editor to provide a framing device of a sort he would often use in future.

In his articles on animal magnetism he emphasised how he had researched the subject in scientific books. His background reading was also clear when he tackled 'monomania' in *The Monktons of Wincot Abbey*, a less successful tale about a family afflicted by hereditary madness and an ancient curse. Wilkie injected considerable suspense into his account of the narrator's efforts to repatriate to England the body of his uncle, who had been killed in a duel in Italy. However, when he sent it to *Household Words*, his first submission there, Dickens surprisingly baulked at the lurid content, and Wilkie had to wait another three years before it was published in *Fraser's Magazine*.

Undeterred, Wilkie offered Dickens's paper something else, '(The Traveller's Story of) a Terribly Strange Bed'. This was scarier in content but lighter in touch, a tale in the style of Edgar Allan Poe about a man who, after breaking the bank in a sleazy Parisian gambling house, is encouraged by the management not to venture home because they are situated in a dangerous area (at the back of the Palais Royale) and his winnings could be stolen. Instead he is invited to stay in an adjoining room, where he wakes up during the night to find himself the victim of an attempted and clearly premeditated murder, as the canopy of his four poster bed bears terrifyingly down on him, impelled by a screw mechanism. This time Dickens was more enthusiastic and offered Wilkie £7 10s to publish it in *Household Words*.

Away from his writing desk, Wilkie continued to indulge his Francophilia as he dragged his friends to French plays. He became intrigued by the realist novelist Honoré de Balzac, who died two years earlier. Around the time he was arguing with Lewes over animal magnetism, he saw, apparently twice, *A Game of Speculation*, the latter's dramatisation of a Balzac comedy at the Royal Lyceum Theatre. And he helped an unidentified friend (possibly Charles Ward) get a translation of Balzac's short story 'Un Episode sous la Terreur' published in *Bentley's Miscellany*.

As he became more prolific, Wilkie took more interest in the professional side of authorship, and this was encouraged through his involvement with the Guild of Literature and Art. In May 1852 he joined Dickens at a public meeting convened by George Eliot's employer, the publisher John Chapman, to protest against restrictive practices in the book trade. This was an emotional issue for writers: the combination of growing literacy and improved printing technology was making the business increasingly competitive, and established publishers such as Longman and John Murray were lobbying hard to maintain their positions by preventing widespread discounting. Wilkie was a free marketer in this respect, his attitude informed by a keen sense of the politics and economics of his profession, and how he could best make them work on his behalf. He would be tenacious in securing the best publishing deals for himself, and would campaign for the adoption of international copyright laws.

Meanwhile, Dickens was getting to know Wilkie's family. The previous month he had attended Harriet Collins's dance in Hanover Terrace for around seventy people. John Millais reported to Mrs Combe in Oxford on 'a delightful evening' at which Charley 'never got beyond a very solemn quadrille' but showed great flair at the waltz and polka. His hostess had lost her voice as a result of a bout of influenza, but she was delighted that 'there were many lions, amongst others the famous Dickens, who came for about half an hour and officiated as principal carver at supper.'

When Harriet went on holiday to Southsea, she took a second-class train, which Wilkie, with the arrogance of youth, considered beneath him. 'I am glad to hear that you could travel comfortably by second class', he declared. 'I cannot. I must either pay 1st Class fare, or defer the pleasure of going to Southsea.' His youthful restlessness was clear from the way he gloated over thrashing Chops, the latest household cat, for daring to sip some milk off the breakfast table. But he was able to lay in a leg of lamb and some gooseberry pudding, so he could entertain his friends Henry Bullar and George Agar Thompson, son of the Irvingite John.

During the summer, Wilkie was again asked to perform on stage with Dickens's Guild company. Following the withdrawal of

Douglas Jerrold from the cast of *Not So Bad As We Seem*, Wilkie took over his rather more substantial part as the upwardly mobile Shadowly Softhead, which he played eleven times in various provincial cities. As usual, when Dickens was involved, the actors lived in style. Wilkie was impressed by the company's reception in Manchester, where it drew an audience of two thousand seven hundred and was feted by the mayor at a magnificent dinner with 'French dishes that would make you turn pale if you looked at them'.

For Wilkie the highlight was the Guild's visit to Newcastle, where he stayed with the Brandlings at their estate, Gosforth Hall. Theatrical company brought out his frisky side, for he decided that Mary, the eldest Brandling daughter, was 'the cleverest and the most agreeable woman I think I ever met with – all the elegance and vivacity of a Frenchwoman – and all the sincerity and warmheartedness of an Englishwoman.'

Mary was not his only female interest in the north-east. Visiting friends there at that time was the sparkling, dark-haired Nina Chambers from Edinburgh. Her father, the writer and publisher, Robert Chambers, was a beacon of Scottish intellectual life. As well as pioneering the influential *Chambers's Encyclopaedia* and the *Edinburgh Journal*, he wrote *Vestiges of the Natural History of Creation*, which promulgated one of the most important and popular pre-Darwinian theories of evolution.

Nina was one of eight sisters (eleven children in all) who lived at 1 Doune Terrace, a substantial Georgian house in Edinburgh's New Town, where the Chambers family was famous for its hospitality, particularly towards artists and writers. She met Wilkie through her sister, Janet, who had married William Wills, Dickens's right-hand man at *Household Words*.

Wilkie and Nina had already struck up a flirtatious friendship, as is clear from a poem he wrote for her earlier in the year:

Miss Chambers has sent me a very sharp letter
With a gift of some toffy (I never sucked better!)
'Tis plain, from her note, she would have me infer
That I should have first sent the toffy to her.
I will only observe, on the present occasion,
(Thinking first gifts of sweets, so much sugar'd temptation),
That in tempting of all kinds, I still must believe
The men act like Adam – the women like Eve:
From mere mortal frailties I don't stand exempted,
So I waited, like Adam, by Eve to be tempted –
But, more fitted than he with "The Woman" to grapple
I return her (in Toffy) my bite of "The Apple"!

Nina subsequently became engaged to Frederick Lehmann, a cultivated young German-born businessman who attended her parents' regular musical evenings. However, his job at Naylor Vickers, one of Britain's largest steel manufacturing firms, regularly took him abroad, and towards the end of August 1852, she found herself visiting friends in Newcastle when Dickens's theatre group was in town.

From there she described the Guild's performance to her fiancé in Berlin: 'We got home in time to dress for the perfor-mance of Dickens's company to which I went in a sort of a dream and I remember only of it – very very hard seats without backs, a stifling atmosphere, Wilkie Collins' really lovely face, Augustus Egg's accommodating bows to myself when he found me out, and my uncle [Wills] (who is the secretary to the Society) suddenly breaking out in three new characters during the perfor-mance & then rushing out & saying 'God bless you my darling Nina'.

Nina was not the only person to remark on Wilkie's pleasing presence on stage. An article in the *New York Daily Times* noted how, after Jerrold dropped out, 'The amateurs did not lose for

Wilkie Collins' who 'studied the part and made it nearly the most effective in the play. His low stature, pretty features and juvenile appearance were all in his favour, no doubt, but the natural ease with which he individualized the character was inimitable.' Dickens agreed, telling his friend John Forster, 'You have no idea how good Tenniel, Topham and Collins have been in what they had to do.'

Having worked closely with Dickens on tour and started to get to know him socially, Wilkie was gratified shortly afterwards to be invited to join the Dickens family on holiday in Dover, where he gave an idea of the palliative drugs he had been using for his nervous condition when he declared that he found 'the sea air acts on me as if it was all distilled from laudanum.' Both he and his host had novels to complete (*Basil* and *Bleak House* respectively). Wilkie took advantage of a disciplined environment, putting in regular hours of work, interspersed with long walks and plenty of bathing in the sea, followed by unusually early nights. After two weeks of this regime, he expressed his delight at having finished his 'hitherto interminable book', declaring to Pigott, 'Yesterday morning [15 September] I wrote those two last welcome words "The End".'

   Basil had taken two years to reach this stage. It was his first effort at writing about the modern world at this length, and he found it a struggle. But it had been worthwhile, for he had produced an adult novel, dealing with sex, class and society. The story told of the consequences of the instant passion stirred in Basil, a wealthy young man of noble birth, after he sees Margaret Sherwin, a draper's daughter, on an omnibus. Driven by an obsession (something Wilkie had written about in 'The Twin Sisters'), Basil finds out where she lives, courts her and makes clear his intention to marry her. But this all has to be done in secret because he knows his father will disinherit him if he finds out about his affair with a girl of inferior status. Mr Sherwin agrees to give Basil his daughter's hand, but stipulates that their relationship cannot be consummated for a year, as she is only seventeen (though Basil suggests lasciviously that she could pass for a girl three years older). The night before her eighteenth birthday, with his wedding still unknown to his family, Basil goes to Margaret's house and finds that she has gone to a party with the mysterious Robert Mannion, who has infiltrated himself into her family as Sherwin's confidential clerk. Basil follows them to a hotel where he overhears them making love. In his fury he attacks and disfigures Mannion, causing him to lose an eye.

It emerges that his victim is the son of a forger, once patronised by Basil's father. When the older Mannion was tried and sentenced to be hanged, Basil's father refused to help. After many setbacks, Robert Mannion found work with Mr Sherwin, making himself indispensable and looking on the nubile Margaret as his eventual prize. Basil's appearance only compounded the earlier family offence and encouraged Mannion to seek revenge, using his sexual powers to seduce the woman for whom Basil was willing to give up his entire inheritance.

In dedicating the book to Charles Ward, Wilkie stated that he had 'founded the main event out of which this story springs on a fact within my own knowledge'. This has led to speculation about who or what he had in mind. One deduction is that he himself had experienced the *coup de foudre* on the omnibus. Although he was impressionable enough for such a thing, no obvious instance is known. In a letter to Edward Pigott around this time, he expressed a yearning for a 'sweet-tempered and lovely' girl called Alice. However, she would have had to perform a change of character, for, in the novel, her alter ego Margaret is a dark-haired beauty who turns out to be shallow, manipulative and self-centred.

Wilkie was determined to situate his story firmly in contemporary London where the main means of transport, the horse-drawn omnibus, symbolised the energy of the modern metropolis. Wilkie commented in the book on the 'mighty vitality of the great city renewing itself in every direction'. Part of this process involved new suburban developments, such as the Sherwin's North Villas, which was not so far from Wilkie's own stomping ground of Regent's Park. Far from being oases of peace and respectability, these places stood in 'wretched patches of waste, half built over', amid unfinished streets and squares.

More unexpectedly, Basil was introduced to a world of carefully guarded secrets. These modern castles were riddled with extraordinary stories of deception, intrigue and domestic oppression. As a writer, Wilkie would now begin to concentrate on this kind of material, partly because he was canny enough to realise that the suburbs, with their aspiring middle classes, were where his core market now lay. He would try to bring the sense of drama and romance found in traditional adventure tales to the job of probing the mysteries and lies of conventional domesticity.

One way of ruffling the closed curtains of the home was to shock and, in *Basil*, Wilkie did this by focusing on sex. From his first encounter with the femme fatale Margaret, Basil is consumed with lust. As she enters the omnibus, she momentarily touches him. 'But how the sense of that touch was prolonged! I felt it thrilling through me – thrilling in every nerve, in every pulsation of my fast-throbbing heart.' She wears a veil but, like curtains in a house, it provides little real protection. Behind it, he thinks he sees slight movement as her lips 'ripened to a smile', but 'still there was enough left to see – enough to charm', as

Basil muses about 'the little rim of delicate white lace, encircling the lovely, dusky throat' and concludes, 'The veil! how little of the woman does it hide, when the man really loves her!'

After this introduction, he is impelled to pursue her, with the soft erotic tone continuing until he spies her and Mannion in the blunter act of sexual intercourse: 'I listened; and through the thin partition, I heard voices – *her* voice, and *his* voice. *I heard and I knew* – knew my degradation in all its infamy, knew my wrongs in all their nameless horror.'

In the process, Wilkie contrasts this dark-haired sexual adventurer, Margaret, with Basil's pure, fair-looking sister, Clara. The two women appear to him as archetypes in a dream to which there is only one possible conclusion. 'I was drawn along in the arms of the dark woman, with my blood burning and my breath failing me, until we entered the secret recesses that lay amid the unfathomable depths of trees. There, she encircled me in the folds of her dusky robe, and laid her cheek close to mine, and murmured a mysterious music in my ear, amid the midnight silence and darkness of all around us. And I had no thought of returning to the plain again; for I had forgotten the woman from the fair hills, and had given myself up, heart, and soul, and body, to the woman from the dark woods.'

As was often the case in Pre-Raphaelite art, the idealised angel in the house was powerless against the immediacy of sexual lust. But, also like the Pre-Raphaelites, the message of Wilkie's novel was ultimately moralistic. Margaret is manifestly punished for her sexual transgression. She contracts typhus when visiting Mannion in hospital and later dies.

Such sharp comparisons provided the tension that gave *Basil* its vitality. Wilkie was fascinated by opposites, like the twins in his earlier story. Here he set about highlighting the differences not only between domesticity and promiscuity, but between the suburbs and the city, the aristocracy and the middle classes, and romance and realism. He set up a nice distinction between the worthy Basil and his rakish brother, Ralph, who, after a life of frivolity, opts for a contented morganatic marriage with an older woman. Ralph tells Basil that he too has enjoyed affairs with 'ladies of the counter', but has never been mad enough to marry them.

Wilkie's most significant set of contrasts was between appearances and reality, a theme he would pick at throughout his working life. People are not who they seem; respectable houses can obscure dangerous secrets. As a writer, he had been fascinated to discover how this truth could be explored in that factory of illusions, the theatre, and he was now intent on examining it further in his novels. But here, to confuse matters, were two apparent opposites that Wilkie regarded as very similar. As he stated in his letter dedicating *Basil* to Charles Ward, he believed 'that the Novel and the Play are twin-sisters in the family of Fiction, that the one is drama narrated, as the other is a drama acted.' Once again, the truth was not quite as it appeared.

Wilkie, the literary magpie, drew on various influences in his quest. In *Basil*, he turned to the Gothic tradition to portray the process of revenge, with ancient grievances coming back to haunt successive generations. Always an eerie figure, Mannion, following his disfigurement, looks and behaves like Frankenstein's monster – to the point of asking his assailant Basil, 'Do you know the work of your own hands, now you see it?'

This reflected Wilkie's growing interest in science, particularly psychology. In recent months he had written about mesmerism and how it could override the rational mind. Now he recorded how sexual infatuation could suspend time and thought. 'From the time when she entered the omnibus,' mused

Basil, 'I have no recollection of anything more that occurred in it. I neither remember what passengers got out, or what passengers got in. My powers of observation, hitherto active enough, had now wholly deserted me.' Later he asked, 'Among the workings of the hidden life within us which we may experience but cannot explain, are there any more remarkable than those mysterious moral influences constantly exercised, either for attraction or repulsion, by one human being over another?' Wilkie was beginning to think seriously about perception and understanding, and to consider the relationship between sensations, thoughts and visions. Put this together with Wilkie's compulsion to stir his readers, and the building blocks of what would later be called sensation fiction were settling in place.

By the end of September Wilkie was ready to offer the manuscript to Bentley for publication. Taking courage from Dickens, he was clear about his terms: he wanted £350 for the full copyright. Bentley initially demurred, but eventually agreed, though he demanded some changes. For example, the premises where Margaret and Mannion went for their sexual tryst became a hotel rather than a house (by implication a brothel).

The book was published in three volumes on 16 November 1852 as *Basil; A Story of Modern Life*. (The manuscript shows earlier discarded titles, including *Basil; or The Love Secret*.) The reviews were generally favourable, though there were dissenting voices, such as the critic of the *Athenaeum* who complained of 'a tale of criminality, almost revolting from its domestic horrors', and said that Wilkie, as the son of an eminent painter, 'should know that the proper office of Art is to elevate and purify in pleasing'.

Wilkie enjoyed creating a stir. With some satisfaction, he told a correspondent that his book had 'been vehemently objected to as immoral (!) by some of those virtuously inflammable ladies and gentlemen of Modern Times who are gifted with particularly sharp noses for smelling out supposititious *[sic]* filth in particularly unlikely places. As I never have written for these people and never will, then their condemnation is infinitely more acceptable than their approval.'

6

REDISCOVERING EUROPE

W RITING *BASIL* HAD taken its toll. Although not yet thirty, Wilkie was already showing signs of wear. In the early summer of 1853 he was unwell and confined to Hanover Terrace. When he began to recover in late June, he needed to walk with a stick and was 'not strong enough yet to do more than "toddle" out for half an hour at a time'. More worryingly, he noted how 'my illness and long confinement have muddled my brains dreadfully – I am still in very bad trim for anything that deserves the name of work.'

The following month Wilkie was feeling much better. He was staying in Maidenhead and had, as he put it, 'begun the great reformation', his way of saying he was taking a rest cure. He was rising earlier and paying more attention to his health. 'Observe the hour above written,' he crowed in a letter to his mother, and underlined for emphasis 'Thursday morning 10 minutes to 9'. He was already dressed and waiting for breakfast, 'a position I never remember to have been placed in before in the whole course of my life'. He added, 'I feel better already – I take no beer – and I stop short at my three glasses of wine.' This passed for abstemiousness in Wilkie's book, and was all the more odd since his hosts were the Langtons, the leading brewers in this Berkshire town. They were friends of Harriet's, living in an area – beside the Thames, within striking distance of London – favoured by the Collinses and their associates. It was not far from Iver, where his father had gone shortly before his death, or from Slough, where Ned and Henrietta Ward had recently moved, with their two children, including Alice, who was Wilkie's goddaughter.

On one level Wilkie's body had simply let him down. With his various physical irregularities, he was never a particularly healthy specimen. He did not help himself by over-indulging in food and drink, and taking little exercise. As a result he had developed early symptoms of gout and rheumatism. This painful combination raises the possibility that he had rheumatoid arthritis (sometimes known as rheumatic gout). Since this disease often has a genetic component, he might have inherited it from his father. However, at this stage rheumatoid arthritis had yet to be named. Although Wilkie's symptoms were frequently rheumatic, they are probably best identified as gout, which also attacks the eyes, as William Collins had experienced and as Wilkie would soon discover. Certainly they were always treated as gout; there was little sense of Wilkie's immune system being attacked, as scientists would later learn was the case with rheumatoid arthritis.

He was suffering considerable pain, which he tried to mask by taking laudanum. This is the inference from his casual references to the drug, such as his comment to his mother the previous year about the effects of the sea air in Dover. She, for all her foibles, had a relaxed attitude to drugs. Once when her late husband's friend Coleridge had bemoaned his opium habit, she consoled him, 'Mr Coleridge, do not cry. If the opium does you good and you must have it, why don't you go and get it?'

Laudanum, a ten per cent solution of opium in alcohol, was

widely available over the counter at chemists. But it could easily become addictive, particularly if taken regularly. At this stage, however, Wilkie's use was mildly therapeutic.

Gout is actually caused by the build-up of uric acid in the body, and the subsequent accumulation of sodium urate crystals in the joints. However, hereditary factors can also play a part, as can diet and stress, the last of which was significant in Wilkie's case. The psychosomatic element in the illness was clear from the way it was often used as a catch-all diagnosis – something Wilkie himself understood and alluded to in his 1873 novel *The New Magdalen* where Lady Janet remarks that 'the medical profession thrives on two incurable diseases in these modern days – a He-disease and a She-disease. She-disease – nervous depression; He-disease – suppressed gout.'

He had no obvious cause for stress, since in the previous two years he had published a successful novel, developed a friendship with Britain's best-known author, and won plaudits for his acting. However, he had been working extremely hard on *Basil* at a time when, on an emotional level, he was also trying to distance himself from his late father. In the early months of 1853 he was beginning to think about a new novel, *Hide and Seek*, in which he would address more directly some of the problems in their relationship. At the same time his mother was preparing her own memoir, which required her to reach some accommodation with her past. And all the while Wilkie was trying to build his friendship with Dickens without being overwhelmed by the latter's personality or reputation.

One area where Wilkie was still floundering was sex. He claimed to have been initiated into lovemaking at an early age, and he had demonstrated a keen young man's interest in women and the demi-monde. He was clearly not unattractive to females, as Nina Chambers's breathy reaction showed, but he had yet to develop any significant relationship. He gives the impression of a man with a strong libido but, when undirected, prone to frustration and perhaps depression.

Part of his problem was that, like many Victorian men, he found it hard to move beyond prevailing sexual stereotypes that cast women as either angels or whores – the dichotomy high-lighted in *Basil* between Clara and Margaret. Wilkie's Pre-Raphaelite friends were particularly susceptible in this respect. In their case, matters were complicated by their religious convictions, as was evident in works such as Charley's *Convent Thoughts*.

The Brotherhood had been on Wilkie's mind because of the recent Summer Exhibition at the Royal Academy, where its members had been cast as bad boys and thus legitimate targets by the Establishment press. The *Era* could not refrain from poking fun at Holman Hunt's *Our English Coasts* for its expanses of grass and sheep, where 'every "tit" of wool is produced so carefully that a Yorkshireman could value it to a farthing in the pound'. Fringe member Charley Collins avoided the limelight with his particularly devout work, *The Christian Year*. But the show-stopper, the painting everyone crowded around, was *The Order of Release*, *1746* by Millais.

This canvas was notable for its depiction of Effie – the gorgeous, brown-haired Scottish wife of the Pre-Raphaelites' once reluctant but now enthusiastic promoter John Ruskin – as the grim, bare-footed wife of an imprisoned Jacobite soldier presenting a gaoler with the order for her husband's release. Effie's involvement was regarded as scandalous in conservative sections of the London art world. Artists normally used working-class girls, such as Rossetti's red-headed muse Lizzie Siddal, but the offence of this particular work was that

Millais had visited the well-born Effie at the Ruskins' home in Tulse Hill and painted her for long periods while her husband was absent.

The unworldly Ruskin did not seem to mind. Indeed, he invited Millais to join him and Effie on an extended painting holiday in Scotland in late June. After a few more weeks together, Millais realised he had fallen deeply in love with Effie, whom he described as 'the most delightful unselfish kind hearted creature I ever knew', while Ruskin had become 'unworthy – with his great talents – of any woman possessing affection and sensibility'.

While he was away Millais wrote regularly to Charley Collins. However, substantial passages of his text were later carefully rendered illegible by Dickens's daughter Katey, who would marry Charley. These might have contained references by Millais to his love life, though, from what remains, it seems unlikely, for, rather than discuss Effie or Pre-Raphaelite stunners, he preferred to engage Charley on the finer theological points of Tennyson.

Religion and art did indeed feature strongly in the two men's complex relationship. Millais was wary of Charley's asceticism, but he was happy to accompany him regularly to services at the Tractarian St Andrew's Church in Marylebone. At times he found Wilkie's brother positively 'chilling', his description to Holman Hunt the previous autumn when, at a loose end, he had wandered over to Hanover Terrace from his parents' house in Gower Street. Once there, Millais had done no more than 'jest with the old lady, say about a dozen words to her layfigure son, and tumble out into the freezing night miserable'. (The old lady referred to so off-handedly was, of course, Mrs Collins, and her layfigure son, Charley, who was compared to a lifeless mannequin or artist's dummy.)

This emphasises how much Millais regarded the Collinses

as 'family'. He described Mrs Collins as his 'second mother', delighting in calling her by silly names, such as 'Mrs Bluebird' or, to Charley, 'your Cardinal mother'. Millais was also very friendly with Wilkie, and was one of the few people to use his first name in correspondence. He had painted his portrait and illustrated his Christmas story *Mr Wray's Cash-Box*.

The two men shared an interest in scientific and philosophical questions, such as the nature of observation. The Pre-Raphaelites had always stressed the importance of looking and seeing correctly. Millais took this further, producing a series of drawings which concentrated on the physical attributes of sight, the best-known of which was *The Blind Man*. At around the same time, his drawing *A Ghost Appearing at a Wedding Ceremony* dealt with another aspect of the same subject – how was it possible to see a spectral being? This was a relevant query at a time when a vogue for spiritualism and séances was emerging from the United States. Wilkie would take up such phenomenological questions as he began to introduce supernatural elements into his stories. Sight would also feature as an important theme in his later novels, such as *Poor Miss Finch*.

It is entirely possible that Millais would have discussed his feelings for Effie with Wilkie. When exactly these arose is not clear, but he was probably aware of them earlier in the year when painting *The Order of Release*. And while he would have been unlikely to mention them to the fastidious Charley, he might well have done so to the more worldly Wilkie, who had recently written so eloquently about sexual passion in *Basil*. However, for all his imaginings about love, Wilkie was by no means an expert. Even *Basil* was more about sexual yearning than gratification. The eponymous hero does not pursue Margaret with the intention of taking her to bed. His only conceivable – and honourable – course is to marry her. In this respect Wilkie offers a more secular version of the Pre-Raphaelite anxiety about sex.

Aside from Millais, the Pre-Raphaelites were surprisingly tentative in their relations with the opposite sex. Far from being the great seducer of popular mythology, Dante Gabriel Rossetti went through endless agonies of sexual denial in his relationship with Lizzie Siddal – to the extent that his biographer Jan Marsh suggests that he was still a virgin at the age of thirty in 1858. And the more religious Holman Hunt had a similarly intense, unhappy and ultimately celibate affair with his model and love, the former bar-girl, Annie Miller.

Throughout 1853 Hunt talked of visiting the Holy Land in search of inspiration. He seemed to want to put some distance between himself and Annie, whom he optimistically intended to leave in the care of his artist friends to be educated into the role of his future wife. Prior to departing, in August 1853, he started work on *The Awakening Conscience*, which, more than any other painting, epitomised the conflicted Pre-Raphaelite attitude to sex. It shows a young woman arising, with a startled look on her face, from the lap of her sexually satisfied lover. This reflected, in graphic pre-Raphaelite fashion, a common enough mid-Victorian phenomenon – a man entertaining his mistress (clearly unmarried because she has no ring on her wedding finger) in a house that is not his family home. Indeed, in order to get the right atmosphere, Hunt rented a room in a '*maison de convenance*' owned by a courtesan in St John's Wood.

Although the painting's realism made it shocking to Victorian sensibilities, Hunt intended it as a morality tale. Initially he wanted to call it *The Still Small Voice* (the words 'of conscience' are assumed) and to emphasise that redemption was possible, even in such sorry circumstances, though some details, such as the cat playing with the mouse, indicated that the artist was signalling that this liaison would not end happily. By comparison, Millais's affair with Effie would turn out to be relatively straightforward.

Wilkie, of course, had other role models for irregular relations with the opposite sex. Ned Ward had led the field by opting for an underage bride. Ned's fellow Clique member William Powell Frith was one of several men who openly defied the conventions of his age and lived with two separate families, at Park Village West and Pembridge Road Villas. Another Clique artist, Augustus Egg, who had introduced Wilkie to Dickens, was known for his hearty bachelor gatherings. But he too would express ambivalence about sex and matrimony in his fascinating, and very Victorian, triptych *Past and Present* (1858), which told the harrowing story of a woman's fall from respectable family life, via infidelity to destitution under the arches by the River Thames.

And then there was Dickens.

As Wilkie began to feel better during the summer of 1853, he was again able to contemplate the future. A return trip to Italy was mooted for the autumn, this time in the company of Dickens and Egg. As a trial run, he was asked to join the Dickens family on its summer holiday in Boulogne. Dickens was clearly ignorant of the extent of his friend's problems for, in extending his invitation on 24 June, he simply enquired if Wilkie had 'shaken off all (his) ailings'. Less than a week later, after Wilkie had obviously provided chapter and verse, Dickens wrote, 'I am very sorry indeed to hear so bad an account of your illness, and had no idea it had been so severe'. He then built up the attractions of Boulogne, where he had rented Chateau de Molineaux, 'a doll's country house of many rooms, in a delightful garden', and where he promised Wilkie 'a Pavilion room . . . with a delicious view, where you may write no end of Basils.'

Once again it was a working trip, with Wilkie struggling to make inroads into his new novel *Hide and Seek*, while Dickens put the finishing touches to *Bleak House*. Apart from a brief sortie to Beauvais and Amiens, Wilkie stayed firmly in Boulogne. However, as soon as Dickens had finished his book, the atmosphere at the chateau changed, and he played host to Forster, Wills, Lemon and various other writers, publishers and illustrators. To add to the mix, Frank Stone was living up the road and there was a flying visit from Angela Burdett-Coutts, Dickens's partner (and financier) in the Urania project for fallen women. Wilkie rather took to her, telling his mother that even if she had not possessed a farthing, he would still have deemed her 'really, and not conventionally, a very "charming person"'.

Despite a punishing work schedule, Wilkie's personality and prejudices could not help asserting themselves. In Boulogne he was reminded of his ambivalent position as someone who felt largely detached from religion, certainly organised religion, but retained atavistic anti-Catholic sentiments. When he visited a votive chapel used by the fishing community, he found the smell of candles and incense so oppressive that he had to escape before he could even look 'at half the sacred Roman Catholic frippery with which the inside of the chapel is decorated from floor to ceiling'. He also made clear his attitude to matrimony when he heard that an artist acquaintance, John Sleigh, was getting married. He asked Charley to convey his best wishes, 'and say I wish him long life and loads of children. He is one of those fresh-complexioned men with a low forehead and a meek character, who always take kindly to the institution of marriage. He will get domestic happiness, a large paunch, and a numerous family in the enjoyment of which advantages he will live respected and die happy.' This was not a future he envisaged for himself.

By the time he left Boulogne for London in early September, Wilkie had written only one volume of *Hide and Seek*, and wanted to talk to his publisher about his future. Bentley, who continued to flounder financially, had plans to shake up the books industry through various marketing ploys, one of which was to cut the price of the traditional three-volume novel. Earlier, he had hoped to put out *Basil* in two volumes, but Wilkie, for all his free trade instincts, was not ready for this innovation and the book came out as a 'triple-decker'.

He had no problem with Bentley's suggestion that a cut in the price of any edition, triple-decker or not, would lead to increased sales to popular lending libraries, such as Mudie's, which dominated the retail market. However, he was not prepared to go along with another of Bentley's proposals – that author and publisher should share profits – since it was generally considered to act against the interests of the former. Feeling eager to compromise if he could, Wilkie added that 'the only real difficulty that I see in our way' was the fact he had lost two months to illness. As a result, he was painfully behind with his book and unable to make much progress before the end of the year since he was committed to travelling abroad with Dickens.

A month later Wilkie was back at the chateau in Boulogne, waiting to start his autumn journey to Italy with Egg and Dickens, who made a point of packing various medicines, including a bottle of laudanum, which he doubtless thought

might be useful for Wilkie. Accompanied by a factotum called
Edward, the three of them set off, spending an enjoyable few
days in a lively Second Empire Paris (where they again met
Angela Burdett-Coutts), before taking what Wilkie described
as the best railway he had ever known to Strasbourg. Next
stop was Lausanne, an old haunt of Dickens's, where they
stayed in a comfortable house, overlooking Lake Geneva,
belonging to his friend, the very rich cleric and poet, the
Reverend Chauncy Townshend, who was a strong advocate of
mesmerism and spiritualism. Townshend provided another
example of the diverse state of British marriage, having gained
a deed of separation from his wife in 1845 on grounds of
'unhappy differences'. Bulwer-Lytton suggested something of
the causes when he described Townshend as 'an accomplished
man – but effeminate and mildly selfish'.

Since there was a sizeable British community in Lausanne,
Dickens was duly dined and feted. However, he found time to
take his travelling companions to an institution for the blind,
which had achieved success in rehabilitating young people who
were not only blind but deaf and dumb – an experience Wilkie
integrated into his ongoing novel *Hide and Seek*.

The 'triumvirate', as Dickens called them, had been informed
authoritatively in Paris that they would not be able to enter
Austrian-held Italy from Switzerland as the latter was regarded
by the former as a nest of spies and revolution. But this proved
to be untrue and they were able to proceed on a route that took
them across the Simplon Pass. Once in Italy, Wilkie visibly
relaxed and began to feel at home. He admitted to almost crying
when he heard a blind fiddler playing Italian folk tunes (he
emphasised the musician's lack of sight, adding that the man
had two blind children). Over the border, his services as an
interpreter were more than ever in demand. The final stage of
the journey to Milan involved travelling through bandit country

and, to ensure nothing was stolen, they were advised to tie string to their luggage on the roof of the carriage and hold onto it through the window.

Wilkie was impressed by the city of Milan, but not by La Scala opera house, where they saw *Il Trovatore*, 'Verdi's last and noisiest production', which was 'miserably lighted, wretchedly dirty, mournfully empty, and desecrated by some of the very worst singers I ever heard, and some of the mouldiest scenery I ever saw exposed to gaslight.' Reaching the coast at Genoa, they boarded the SS *Valetta*, an overcrowded mail boat owned by the P&O company, for the voyage to Naples. Wilkie spent the first night on deck before prevailing on the captain to allow him to sleep on a dresser in the store room, surrounded by flour, figs and spices.

Since they were already behind schedule, the three friends decided not to proceed from Naples to Sicily as intended. Instead, they travelled straight to Rome, which Wilkie was happy to discover was truly the Eternal City. Nothing had changed since he had lived there fifteen years earlier: the Pincian Hill was the same, the Madonna still stood in a niche outside the Collinses' old house in the via Felice. He was amused when his tendency to procrastination led to an encounter with the Pope. Wilkie was delayed at his hotel when his companions went to St Peter's Basilica. Trying to catch them up, he was passed by the papal carriage. When everyone dropped to his or her knees, Wilkie remained on his feet, though he did doff his hat, a gesture acknowledged by a gracious wave from the Pontiff.

The party carried on to Florence, where Wilkie seems to have made his first acquaintance with Frances Dickinson, a woman to whom he would grow very close. She was an unusually spirited and intelligent woman in her early forties, who was trying to keep out of the public eye after one of the most lurid

divorce cases of recent years. The only child of a Somerset
landowner who died when she was six, she was a wealthy heiress
when, aged eighteen, she married a Scottish soldier, Lieutenant
John-Edward Geils, and went to live with him on his heavily
mortgaged estate near Glasgow. However, he regularly abused
Dickinson and, after he committed adultery with the servant
girls, she sued for divorce in a case that was pruriently reported
as it dragged through a succession of ecclesiastical courts. In the
course of these actions, the differences in the finer points between
English and Scottish matrimonial law were endlessly aired –
points that would fascinate Wilkie and provide copy and plots
for his later novels.

For the last few years Dickinson had been trying to reinvent
herself as an author. In 1851 she wrote a rabidly anti-Roman
Catholic book for Richard Bentley, entitled *The Priest Miracles
of Rome, a Memoir for the Present Times*. This comprised an
attack on the 'papal aggression' – the Pope's re-establishment
the previous year of the Catholic episcopal hierarchy in Britain,
under the newly appointed Archbishop of Westminster,
Cardinal Wiseman. This unilateral action fuelled considerable
controversy in the febrile world of religious politics, coming
so soon after Newman's defection to Rome. Wilkie, with his
inbred Protestant ideology, would no doubt have applauded
her stand.

After a short stay in Venice (more opera, more Verdi – this
time *Nabucco*), the party began its homeward journey, stopping
again in Genoa to see Dickens's friends, the de la Rues. When
Dickens had visited the Continent in 1844–5, he had tried to
mesmerise Augusta de la Rue, a local banker's wife, in an attempt
to cure her of her various nervous complaints, which have been
likened to the symptoms of what later in the century was
described as hysteria. However, Catherine Dickens had not
been amused: so far as she was concerned, her husband had

seemed rather too keen on this intimate manner of relating to a comely lady. Now, nearly a decade later, Dickens returned to the subject in an insensitive manner, calling on his wife to write what amounted to a letter of apology to Madame de la Rue, and also to recognise that 'the intense pursuit of any idea that takes complete possession of me, is one of the qualities which makes me different – sometimes for good; sometimes I dare say for evil – from other men.' This uncompromising statement of his independence was an early sign of problems in his marriage. It was significant that it came towards the end of his bachelor-style travels when, as he later jested to Augusta's husband, Emile, his own wife had been 'excruciatingly jealous of, and has obtained positive proofs of my being on the most confidential terms with, at least Fifteen Thousand Women'.

Along the way Wilkie picked up some gifts – bracelets for his mother, a snuff box for Charles Ward, and a brooch for Ward's wife Jane. However, he had difficulty deciding what to buy for his devout brother. Eventually, with a sense of mischief, he bought him a Roman crucifix. Charley had clearly thought that Wilkie's soul needed sustenance, because he had earlier pressed on him a book by Jeremy Taylor, a seventeenth-century divine known for his Laudian anti-papist sentiments. Wilkie had to report to his mother that he had found this hard going 'because my present course of life is not favourable to theological studies, and Jeremy is rather involved and hard to understand after a day's rolling over rough high roads in a travelling carriage'.

Wilkie recorded his progress in letters, mainly to his mother, brother and Edward Pigott. He hoped to call on these later when he came to write up his travels in a series of articles or perhaps a book. The picture he painted helped complement Dickens's accounts to his wife Catherine and others. It was clear that the triumvirate got on well. Wilkie enjoyed his role as the party's linguist, which meant he did much of the necessary haggling, though Dickens thought him slightly mean with his tips and other payments. He sometimes annoyed Dickens with his habit of whistling opera hits, particularly as he was so often out of tune. But there was no lasting ill feeling.

Dickens's recollections were generally more humorous than Wilkie's, recounting the shambolic progress of three Englishmen in Europe and making fun of their various eccentricities. In Venice, Dickens painted a delightful picture of the trio attending the opera: 'Imagine the procession – led by Collins with incipient moustache, spectacles, slender legs, and extremely dirty dress gloves – Egg second, in a white hat and a straggly mean little beard – Inimitable bringing up the rear, in full dress and big sleeved coat, rather considerably ashamed.' ('Inimitable' was a nickname that Dickens rather liked for himself.)

A running gag was the men's facial hair, which they tried to grow in competition with each other. Apropos Wilkie's moustache, Dickens informed Catherine, 'You remember how the corners of his mouth go down, and how he looks through his spectacles and manages his legs. I don't know how it is, but the moustache is a horrible aggravation of all this. He smooths it down over his mouth, in imitation of the present great Original.' Having done this, Wilkie would then tell Egg he ought to cut his moustache because it was likely to get in his mouth.

In his despatches Dickens presented Wilkie as an amiable fantasist who regaled his companions with colourful stories recalling, for example, the copious amounts of Montepulciano he drank when last in Italy, 'and what distinguished people said to him in the way of taking his opinion, and what advice he gave them and so forth – being then thirteen years old.' Dickens noted that Egg would make him laugh by poking fun at these 'absurdities'.

He also remarked how Wilkie had talked of his 'first love adventure' during his 1837–38 trip to Italy. Dickens was sceptical of this tale too. Indeed, context was all: in the same way that Wilkie's recollections of his youthful drinking bouts came while the triumvirate were carousing, his memories of his amorous exploits may well have occurred when he and his companions were dallying with members of the opposite sex.

In a curious admission, Dickens told Catherine that Wilkie 'occasionally expands a code of morals, taken from modern French Novels; which I instantly and with becoming gravity Smash.' There is no escaping his tone of disapproval, though he might have been trying to mollify his jealous wife. He also wrote of Wilkie's growing enthusiasm for French authors such as Balzac. The code of morals Dickens referred to was the bourgeois realism of *La Comédie Humaine*, Balzac's collection of novels portraying a ruthless, immoral world driven by material avarice and sexual passion. Wilkie was doubtless indicating the kind of books he wanted to write, but the implication was that he sometimes tried to introduce elements of this code into their lives on the road.

7

LEAVING HOME

WHISKERS WERE NOT merely an amusing diversion for the 'triumvirate', but a cultural and even political statement. Wilkie was clean-shaven in two portraits in the early 1850s – one by Millais in 1850, the other by Charley three years later. But by the time Wilkie was photographed in 1857, he was heavily bearded. Dickens similarly had no facial hair in a daguerreotype of 1852, but sported a moustache by 1854, a wispy beard the following year, and a full growth in 1856.

This hirsuteness was an expression of the cult of manliness that developed during the decade as the confidence of the Great Exhibition dissipated in the face of a series of threats to national security. First there was a fear that France might invade following the coup d'état by the new Emperor, Napoleon III. (Hunt's painting *Our English Coasts* has been interpreted as an artistic statement of this concern.) In response, the government of Lord John Russell proposed reconstituting the militia, but the passage of his Militia Bill proved so fraught that Russell was forced to resign. The death of the Duke of Wellington, the hero of Waterloo, in September 1852 added to the unease. William Rossetti was adopting a widely-held point of view when, to Millais's horror, he stated that he was in favour of war because 'it would do much good'. The following year the tables were turned, and Britain and France found common ground once more as Russian aggression in the Balkans ratcheted up the diplomatic tension prior to the start of the Crimean War in March 1854.

The extreme cold of the Crimea encouraged a trend noted by Dickens in an article in *Household Words* a few months earlier. In 'Why Shave?' he promoted the cause of beards, arguing that they had a public health role in preventing the spread of germs and quoting Socrates as an example of the 'connection between a man's vigour of mind and body, and the vigour of growth in his beard'. *Punch* ran cartoons about the vogue for facial hair. The coming together of beards, manliness and, it was generally thought, success with women was too powerful to argue against.

For Wilkie, as a pacifist and a contrarian, his hair had more to do with fashion than political sentiment. True to form, he rejected the popular martial mood, telling Charles Ward succinctly, 'My sentiments on the subject of the approaching Russian War, are dictated by the most disinterested feelings of Patriotism.' He would continue to oppose the hostilities, to the extent of expressing support for John Bright, the anti-war campaigner. However, he could not help being affected by the general mood. As he told Richard Bentley, 'If this war continues, the prospects of Fiction are likely to be very uncertain to say the least of it.'

As he eased himself back into London life in early 1854, Wilkie found that several other things had changed. For one, the Pre-Raphaelite Brotherhood had pretty much ceased to exist. This was underlined by Millais's election as an Associate of the Royal Academy the previous November, leading Dante Gabriel Rossetti to pronounce to his sister Christina that 'now the whole Round Table has been dissolved'. Nevertheless, Hunt's *The Awakening Conscience* would create an appropriate furore when it was shown at the Royal Academy Summer Exhibition that year. The artist himself was still in the Middle East, where Charley spun him the unlikely tale that Wilkie wanted him to 'go to Thebes & Memphis & Philae & Carnac & the 1st & the 2nd cataracts of the Nile & the Negro kingdom of the Shillooks & the Lotos eating & unexplored parts of Central Africa that he might have the benefit of your experience previous to going there himself.'

More immediately, Millais's affair with Effie was not only flourishing but causing major problems. With divorce or some form of annulment now on the cards, her husband John Ruskin had begun to accuse her of insanity. In despair, Effie was forced to confide in a couple of female friends that her marriage had never been consummated. They were affronted on her behalf, not so much because she had been denied the delights of sexual intercourse but because she had been prevented having children – the goal of all Victorian women, and a constant ingredient in the debate about their role in society.

Wilkie was in touch with Millais during this time, and records a meeting at his house in February. But not a jot of his friend's affair came to light in any of Wilkie's public declarations or correspondence. As he began to develop a running theme of secrets in his novels, he remained adept at keeping mum about his own confidences and those of the circle around him.

On his return to London, Wilkie offered Bentley's son George a series of six articles on Italy, which he puffed as a lively concoction about art, papist ceremonies and love. But *Bentley's Miscellany* had recently run similar pieces and declined the offer, as did Dickens's *Household Words*.

His recent travels were still on his mind in May when he sent Samuel Carter Hall at the *Art Journal* an article about Italian art by his new friend Frances Dickinson. This time he was more successful and Dickinson's offering would prove the first of a number she wrote for that outlet over the next year or so under the pseudonym Florentia. She regularly travelled back to England where she owned large houses near Bath and Reading. The latter, Farley Court, was home to her mother, who soon became a good friend of Harriet Collins.

With Wilkie's artist friends otherwise engaged, Dickens working on his novel *Hard Times*, and Pigott occupied with his family estate (which was a mess, following his father's death and his elder brother Henry's dementia), Wilkie was now making headway on his new book, *Hide and Seek*. This was turning out to be quite different from *Basil*. It was still ostensibly 'modern' but, dismayed by the less than whole-hearted response to his previous offering, Wilkie wanted to make it lighter in tone than its predecessor. So he sought to satirise the emerging middle classes, with their sterile suburban construction projects, where 'the cry of the costermonger and the screech of the vagabond London boy were banished out of hearing'.

At the same time, like Dickens and Mrs Gaskell, he hoped to say something about the social condition of Britain. In *Hide and Seek* he addressed the problems of one particular disadvantaged group – deaf and dumb children. He also began to look critically at the law as it related to aspects of matrimony, adoption and legitimacy.

However, the novel's edge came from its personal input, as Wilkie began to work through unresolved issues with his father. Only six years after dutifully writing the *Memoirs*, he was now prepared to expose the traumas he had experienced as a result of William Collins's fundamentalism.

Hide and Seek shows the feckless Zack Thorpe trying to escape from his over-zealous father by apprenticing himself to a gentleman artist, Valentine Blyth. Wilkie emphasises the autobiographical elements by giving Zack a stultifying job in the tea business and making him subject to a domestic curfew, which he regularly breaks to frolic in late-night taverns. Old Mr Thorpe is predictably uncompromising in his religious views, which are more Evangelical than Tractarian. He uses the same kind of moral blackmail as William Collins when he tells his son, 'I want you to learn your lesson, because you will please me by obeying your papa. I have always been kind to *you*, – now I want you to be kind to *me*.'

Wilkie showed another side of his father in the more sympathetic Blyth, who has a similar studio and a cat called (in the initial 1854 version) Snooks, the name of an earlier much-loved Collins family pet. Wilkie's two-pronged approach extended not only to the title, *Hide and Seek*, but to its format, with a first part establishing the characters and their mysterious backstories, and a second teasing out and gathering together disparate narrative strands. In this way the novel followed *Basil* in its emphasis on the unlocking of secrets.

The main story revolves around the origins of a deaf and dumb girl, Mary, otherwise known as Madonna, who lost her hearing in an accident at the circus. Subsequently adopted by the artist Valentine Blyth, she is treasured by him and his wife, a woman with her own disability, an injury to her spine. Meanwhile, on one of his nightly revels, the would-be artist Zack befriends Mat Marksman, a maverick figure who spent years living wild in the Americas (where he was partially scalped by an Indian). Mat is keen to rediscover his British roots, which he does through a mixture of perseverance, good fortune and amazing coincidence.

After finding that his sister has been forced to leave home because she gave birth to a bastard child by the mysterious Arthur Carr, Mat, acting on a hunch, gains access to a locked bureau where Blyth has hidden a hair bracelet belonging to Madonna. An inscription on the bracelet confirms to Mat that Madonna is his niece (the illegitimate daughter of his long-lost sister), while the hair itself seems so similar to Zack's that Mat suspects his friend and Madonna may be siblings. When he confronts Zack's father, Mr Thorpe breaks down, admits his 'guilty secret' – that he is indeed Arthur Carr – and begs Mat not to divulge it to his wife or son.

During the course of unravelling this intricate web of deception, Wilkie deals with topics he was familiar with, particularly art and fundamentalist religion, as well as others in which he was less well versed, including the outdoors world of Mat Marksman and the finer points of disability. To understand these, Wilkie relied mainly on literary sources: his details of the American frontier drew on the novels of James Fenimore Cooper, while his understanding of deafness and dumbness came partly from his visit to the institute in Lausanne and more specifically from John Kitto's 1845 study, *The Lost Senses*, to which he had probably been introduced by Dickens, a correspondent of the author.

Although *Hide and Seek* provides insights into Wilkie's struggles with his father, it should not be read, as some have done, as gospel truth. However, its charting of Zack's voyage of self-discovery has many parallels with Wilkie's. At one stage the young man is too callow to respond to Madonna's modest gestures of affection. With the help of three father figures (his own, Blyth and Mat), Zack grows to maturity. In Wilkie's case, similar roles were played by William Collins, his artist friend Ned Ward, and now Dickens, the man of the world who took him under his wing. (Dickens reportedly saw a resemblance to himself in Mat.)

How far can one take these parallels? Zack's father, the religious fanatic, turns out to be a hypocrite with a 'guilty secret' of the kind Wilkie would regularly root out in his novels. Although William Collins did not, so far as is known, have a child out of wedlock, the book does throw light on Wilkie's parents, when Zack's father admits, 'I married, under circumstances not of an ordinary kind'. A passage, removed from the second 1861 edition, elaborates on this, suggesting that Mrs Thorpe had 'misconstrued some very ordinary attentions paid her by Mr Thorpe, had fallen in love with him, and had long pined for him in secret, before he discovered it, and – more out of honour than affection – made his proposals to her.' This revisionist interpretation of the courtship of William and Harriet Collins was doubtless discussed in Hanover Terrace when Harriet was writing her memoir. If nothing else, Wilkie was hinting that his own family had secrets that still bore unravelling.

Since he was working furiously to complete *Hide and Seek*, Wilkie did not get round to discussing it again with Bentley until early April and he did not conclude a publishing agreement until mid-May, when he had only seventy pages left to write. Bentley's terms were not particularly generous, certainly not financially – £150, to be paid in two parts, for a three-volume edition of 500 copies, with an option for reprints over the next eighteen months. Nevertheless, Bentley was fast and professional and the novel was, remarkably, ready for sale by the end of the month, complete with a dedication to Dickens 'as a token of admiration and affection'.

It was soon gathering favourable notices in the *Spectator*, the *Athenaeum* and, not surprisingly, *Bentley's Miscellany*. Reviewing it for the *Morning Post*, William Rossetti compared it to the works of Dickens and Thackeray 'and not inferior in our judgement, to any of the productions of these popular writers . . . It is the matured work of a mastermind.' Dickens was equally laudatory, chiding his sister-in-law, Georgina Hogarth, for not taking it seriously and telling her that he thought it was 'far away the cleverest Novel I have ever seen written by a new hand. It is much beyond Mrs Gaskell, and is in some respects masterly.' However, sales were again sluggish – something Wilkie attributed to the competing attentions of the Crimean War. He also gave this as the reason for the book being ignored in the review columns of *The Times*.

Wilkie celebrated *Hide and Seek*'s publication by joining the Garrick Club, a leading watering hole for writers and actors, then based in King Street, Covent Garden. He was proposed by Dickens, who had only recently rejoined after a period of exile, and seconded by Shirley Brooks, one of the many multi-faceted Victorian men of letters noted as a journalist, author and playwright. Brooks lived at Kent Terrace, directly behind Hanover Terrace, so was a near neighbour. The names of Wilkie's numerous supporters spill out in higgledy-piggledy fashion in the candidates' book. However, it is possible to make out well-known literary and artistic figures such as William Makepeace Thackeray, David Roberts, John Leech, Tom Taylor and Mark Lemon, as well as trusted friends including Edward Pigott and Augustus Egg.

Wilkie could now ply between his club, his bank Coutts in the Strand (still, technically, the bank of the executors of his father's will), the *Leader* offices, close to *Household Words* in nearby Wellington Street, the Royal Academy in Trafalgar Square, and the inviting theatreland in and around Covent Garden. With time on his hands, he was keen to review not only books but plays. But theatres were choosy about the names on their free lists, so Wilkie, who was discomfited by the claims of a rival journalist called Collins, asked Pigott, as editor of the *Leader*, to help him obtain tickets as a reviewer for that paper.

He tended to opt for slightly outré productions with a French flavour, such as *La Joie Fait Peur* by Delphine de Girardin, an extraordinary Frenchwoman of impeccable literary pedigree, who had written about Balzac. Her husband, Emile, was a radical journalist and friend of Dickens. After the original

French version of this play opened at the St James's Theatre at the end of May, an English adaptation (*Sunshine Through the Clouds*) by George Henry Lewes followed at the Royal Lyceum. Lewes's work on the play was one of his last commitments before going into voluntary exile in Europe with his lover Marian Evans. Tongues had been wagging about unorthodox sexual relationships in the *Leader* offices, and Pigott was having to answer awkward questions. Wilkie lent him support in his 'troubles', as he tried to sample whatever French culture he could.

Wilkie was at an important turning point in his career. His novels were winning plaudits in literary circles but, for all Bentley's energy, this success had yet to be translated into appreciable sales. His situation was not helped by the financial difficulties both he and his publisher were now experiencing. Offered an opportunity to buy back the copyrights of *Antonina* and *Basil*, Wilkie did not have the spare £200. Bentley then rather desperately suggested a deal where Wilkie paid £100, with the rest to come when he had the money. But Wilkie was still unable to afford it. Before long, Bentley was forced to look elsewhere for funds and sold his *Miscellany* magazine to Harrison Ainsworth.

At this stage, Dickens's support proved important. It is difficult to say exactly what qualities he saw in Wilkie, his junior by a dozen years. Dickens already had plenty of literary and artistic friends, and was particularly close to John Forster, who would write his biography. But Wilkie had certain irrepressible features not found in Forster or the others. As well as sharing Dickens's more cerebral interests, he was an agreeable companion with an unusual capacity for enjoying himself.

The two men's friendship had evolved considerably since

they had larked around in hotels while on the road with the Guild company. They had subsequently taken leisurely holidays together on the south coast of England and in Europe. And they had come to relish their shared pleasure in food, drink and, although they were careful not to commit details to paper, women. When Dickens told Wilkie in July that he was making a brief visit to London from the house he was renting for the summer in Boulogne, there was no mistaking his intentions when he said he wanted to pass his time 'in the career of amiable dissipation and unbounded licence in the metropolis.' He asked Wilkie to join him for breakfast at about midnight 'anywhere – any day – and go to bed no more until we fly to these pastoral retreats.' He added he would 'be delighted to have so vicious an associate,' an unusual adjective, until one recalls that 'vicious' is related to 'vice' and realises that Dickens was proposing a night on the town that would take in not only bars but prostitutes.

Wilkie was happy to oblige, particularly since he was alone at Hanover Terrace, with his mother doing her summer rounds of hospitable friends and Charley away on a painting holiday in Scotland with a blissfully contented Millais, who learned in July that the marriage of his beloved Effie had been annulled in the Ecclesiastical Court.

Dickens had promised to sit for a portrait by Ned Ward who, never having been a Pre-Raphaelite, continued to forge a more conventional career, specialising in history painting (including a commission to decorate the corridor at the rebuilt House of Commons). After completing his London commitments, Dickens invited Wilkie to accompany him back to Boulogne, where he offered the added enticement of copious quantities of 'the celebrated 1846 champagne . . . a very fine wine, and calculated to do us good when weak.' Dickens had earlier sent his sister-in-law Georgina across the Channel to scout out a house for the summer. She had alighted on the Villa du Camp de Droite, on a hill overlooking the main town of Boulogne. Since it was close to an old army encampment that had been revived for the war, Wilkie was unable to ignore what was going on in the Crimea, particularly when Prince Albert paid an official visit to the town. In celebration of the Anglo-French alliance, Dickens, his family and his guests illuminated the front of their house 'in the English way' with 114 candles, and hung the Union Jack and the Tricolor at the top of a tall flagpole in the Villa's garden.

By the middle of September, after nearly two months of leisurely non-activity, Wilkie returned refreshed to Hanover Terrace, where he was soon writing 'The Lawyer's Story of a Stolen Letter', an accomplished tale about the disruptive power of indiscretions and confessions committed to paper in private correspondence. Here a woman's marital happiness is threatened by a blackmailer who gets his hands on a letter in which her father confesses to the forgery of a bill of credit. The lawyer turns detective to retrieve the offending letter and burns it.

Dickens was now producing special portmanteau issues of *Household Words* for Christmas. Wilkie's piece, which is often described as the first British detective story, would appear there alongside a series of linked tales called 'The Seven Poor Travellers' in the Christmas 1854 edition. In this story Wilkie stated, 'If everybody burned everybody's letters, half the courts of justice in this country might shut up shop.' This reflected an ongoing concern: letters could be extraordinarily revealing and, as such, frequently provided the basis for litigation. But although he would often use them in his written work to throw light on hidden aspects of his characters, he took pains in his personal life to ensure that his own correspondence remained private. A few years later Dickens would famously carry out a ritual burning of all his letters, and Wilkie would frequently call on his nearest and dearest to keep his confidences to themselves.

Wilkie was also thinking about what he called his 'dramatic experiments' to turn one of his stories into a play. Worried that he might not be successful, he begged Charles Ward not to mention this to anyone. From his correspondence with Pigott it seems he did write some sort of play. However, it remained experimental and was never staged.

Professional circumstances remained difficult and Wilkie was forced to scrounge around for books and plays to review. One positive result was that he honed his ideas about the Victorian books business. *Hide and Seek* had been published as a triple-decker, which was an expensive purchase in its three separate volumes. Wilkie was reinforced in his view that the way to sell more books was to make them cheaper. Triple-deckers persisted for a variety of reasons, relating to literacy and class, but one was simply market inertia: the reading public knew nothing else, a situation that publishers were happy to perpetuate because they could rely on popular lending libraries to underwrite their excessive costs. Faced with producing a triple-decker, writers often resorted to padding out their material, as was the case with *Hide and Seek*.

When Wilkie cut the book and reissued it in single-volume form in 1861 he enjoyed significantly higher sales. He was supportive when, in early 1855, the enterprising Bentley mooted plans for a new venture to issue single-volume novels at six shillings (about £22 in 2013 money). Wilkie also showed interest in negotiations on copyright, attending meetings of Dickens's Guild of Literature and Art, where at one stage he suggested that artists' works should also be protected. But none of these initiatives could alter his penury. 'I am as poor as Job just now,' he told Pigott, 'and am hard put to it to ride comfortably over the next three or four months.'

Dickens did not help financially but, as an interim measure, he invited Wilkie to take part in a children's entertainment at Tavistock House after Christmas 1854. As well as a small speaking part, Wilkie performed a comic turn which involved devouring some loaves – very appropriate, commented Dickens's son Henry, since 'he had the reputation of being a bit of a gourmand'. But Dickens had problems of his own. He was suffering from an overwhelming feeling of 'restlessness'; were it not for his regular, long, brisk walks, he recently confided in Forster, he felt he would explode. At root was his realisation that he was bored with his marriage but could not yet admit this to anyone else. He was about to start a new novel, an anti-government polemic, later called *Little Dorrit*, but at the time known as *Nobody's Fault*, a title that reflected his disgust at the incompetence of the Aberdeen coalition government and, in particular, its refusal to take responsibility for military reverses in the Crimea. But before embarking on this, he needed a short break in Paris, and for this sort of escapade there was only one companion – Wilkie Collins.

The two men's intentions were again clear enough. Dickens asked his friend François Regnier, an actor in the Comédie-Française, to find him and Wilkie an apartment so that, on their arrival in February 1855, they could throw themselves 'en garçon on the festive diableries of Paris'. Regnier negotiated rooms in the Hotel Le Meurice on the rue de Rivoli, looking out over the Tuileries. As the weather was piercingly cold, Wilkie relished having the 'gorgeously-furnished drawing-room – bedrooms with Turkey carpets – reception room – hall – cupboards – passages – all to ourselves', and being able to make a start on a new story, *A Rogue's Life*, a lively satire more in Thackeray's style than Dickens's, on the phoniness of English society and of the art world in particular. Looking back to *Memoirs of a Picture*, his grandfather's idiosyncratic biography of George Morland,

Wilkie's novella tells of Frank Softly, a would-be young gentleman who, unable to find a settled role in life, drifts from painting to forgery to counterfeiting coins.

Wilkie's progress was held up when he felt unwell and Dr Joseph Olliffe, the British ambassador's physician, was called to see him. According to Dickens, Olliffe gave Wilkie 'strong medicine' and advised him not to go out. The malady was described as influenza but, reading between the lines, Wilkie had picked up a venereal disease. The following month, when Wilkie was back in London, Dickens made comments about coming to 'inspect the Hospital', adding, 'I am afraid this relaxing weather will tell a little faintly on your medicine, but I hope you will soon begin to see land beyond the Hunterian ocean.' Wilkie, but not many others, would have realised that his friend was referring to John Hunter, the great surgeon and anatomist of the previous century, who was also a pioneer in the treatment of venereal diseases. Hunter is believed to have given himself syphilis in order better to understand the symptoms. The 'ocean' was probably a reference to the unpleasant discharge (associated with both syphilis and gonorrhoea) that was curtailing Wilkie's social life.

On his return to London, Wilkie found everyone at Hanover Terrace unwell – his mother had her obligatory winter cold, Millais was staying and was ill, and Charley was labouring under the burden of producing a new picture. No wonder Dickens called it the Hospital. It cannot have been a joyful place.

Wilkie informed Ned Ward opaquely, 'I am in the Doctor's hands again – a long story which I will not bother you with now.' But by mid-April he was feeling better, and was able to meet Dickens at the Garrick Club and to talk of visiting the Ship and Turtle, an East End pub noted more for its links with Freemasonry than for any suggestion of ill repute. Dickens found him 'an amiably, corroded hermit' – an odd description of a man in his early thirties. He left Wilkie to get on with his affairs, while he himself continued to lobby for his various social and political causes – inside and outside the pages of *Household Words*.

Wilkie's main writing commitment was *Sister Rose*, a bloated tale of family intrigues at the time of the French Revolution. Dickens approved of the outcome, which ran for four weeks in *Household Words* and, four years later, helped inspire his own *A Tale of Two Cities*.

Wilkie was otherwise concentrating on freelance journalism, covering books and the arts for the *Leader*. But making ends meet remained a struggle. On more than one occasion he had to chase payments from Pigott, who, as a result of the problems associated with his family estate, was also surprisingly strapped for cash.

Wilkie was particularly active with his journalistic pen in May, following the opening of the Royal Academy summer exhibition. Even before the event, Millais had objected furiously to the poor hanging of his new painting *The Rescue*, which showed a swarthy fireman saving three children from a blazing house. Based on a fire that he had witnessed at Meux's Brewery on the corner of Tottenham Court Road and Oxford Street, this advertisement for a new public service was as near as Millais got to social commentary. Wilkie showed he had lost none of his antipathy towards his father's revered institution when he took up the attack on the exhibition in three scabrous articles in consecutive weeks in the *Leader*, concluding that it was 'the worst we remember to have seen since the building in Trafalgar-square was first opened to the public'. He was not above using his piece to puff not only Millais, but his brother Charley, whose poignant *The Good Harvest of 1854* he described as 'the best piece of earnest conscientious painting the artist had produced', and also Ned Ward, whose less inspired *General Hearsay in the Dress of the Irregular Native Cavalry E.I.C.S.* he deemed 'a most refreshingly-original picture to turn to, after looking at the yards of conventional portrait-painting'. This last comment was an unusually barbed jibe at his aunt, Margaret Carpenter, who, from her grace and favour house at the British Museum, continued to turn out portraits, four of which were shown in the exhibition.

Wilkie had now completed *The Lighthouse*, the play he had been ruminating about for some time. This was a theatrical rendering of his earlier story 'Gabriel's Marriage', rewritten in a British context and given dramatic intensity by a confined new setting in the Eddystone Lighthouse. Dickens liked what he described as 'a regular old-style Melo Drama' and, seeing a good role for himself as Aaron Gurnock, an old lighthouse keeper haunted by memories of his part in a woman's murder, set about staging it at Tavistock House. He spared no expense in arranging for Clarkson Stanfield to paint the backdrop, Francesco Berger to compose some music, and the cream of London's theatrical outfitters to provide costumes and props. He even made sure he had the right sound effects (half a dozen cannonballs rolling about on the floor) for the sea lashing against the lighthouse. He then gave rein to a small company of players, comprising Wilkie, Lemon, Egg, himself and members of his wider family, including Georgina as the female lead, Lady Grace (in which role she was painted by Charley Collins).

After running for four nights at Tavistock House in mid-June, *The Lighthouse* was resurrected the following month for a single public performance in aid of charity at Campden House, Kensington, a vast palazzo around the corner from where Egg was now living. One member of the audience, Janet Wills, the wife of Dickens's colleague at *Household Words*, was the first person to question Wilkie's acting ability when she noted, 'Mrs Collins sat next to me and got every now and then so excited applauding her son Wilkie that I thought the respectable, comely old woman would explode, he all the time looking and acting most muffishly. Nothing could be better than the drama as drama, but oh, he makes a most unloving and unlovable lover.'

Neither Dickens nor Wilkie was aware that they were dupes in a giant mid-Victorian sting. Colonel Waugh, formerly of the 10th Light Dragoons and apparently a successful businessman, had rented the house earlier that year and was using it as a vehicle for self-promotion. Situated in beautiful grounds with views over London, the house had served as a palace for Princess, later Queen, Anne and her husband Prince George of Denmark. She had added a separate dwelling, initially called Little Campden House, to the west of the main building. This was later renamed The Elms and was in the 1850s the home of Augustus Egg, which may explain why the venue was chosen.

On 7 July 1855, Campden House, with its twenty main rooms, was the venue for a sumptuous reception for Colonel Waugh's stepson Francis Carew when he married Mary Fanny Cornwell at a ceremony attended by the Duke and Duchess of Richmond, the Duchess of St Albans and other titled ladies and gentlemen. For several days previously, newspapers were full of advertisements for the charity performance of *The Lighthouse* at Campden House the following week.

But less than a year later, the Waugh bubble burst. It emerged that the Colonel, who also lived at Branksea Castle on Branksea (now Brownsea) Island in the middle of Poole Harbour, had defrauded his fellow directors at the London and Eastern Banking Corporation of over £250,000. At his bankruptcy proceedings details were revealed of how his wife, the former Mrs Carew, had run up a bill of £1,854 with Jane Clark, a milliner in Regent Street. Included in this was about £1,200 for her daughter's wedding trousseau. At one stage Waugh was declared to have debts of over £333,000.

Although the reviews for *The Lighthouse* were mixed, Wilkie, inspired by the smell of the greasepaint, was determined to persevere with the theatre, a medium where he could experience the visceral impact he was striving for in his fiction. He enlisted friends to help him get *The Lighthouse* staged in the West End, even presuming to lay down terms to the established actor-manager Benjamin Webster (an option on the piece for twelve months, plus a payment of five pounds a night for each of the first twenty nights of its run). However, he received little response and had to wait three more years before his career as a playwright took off.

On 3 July 1855, Millais finally married Ruskin's former wife, Effie. The Collins family had, in their different ways, helped him to the altar. Until the end of the previous year, Millais had been frantically finishing his portrait of Ruskin. For this he used Charley's studio in Hanover Terrace, where he acknowledged he 'half reside[d]'. In January, Millais had attended a dinner given by 'that strong-minded old lady' Harriet Collins at Hanover Terrace, where he buried the hatchet with his fellow guest Dickens, who finally made his peace with Pre-Raphaelitism. Charley again helped as Millais worked until the last minute to complete *The Rescue* for the 1855 Summer Exhibition. Charley's contribution was to paint the fire hose.

The wedding at Bowerswell, Effie's family's house in Scotland, was low-key. Wilkie did not attend; instead he invited mutual friends – Charles and Jane Ward, Pigott and John Luard, an army officer turned artist, whom Wilkie had helped put up for the Garrick Club – to a celebratory dinner that evening in Hanover Terrace. Amid the high spirits, Wilkie declared, 'May he consummate successfully! and have the best cause in the world to lie late on Wednesday morning!' He added that he couldn't 'resist jesting on the marriages of my friends. It is such a dreadfully serious thing afterwards, that one ought to joke about it as long as one can.' This might have been Wilkie's jaundiced view, but it was not Millais's. Although he had been apprehensive about his course of action, he was soon telling Hunt how happy he now was and how he hoped soon to be a paterfamilias: 'I cannot help touting for matrimony, it is such a healthy, manly and right kind of life.'

Having few such ambitions, Wilkie was grateful to receive an invitation to spend August and part of September with the Dickens family in a quieter holiday house in Folkestone, Kent. Even now he could not escape the war, since the Queen came to Folkestone to review the (in his eyes) particularly scruffy members of the German Foreign Legion recruited for service in the Crimea. There was another contingent he disliked: 'This place is full – troops of hideous women stagger about in the fresh breezes under hats as wide as umbrellas and as ugly as inverted washhand basins. The older, uglier, and fatter they are the bigger hats they put on – and the more execrably they dress themselves. My soul is sick of the seaside women of England.' However, he enjoyed meeting the usual flock of pilgrims who made their way to the Dickens shrine, including Thackeray, Lemon and Pigott.

While walking around town, he frequently ran into George Murray Smith, proprietor of the publishing firm Smith, Elder, who was also holidaying on the Kent coast. This was the company, started by Smith's father, that had turned down *Antonina*. Wilkie's holiday contact paid off, however, for he was commissioned by Smith, Elder to gather his more recent stories, originally written mainly for *Household Words*, in a collection called *After Dark*.

In Folkestone he spent some time editing his mother's memoir, but he regretfully concluded that it lacked a compelling enough narrative. Nevertheless, there were signs of this memoir in *After Dark*, where he expanded on his idea in 'A Terribly Strange Bed' of having a painter introduce the main story of bizarre goings-on in France. This time, in his determination to find a convincing framing device (and so emphasise the artistic context), he doubled this effect by having the painter's wife Leah (based on his mother) present the introducer.

Although he complained of financial worries while in Folkestone, Wilkie still found the time and resources to join Edward Pigott in October on a much discussed voyage around the south-west coast to the Scilly Islands. While Edward's family was known for its seamanship, as champions of the newish sport of yachting, Wilkie had never been identified with any particular physical rigours. However, he had always enjoyed the ocean and jumped at a chance to show off his skills as a sailor.

Pigott needed the break more than Wilkie. Aside from the *Leader*, he was still tied up with family problems. Indeed, the unconventionality of the Smyth Pigotts had never been clearer than in the years following the death of Edward's father. The eldest son and heir to the estates, John, preferred to remain abroad with his mistress rather than return to Somerset. The more reliable Edward had been appointed as executor of the estates, together with his brother Henry, but the latter was now suffering the worst effects of dementia associated with syphilis. Edward was involved in endless legal cases, including a complaint against John, who had gambling debts of £10,000, and protracted efforts to replace Henry with another trustee. Matters were complicated because their late father's mistress had also entered the legal fray. Edward managed to sell his father's valuable books and paintings, but his brother John's debts necessitated a massive auction of Smyth Pigott property, which took place gradually over three years from 1854.

Eager to leave these worries behind, Pigott threw himself into preparations for the voyage. Wilkie started to get cold feet after friends told him they felt he was being foolhardy sailing such a distance in squally autumnal conditions. He told Pigott he had been consulting his *Almanack* and wondered if they might not be 'tempting Providence' in embarking on a voyage in an eight-ton boat at the time of the 'equinoctial gale'. But Pigott was determined and overruled these objections. With Wilkie's help, he secured provisions, first in Bristol and then from the well-stocked larders at his family home Brockley Hall. The two men added their personal stashes of tobacco, French novels and Egyptian cigars. Then, after visiting their friend Dr Stringfield in Weston-Super-Mare, they set sail in a slightly larger cutter, the *Tomtit*, having hired three local sailors as crew.

After two nights at sea, they reached the Scilly Islands. Even more than with the Smyth Pigotts in Weston-super-Mare, these south-westerly outposts were the dominion of one man, Augustus Smith, a scion of the family that owned Smith's Bank. Having leased the islands from the Duchy of Cornwall, he was determined to make them productive. That year, he had caused a furore by evicting the last of ten inhabitants from one of the islands, Samson, which he intended turning into a deer park – an experiment that failed as the deer kept trying to swim away.

Wilkie saw fit to describe this autocracy as 'benevolent' when he wrote up the trip for *Household Words* as 'The Cruise of the Tomtit'. This was a comic travelogue, not unlike *Rambles Beyond Railways*, featuring two very familiar protagonists, Jollins and Migott, who sailed from Mangerton in the Mud. At the start Wilkie announced his intention to 'tell things just as they happened. What some people call smart writing, comic colouring, and graphic describing, are departments of authorship at which I snap my fingers in contempt.' He recorded how Jollins treated any of the crew who felt sick with his patent medicine: 'Two tea spoonsful of essence of ginger, two dessert spoonsful of brown brandy, two table spoonsful of strong tea.' He emphasised the leisurely nature of the on-board regime: 'We have no stated hours, and we are well ahead of all rules and regulations.' And he took pride that the five of them were able to coexist in 'a pure republic' with no particular master. They shared a twelve-foot by eight-foot cabin, which provided just enough space for their hammocks. Otherwise, 'the man who can do at the right time, and in the best way, the thing that is most wanted, is always the hero of the situation among us.'

This amiable on-board democracy made for entertaining newspaper copy. But the voyage was little more than a nautical interlude in the increasingly fraught lives of Wilkie and his close friends. For all his intention to 'tell things just as they happened', his account ignored the problems that Pigott, Dickens and he himself were experiencing in their personal lives.

Pigott's immediate task, after the voyage, was to go to Genoa to bail out his hapless elder brother, who had become emotion-ally attached to a foreign woman – something that both Wilkie and Dickens had managed to avoid. Little is known about the lady, except that she was Polish and Jewish. With the help of Dickens's banking friend Emile de la Rue in Genoa and the local British Consul, Timothy Yeats-Brown, Pigott paid her £600 (around £43,700 in today's money).

For Dickens, matters were hardly less complicated. He had been living in Paris since October. Without consulting his wife, he had decided to leave Tavistock House and was considering a possible move to Gad's Hill Place, a large house outside Rochester in Kent, which he had known and loved as a child. But, still troubled by his 'restlessness', he acted on his often stated intention – some might say threat – to uproot his family and settle them in the French capital for six months. Although working hard to finish *Little Dorrit*, he was able to assist in efforts to extricate Pigott's brother, while Wilkie in London could only file away second-hand information about a landed gentleman's peccadillos and hope to use it in some future fiction.

In February 1856, Wilkie joined his friend in Paris, where Dickens arranged for him to stay in a 'perfect little bachelor apartment' at 63 Avenue des Champs-Elysées, close to his own entourage in the same street. Wilkie had a bedroom, sitting-room, dressing-room and kitchen, all in one little building 'like a cottage in a ballet'. He was able to observe a fast-moving city, where old buildings were being demolished and boulevards widened in accordance with Baron Haussmann's radical urban planning initiatives.

However, Wilkie's trip was shrouded in mystery. He was delayed, though the reason was unclear, and Dickens was forced to dissemble to his own family. 'I told them at home that you had a touch of your "old complaint",' he informed Wilkie by letter on 12 February, 'and had turned back to consult your Doctor. Thought it best, in case of any contretemps hereafter, with your mother on one hand and my people on the other.'

Wilkie finally surfaced in Paris more than two weeks later, when he informed his mother on 28 February about his safe arrival. What had he been doing in the meantime that Dickens clearly thought it politic not to divulge? In the light of developments on Wilkie's return from Paris six weeks later, it could have been one of three things. It might have related to Harriet Collins's tenancy at Hanover Terrace. While her son was in Paris, she surprised him with a plan to up sticks to Harley Place on the New Road, as Marylebone Road was still called at the time. However, this news cannot have come out of the blue since the lease was drawing to a close and the matter must have been discussed.

Alternatively, Wilkie's delayed arrival in Paris was probably a consequence of his unorthodox love life – perhaps a flare-up of his venereal disease. More likely, it was the first intimations of a new romantic liaison which he would pick up on his return to London, and which, despite his mother's continual opposition, would last a lifetime. Whatever Dickens was referring to in his letter of 12 February, it was something which Georgina Hogarth later thought best not to include in her edition of her brother-in-law's letters.

Having established himself in what he liked to call his 'pavilion' in the Champs-Elysées, Wilkie soon succumbed to persistent 'rheumatic pains and aguish shiverings', which really did sound like his 'old complaint'. But his condition soon improved, and before long he was feeling only 'a little weakness'.

A week later, Wilkie heard that his mother had taken a lease on the house in Harley Place. He counselled her to check the lease and taxes and to ensure that the place was properly surveyed. But he was soon purring, 'I like the situation of the house so much that I am sure to like the house itself.' His concern about what would happen to his papers was removed when Ned Ward and his family took a short lease on Hanover Terrace. His only other worry was that his mother and brother should have places to go to until Harley Place became available in June. He himself could stay with Pigott, Stringfield or even old Mrs Dickinson. There was also an offer from Dickens to park himself at Tavistock House.

Wilkie used his time in Paris for some energetic writing. Before he left London, his collection of stories, *After Dark*, had been published to acclaim by Smith, Elder, but he still had work to do completing the last, difficult section of *A Rogue's Life* (the earlier chapters of which were being printed in *Household Words* even as he wrote). The story picked up on his current fascination with painting and forgery to produce some of his most penetrating analysis of his father's profession. He told his mother he was 'rather proud' of chapters four and five and asked her to read them attentively. These laid bare the tricks of the art forger, a trade which, he argued, had been made easier by the deeply conservative taste of the mindless aristocratic patrons his father had put up with. More recently, this kind of deceit had become more difficult because art buyers now tended to be self-made entrepreneurs, not bound by rules and precedents, but keen on acquiring art they liked. 'They saw that trees were green in nature, and brown in the Old Masters, and they thought the latter colour not an improvement on the former – and said so.'

Along the way Softly, the eponymous rogue, is redeemed by his love for Laura Knapton, the daughter of a master counter-feiter. This affair again allows Wilkie to wax lyrical (and seem-ingly knowledgeably) on the power of romantic obsession. He remarks, 'Love is generally described I believe as the tender passion. When I remember the insidiously relaxing effect of it on all my faculties, I feel inclined to alter the popular definition, and to call it a moral vapour-bath.'

He is forced to flee, ahead of the Bow Street Runners, leading to his marrying Laura across the border in Scotland, where the law on matrimony requires no official banns, but only a personal declaration of troth. Softly does not escape trial for his forgery, however, and is sentenced to transportation to Australia, where Laura follows him and later, in the guise of a widow, hires him as her indentured servant or 'ticket of leave man', after his partial release for good conduct. Wilkie concludes his story by showing Softly prospering and becoming respectable Down Under – another dig at the shaky foundations of Victorian propriety. Although unambitious in design, *A Rogue's Life* tackled a number of themes to which Wilkie would return, including the mutability of form and personality, the nature of criminality, and variations on the marriage law. Dickens was delighted at the finished product, which appeared as a short serial in five consecutive editions of *Household Words* in March.

Having finished this assignment, Wilkie began thinking about his new novel, *The Dead Secret*, and was encouraged to receive enthusiastic feedback from Dickens about the plot. However, he asked his mother not to mention this to anyone except Charley. Clearly responding defensively to something that had been written or said, he feared that people might think he was dependent for his success on his more experienced friend. He pointed out that Dickens had simply alerted him to some of the weak points in his story and helped him strengthen them.

It was not all work in the Champs-Elysées. In the evenings Wilkie accompanied Dickens to literary dinners and was introduced to Ary Scheffer, the Dutch-born painter of Dickens's latest portrait. In Dickens's telling, Wilkie, 'who has a good eye for pictures', did not like the end result, commenting that there was 'no man living who could do the painting about the eyes'. Wilkie was more positive in a letter to Ned Ward, though his antipathy towards the Royal Academy remained as strong as ever, for he could not help adding, only half-jokingly, 'The picture is to be exhibited in the rooms of the corrupt Institution to which you belong.'

As usual, the two friends enjoyed their visits to the theatre. One evening they attended a new production of *Paradise Lost*, which was attracting advance publicity based on speculation that Eve would appear naked. In the event, Dickens was disappointed to find that the producers had scoured Paris for a woman whose vast expanse of hair fell to her knees and so obscured her charms.

There was, however, another dimension to this friendship. Dickens was now convinced that his 'restlessness' was linked to problems in his relationship with Catherine. Wilkie's carefree ways had helped him throw off some of the worries of married life as the two men continued to explore the Parisian underworld. The more severe John Forster had been superseded in this respect, though Dickens still valued his friendship, recalling the 'old days' in a letter, and adding, 'I find that the skeleton in my domestic closet is becoming a pretty big one.' There is no doubt he was referring to his difficulties with Catherine.

After Wilkie returned to London, Dickens threw his usual

epistolary discretion to the winds and reminded his friend of their ebullient times together. Writing from Paris, he recorded how he had revisited a seedy dive where they had both recently watched a wrestling match. He described the place as similar to 'our own National Argyll Rooms'. In this he seemed to be mixing up two similar dance halls, the Argyll Rooms in Great Windmill Street and the National Assembly Rooms in High Holborn. The former in particular was known as a gathering place for prostitutes. Dickens said he had seen 'some pretty faces, all of two classes – wicked and coldly calculating, or haggard and wretched in their worn beauty'. Among the latter he had alighted on a woman of around thirty in an Indian shawl. Fancying something about the nobility of her forehead, he reported, 'I mean to walk about tonight, and look for her. I didn't speak to her there, and I have a fancy that I should like to know more about her.' It sounds as though this sort of pick-up procedure was a regular practice of the two men.

Back in London, Wilkie was still suffering from a cold and rheumatic symptoms. Developments at the Collins house remained uncertain, so Wilkie had taken the precaution of addressing his last letter from Paris to his mother, care of her neighbour Elizabeth Gibbons at number 16 Hanover Terrace. Charley had already moved out and was renting a studio in 2 Percy Street, off Tottenham Court Road. This caused some of his friends to think he had taken a mistress. But they were mistaken; Charley was not that type. As soon as he was in Percy Street he was having a crisis of conscience typical of his highly sensitive nature. He was worried about a painting he was attempting, which depicted a wife using the electric telegraph to try and find out about her husband who has been involved in a railway accident. He had been working on this for nearly two years, but had become concerned that it reflected too much of the influence of his friend Millais. On 22 April, he wrote a distressingly pained account of this matter, in which he tried to work out where he stood. The idea for the work was not unlike Millais's *The Rescue*, not merely in the way it tried to marry a Pre-Raphaelite aesthetic to a modern subject, but also in its depiction of the tribulations of a modern wife. Charley claimed that the idea for the painting had been his, but admitted that Millais had made several useful suggestions. (The parallels in his brother Wilkie's relationship with Dickens are clear.)

While Charley was wrestling with these problems, Wilkie also moved out of the family home. He stayed one night in a hotel, before establishing himself in a lodging house at 22 Howland Street, one of the less salubrious thoroughfares in Marylebone, but close to the new woman in his life.

THIRD EPOCH

8

ENCOUNTERING CAROLINE

A T THE AGE of thirty-two, Wilkie was finally escaping the ghosts of feuding Academicians and pious Tractarians and establishing himself as his own man, a literary Bohemian worthy of the company of Dickens. The results would show in a more confident tone to his writing. And the catalyst for these changes was an enigmatic young woman who lived in the same warren of run-down streets as Wilkie now did.

Twenty-six-year-old Caroline Graves was a pretty, capricious widow from a humble background who was particularly down on her luck, following the death of her husband three years earlier. Left with a baby daughter, she was trying to avoid the fate of many similar down-at-heel women who were forced to sell their bodies. This was not easy in an area of London which – as a glance at *London Labour and the London Poor*, Henry Mayhew's contemporary sociological survey, confirms – was thick with prostitutes. In her efforts to claw her way to respectability, Caroline had reinvented herself in a manner that would have done credit to Wilkie's skills as a novelist.

For a start, Caroline was not her real name. She was born in late 1829, and for her first twenty years she was called Elizabeth, until she saw the advantages of adopting the arguably more genteel moniker, Caroline. Her age was also a matter of debate, as she liked to suggest she was five years younger than she was. Then there was the matter of her origins. She described her father as a gentleman (or sometimes an army captain) with the delightfully aristocratic name of John Courtenay, while in fact he was John Compton, a jobbing carpenter. At the time of her birth he was living in Toddington, on the edge of the Cotswolds, not far from Cheltenham, in Gloucestershire, but he originally came from Combe Hay, on the other side of Bath, in Somerset, where he returned in the early 1840s.

Caroline's lifelong efforts to present herself as better born than she was covered over her most closely guarded and potentially most damaging secret: she was born out of wedlock. Biographers have hitherto known about her family from censuses but have skated over her birth since there was no certificate. However, so far as it can be read, the register of baptisms in the parish of Toddington shows that on the 8th November 1829 Elizabeth Compton, the illegitimate daughter of Sarah Pully (in fact Pulley) of Grovelays in the neighbouring parish of Hailes, was baptised by the vicar, John Eddy. So Elizabeth was born some time in the preceding weeks. There is no specific mention of a father, though it does state her name as 'Compton, illegitimate daughter of'.

The register goes on to show that her sister Teresa was baptised in May 1832, by which time John and Sarah Compton were described as married (though probably in an unofficial ceremony rather than according to ecclesiastical law, since there is again no record of any union, in the parish or elsewhere). Teresa was followed by four more siblings.

A decade later John Compton had moved back to his native Combe Hay and was living there with his wife Sarah and four additional locally born children. In the meantime, Elizabeth (or Caroline as we shall call her) had been brought up between Toddington and nearby Hailes, the home of her mother's family, the Pulleys. They had all been attracted by the employment opportunities at the main estate in the vicinity, Toddington Manor, seat of the Hanbury-Tracy family, who had made a fortune from ironworks in Wales. (Today the Manor is owned by the wealthy artist Damien Hirst.)

In the early to mid-1840s, Sarah Compton joined her husband in Combe Hay, taking her young family with her. Towards the end of the decade her daughter Caroline moved to Bath, which was still prosperous despite having lost some of its Georgian lustre. It is not clear how she was employed, but she almost certainly had a lowly job, not unlike her younger sister Martha, who in 1851 was working there as a servant in the house of Henry Roberts, a silk merchant in Gay Street, where both Jane Austen and Dr Johnson's friend, Hester Thrale, had once lived.

The city offered Caroline an opportunity first to lose herself and then to put her bastardy behind her by finding respectability through marriage. She was quartered in Burdett Buildings, a tenement house in the Walcot district, when, on 30 March 1850, she married George Robert Graves, an accountant, in the local parish church, St Swithin's, where Jane Austen's parents and brother were buried. Also lowly born, the son of a mason, George gave his address as Clerkenwell in London.

However, he had links with Bath, having been educated at Portway House Academy in Weston on the Bristol side of the city. Since his widowed mother could not have afforded this education, he was certainly a scholarship boy. He stayed in touch with his old school: Thomas Cousins, the headmaster, was a witness when George married Caroline. Indeed, the establishment played a significant part in their relationship and the 1851 census lists, among the sixty or so pupils, an eleven-year-old boy called William Compton, who was born in Toddington, Gloucestershire, and who was almost certainly Caroline's younger brother.

Shortly after their marriage, the Graveses moved to London,

to Cumming Street, just north of the Pentonville Road, close to where the new King's Cross railway station was being built. Their future looked rosy when George, who had shorthand skills, found a job as a clerk in a solicitor's office. Early in 1851, barely nine months after her wedding, Caroline gave birth to a daughter, Elizabeth Harriet. The census a couple of months later shows that the young family was also playing host to George's widowed mother, Mary Ann Graves, who doubtless helped in looking after the baby.

Caroline's determined efforts to improve her lot suffered various setbacks over the next couple of years. On 30 January 1852 she had to cope with the devastating loss of her husband George from tuberculosis in Bath. At the time he was staying at Moravian Cottages, on the Weston Road, close to his old school. Caroline does not seem to have been there; perhaps she remained with her daughter in London. As a result George's death was reported to the authorities not by his wife, but by his mother. Less than three months later, Caroline's own mother died in Combe Hay. Sarah Compton was only forty-three, and the number of her children was in double figures. Officially the reason was the 'escape of the contents of the stomach into the abdomen'. This suggests stomach cancer, but may have been related to the birth, only the previous year, of her son, Levi.

Mary Ann Graves duly returned to London where she opened a tobacconist's shop in Hertford Street in the heart of what came to be called Fitzrovia, the favourite stamping ground of so many of Wilkie's artist and writer friends over the years. Caroline soon followed, but must have considered that her efforts to better herself were doomed when she was forced to open a marine or junk store in the rather seedier Charlton Street nearby. This was a lowly form of mercantile life, even by Victorian standards, in a rough area that accommodated labourers, carpenters, charwomen, seam-stresses and prostitutes.

Wilkie portrayed these surroundings in an article for *Household Words* in June 1856, two months after he moved to Howland Street. 'Laid up in Two Lodgings' contrasted his experiences in two hostelries – one in Paris, where he delighted in the view from his window, and the other in London, where he 'looked out upon drab-coloured walls and serious faces through a smoke-laden atmosphere'. In 'Smeary Street', his name for Howland Street, his room was flea-ridden, dirty and uncomfortable; the other tenants passed through rapidly (as did the maids).

Wilkie made a point of saying that he had chosen this particular location because it was close to his doctor. But this was typical dissimulation. In fact, 22 Howland Street was bang in the middle of the walk Caroline took from her marine store in Charlton Street to her mother-in-law's tobacconist's shop in Hertford Street. And if he wanted to stroll home to see his mother, he was likely to pass through Charlton Street.

The circumstances of his first meeting with Caroline are not known, but the encounter has since taken on significance since she has been identified – in most detail by John Guille Millais, the son of Wilkie's artist friend – as the model for the eponymous character at the centre of one of his greatest novels, *The Woman in White*, published in 1859–60. The elder Millais told his son of the evening he had accompanied the Collins brothers on a walk back from their mother's house in Hanover Terrace to his own family house in Gower Street. Suddenly the three of them were stopped in their tracks by the sound of a scream coming from the garden of a house they were passing. Their initial fears that a woman was in considerable distress were confirmed when an iron gate was flung open, and they were presented with the extraordinary sight of a beautiful young woman dressed in flowing white robes that shone in the moonlight.

She then fled into the shadows and, according to Millais, Wilkie ran after her, saying he must see what he could do to help. The other two heard no more until the next day when a sheepish Wilkie told them how he had caught up with the woman and discovered she had somehow fallen into the hands of an unscrupulous man who lived in a villa in Regent's Park. For several months this person had controlled her by mesmerism and kept her prisoner. It was only when he threatened to kill her with a poker that she decided she must escape.

Couple this dramatic story with the observation from Dickens's daughter Katey that Wilkie (later her brother-in-law) had a mistress called Caroline who was the inspiration for *The Woman in White*, and one can easily see why this moonlit apparition has been linked to the young widow from Gloucestershire.

However, both these sources are suspect. By the time their accounts were made public, the protagonists were all dead. There is no evidence for Caroline having been kept captive, let alone by an evil mesmerist. The story has the air of an engaging fantasy spun by Wilkie for the amusement of fellow dinner guests, and hints at just enough of the truth to be taken for the real thing.

Wilkie probably liked to imagine that, in Caroline, he was helping a woman who was suffering, both mentally and physically. The fact that she was illegitimate only added to her déclassée allure. Her living quarters suggest she was on the verge of becoming a 'fallen woman' of the type that so fascinated Victorian artists and writers in the abstract, but that in reality required financial assistance from philanthropists such as Angela Burdett-Coutts. He had helped Caroline avoid the drop into prostitution. As a quid pro quo, he wove a web of fantasy around her, using her as a model for many of the wilful but disadvantaged women who featured so prominently in his fiction.

The progress of Wilkie's relationship with Caroline is nevertheless difficult to follow as no correspondence between them has survived. Over time he would introduce her to his closest friends, usually at his home. Dickens had little time for her, though Frederick Lehmann hinted at her coquettish appeal when he recalled her emerging from the kitchen in a 'very *décolleté* white silk gown'. Such occasions were seldom repeated; aside from the occasional visit to the theatre, Wilkie and Caroline were never seen in public together. Although his work showed considerable empathy with disadvantaged women like her, he kept his new mistress in the shadows, preferring the easy-going bachelor lifestyle to which he was accustomed.

Wilkie's stay in Howland Street was short-lived. Dickens visited him there in early May 1856, but by the end of the following month his mother was ensconced in her new house at 2 Harley Place. Wilkie did not join her immediately, but he used this as an accommodation address while he contrived to follow a care-free peripatetic existence.

He made little obvious effort to help Harriet with her move, preferring to go sailing with the Pigott brothers, John and Edward (the 'Ancient Mariner', as Dickens called him). Having been clawed back from Italy, John was beginning to settle as lord of the manor in Weston and Brockley. As a treat to himself, he bought a 47-ton schooner called the *Coquette*, a toy he shared with Edward for the next year, until he unexpectedly married Blanche Arundell, a member of a leading Roman Catholic family, and adopted her religion.

There was no place for Caroline Graves, or any other women, on this bachelors' voyage on the *Coquette* which sailed from Gravesend to the Isle of Wight – then, as now, the headquarters of yachting – and across the Channel to Cherbourg, where it loaded some fine wines, before returning to its home port of

Weston. Edward Pigott had been introducing several literary friends to a taste of this nautical life: he had already taken Thornton Leigh Hunt and Herbert Spencer to Cherbourg, and later in July he promised George Lewes and Marian Evans a trip across the Bristol Channel from Tenby, though this did not materialise.

Wilkie liked feeling the wind in his hair and forgetting his cares. However, his experience of seamy urban life and of Caroline's predicament had affected him. He was genuinely touched by the situation of a maid at Howland Street who could only look forward to 'dirty work, small wages, hard words, no holidays, no social station, no future'. In his piece for *Household Words*, he added in Dickensian mode, 'No human being ever was created for this. No state of society which composedly accepts this, in the cases of thousands, as one of the necessary conditions of its selfish comforts, can pass itself off as civilised.' He concluded, 'I have witnessed some sad sights during my stay in Smeary Street, which have taught me to feel for my poor and forlorn fellow-creatures as I do not think I ever felt for them before.'

This more compassionate and socially aware Wilkie was evident in 'The Diary of Anne Rodway', his next assignment for *Household Words*. This unfussy piece broke new ground in several ways, notably as a detective story (the first ever to feature a woman as the sleuth) that drew cleverly on the media frenzy surrounding a recent murder case to ratchet up tension.

Its real-life forerunner was the Rugeley murder trial, which had taken place in May 1856, resulting in the conviction of the surgeon William Palmer for killing a gambling colleague. This was the first criminal prosecution to use forensic evidence – in this instance, to prove that the victim had been poisoned. Wilkie attended the trial and was fascinated by the way various pieces of conflicting evidence came together to present a convincing case.

The general public was familiar with the Rugeley murders (Palmer was suspected of others) because the circulations of newspapers had risen sharply following the abolition of the stamp tax the previous year. As papers competed to report the gruesome details, the doctor's name became synonymous with evil.

Wilkie's story for *Household Words* centred on Anne Rodway, an impoverished seamstress, living in the manner of Caroline Graves in a run-down lodging house in a road similar to 'Smeary Street'. Significantly perhaps, Anne is the same age as Caroline, twenty-six. She has a fellow lodger called Mary Mallison, who has low self-esteem and a problem with drink and laudanum. One night, after a prolonged absence, Mary returns home, the bedraggled victim of a violent assault, and dies shortly afterwards. When Anne seeks to discover her friend's killer, all she has to go on, her only clue, is a black silk strand from a man's cravat.

On her way back from work, she stops to buy candles at an emporium which, in Wilkie's description, is a mixture of Caroline's workplace and that of her mother-in-law, Mary Ann Graves – 'a small shop with two counters, which did business on one side in the general grocery way, and on the other in the rag and bottle and old iron line.' Having bought her candles, Anne is told there is no paper to wrap them in. At this point she spies by chance, among some rags, a cravat which matches the strand she has found on Mary. She contrives not only to have her candles wrapped in this piece of cloth, but also to discover where it came from. As a result she is able to follow the trail further and find out who murdered her friend. The details of the story emerge fluidly in the form of diary entries by Anne.

This slightly self-conscious process shows Wilkie writing a new type of detective story. Halfway through Anne's tale, she relates a dream about the strand of cravat: 'I thought it was lengthened into a long clue, like the silken thread that led to

Rosamond's Bower. I thought I took hold of it, and followed it a little way, and then got frightened and tried to go back, but found that I was obliged, in spite of myself, to go on.' Wilkie is here picking up on a new meaning for the word clue (or clew) – originally a thread of yarn, but, more recently, by extension, something which guides you from one place or idea to another. Clues in this latter sense had started to appear in the detective fiction of writers such as Edgar Allan Poe, who used the word in 'The Purloined Letter' in 1845.

The first part of 'The Diary of Anne Rodway' was published on 19 July, a month after Palmer's execution. Dickens recognised its importance in Wilkie's literary development. He told him how much he admired it, adding that it gave him 'a personal pride and pleasure', which suggests he saw his own influence having a positive effect on Wilkie's work. Always an emotional man, Dickens was so moved when he originally read the story in a railway carriage that, to the consternation of his fellow passengers, he broke down and cried. He described it to his actor friend William Macready as having 'great merit, and real pathos' and asked his colleague Wills to give Wilkie a £20 bonus as he 'wished to remove it from ordinary calculations'.

Wilkie devoted the rest of the month to his personal affairs in London before departing on holiday with the Dickenses in Boulogne. After his recent literary successes, his standing with his friend was high. However, the general holiday spirit was dampened by an outbreak of diphtheria, which killed several local people, including two members of the Dickens circle, the humorist Gilbert à Beckett and his son Walter. Although staying comfortably outside the town, Dickens swiftly sent his family home, though he prolonged his own homeward journey by walking most of the way from Dover to London in the company of Wilkie and Pigott. One reason was that he wanted to show his friends Gad's Hill Place, the country house set in twenty-six acres of grounds outside Rochester, which he had finally committed himself to buying for £1,790 in March. The vendor was Mrs Eliza Lynn Linton, a formidable anti-feminist writer and journalist, who had worked for *Household Words*. She wrote one of the stories in *The Seven Poor Travellers*, the Christmas omnibus issue of 1854, which also included one of Wilkie's first contributions to the magazine. After months of uncertainty about what Dickens would do with Gad's Hill, he finally decided to live there. It was clear that he was just as unsettled as Wilkie, as he moved from house to house, in search of distraction from his failing marriage.

Wilkie hoped to stay at Harley Place when he returned to London, but his mother was away visiting the Langtons in Maidenhead. He had clearly spent very little time at her new house, since he had to ask her for the names of the servants. Nevertheless, he took the opportunity to soldier on with the new play that he and Dickens had been discussing since Paris in April. Dickens had the original idea for a production to be staged at Tavistock House the following January – on Twelfth Night, his son Charley's twentieth birthday. He wanted to base it on Captain Sir John Franklin's 1845 expedition through frozen Canadian waters to find a north-west passage to Asia. Like its predecessors, this quest was unsuccessful, and worse, since no one returned.

Wilkie and Dickens developed a storyline about two members of a rescue party for a similar expedition and their rivalry for the hand of the beautiful Clara Burnham. As a result of regular discussions about the play during the summer, Dickens had identified one of these men, Richard Wardour, as an excellent part for his acting talents, while Wilkie would play the other,

Frank Aldersley. By early October, when Wilkie had almost finished writing the script, Dickens was visibly excited. He grew his beard and set about transforming the school room at Tavistock House into a suitable theatre. (Wilkie almost certainly followed suit tonsorially at this stage.) With his usual forceful-ness, Dickens then roped family and friends into acting, designing and staging the play. The intensity of the fictional relationship between Wardour and Aldersley seemed to mirror that between him and his collaborator.

Wilkie was now entering a period of great industry as he poured out both fiction and non-fiction copy for *Household Words* and other publications. Impressed by this output, Dickens invited him in October to join the staff of his magazine, describing him to Wills as 'exceedingly quick to take my notions . . . industrious and reliable besides,' and justifying his employment as an economy measure: given the amount of work Wilkie was producing, paying him a salary of five guineas a week would be cheaper. Wilkie was initially underwhelmed, worrying that his contributions – which appeared anonymously in *Household Words* – would be muddled with Dickens's. But Dickens worked out an acceptable compromise, so that at least some of these pieces would be advertised with Wilkie's name attached.

As rehearsals of *The Frozen Deep* began, Wilkie was collabor-ating with Dickens on the next *Household Words* Christmas number. This year the 'conductor', as Dickens termed himself, wanted a nautical theme, and Wilkie, with his yachting experi-ence and knowledge of John Franklin's ill-fated expedition, was just the man to help with a series of related stories about a ship that went down after hitting an iceberg in the freezing waters of the Southern Ocean bordering Antarctica. Dickens started 'The Wreck of the Golden Mary' in the voice of the ship's captain. But still preoccupied with *Little Dorrit*, he handed over narration to Wilkie who, as the first mate, related the tribulations of the passengers and crew, as well as providing the account of their eventual rescue.

In commending the festive issue to Angela Burdett-Coutts, Dickens specifically noted, 'I am the Captain of the Golden Mary; Mr Collins is the Mate.' However, Wilkie was responsible for the bulk of the writing and, though Dickens had the final word, the balance of power in the two men's professional relationship was beginning to shift.

One of Wilkie's recent pieces, 'My Black Mirror', drew on his experience of the delights (particularly the food) and miseries (the bureaucracy and discomfort) of travel in Europe, but concluded that he preferred being at sea 'in the fastest fairest schooner-yacht afloat . . . taking our pleasures along the southern shores of the English coast'. He was recalling his trip on the *Coquette*: 'Here is no hurrying to accommodate yourself to other people's hours for starting, no scrambling for places, no wearisome watchfulness over baggage.' Instead, there was the sense of freedom he had revelled in over the years. 'We can make our own road, and trespass nowhere. The bores we dread, the letters we don't want to answer, cannot follow and annoy us. We are the freest travellers under Heaven.'

Now he was employed by *Household Words*, his articles became more personal, even if one has to read between the lines to understand this. In 'To Think, or Be Thought For', Wilkie showed how far he had moved from his father's Academicism as he canvassed a populist approach to art, attacking the waffle of professional critics with their admiration of old masters, and pleading for art to be enjoyed by the common man. He could not have put his case more forcefully when he declared, 'The sort of High Art which is professedly bought *for us* and which does actually address itself to nobody but painters, critics and connoisseurs is not High Art at all, but the lowest of the Low, because it is the narrowest as to its sphere of action.'

'A Petition to the Novel-Writers' was an opinionated piece about trends in modern fiction. Wilkie lampooned the average reader who was put off by the occasional licence, even frisson of excitement, he or she found in the novels and preferred the tedium of traditional long-winded travel books. Offering advice he did not always follow himself, he also took authors to task, calling on them to banish clichés, such as putting heroes on horseback and limiting their readers to a choice between two leading ladies – invariably a tall dark one who is serious and unfortunate and a short fair one who is flirtatious and happy.

In this context, Wilkie could not avoid airing his prejudices – jokingly presented but no less firmly felt – as he noted disapprovingly the emergence of a new type of literary heroine: the lip-curling man-hater. He suggested that such a woman could never be a suitable wife for any son of his, who would be better purchasing a Circassian slave in Istanbul. At least then she would not despise him for his masculinity. His own fantasy wife was flutteringly submissive: 'Can I ever forget the mixture of modest confusion and perfect politeness with which that admirable woman heard me utter the most absolute nonsense that ever issued from my lips?'

He left his most outspoken comment on Victorian sexual politics until the end of the year when, in 'Bold Words by a Bachelor', he made a passionate plea for traditional male friendship. He argued, with a touch of irony, that a certain type of modern woman was so demanding of the attentions of her husband that the latter had no time, let alone emotional energy, to share with his friends. Such exclusive marriages were selfish, he wrote, because they led to a married man 'leaving all his sympathies in his wife's boudoir, and all his affections upstairs in the nursery, and giving to his friends such shreds and patches of formal recognition, in place of true love and regard, as consist in asking them to an occasional dinner-party, and granting them the privilege of presenting his children with silver mugs.'

Wilkie might have been thinking about Dickens or another of his male friends. But, more likely, he was setting out his stall with Caroline. She had made a strong impression on him, but he wanted to reinforce his position that he had no intention of giving up his bachelor ways, which involved evenings at the Garrick Club, visits to friends in the country, and leisurely trips *en garçon* with Dickens.

His attitude to his leisure time was not purely selfish. He had strong views on the institution of marriage, whose 'scope and purpose' he felt was 'miserably narrow'. And in the 'Bold Words' article he introduced a theme he would often return to in his writings – the stupidity of the divorce laws, which meant that some people 'would rather see murder committed under their own eyes than approve of any project for obtaining a law of divorce which shall be equal in its operation on husbands and wives of all ranks who cannot live together'. He claimed to have a higher idea of marriage: 'The light of its beauty must not be shut up within the four walls which enclose the parents and family, but must flow out into the world, and shine upon the childless and solitary, because it has warmth enough and to spare, and because it may make them, even in their way, happy too.'

These were not idle words. He had an equally strong sense of how the institution might not work for the opposite sex. He knew how disastrous it had been for friends such as Frances Dickinson, and he understood that it could be as much of a trap for women as for men. So this was another subject for his fiction, as marriage and divorce came increasingly under the same rational scrutiny as other issues in society. In 1857, the Matrimonial Causes Act would remove divorce from ecclesiastical courts, making it a civil rather than church issue. It would also give married women partial protection of their earnings.

However, the law remained heavily weighted in favour of men, who retained rights to their wives' property and enjoyed less onerous requirements of proof in divorce. These continuing inconsistencies and inequalities would provide Wilkie with ample scope for cliffhanging plotlines over the following years.

Wilkie as a child, drawn by his father William Collins.

Wilkie and his brother Charles, aged nine and five, painted by their father's friend, Andrew Geddes, in 1833.

William Collins, Wilkie's father,
painted by his friend John Linnell,
who lived near the Collins family
in Hampstead and Bayswater.

Harriet Collins, Wilkie's mother, also
painted by John Linnell.

Margaret
Carpenter,
Wilkie's aunt,
painted by her
son William
Carpenter Jr.
in 1846.

alian boats at Sorrento, sketched in a pen and black ink drawing by Wilkie,
ʒed thirteen, while he was visiting Italy with his parents and brother in 1837.

he Caves of Ulysses at Sorrento, Naples depicted in an oil painting by
Villiam Collins, as recalled by him in 1843.

Charles Allston Collins on the steps of Charles Dickens's home at Gad's Hill Place in Kent.

Wilkie Collins, painted by his friend John Everett Millais in 1850.

May, in the Regent's Park, painted by Charles Allston Collins in 1851, showing the view from his studio in the family house at 17 Hanover Terrace

Mr Honeywood Introduces the Bailiffs to Miss Richland as his Friends – Act III, Scene 1 from Goldsmith's play, *The Good-Natured Man* – painted by William Powell Frith in 1850. It was performed in the 'Theatre Royal, Back Drawing Room' at the Collinses' house in Blandford Square. The bailiff on the right may well portray Wilkie Collins.

RIGHT: Scene from *The Lighthouse* at Campden House, 10 July 1855, with (*left to right*) Wilkie Collins as Martin Gurncock, Georgina Hogarth as Lady Grace and Charles Dickens, kneeling, as Aaron Gurncock.

LEFT: Scene from *No Thoroughfare* at the Adelphi Theatre, 1867, showing the actor Charles Fechter as Obenreizer (*fourth from left*). Also in the picture (*far left*), is the actor and manager Benjamin Webster.

Sketch by John Everett Millais of a young Wilkie Collins (*seated right*) and Richard Doyle (*back to the artist*) with three women.

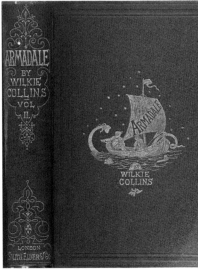

Armadale: the cover and spine of the first edition of Wilkie's novel, published in two volumes by Smith, Elder in 1866.

Frontispiece drawing by John Everet Millais for Wilkie's 1851 Christmas story, *Mr Wray's Cash-Box*.

ehearsal for *The Frozen Deep* at Walham Green, 1857. From left to right:
ack row) artist William Telbin, Mr Evans, novelist Shirley Brooks, Mark
emon Jr., printer W. Jones, publisher Frederick Evans, artist Marcus Stone,
usician Francesco Berger, *Punch* editor Mark Lemon and artist Augustus
gg; (*middle row*) author Albert Smith, artist Clarkson Frederick Stanfield,
liss Evans, journalist Edward Smyth Pigott, Mrs Francis and artist John
uard; (*bottom row*) Charles Dickens Jr., Kate Dickens, Miss Hogarth, Mary
ickens, Wilkie Collins, Miss H. Hogarth. Charles Dickens is stretched out
the front of the group.

hn Everett Millais: from the frontis-
ece to *The Life and Letters of Sir John
verett Millais*, the biography written
y his son, J. G. Millais, in 1899.

William Holman Hunt: a self-
portrait that appeared in his book,
*Pre-Raphaelitism and the Pre-
Raphaelite Brotherhood*, in 1905.

First known photograph of Wilkie Collins, produced in 1857 by Herbert Watkins, who had a studio at 215 Regent Street, London.

Hotel bill for Wilkie and Charles Dickens from the Ship Inn, Allonby – now in Cumbria – dated 9–1 September 1857. The two authors rested here after Wilkie was injured climbing Carrock Fell. They later wrote an accoun of their travels, *The Lazy Tour of Two Idle Apprentices*.

9

THE UNKNOWN PUBLIC

WILKIE'S RELATIONSHIP WITH Caroline Graves was unusual but by no means unique. He knew several men with girlfriends and mistresses, often from a lower class. But his liaison was not public, and it betrayed his own tendency to secretiveness, a feature of the age at variance with another contemporary phenomenon – the thirst for knowledge and exactitude. Now, with a mixture of perverseness and intuitive brilliance, Wilkie was to make the dichotomy between these two trends a centrepiece of his work.

His new novel, *The Dead Secret*, showed the way. Its subject was no ordinary secret but an ancient family mystery, details of which had been committed to paper and deliberately hidden. For the task of investigation, Wilkie opted for a plucky young woman. The fact that the secret related to her own legitimacy and thus her right to inherit the part-ruined Porthgenna Tower in Cornwall added poignancy and made the story a particularly gripping page-turner. It could almost be read as an alternative version of how life might have turned out differently for Caroline at Toddington Manor in Gloucestershire.

Wilkie's previous novels *Hide and Seek* and *A Rogue's Life* had featured painters. *The Dead Secret* focused on a different branch of the arts, the theatre, which excited him in a way his father's profession no longer did. He originally wrote the story in a series of 'acts', starting with the dying chatelaine of Porthgenna, a one-time 'play-actress', Mrs Treverton, who sets the plot in motion by confiding her secret in a letter she entrusts to her maid Sarah Leeson to give to her absent seagoing husband.

The secret, it transpires, is about the parentage of the Trevertons' daughter, Rosamond, who is really the maid Sarah's daughter by a lover who had died while she was pregnant. Because of Captain Treverton's desire for a child, his wife and Sarah passed the now fatherless infant off as his own. The dying Mrs Treverton's letter is intended to inform her husband about this. But Sarah is emotionally disturbed by the contents and she decides to bury it in the Myrtle Room in the derelict north wing of the house, hoping it will be forgotten. The novel takes Sarah through a series of adventures in which she acts essentially as a detective, until she finally discovers the letter, and the truth about her birth and her inheritance.

The year 1857 started briskly for Wilkie with the serialisation of the first part of *The Dead Secret* in *Household Words* on 3 January, followed two days later by the dress rehearsal of *The Frozen Deep* at Tavistock House, where his fellow cast members included not only Dickens and members of his family but also Mark Lemon, Augustus Egg and Edward Pigott. The first full performance took place, as planned, on Twelfth Night, followed by four more shows over the next eight days.

The play proved so distracting that Wilkie had to lock himself away in a house overlooking Richmond Park for the next month or so, so he could keep up with his punishing weekly schedule for serialisation of *The Dead Secret*. (This was the first time he had published a full-length novel in this manner, and it was a struggle.) Dickens was equally under pressure to complete not only *Little Dorrit* but also construction work at his new house at Gad's Hill. The two men typically sought some distraction in early March and want to stay at the Bedford Hotel in Brighton, from where the only information that emerged was that they both got soaked walking on the Downs.

Wilkie's literary and theatre productions now progressed in tandem. He had a following in the United States, where *The Dead Secret* was serialised in *Harper's Weekly*, a new outlet based on the *Illustrated London News* from the stable of Harper and Brothers, a leading New York publisher. But he needed a firm to get behind his books in Britain, so, with Bentley still financially strapped and Smith, Elder not interested, he plumped for Dickens's (and Thackeray's) publishers Bradbury and Evans, who were on hand as the printers of *Household Words*.

Wilkie took time off on 19 May to attend a party at Gad's Hill, which must have been a bizarre occasion as it was both a house warming and a celebration of worn-down Catherine Dickens's forty-second birthday. He allowed himself only a short break as he still had work to do: until almost publication day in mid-June, he was correcting proofs of *The Dead Secret* as soon as they arrived from *Household Words* and sending them on immediately to his new publisher, Frederick Evans. The dedicatee of the finished volume this time was Edward Pigott, in whose company he had spent a lot of time while writing it. (It seems that the house where he holed up in Richmond Park belonged to either Pigott or one of his close friends.)

Critics were muted in their response, and thought that Wilkie had spoiled the plot by giving away the secret at the start. In his preface to a revised version in 1861 he acknowledged the risks, but said he wanted to draw out the process of the investigation, or as he put it, 'to let the effect of the story depend on expectation rather than surprise'.

Wilkie was now influential enough to elicit support from his and, particularly, Dickens's circle of friends. The prolific Edmund Yates obliged with a favourable profile in his ephemeral weekly, the *Train*. When this appeared in June, it was illustrated by a studio photograph of a now extremely hirsute Wilkie, taken by Herbert Watkins of Regent Street. Yates emphasised his subject's conscientiousness and industry, as well as his mastery of the art of plotting a novel. He declared him to be the fourth best English novelist, behind Dickens, Thackeray and Charlotte Brontë. Wilkie was, in modern parlance, running a public relations campaign, for that same month his portrait by Millais was shown at an exclusive exhibition of Pre-Raphaelite art at 4 Russell Place, Fitzroy Square.

There were persistent rumours that Queen Victoria wanted to see *The Frozen Deep*, but Dickens, with his radical sympathies, did not make it easy. He declined to put on a performance at Windsor Castle on the unconvincing grounds that his daughters, who were yet to be formally presented at court, might suffer socially from appearing there as mere actresses. The Queen agreed instead to attend a special private performance on 4 July at the Royal Gallery of Illustration in Lower Regent Street, where she took a large party, including her four eldest children and her uncle, the visiting King Leopold I of Belgium. Among Dickens's own guests was Hans Christian Andersen, the Danish author best known for his fairy tales, who was beginning to outstay his welcome at Gad's Hill, where he had annoyed Wilkie by surreptitiously attaching some daisies to his hat and allowing him to walk thus into the village.

The cast had seen some minor changes since the start of the year, with Wilkie's friend Frances Dickinson now taking over the role of the Scottish nurse from Wills's wife Janet, who had become lame. Frances had at least picked up the right accent during her problematic marriage. Once again Dickens made life difficult for himself, declining an invitation to receive the Queen's personal congratulations because, he claimed, he was inappropriately dressed in his actor's costume. The Queen was unfazed, professing to find the play 'most interesting, intensely dramatic, & most touching & moving, at the end'. She asked an equerry to convey her 'high approval' of Wilkie's performance.

Dickens was enjoying his acting so much that he seized an opportunity to present extra performances at the Gallery of Illustration to raise money for the family of his early mentor, Douglas Jerrold, who had recently died. Though the Jerrolds protested that they had been well provided for, they were not too unhappy to pocket the proceeds.

Dickens was not finished yet. He had promised his friend's family a sum of £2000, and when that total fell short, he readily accepted another invitation to stage the play in Manchester's vast Free Trade Hall. Adjudging that the women in the cast were not up to this task, he took advice from his actor-manager friend Alfred Wigan, and hired the seasoned actress Mrs (Frances) Ternan. She had three daughters with stage experience, two of whom also joined the company, including the youngest, a pretty, blue-eyed slip of a girl called Ellen (known as Nelly).

The upshot, Dickens informed his friends, was an extremely emotional series of performances, with many of the actors breaking down in tears at the sadness of the final scene. He neglected to reveal that, in this heightened atmosphere, he had fallen deeply, if not obsessively, in love with Nelly Ternan. For two years he had been looking for someone or something to fill a void in his life. Now he believed he had found it in this unassuming eighteen-year-old, young enough to be his daughter.

Wilkie was temporarily distracted by the professional premiere of *The Lighthouse* on 10 August. He had long wanted to see one of his plays produced on the London stage proper. At last the actor-managers Frederick Robson and W.S. Emden had found a slot for his melodrama at their Royal Olympic Theatre, off the Strand. Wilkie was so delighted by the enthusiastic reaction of the first-night audience that he felt he had to share the news immediately with his mother. Even while celebrating after the performance in the supper room of the Albion Tavern in Great Russell Street, he grabbed some paper and wrote to tell her of the calls for him at the end of the first act, and then 'a perfect hurricane of applause at the end of the play – which I had to acknowledge from a private box. Dickens, Thackeray, Mark Lemon, publicly appearing in my box. In short an immense success.' This was the general consensus, and the play would run for over two months, though his own takings were limited to a modest advance of £100.

In early September, Wilkie again turned his attention to Dickens, whom he found in a depressed mood, having finally steeled himself to admit to John Forster that his marriage was over. However, Dickens's passion for Nelly was so novel and so overwhelming that he had no idea how to proceed. His solution was to call on Wilkie, who was more tolerant of his foibles than Forster, to join him on a diversionary trip, which he hoped would jolt him out of his listlessness and allow them jointly to pen a light travelogue for the somewhat neglected *Household Words*.

Wilkie suggested Norfolk as a destination, but Dickens insisted they should go to Cumberland and then proceed to Doncaster, where he claimed he wanted to attend the annual St Leger race meeting. However, his real motive was that Nelly Ternan and her sister Maria would be acting there at the Theatre Royal at the very same time. Even before he and Wilkie set out from Euston station on 7 September, he had already booked two bedrooms and a sitting-room at the Angel Hotel in Doncaster.

Having acquired a smart new brown suit for the trip, Wilkie had only been on the road for two days when he suffered a slight accident of a type to which he was prone. He and Dickens decided to climb Carrock Fell, an undistinguished but still challenging peak of 2,169 feet. Wilkie was disappointed to reach what he was told was the top and find that he could see nothing: the view was entirely obscured by mist. On his descent, calamity struck when he tripped and fell into a rivulet, from which he emerged with a badly sprained ankle. Dickens had to support him all the way down, an intimate process he compared to his experience as Richard Wardour holding up Frank Aldersley in *The Frozen Deep*. Over the next few days, as they continued gingerly to Wigton, Allenby on the Solway Firth and back to Lancaster, he became irritated with having to act as nurse-maid, particularly when the invalid Wilkie created a lake of potions and healing baths around him in their hotel, and later when he showed signs of his old stinginess in complaining about the price of a meal.

The ankle soon began to heal and, shortly after arriving in Doncaster, Wilkie was able to hobble around on a stick (Dickens called him the 'gouty admiral', after a character in Jane Austen's *Persuasion*). On the day of the St Leger, Dickens hired an open carriage and took the redoubtable Mrs Ternan and her nubile daughters, Maria and Nelly, to the racecourse. Dickens then invited Nelly to join him on a jaunt in the country, but she – or more likely her mother – objected, and he returned to London more emotionally confused than ever, while Wilkie made his way to Scarborough, ostensibly for further convalescence, but perhaps also to buy time at a difficult juncture in his affair with Caroline Graves.

Indications of niggles in Wilkie's relationship with Caroline can be discerned in his story 'Mrs Badgery', which appeared in *Household Words* at the end of September. It took the form of a plea by an exasperated bachelor with 'a large circle of acquaintance' who wants to buy a house owned by a widow (the eponymous Mrs B). But she is 'too fond of the memory of her late husband' whose presence she keeps recalling in every room. This scenario, involving the purchase of a suburban villa, was far removed from Caroline's world. But her loyalty to George Graves, and perhaps the position of her young daughter, Harriet, may have created tension with Wilkie.

Wilkie and Dickens wrote up their recent journey as 'The Lazy Tour of Two Idle Apprentices', a title that drew on 'Industry and Idleness', a series of William Hogarth engravings which contrasted the lives of two apprentice weavers – one hard-working and virtuous (the persona adopted by Dickens) and the other feckless and no good (Wilkie). 'The Lazy Tour' played off these two different personalities against each other, and provided a lively commentary on contemporary modes of travel, and in particular the paradox of the express train, which caused the world to flash by, without providing much comfort, relaxation or indeed opportunity for laziness.

Wilkie's professional skills were appreciated at *Household Words* and in October he was given a salary rise of £50 a year. His easy, non-judgemental companionship was also valuable to Dickens, who, on his return from Doncaster, had grumpily ordered a solid partition to be built between his dressing room and the matrimonial bedroom at Gad's Hill. The message to Catherine was that he intended to continue his life in peace in his own space. In stark contrast, a new personal closeness was acknowledged the next time Dickens wrote to his friend, addressing him as 'My Dear Wilkie' rather than 'My Dear Collins'.

Dickens vented his personal frustrations in an unseemly invective against Indians, which appeared not only in his letters but in his latest Christmas collaboration with Wilkie, entitled 'The Perils of Certain English Prisoners'. He was infuriated by what he had heard about the atrocities committed earlier in the year during the Indian Mutiny. He was particularly exercised because, only a few months earlier, his son Alfred had joined the East India Company in Calcutta. Wilkie also had a personal link through his cousin William Carpenter, who had recently returned after spending most of the decade in India, where he gained a reputation as a water-colourist with close ties to the Mughal court. In Wilkie's case, this connection helped mitigate his attitude to events in the subcontinent, and he prevailed on Dickens to change the location of these latest tales of British heroism in the face of native brutalities from India to some unspecified island in the Caribbean.

Wilkie maintained this emollient line towards India the following February when, at the start of another phase of prolific writing for *Household Words*, he penned 'A Sermon for Sepoys', which suggested that Indians did not need Christian missionaries since they had perfectly good and morally uplifting myths of their own. This did not mean that Wilkie was opposed to all British forays abroad. Only the previous month he had turned in a piece praising the bravery and spirit of adventure shown by the missionary and explorer Dr Livingstone in Africa.

But Wilkie was not known for consistency in either his opinions or his private life, which remained unsettled as he flitted between addresses, using his mother's house in Harley Place as his principal abode, and, as far as is possible to discern, leaving Caroline and her daughter to fend for themselves.

For the time being he had a more important role to fulfil as Dickens's friend, rather than employee. In early February 1858, he was one of only two people (the other was Forster) invited to celebrate Dickens's birthday in Gravesend. 'The Inimitable' seemed happy to steer clear of Gad's Hill as long as his domestic circumstances remained fraught, causing him to mope to Wilkie that he had not enjoyed 'a moment's peace or content' since his 'Doncaster unhappiness'.

Since he was arranging a nationwide reading tour and tongues were starting to wag about his marriage, Dickens decided to tell his agent, Arthur Smith, what was going on. He wrote to him explaining the background to his forthcoming separation from Catherine, in case the matter was raised by any of Smith's clients. What became known as the 'violated letter' was somehow published in the United States and the details seeped back to the British press. As a result, Dickens was forced to pen an extraordinary denial, which he pressured potential allies to print. When Mark Lemon, the editor of *Punch*, and Frederick Evans and William Bradbury, the magazine's owners (and also the publishers of both Dickens and Wilkie), declined, Dickens was furious and cut them all from his life.

This vengeful act was followed shortly afterwards by another impulsive gesture. After hearing someone at the Garrick Club repeat the common enough rumour that Dickens was having an affair with his sister-in-law, Georgina Hogarth, Thackeray retorted that the woman was actually an actress. Dickens did not take this kindly, and a smouldering feud became worse after Thackeray objected to a profile of himself in the magazine *Town Talk*, owned and edited by Edmund Yates. Since Yates was not only a member of the Garrick but a friend of Dickens, Thackeray complained to the Club committee, which saw fit to expel Yates. At this juncture, while remaining a member of the Club, Dickens resigned from the committee, ostensibly in sympathy with Yates, but really as a gesture against Thackeray who, for a while at least, joined his circle of the damned.

Meanwhile, Wilkie continued to provide unobtrusive support. Dickens may have used Forster, his literary executor, as his preferred go-between when his solicitor Frederic Ouvry drew up a legal deed of separation from Catherine. But as soon as this official business was completed in mid-May, Dickens contacted Wilkie, thanking him for his friendship and asking him to come and see him. 'I can then tell you all in lieu of writing. It is rather a long story – over, I hope, now.' It was typical of Wilkie that, despite his closeness to Dickens, he remained on good terms with Catherine, whom he later visited in her new house in Gloucester Crescent in Camden, across Regent's Park from his mother.

There is no record of Wilkie reciprocating and telling Dickens about his relationship with Caroline, although he must have done so. One can only imagine how Dickens's separation, and Wilkie's role in it, appeared to her. At a time when, to Wilkie's intense interest, the subjects of marriage and divorce were firmly on the public agenda as the first cases began to be heard in the civil courts following the passage of the 1857 Matrimonial Causes Act, the widowed Caroline must have wondered about her own status and future.

Wilkie's mobility was restricted owing to his still unstable ankle, and not helped by a flare-up of gout. However, his pain did not prevent him joining Pigott on a sailing trip in June. There is no evidence of any women accompanying the two friends on a voyage that took them to Wales, where Wilkie was amused to be introduced to a local Bard as Dr Collins. A couple of months later, he again took time off in Broadstairs.

Wilkie's leisure allowed him to work on various projects he had been contemplating, such as a play Frederick Robson of the Olympic Theatre had asked him to write following the relative success of *The Lighthouse* the previous year. Wilkie came up with *The Red Vial*, a mish-mash of theatrical hyperbole in three acts, taking in lunacy, poison, murder and intrigue, as it moved disjointedly from a German merchant house in London to a Frankfurt morgue. Although it ran for four weeks in October, it was panned by the critics, most damningly by the *Daily Telegraph*, which accused it of 'transgress[ing] all the limits which good taste and propriety suggest'. The paper added that the play's excesses might have been mitigated if it had been written as 'a series of chapters', rather than committed to stage. Wilkie bridled at this criticism, but took the advice to heart, endeavouring to introduce a theatrical sense of immoderation and surprise into his novels. (Years later he reworked *The Red Vial* as the novel *Jezebel's Daughter*.)

Although Wilkie again craved success in the theatre, he had not given up on his fiction, which was in demand in the American market. Earlier in the year he had written 'A Marriage Tragedy' for *Harper's Monthly*. When collected in *The Queen of Hearts* in 1859, this was called '(Brother Griffith's Story of) a Plot in Private Life', a title that pointed less at the contents than at the type of fiction Wilkie was aiming for – an intricate domestic mystery, requiring a sleuth of some sort to gather and resolve the loose ends. It told of James Smith, a landowner with a passion for yachting. After leaving his wife, Smith makes a bigamous second marriage with a woman he meets while sailing his schooner in Scotland. Returning to his original home, he quarrels with his first wife and then disappears, leaving a blood-stained undergown. This allows a malevolent maid to try to pin a charge of murder on a faithful servant who, with the help of a lawyer's clerk in the role of a quasi-detective, had earlier pursued Smith and tracked down his movements. This heady mixture of bigamy, suspected murder and dogged investigation showed the direction in which Wilkie wanted to take his fiction. Drawing on aspects of his earlier story 'The Diary of Anne Rodway', 'A Marriage Tragedy' looked ahead to *The Moonstone* a decade later, not least in its domestic setting and its use of a stained piece of clothing as a clue.

Wilkie followed this up with 'Who is the Thief?' (later known as 'The Biter Bit'), also written for an American magazine. Adopting a light-hearted epistolary form, this early police procedural exposed incompetence and rivalry within the emerging detective force as it pitted an ambitious young trainee against a seasoned sergeant, both trying to solve a theft while under the baleful eye of a chief inspector.

In the early autumn he added 'The Poisoned Meal' to his output of detective stories. This was a gripping study, set in eighteenth-century France, of an investigation into a death involving arsenic, which, because of its widespread availability, had become the poison of choice for mid-Victorian murderers. It was subtitled 'from the Records of the French Courts', but the details were similar to the tale of Eliza Fenning, a servant who was controversially executed for attempted murder in 1815, after adding arsenic to a family's dumplings. Wilkie's imagination may also have been stimulated by the recent trial of Madeleine Smith, a middle-class Glaswegian alleged to have poisoned her former lover, a Frenchman, when he threatened to expose details of their affair. Wilkie was clearly intrigued by this case since he drew directly on it for his 1875 novel *The Law and the Lady*.

Before the end of the year he again went back in history, to the theme of bank forgery in 'A Paradoxical Experience', a gentle fiction based on the story of Henry Fauntleroy, the last Briton to be hanged for this crime in 1824. He also worked on a new Christmas issue of *Household Words* with Dickens, who had completed his intensive reading tour in mid-November. Dickens was still so angry with Bradbury and Evans's refusal to publish his 'personal statement' about his marriage that he was planning to close his magazine and start another. That did not stop him and Wilkie collaborating (together with Elizabeth Gaskell and the writer Barry Cornwall's feminist daughter Adelaide Anne Procter) on the Christmas offering 'A House to Let', about strange happenings in a house supposedly for rent.

Otherwise, Wilkie concentrated on his journalistic work for *Household Words*, where he certainly earned his salary increase during 1858. With Dickens involved in personal matters, Wilkie revelled in his job requirement to be opinionated, prolific and essentially lightweight. He could turn out amusing lifestyle articles, such as his protestations about the proliferation of crinolines (and the vast amount of space they took up). He could do quirky political pieces, including his advocacy of a series of consumer strikes to protest against poor service on trains and buses. And as was clear from his fiction, he was not afraid to enter the realm of sexual politics, taking on the persona of a woman to address the problem of female bores. He liked the freedom of adopting different personalities, talking about his (fictional) wife and daughters in his crinolines piece, before reverting firmly to bachelor mode when he examined the problems of shyness when proposing marriage.

Occasionally he took on a more serious persona, particularly when he tackled aspects of his profession. Ruminating on the poor state of English theatre, he attributed it to the inadequate financial returns it gave writers. He suggested that the situation was different in France, where famous writers were properly rewarded.

On the whole, Wilkie now rarely reviewed books, but in one piece he took strongly against *The Heir of Redclyffe*, a popular novel by the Tractarian author Charlotte M. Yonge, after discovering that Sidney Herbert, the former secretary of war who had championed Florence Nightingale in the Crimea, had promoted it as an example of great literature, and had quoted in his support the French historian and statesman François Guizot, who had observed that this kind of 'domestic novel' was the only type of book in which England was superior to France. Wilkie attacked Herbert for his hypocrisy in taking on a subject he knew nothing about, but his real vitriol was reserved for Yonge's novel, which he dismissed as a hodgepodge of sentimental religious tosh, calling it a 'Pusey-Novel'. Wilkie's tirade suggested he was still troubled by his Tractarian demons, which was all the more remarkable since his mother retained close links with this faction of the Anglican Church. He was also genuinely concerned that Yonge's medieval religiosity (her book was much praised by the Pre-Raphaelites) should be feted as an example of the British domestic novel at a time when he and other authors, such as Dickens and Thackeray, were trying to steer it in more challenging directions. Even Dickens thought Wilkie's criticism excessive, and asked his colleague Wills to tone it down.

Wilkie's interest in the publishing business was again clear from one of his most influential articles, 'The Unknown Public', published in August 1858. It argued that a vast market for books was being ignored. Estimates of the number of readers in Britain had been artificially low, he believed, since they failed to include the newly literate working classes who bought penny journals at railway stations and cheap stores. He calculated that journals such as *Reynolds's Miscellany* and the *Family Herald*, which offered a mixture of suspense, romance and titbits of educational information, had a weekly circulation of one million, with each copy read by three people. Although he mocked their often homely content, he understood the significance of their readers, whose appetite for diversion would play an important part in the development of his own approach to novel writing.

Underlying his thesis was a thorough understanding of how changes in society were affecting his market. Increases in population and disposable income inevitably created a wider readership, whose tastes might not be as elevated as before, but who were eager for print of some kind. This process was helped by other factors, including the Public Libraries Act of 1850, which encouraged councils to set up free libraries (the first was in Manchester), increased discounting of books following John Chapman's campaign against restrictive practices earlier in the decade, and the success of W.H. Smith's railway bookstalls, which spawned a variety of cheap editions such as George Routledge's shilling Railway Library. The market domination of Mudie's and their subscribers would continue for some time, and the tripledecker would die out only in the 1890s. Over the next three decades, publishers would be forced to adopt new approaches, and Wilkie would only benefit.

After this heavy schedule of work, he was happy to put aside his prejudices and on 4 November attended the wedding of Joseph Stringfield, the Weston-super-Mare doctor he had befriended through Pigott. Not only that, but Wilkie signed the official register after Stringfield had married his second wife Mary Ann (Teresa) Garment at St Luke's Church, Chelsea on 4 November, 1858. His brother Charley tried unsuccessfully to see the newly-wed Stringfields when they passed through Paris on their honeymoon a few days later. Charley had given up painting (it only caused him 'extreme suffering and anxiety', he told Holman Hunt) and was visiting the French capital, with a view to developing a career as a writer. He was already producing articles for *Household Words* and seemed to be enjoying himself, as he called on his mother to 'caution Willie against committing himself to London lodging before he has tried Paris again'.

This suggests that Wilkie's domestic arrangements with Caroline were still far from resolved. After so much frenetic creative activity, there was something sad about the way he felt obliged to turn down an invitation from his cousin Jane Ward to join her and her husband Charles over Christmas 1858. 'My term, at my own house, is up this Christmas,' he told Jane, referring to the end of his mother's lease at Harley Place. 'I have no idea where to go to – and I think it quite likely that I may be at Paris, or by the seaside, in search of relief to body and mind, or in bed on Christmas Day. I never felt less certain of my future proceedings than I do at this moment – and I should, on that account, have been afraid of engaging myself to you, even if I had been a free man, this year, so far as the social proceedings of the 25th are concerned.' It sounds as though he was, somewhat reluctantly, committed to spending the festive season with Caroline and her daughter Harriet.

10

LUNACY PANIC

FOR HIS HOLIDAY in August 1859 Wilkie opted again for the sea breezes and intermittent sunshine of Broadstairs. The previous year he had parked himself in the centre of town, but this time he rented Church Hill Cottage, which looked out over the sea on the road towards Ramsgate. One reason was that he was tired of the noise of tourists: he wanted peace and quiet, for he had work to do. More significantly, he had family in tow: Caroline and her eight-year-old daughter.

In February he began for the first time to live openly with Caroline and Harriet at 124 Albany Street, a lodging house with a dubious reputation close to the church where William Collins had once worshipped. Only eighteen months earlier, *Reynolds's Newspaper* had published a titillating news item under the headline 'The Dashing Widow and the Amorous Colonel', which reported a court case involving a well-born woman who had had an illegitimate child by a retired army officer, Colonel D'Aguilar. When she sued for financial support, he claimed that he had thought she was a prostitute. At one time she had lived at 124 Albany Street but had been thrown out after her landlady found her in her room with an unknown man.

But this unsavoury place was only a staging post: two months later Wilkie and his fledgling family moved again to a similar establishment, 2A New Cavendish Street, along the road from where he was born. (The Collinses clearly liked pirouetting around Regent's Park: his mother had recently settled into a new house at 2 Clarence Terrace, another elegant Regency development around the Park, and close to where she had once lived in Hanover Terrace.)

Caroline was now not only participating in Wilkie's life but being recognised as doing so. In early May, he asked Charles Ward to dinner but, at the last minute, was invited to the opera. He requested Ward to come anyway; they would be able to spend a couple of hours together before he had to go, and then he would leave his guest with Caroline who, he promised, 'keeps you company and makes you your grog – and you stay as long as you feel inclined'.

Earlier in the year Wilkie had struggled with his health. In February, he declined an invitation to a dance at the (Henry) Bullars, citing continuing problems with his ankle. But he always perked up in the comfortable surroundings of Gad's Hill, where Dickens celebrated his new life – without Catherine – by commissioning a handsome portrait by his friend William Powell Frith. For some time Dickens had been underwriting the Ternans' expenses. He almost certainly paid for the lease on their four-storeyed house in Mornington Crescent, not far from Wilkie in Albany Street, and for singing lessons for Nelly's sister Fanny in Florence. His bank account coyly recorded payments to 'N'. To add to his emotional turmoil, his brother Augustus had recently abandoned his wife and decamped to America.

On the work front, Dickens was still furious with the 'Whitefriars Gang', as he called Bradbury and Evans, for refusing to print his 'personal statement' in *Punch*. Drawing inspiration from Wilkie's essay 'The Unknown Public', he began planning a rival journal, *All the Year Round*, and made clear he would cease 'conducting' *Household Words* after May 1859. Having acquired

an office for his new publication in Wellington Street, a few
doors from the old one, he did exactly as he had threatened.
The first issue of *All the Year Round* (a 75:25 per cent joint
venture between him and Wills) was published on 30 April and,
by the time *Household Words* duly closed at the end of the
following month, Dickens was ready to tempt its readers with
the first episode of his new novel *A Tale of Two Cities*.

Wilkie duly followed him into the new venture, where
Dickens soon approached him to produce an exciting new serial
that would follow immediately after his own and so maintain its
robust circulation – at one stage running three times higher
than its predecessor's.

When Wilkie visited Gad's Hill in July, Dickens was suffering
from 'a small malady' he claimed had been 'engendered' by his
'bachelor state'. This is likely to have been a dose of gonorrhoea,
since he joked that there was no silver nitrate (a cure for the
disease) in the sea at Broadstairs, where Wilkie soon went on
holiday.

For a while, until they were joined by Wilkie's brother
Charley, the only other guests at Gad's Hill were Anne and
Adelaide Procter, wife and daughter of Dickens's affable long-
term friend, Bryan Waller Procter, otherwise known as the writer
Barry Cornwall. Wilkie had seen a lot of this family in recent
months. Anne had a reputation as a literary hostess, while her
daughter Adelaide was a poet and regular contributor to
Household Words. Adelaide was also a leading member of the
Langham Place group of moderate but committed feminists who
lobbied strongly for greater opportunities for women, particularly in education. She had been involved in two of their recent
initiatives, the *English Woman's Journal* and the Society for the
Promotion of Employment for Women.

Wilkie was uncertain where he would take his main summer
vacation. He toyed with the Isle of Man, the Isle of Wight,

Hastings, Wales and Yorkshire, all of which had their attractions. But, as he told Charles Ward, 'I have nothing particular to record but the history of my own doubts.' His indecision may well have resulted from having to consider Caroline and her daughter. But if he hankered after a bachelor jaunt, Caroline put her foot down and demanded a family holiday. The compromise was six weeks by the seaside in Kent.

He was still not clear where he would stay. Once he had made up his mind about Broadstairs, he travelled the short distance to reconnoitre there on Saturday 23 July. Through Dickens he knew James Ballard, landlord of the Albion Hotel, who directed him slightly out of town to the tranquil Church Hill Cottage. But it was still occupied and he could not immediately move in. So Wilkie made his way back to London, which would have enabled him to check on the progress of *The Queen of Hearts*, a collection of his recent stories which was going through various stages of production before being published by Hurst & Blackett in October. This volume, which included neatly framed tales like 'The Diary of Anne Rodway', was dedicated to Emile Forgues, a Paris-based critic and friend of Dickens, who had done much to introduce Wilkie's writings to the French market. Forgues's piece 'Etude sur le roman anglais' in the *Revue des Deux Mondes* led the way in this respect, and he went on to translate several works of Wilkie's including *The Woman in White* and *The Moonstone*. Wilkie would describe him as 'a gentleman, an admirable English scholar, and a translator who has not his equal in France'.

After picking up Caroline and Harriet, he returned to Broadstairs to start his tenancy on 3 August. When he informed his mother about his plans, he was careful to use the first person singular, because it seems clear that she had taken against Caroline, and Wilkie had no desire to provoke her wrath further. Since Harriet left no record of her reasons for this coolness towards her son's lover, it must be assumed that she did not consider this illegitimate widow with a young child a good enough catch for her dear son.

Mindful of Dickens's requirements for *All the Year Round*, Wilkie was soon at work on *The Woman in White*, the novel he had been contemplating for well over a year. As far back as April 1858 he had mentioned having to write a long serial story, at that stage for *Household Words*, and claimed that the plan was 'all drawn out'. In August that year, on his previous holiday in Broadstairs, he had enthused about having 'hit on what is (so far as I know) an *entirely new form of narrative*' for this work. But the conflicting demands of theatre, journalism and domestic responsibilities had allowed little progress.

According to a note he later appended to the original manuscript, he began writing the new book on 15 August 1859. However, he had obviously started earlier, since that same day he posted a registered packet to Wills, saying he would 'go distracted if it was lost'. It contained the first eight or nine pages of his closely written text, describing Walter Hartright's first meeting with the distraught Anne Catherick, the eponymous woman in white. Wilkie apologised if it was on the long side, but added, 'I must stagger the public into attention, if possible, at the outset.'

His letter to Wills contained his first reference to the title of his new book, which he claimed had come to him while walking at night on the North Foreland. Edmund Yates later expanded on this to reveal how, after an extended hike around Broadstairs, Wilkie flopped down, exhausted, on a grassy headland looking out over the North Foreland Lighthouse, which warned of the dangers of the nearby Margate Sands. According to Yates, the lighthouse looked awkward and stiff in the eerie evening light. Turning this over in his mind, Wilkie thought it looked like Anne Catherick, the 'white woman' or 'woman in white' he had just started writing about. At that point, the penny dropped and he decided this was what he should call his book.

John Forster did not consider it appropriate, but Dickens was enthusiastic, describing it as the 'name of names, and very title of very titles'.

Spurred by Dickens, Wilkie wanted to write a mystery novel that was both psychologically true and socially engaged. He had a great capacity for absorbing contemporary information and trends, and for recycling them in an entertaining manner. In this book, he gathered various strands – crime, lunacy, identity, inheritance, marriage and the sexes – and turned them into compellingly readable art.

The Woman in White focuses on two contrasting types of contemporary women – Laura Glyde (née Fairlie) and her half-sister Marian Halcombe – or three, if one includes Anne Catherick, who also turns out to be a half-sister, though through an illegitimate line. Laura is an heiress – pretty, self-effacing and programmed to make a conventional marriage. Marian is more modern, less obviously attractive (with her shadow of a moustache), but with the intelligence and tenacity to galvanise the phlegmatic 'drawing master' Walter Hartright into helping her unravel a series of mysteries that led to Laura, whom they both love, being incarcerated in a private lunatic asylum in the place of Anne.

In their roles as sleuths (for this is also a variation on a detective story), Marian and Walter are confronted by Count Fosco, one of the most convincing monsters in English literature. An overweight comic grotesque, with delicate Italian manners and a troupe of pet white mice, Fosco befriends his brother-in-law Sir Percival Glyde, the man Laura has reluctantly been forced to marry. As both Sir Percival and Fosco are strapped for cash, they hatch a plan to lay their hands on Laura's £20,000 wedding settlement. Fosco, the prime mover, sees a way of obtaining this money – by swapping the identities of Laura and Anne, who has escaped from an asylum and is making life difficult for Sir Percival by hinting that he is hiding some dark secret.

The Woman in White provides a masterclass in the art of storytelling. From the start, Wilkie played with the idea that he was presenting his tale as if it were evidence in a court of law. Thus different characters put forward their versions of events, leaving the reader to arrive at his or her take on the truth. Wilkie hit on this as a ploy when he attended the Rugeley murder trial three years earlier. It came naturally to him since he had trained as a lawyer. However, he was aware of the related difficulties, such as the fallibility of witness testimony. Even a diary, seemingly a secure repository of the truth, can be questionable, as when Marian's tails off and her intimate thoughts cease to be legible.

Wilkie also introduces a key ingredient into what would soon become known as sensation novels. A feature of mid-Victorian psychology was the idea that individuals are a bundle of sensations and nerves, making them not only irrational but vulnerable to others playing on their anxieties and exciting their emotions by creating sensational effects. The mutability of the human personality was being acknowledged in science and literature for the first time. Added to this were developments in the study of psychology and vision, which confirmed the idea that perceptions were not always what they seemed. Everything took on added significance in an intellectual climate where established truths were under fire from scientific inquiry, particularly in 1859, the year of publication of the ur-text on this process, Charles Darwin's *On the Origin of Species*.

In its effort to achieve social relevance, *The Woman in White* focused on one particular contemporary issue – the role of private lunatic asylums. In recent years there had been many reports of people being wrongly incarcerated and without adequate oversight or supervision.

This scandal was highlighted – and brought painfully close to home – in a heavily publicised court case that concluded at the end of June 1859, just as Wilkie was contemplating the details of his new book. The case in the Court of Queen's Bench was billed as 'Ruck versus Stilwell and Another'. The plaintiff Lawrence Ruck, an Oxford-educated landowner, was seeking damages for being confined against his will in Moorcroft Asylum in Hillingdon, a private institution run by Dr James Stilwell. Ruck's wife had him placed there after he allegedly displayed delusional behaviour, including accusing her of 'general prostitution'. Stilwell was assisted by Dr John Conolly, the 'Another' in the case, who had hitherto been feted as a reforming 'alienist', or mental health doctor, as a result of his work to end the practice of restraining patients in asylums. But he had fallen on hard times and needed money. After having earlier testified that he had nothing to do with this asylum, it transpired that he had been paid regularly and handsomely for referrals to Moorcroft. Not only had he illegally signed the certificate for Ruck's internment but had received a fee of 15 per cent of the internee's boarding costs.

The case was embarrassing for Dickens, who had been one of Conolly's most fervent advocates, in *Household Words* and elsewhere, at a time of intense public debate on reform of the lunacy laws. It also raised questions about the temporary committal a year earlier of Rosina Bulwer-Lytton, the woman who had threatened a rumpus at the premiere of her husband's play *Not So Bad As We Seem*. As the aristocratic owner of Knebworth, Bulwer-Lytton had recently been concentrating on his political rather than literary career, and been appointed colonial secretary in the Conservative government of Lord Derby. Still fuming at her treatment by her estranged husband, Rosina denounced him on the hustings while he was standing for re-election in Hertford in June 1858. His patience worn thin, he responded by having her confined to Inverness Lodge, a private lunatic asylum in Brentford. He was advised on his course of action by none other than John Conolly.

Rosina was visited by the lunacy commissioners, including Bryan Procter, wearing a different hat, and after considerable lobbying from her friends, she was released three weeks later. The case gained wide coverage, particularly as it came in the wake of a recent liberalisation in the divorce laws, which highlighted questions about the rights of women in marriage.

It is inconceivable that Wilkie did not discuss Rosina's case with Dickens and Procter, who significantly was later the dedicatee of *The Woman in White*. Wilkie was unusually well informed about such matters, partly through Dr Joseph Bullar who, being unmarried, lived in the Bullar family house at Basset Wood where Harriet Collins was staying in the summer of 1859. As a notably eclectic doctor, Joseph had promoted the use of opium and chloroform in clinical practice. He was also involved in the certification of lunatics, albeit from a doctor's angle, since he devised a form to ensure that members of his profession were not legally liable if they sent patients to asylums.

Another of Wilkie's sources was Pigott's brother-in-law, Edwin Fox, a surgeon who helped run a well-established lunatic asylum at Brislington, outside Bristol. This was generally considered a benevolent establishment, though inmates did occasionally commit suicide or become involved in legal action, which threw light on its workings. In one case, a woman was committed by her husband because of her spiritualist tendencies. In another, which was rather more influential, John Perceval, son of the assassinated former prime minister, Spencer Perceval, inveighed against the abuses he had experienced there, including physical restraint, beatings and, a particular bugbear, being forced to associate with 'vulgar persons below me in society'. Perceval's complaints played an important role in the agitation for the 1845 Lunacy Act. They were given additional currency, since his brother was a lunacy commissioner and a prominent Irvingite 'apostle'.

The Commission of Lunacy had existed in various guises since the late eighteenth century, before becoming a statutory body in 1845, a centralising initiative by the great reformer Anthony Ashley Cooper, or Lord Shaftesbury, who was its chairman. It consisted of eleven commissioners, six of whom were salaried professionals (three doctors and three lawyers). Wilkie had probably first learned of it from Edmund Southey, his fellow pupil at school, whose father Henry Herbert Southey was a medical commissioner and remained so until his death in 1865.

Wilkie did not lack for background detail about the Commission and the asylums it oversaw. Through Procter and his family, he would have learned about another case with intriguing similarities with *The Woman in White*. In the mid-1840s, Louisa Nottidge and three of her sisters, all heiresses with fortunes of £6,000, had been drawn to a utopian religious sect, The Abode of Love, or Agapemone, which was widely painted as promiscuous and immoral. After the other three girls had been told it was God's will that they should marry elders of the sect (and thus give up their money to the community), their mother feared that Louisa might be forced to follow suit. So, together with her son-in-law, Frederick Ripley, she arranged to have Louisa kidnapped from the sect's headquarters near Bridgwater in Somerset in November 1846. Ripley took Louisa to his house in Marylebone before committing her, like Lawrence Ruck, to Moorcroft House asylum in Hillingdon, run by Dr James Stilwell's uncle, Arthur. Once again, John Conolly was supportive of the woman's confinement. But, like Anne Catherick, she managed to escape in January 1848 and travelled to London to meet William Cobbe, an elder of the sect who had married one of her sisters. Before she could make her way to Somerset, she was apprehended and returned to the asylum. At this stage she applied – not for the first time – to the Commissioners in Lunacy to examine her case.

Since they could not make up their minds, it fell to Bryan Procter, when he visited her in May, to determine that, though she seemed deluded in her religious beliefs, she was no danger to the community and should be released.

By 1858–59, the clamour over the detentions of Rosina Bulwer-Lytton, Lawrence Ruck and others became so loud that commentators would later talk about the 'lunacy panic' of those years. When Wilkie met Procter's wife and daughter at Dickens's house in July 1859, he is likely to have received a feminist perspective on the phenomenon, and particularly on the Nottidge case, since one of Adelaide Procter's associates in the Langham Place group was Frances Power Cobbe, whose brother William was the elder in The Abode of Love married to one of the Nottidge sisters.

A quarter of a century later, Frances Power Cobbe became a regular correspondent of Wilkie's, particularly on the topic of vivisection, against which she lobbied strongly. In the intervening years she emerged as a leading theorist about women and marriage. In *What Shall We Do With Our Old Maids?* she pointed out that, partly because of emigration and deaths in the Crimean War, many more members of her sex were having to fend for themselves. She estimated that three million women were now earning their own living and one in four was destined not to marry. As a result, it was imperative to provide them with employment opportunities. In *Celibacy vs. Marriage*, she expanded on this line when she acknowledged, in a cheery female parallel to Wilkie's views about bachelors, that women needed to get used to co-habiting in amicable spinsterhood (as she herself did). In the same article she argued that the new secular divorce courts had 'revealed secrets which must tend to modify immensely our ideas of English domestic felicity'. Wilkie absorbed these details and wove them into his novels with an evident understanding of the underlying feminist polemics.

He was often reminded about The Abode of Love in years to come. His friend William Hepworth Dixon, the editor of the *Athenaeum* magazine, made it the centre-piece of *Spiritual Wives*, his 1868 study of polygamy in religious communities. Astonishingly, towards the end of the century, The Abode would be led by someone much at home in its Somerset surroundings – Edward Pigott's nephew, John, the son of his brother Henry, who had died of his syphilis.

While Wilkie drew on contemporary Britain for the basic plot of *The Woman in White*, he looked to France for its colour and romance. His story 'The Poisoned Meal', published in *Household Words* the previous autumn, showed his liking for fictionalising snippets of news from France. Throughout 1858 the British press ran a number of stories (often couched in anti-Catholic tones) about a young girl's sighting of a woman in white, alleged to be the Virgin, by the river Gave in the Pyrenees. *The Times* printed a version of this on 26 August 1858, in the same issue as an account of Lawrence Ruck's action against Stilwell and Conolly.

Wilkie claimed that he took the story of *The Woman in White* (along with 'some of my best plots') from Maurice Méjan's 'Receuil des causes célèbres, et des arrêts qui les ont décidées', a collection of French legal cases published at the start of the century and catering for the same market for 'true crime' as the *Newgate Calendar* in Britain. Included in his copy of the book, which he had found on a visit to Paris with Dickens in 1856, was the tale of Adélaide-Marie Rogres Lusignan de Champignelles. In 1764, Marie, as she was known, married the Marquis de Douhault, who lived in a castle at Chazelet in central France. When he proved mentally unstable and tried to kill her, her father managed to have him locked up as a lunatic. Over the years Marie became greatly respected as trustee of the Marquis's estates. However, when her brother Armand began to swindle her, she decided to go to Paris to confront him. En route she stopped in Orléans, where she was refused entry to the house of her usual host, a relation of her husband, and was directed instead to stay with a neighbour she did not know. On the eve of her departure for Paris, she was taken by her hostess for a drive beside the Loire, during which she accepted a pinch of snuff and fell into a deep sleep from which she never awoke. On 18 January 1788, she was declared dead and quickly buried.

Or so one version of the story went. In Paris ten days later, a woman in a white gown was unceremoniously deposited by the police at the Salpêtrière Prison, which served as a dumping ground for the city's down-and-outs, including the insane. She was admitted under the name of Blainville and appeared very dozy, but she recovered her senses and began to question why she was being held there, when she was really the Marquise de Douhault. Members of the prison staff were unimpressed by her protestations since they were used to inmates with various delusions.

Several months later a man claiming a connection with the court of Louis XVI arrived at the Salpêtrière with an order for the release of Madame 'Blainville'. She left, still dressed in white. But on her way home she found that her relations had begun to plunder her estates. Worse, when she met her brother, he claimed not to recognise her. By now, France was in the throes of Revolution; law and order had broken down, and no one was interested in the domestic problems of a minor aristocrat. However, when she finally reached her original home of Champignelles, she was accepted as the Marie of old. And two years later, when she sought to confirm her identity in a court of law, she was supported by the local peasantry, who regarded her detention as another example of the hated *lettres de cachet* system that gave the Ancien Régime arbitrary powers of

arrest. But the court was not convinced, claiming she was Anne
Buiret, a notorious criminal who, after being detained in the
Salpêtrière, had taken advantage of the confusion caused by
the Revolution to impersonate the Marquise de Douhault, whom
she had heard was dead.

After a series of inconclusive law suits, it was generally agreed
that the claimant could not be proved to be Anne Buiret, but
neither could Marie's original death certificate in Orléans be
dismissed as a forgery. It was never determined whether Marie
was the victim of a dastardly plot by her relations or had been
impersonated, in striking white garb, by a fellow inmate in the
Salpêtrière. Marie was left as 'la femme sans nom', or, as she
put it in a despairing plea to the Emperor Napoleon, 'In civil
life, I am neither daughter, wife, French, nor foreigner.' This
idea that one's identity was fragile and easily lost in the cut and
thrust of modern society was one to which Wilkie would
frequently return in his books.

Having alighted on this historical silhouette of a woman in
white, Wilkie needed to introduce her to his readers in
suitably striking circumstances. For this he chose to place
Walter Hartright's moonlit encounter with Anne Catherick in
an area of north London he knew well. The two of them met
at the junction of Pratt's (now Platt's) Lane and Finchley Road
as Hartright walked back into the steaming city one summer
night after visiting his family in Hampstead. Continuing on
his journey, he reached Avenue Road (where Wilkie had once
lived), when he heard two men in a carriage asking a policeman
if he had seen a woman in white who had escaped from their
asylum. John Guille Millais's claim that this fictional concur-
rence was based on a similar event as his father was accompanied
to his home by Wilkie and Charley Collins remains fanciful.
Dickens nevertheless regarded Wilkie's version as one of the
two 'most dramatic' scenes in literature (the other, according

to his son Henry Dickens, was Thomas Carlyle's account of the march of the Paris women to Versailles in *The French Revolution*.

Wilkie's desire to present the ensuing story as if it were evidence in a court of law showed him consciously addressing the issue of crime in the modern world. In making Count Fosco the model of a cultivated Italian gentleman, he touched on a mid-century unease that lawlessness was becoming part of the fabric of society. Whether an act of poisoning or forgery, it (and its silky perpetrators) all too often went undetected. As Fosco himself boasted, 'The fool's crime is the crime that is found out, and the wise man's crime is the crime that is not found out.' And he went on to goad Laura and Marian, 'The machinery [society] has set up for the detection of crime is miserably ineffective . . . and yet only invent a moral epigram, saying that it works well, and you blind everyone to its blunders, from that moment. Crimes cause their own detection, do they? And murder will out (another moral epigram), will it? Ask Coroners who sit at inquests in large towns if that is true, Lady Glyde.'

This challenge to the easy consensus on crime raised many questions. It gave Wilkie an expanded canvas as he tried to enlighten his readers about these cleverer, more elusive transgressions and to guide them through the process of tracking down the villains. All this was vital to the evolution of the detective story. For it required him to draw on the principles of nineteenth-century rational enquiry to probe into the more obscure workings of the community. He and fellow seekers after the truth needed to observe and heed clues in the same way as Marian when she stands in the brambles looking for Laura: 'I saw on one thorny branch some fragments of fringe from a woman's shawl. A closer examination of the fringe satisfied me that it had been torn from a shawl of Laura's, and I instantly followed the second path.' She had discovered another graphic example of a clew or clue.

Wilkie tried to steer clear of the tourists in Broadstairs, but he could not avoid the town's rapacious traders. As he struggled with 'all but insuperable . . . difficulties at the beginning' of his new novel, he complained about the prices he was having to pay in the local market – a skinny chicken cost three shillings and sixpence and vegetables three times the London price. His mood was not helped by a painful boil in his groin. As a result, he could not work for much more than four hours, between ten in the morning and two or three in the afternoon.

At the start of September, Dickens came to visit, though, suffering from a streaming cold, he stayed at the Albion Hotel and later joined Charley Collins at a popular seaside mesmerism show. Owing to the mid-century vogue for spiritualism, the paranormal was now a legitimate subject for entertainment. Wilkie, ever alert to cultural nuances, was keen to reflect this, not only in the mesmeric tricks practised by Count Fosco, but in his representation of the supernatural in stories such as 'The Ghost in the Cupboard Room', his offering for the 1859 Christmas number of *All the Year Round*.

Wherever new, quasi-spiritual ways of experiencing the world were making themselves felt in mid-Victorian England, traditional religion was not far behind, often wagging its finger in disapproval. Dickens told his daughters Mary and Katey how two 'disagreeable' Evangelical girls were going around Broadstairs distributing tracts against the mesmerism show. He and Charley Collins had decided to attend after reading one of these leaflets, though they found the proceedings dire.

However, the Evangelicals did seem to impress young Harriet

Graves, if Dickens's comment to Wilkie is to be interpreted correctly. He told his friend that he was 'charmed with the Butler', a nickname he had given the child, reflecting the withdrawn and formal manner of someone who had lost her father at an early age and was struggling to find herself amid the vicissitudes of her mother's and Wilkie's relationship. Dickens went on, 'O why was she stopped! Ask her flinty mother from me, Why, Why, didn't she let her convert somebody! – And here the question arises – Did she secretly convert the Landlord?'

The implication is that, like many children of her age, Harriet enjoyed imitating people she met. In this case, doubtless to a mixture of horror and amusement in Wilkie, she played the game so convincingly that she appeared to be proselytising herself. Although Dickens did his best to maintain cordial relations with Caroline, his description of her as 'flinty' suggests he regarded her as unsympathetic and as having a chip on her shoulder.

Back in London later in September, Wilkie took time off from his novel to accompany Pigott to one of the latter's regular musical evenings at the house where George Lewes lived with Marian Evans. Pigott brought another friend, George Redford, a surgeon with artistic leanings who had served in the Crimea. Evans (or George Eliot) wrote to Lewes's son Charles about the 'charming' occasion, commending Pigott's 'delicious tenor voice' and Redford's 'fine baritone', which had featured to great effect on Beethoven's 'exquisite song' 'Adelaide'. She did not mention Wilkie's musical interests, which were unsophisticated, but he often attended such gatherings. A year earlier, he had dined with the couple, causing Eliot to remark on 'a sturdy uprightness about him that makes all opinion and all occupation respectable'.

On 26 November, Wilkie's novel started running simultaneously in *All the Year Round* in Britain and *Harper's Weekly* in the United States. In the meantime, his collection *The Queen of*

Hearts had been published by Hurst and Blackett, and he had written his ghost story for the Christmas issue of *All the Year Round*. Intrigued by the subject, in December he accompanied Dickens, Wills and a colleague John Hollingshead on a ghost hunt in an allegedly haunted house in Cheshunt. He was keen to gather as much information as he could about another topic he could turn into page-turning stories.

By early in the New Year, the serial of *The Woman in White* had been appearing long enough to spark considerable interest and it was time for Wilkie to talk to publishers about a volume edition. After toying with Smith, Elder, he signed a contract with Sampson Low, a small, entrepreneurial company with roots in printing and bookselling. George Smith at Smith, Elder had put only £500 on the table and later regretted it, saying he should have offered at least ten times that amount. It can be assumed that Sampson Low's offer was significantly higher (though the exact figure is unknown). They were also prepared to accept Wilkie's terms of a three-year licence, with any reprint to be limited to three volumes. In this way, as was his practice throughout his life, he astutely held onto his copyright.

Having dealt with this important stage in the book's cycle, Wilkie, together with Caroline and her daughter Harriet, moved again in March 1860 into a more permanent rented property at 12 Harley Street, in the heart of the medical district, where their landlord was a dentist called George Gregson. Since the place was a mess and needed refurbishing, Wilkie had to hire a carpenter, who proved a distraction. It was also very cold, which did not help either his health or the smooth progress of *The Woman in White*. He turned down several invitations to dinner, as well as a couple of requests to stage his plays *The Red Vial* and *The Lighthouse*, and was forced to rely more than ever on Charles Ward to pay his bills and generally keep his business affairs in order. In the course of these communications, he also treated Ward to domestic confidences, such as the eccentric behaviour of a temporary maid who liked to watch him go in and out of the lavatory: she tried the door 'every time I make water' and 'I have reason to believe . . . [she] must have seen My Person!'

The big news in the family was that, on his return from France, Charley had begun courting Dickens's flirtatious daughter Katey. It was not exactly a love match, but Charley had decided he needed to marry. Only the previous summer Wilkie had noted that his brother 'continues to spin madly in the social vortex, and is still trying hard to talk himself into believing that he ought to be married'. Now an opportunity had presented itself, since the atmosphere at Gad's Hill had grown so poisonous in the wake of Catherine Dickens's unceremonious ejection from the premises that Katey could no longer bear to live there. With her auburn hair and trim, curvaceous figure she had been muddling along as a model for her artist friends. At the start of the year she sat for Millais as the female interest in his striking painting *The Black Brunswicker*. But she wanted more from life. When in London she often called in to see Harriet Collins, before crossing the park to visit her mother in Gloucester Crescent. At one stage she had been smitten with Edmund Yates, but he had rejected her. So she settled on a marriage with Charley, who seemed to get along well with her father while he forged a new career as a writer on *All the Year Round*.

The wedding took place at Gad's Hill on 17 July 1860. As Wilkie was in the final stages of *The Woman in White*, he was relieved that, from his point of view, the event passed without fuss. He described it to Anne Procter in the chatty, objective style of his letters as 'a pattern wedding in two things – nobody made any speeches and the bride and bridegroom had to go away before the breakfast was over. There was also only the most moderate allowance of tears, at the last moment – and

they were shed to the accompaniment of cheerful howling from
Forster and a shower of old shoes flung after the married pair
as they fled into the carriage.'

Wilkie's friend, Frederick Lehmann, saw it differently. He
had married Nina Chambers and they were now living with
their son in London. He did not like Katey, whom he described
as a 'little hussy'. Having been to Sardou's play *A Scrap of Paper*
the previous evening, he had overslept and missed the special
train taking guests from London Bridge to Higham, the closest
station to Gad's Hill. When he did eventually get there just
before midday (the service had started at eleven), he found the
assembled party streaming from church to the house. He told
his wife, Nina, that certain figures were patently absent: the
bride's mother was cruelly banned, and also, to Katey's consternation, any member of the Thackeray or Lemon families,
following Dickens's falling-out with his former friends over their
attitude to his rift with Catherine.

After their wedding breakfast, Katey and Charley disappeared. When they returned for their going away, she was
wearing a black dress, which annoyed her new mother-in-law,
Harriet Collins. This seemed to signal that something untoward
had happened: according to Lehmann, Katey was 'crying bitterly
on her father's shoulder, Mamie [her sister] dissolved in tears,
Charlie [*sic*] as white as snow. No end of God Bless yous, King
John Forster adding in his d—d stentorian voice, "Take care of
her, Charlie, you have got a most precious treasure."' After the
couple departed for a honeymoon in France, everything seemed
to settle down and the remaining guests had dinner, before
catching the special train back to London at eleven. But all was
not finished: at some stage that evening Mamie found her father
on his knees in Katey's bedroom. He was sobbing into her
wedding dress and saying that he was the reason his daughter
had left home. In retrospect, Katey's black dress might have

been a statement of protest about the ghost in the room – her mother who had not been allowed to attend.

Wilkie must have known about this emotional outburst and its background, but he kept mum. Nor did he or anyone else comment on another obvious absence, that of Caroline Graves and her daughter. He was contemplating another newly-wed couple – Walter and Laura in *The Woman in White* who, following the death of the conniving Sir Percival Glyde in a fire as he is trying to destroy evidence of his illegitimacy, are finally able to set the seal on their long-simmering romance. It was ironic that Wilkie, with his attachment to bachelorhood, should conclude his novel with a traditional marriage in this way.

On 26 July, little more than a week after Charley and Katey's nuptials, Wilkie finished *The Woman in White*. He immediately wrote to his mother, 'Hooray!!!!! I have this instant written at the bottom of the four hundred and ninetieth page of my manuscript the two noblest words in the English language – The End – and, what is more, I have wound the story up in a very new and very pretty manner.' At the start of the following week he received a letter that crowned his achievement. It came from Gad's Hill and contained Dickens's congratulations on 'having triumphantly finished your best book'.

II

BASKING IN SUCCESS

H AVING COMPLETED *The Woman in White*, Wilkie needed to think carefully about his future. At the age of thirty-six, he was finally settling down with a woman in a proper house of his own, and that meant he had to take responsibility not only for her, but for her chubby, good-natured daughter Harriet, who was now nine.

Wilkie's experience of children was limited. He was invariably kind to those he knew, such as Ned and Henrietta Ward's daughter Alice, who was his god-daughter, but the truth was that most young people found his appearance and behaviour a trifle daunting. This was certainly the impression of Alice's brother Leslie, who was discomfited by Wilkie's unfocused and often inflamed gouty eye. Leslie preferred Charley Collins, who he remembered as 'surrounded by a halo of mystery and wonder'.

Wilkie took a more pragmatic approach to the younger generation. Leslie recalled with pleasure how, the previous year, Wilkie and Pigott had taken him to Astley's Theatre in Westminster Bridge Road. The occasion was Tom Taylor's play *Garibaldi*, which was advertised as a 'hippodrome on the life' of the Italian patriot, involving 'full company of the greatest riders from all quarters of the globe', including the 'premiere equestrians' of St Petersburg, Monsieur and Madame Zempo. Young

Leslie thought it was magical, and the taste of his first ever
strawberry ice cream bought by Wilkie remained with him for
ever. Another youngster who came within Wilkie's orbit was
Nina and Frederick Lehmann's son, Rudolph, who recalled
Wilkie helping him in his schoolwork with an effortless translation of Horace's Odes from Latin into English.

Wilkie now prepared himself to act more formally *in loco
parentis* to Harriet Graves. He must have treated her well
because she remained devoted to him throughout his life. He
was helped in this since, following his brother's marriage to
Katey, he was now officially part of a wider family centred at
Gad's Hill. Not that Dickens had much time for Caroline, nor
did he have much faith in the potential of their relationship
to endure, as was clear from his barbed comment to Frances
Dickinson, 'Wilkie has finished his White Woman (if he had
done with his flesh-coloured one, I should mention that too).'

Nevertheless, Wilkie's long-term future was becoming slightly
clearer. A useful, if unintended, consequence of Charley's dash into
matrimony was that Wilkie now had a bank account of his own.
Until recently, both brothers had more or less helped themselves
from the family deposits at Coutts, which were formally held by
their father's executors. But Charley now required a separate facility
for his affairs. It was natural for Wilkie to follow suit, and it made
particular sense, not only because he was also setting up home,
but because he needed a secure repository for his substantial
earnings.

At this stage, Wilkie might have felt confident enough to
branch out and concentrate on his novels. But, conscious of his
domestic commitments, he decided he still needed the double
safeguard of regular employment and proximity to Dickens. So
on 7 August 1860, he agreed a new two-year contract with *All
the Year Round*. For a salary of seven guineas a week (an appreciable advance on the five guineas of four years earlier), plus

one eighth of the annual profits of the business, he would continue to produce a mixture of articles and a serial of similar length to *The Woman in White*. However, he would be allowed to retain his copyrights and would be given five months free of other commitments to produce this serial.

Once the agreement was in place Wilkie was able to relax, and accept dinner and travel invitations. His first culinary blow-out was at home – a celebratory dinner at Harley Street, where he could now afford to employ a temporary chef (from Genoa). He invited several of his best friends, including Holman Hunt, Ned Ward and Augustus Egg, and asked Charles Ward to arrange the wines: he had enough champagne to last him a year, but was keen to lay in some Chateau Lafite, which Wilkie later admitted he found 'very genuine and good – but, to my taste, rather thin'. The meal itself could not have been better: 'The Genoese cook really did wonders. I never eat [*sic*] a more perfect dinner in Paris.'

Before this indulgence, he had been to pay his respects to the Procters. No doubt *The Woman in White* and the Lunacy Commission were discussed. Afterwards he went in mid-August to stay in great style at Fryston Hall in Yorkshire with the literary-minded MP Richard Monckton Milnes. Among the other guests was Ricciotti Garibaldi, the sickly son of the Italian patriot, whom Wilkie uncharitably found 'remarkably stupid'. Before the end of the month he went south again to visit the Lehmanns at their holiday house at Franklin on the Isle of Wight.

Frederick Lehmann and his wife Nina were fast becoming his very good friends. Wilkie enjoyed their engaging mixture of cosmopolitanism, culture and opulence. He had always been fond of Nina, one of several lively, intelligent women he admired. Over the years he had grown close to her husband, Frederick, who came from a family of gifted German-Jewish artists. His father Leo was a well-known portrait painter in Hamburg. Two of his brothers – Heinrich (later Henri) and Rudolf – had followed in this business. (Another brother, Emil, worked as a translator, in which capacity he later rendered Wilkie's books into German.) Despite showing talent as a violinist, Frederick was encouraged to follow a business career by a cousin, Ernest Schlesinger Benzon, a successful *homme d'affaires* who came from an equally cultured background in Germany, where his father, Adolf Martin Schlesinger, founded a famous Berlin music publishing house that numbered Beethoven and Mendelssohn among its clients. Ernest Schlesinger was more geared for the cut and thrust of industry. After travelling to New York, he became the United States agent for the Sheffield iron and steel manufacturer Naylor, Vickers, in 1840. So successful was he in introducing Yorkshire-made steel to the burgeoning American market that he was made a partner.As a result he was able to bring Frederick, his ambitious kinsman (and before long his brother-in-law, since he had married Frederick's sister, Elizabeth Lehmann), into this company. Frederick was posted to Edinburgh's port of Leith, with responsibility for expediting Naylor Vickers's shipments of iron ore from Northern Europe, a job which suited him well as it allowed him to lead a peripatetic and often libertine bachelor existence. At one stage, he plucked an English-born prostitute from a Hamburg brothel and set her up as his mistress in St John's Wood.

In 1859, Lehmann, now a partner in Naylor Vickers and married to Nina, settled in London. They could afford a substantial house at 139 Westbourne Terrace, Bayswater, as well as a place in what they called the country – actually, a seven-acre estate called Woodlands in Muswell Hill, close to Highgate Woods and Hampstead Heath in North London. They also had their seaside cottage on the Isle of Wight. Wherever they went they liked to surround themselves with writers, artists and musicians. Several times a week they would invite between twelve and twenty people to Westbourne Terrace for dinner, after which a further twenty or thirty others would join them for a musical soirée. This was usually of the highest quality, because Frederick knew many top immigrant composers and instrumentalists, including Joseph Joachim, Karl Hallé, Giacomo Meyerbeer and Clara (widow of Robert) Schumann. Any impromptu concert was often enhanced by turns from the hosts – Frederick on the violin and Nina at the piano. (Wilkie once joked that Hallé, the founder of the eponymous orchestra, was the second-best piano player in England, after Nina.)

Although Wilkie himself had little real feeling for classical music, aside from the opera, such events extended his knowledge and provided him with material for the musical references that resonate through his books. In *The Woman in White*, Count Fosco emerges as an advocate of Rossini. He accompanies himself on the concertina in a rendering of Figaro's aria from *The Barber of Seville*, where the words 'Figaro qua, Figaro la, Figaro qua, Figaro la' reflect his own elusiveness. Later the Count takes to the piano to try to prove that *Moses in Egypt* is the equal of any German opera. Meanwhile, Laura Fairlie woos Walter Hartright with 'the heavenly tenderness of the music of Mozart', in the same way that Magdalen Vanstone in *No Name* plays a selection of pieces from Mendelssohn, Chopin, Verdi and Mozart to evoke the spirit of her love for Frank Clare. Wilkie uses music in this way to give an added sensory dimension to his search for dramatic effect.

Frederick Lehmann's influence was significant in other ways, since he approached life with a degree of European sophistication that the well-travelled Wilkie respected. Despite having indulged in some racial caricature in *A Rogue's Life*, Wilkie was now notably philo-Semitic (a legacy partly from having had a Jewish tutor in Nice). During the 1860s, he became friends with a number of highly distinguished Jews, not only Lehmann and his artist brother Rudolf, who would marry Nina's sister Amelia in 1861 and settle in England, but also Sir Francis and Lady Goldsmid, Sir David Salomons, Charles Oppenheim and, Frederick's cousin and business partner, Ernest Schlesinger Benzon.

Goldsmid and Salomons were particularly prominent in the fight for Jewish rights and causes in Victorian England. Scion of a prominent banking family, Sir Francis was a philanthropist who had been Britain's first Jewish barrister and later became an MP. His wife Louisa sought out Wilkie's opinion on literary matters and did much to promote women's education. Also originally a banker, Sir David was sheriff and later Lord Mayor of London, an MP and High Sheriff of Kent, who at every stage overcame prejudice to secure his place in public life.

Wilkie liked the relaxed company of such people, who were prepared to indulge his foibles and did not expect him to change for dinner. One of his enduring habits was that he abhorred full evening dress of tailcoats, wing collars and silk top hats. He considered such sartorial paraphernalia pretentious, so 'he would sit down to dinner in a light camel hair or tweed suit, with a broad pink or blue striped shirt, and perhaps a red tie, quite as often as he would in a dark suit or regulation evening dress.' These were the clothes of someone who preferred to please himself rather than society. They helped develop his standing among his friends as a man who was eccentric and fun to be with, a civilised flâneur but definitely not a dandy.

As he travelled around the country during the summer of 1860, Wilkie basked in the success of his new novel, which was published in three-volume form by Sampson Low on 15 August, and quickly went into a second impression. (There would be seven in all, plus a new edition before the end of the year.) It was almost an anti-climax when the last instalment of *The Woman in White* appeared across a dozen pages in *All the Year Round* on Saturday 25 August.

But while Wilkie was prospering, Dickens was less upbeat.

Soon after his bout of self-recrimination over Katey's departure, his mood was further blackened by the death of his brother Alfred. The move to Kent meant that he had to give up Tavistock House in London by the first week in September, which required considerable organisation, particularly to ensure that all his cherished paintings came to Gad's Hill. It also meant the discarding of memories. At the start of the month, Dickens gathered together all the personal letters he had received over the years (from political and literary figures, as well as from members of his family) and set fire to them in a field behind Gad's Hill. He later intimated that he disliked the way that the confidential correspondence of famous men was being misused. In retrospect, this wilful act of arson dealt a cruel blow to Wilkie Collins studies. One hundred and sixty letters from Dickens to Wilkie exist and have been published. This suggests that there would have been an equal number in reply, but of these only three are known to survive.

The following week, Wilkie went to Gad's Hill, ostensibly to discuss his collaboration with Dickens on the forthcoming Christmas issue of *All the Year Round*. Competition among the middle-market weeklies was now fierce, and he found himself taking part in a 'council of war' over the future of the magazine. By then it was already clear that Wilkie's successor in the serial spot, *A Day's Ride: A Life's Romance*, by the Irish novelist Charles Lever, was not attracting sufficient readers. Looking for a big name, Dickens approached Bulwer-Lytton but received no reply. He also called on Charles Reade, but quickly realised that he himself would have to 'strike in' (as he put it to Forster) and come up with another blockbuster, which turned out to be *Great Expectations*.

Back in London, Wilkie's book had become a genuinely popular phenomenon. He could boast to his mother that, on the basis of his postbag, he knew that *The Woman in White* was 'soothing the dying moments of a <u>young</u> lady – it is helping (by homeopathic doses of a chapter at a time) to keep an <u>old</u> lady out of the grave – and it is the first literary performance which has succeeded in fixing the attention of a deranged gentleman in his lucid intervals!!'

Correspondents sent him themed poems and songs. While no examples of reported spin-off merchandise – including 'Woman in White' cloaks and bonnets, as well as the perfumes and toiletries – have survived, his characters were celebrated in the 'Woman in White Waltz' and later 'The Fosco Galop'. Further evidence of his book's popularity came in an unauthorised play version at the Surrey Theatre in Lambeth towards the end of the year. Few people were convinced by James Whistler's claim that his 1862 painting *The White Girl* had nothing to do with Wilkie's book. It was originally displayed at the Berners Street Gallery as *The Woman in White*, before an outcry caused Whistler to alter the title to *Symphony in White, No 1: The White Girl.*

The critics were initially slow to pontificate and, when they did, they were not always as well-disposed as the general public. Wilkie, the sharp literary operator, had already asked Charles Ward to intercede with his friend John Walter, the proprietor of *The Times*, to see if the paper might run an early notice. One of the first full-length pieces, published anonymously in the high-minded *Saturday Review* on 25 August 1860, was sniffy about the book's main protagonists ('they have characteristics, but not character') and about what it considered its all too visible structural underpinnings. It described Wilkie as 'a very ingenious constructor, but ingenious construction is not high art, just as cabinet-making and joining is not high art', and added for good measure that he was 'an admirable story-teller, though . . . not a great novelist'. The idea that Wilkie's novels concentrated on plot at the expense of character would become a staple of commentary on his work over the next thirty years. However, the *Spectator* disagreed, describing *The Woman in White* two weeks later, in what was clearly a rejoinder, as 'the latest, and by many degrees the best work of an author who had already written so many singularly good ones'. Taking issue with the criticism of over-plotting, it said, 'If *The Woman in White* were indeed a protracted puzzle and nothing more, the reader's attention would often grow languid over its pages.'

Like many authors, Wilkie reacted in schizophrenic fashion to such opinions. 'I see no reviews,' he professed to his mother in September, yet added in the same letter, 'I send the *Spectator* by this post. Look at page 864. A review of *The Woman in White* answering the *Saturday Review*.' Not that he needed to worry. He had already made £1,400 (the equivalent of well over £100,000 in 2013), he retained the copyright, and, having sold out the expensive guinea and a half edition, Sampson Low was now talking of cheaper editions. 'Cock-a-doodle-doo!' Wilkie chirrupped. 'The critics may go to the devil.'

In the manner of his father three decades earlier, Wilkie continued his progress around the British countryside in September, spending a leisurely few days with a doctor friend, George Gregory, just outside Stroud in Gloucestershire, and a night with Pigott's relation Edwin Fox at his family-run asylum at Brislington. Then at the end of the month he could not resist the lure of another voyage with Pigott and a companion, Charles Benham. The three of them had hoped to sail to Ireland, but gales prevented them getting beyond the Bristol Channel.

Twenty-eight-year-old Benham is a difficult man to

pigeonhole. He was born in Uxbridge, the home of Pigott's
doctor friend George Redford, who had introduced him to the
circle. Redford's son, also called George, would marry into the
Benham family and take over from Pigott when the latter was
appointed official Examiner, or censor, of Plays. Later in the
decade, Wilkie began to deal with a firm of solicitors called
Benham & Tindell, based in Essex Street off the Strand. This
has given rise to the erroneous idea that Charles Benham was
a solicitor, when in fact he did very little, except, almost certainly,
introduce Wilkie to his kinsman, Ebenezer, the principal of
Benham & Tindell. Indeed, the name Benham crops up with
confusing regularity in Wilkie's life around this time, since he
was in touch with Ebenezer's sister, Jane Benham Hay, a
Bloomsbury-based artist who, after a brief career on the fringes
of the Pre-Raphaelites, had married young but had subsequently
abandoned her family and decamped to Florence with her Italian
lover. The father of Ebenezer Benham, the solicitor, had once
been an ironmonger and appears to have been linked to the
Benhams who ran a celebrated kitchenware shop in Wigmore
Street. As a result Wilkie's references this year to substantial
payments to Benham & Sons had nothing to do with legal
services but relate rather to purchases of pots and grates for
his Harley Street house.

Around this time the town of Farnham began to feature in
Wilkie's letters. This had nothing to do with his recreational
tours. Rather he and Caroline chose a small school in this distant
corner of Surrey to educate Harriet. The establishment, which
boasted only nine pupils, was run by Suzanne Milne, a woman
in her early sixties, with help from her unmarried daughter Ann.
Harriet would attend it until August 1863 – a detail which is
clear because Wilkie's bank account shows that he regularly paid
her school fees by cheque, starting with £15 8s 6d in January
1861.

Harriet had not played a prominent role in Wilkie's life until now. She accompanied him and her mother on holidays, where her skills as a mimic suggested some artistic talent. Sending her away to boarding school could be interpreted as a sign of his wanting her out of the newly established house, but given his generally sympathetic attitude towards women, he was almost certainly acting in a more positive manner. He cannot be faulted for wanting to contribute to Harriet's education.

Wilkie's wealth made such financial commitment easier to afford, along with the regular purchases of groceries from Fortnum and Mason and of wine from Justerini and Brooks. It also inspired him to make an unusually expansive gesture and invite Caroline on a two-week trip to Paris in mid-October, with no expense spared. He had been away frequently during the summer and perhaps felt he needed to woo her with a taste of the good life. Their decision over Harriet's schooling was indicative of a new stability in their relationship, a statement of their determination that, even if they did not marry (and Wilkie still seemed averse to this), they were committed to a future together.

Because of the emotional significance of all this, Wilkie told his mother very little about his forthcoming trip. Even on 3 October he appeared to be hedging when he wrote, 'I am going abroad next week (probably).' As usual, he made no reference to Caroline or Harriet; indeed he again stuck firmly to the first person singular when he added, 'Only to Paris – and first class all the way, with my own sitting room at the best hotel when I get there – and every other luxury that the Capital of the civilized world can afford. No horseflesh for me – unless in the form of cookery, in which case (with a satisfactory sauce) I see no objection to it.' 'Horseflesh' was a reference to the enterprising honeymoon journey on which Charley and Katey had embarked, travelling with their own horse and cabriolet to Paris and then on to Lausanne. Wilkie never failed to mock this venture, even though it led to the publication of Charley's most successful book, *A Cruise Upon Wheels: The Chronicle of Some Autumn Wanderings among the Deserted Post-Roads of France*.

Once in Paris, Wilkie made sure that Caroline enjoyed the best the city could offer. He booked them both into the Hotel Le Meurice, the favourite of rich and discerning English visitors, and he took her to restaurants such as Les Trois Frères Provençaux, presided over by the great chef Adolphe Dugléré, who had learned his trade working for the Rothschild family. Unusually, but perhaps not unsurprisingly, he did not send an account of his trip to his mother (or, at least, nothing survives). However, he was careful to ensure that he also returned with a gift for her – a fashionable Parisian cap, which was a cause of family mirth as Harriet had a habit of enlarging her bonnets and decorating them with what her new daughter-in-law Katey described as cauliflowers. Katey urged her not to 'disfigure Wilkie's cap in that way and . . . not to make it so large as to overshadow your body'. However, Charley told her that his mother would already have done this.

Indeed, Harriet seems to have given up all pretence at fashion. Young Leslie Ward, the son of Ned and Henrietta, who would make his name as Spy, the cartoonist in *Vanity Fair*, recalled her wearing her kid boots carefully down on one side, then reversing them and wearing them down on the other. This 'quaint old lady', as he put it, 'had a horror of Highlanders because they wore kilts, which she considered scandalous'. Old Mrs Collins, who had always been her own woman, was getting more eccentric by the year.

On their return to London, the best-selling Wilkie was inundated with offers from publishers to reprint his back list. He also found that *The Woman in White* had been seized on by the book trade to challenge the virtual monopoly enjoyed by Mudie's circulating library. Because of its dominant position, Mudie's demanded generous terms from publishers. But now the smaller libraries, acting in concert, protested that they would not stock Wilkie's book unless given the same terms as Mudie's. One such minnow, Cawthorn and Hutt, said it would take fifty copies if offered them on Mudie's terms, but none if not. Sampson Low refused to buckle and the smaller libraries soon gave in. Wilkie somehow forgot his free trade principles and his enthusiasm for the unknown public. As he no doubt foresaw, he was rewarded with greater sales than ever, followed before Christmas with a personal invitation to the grand opening of the vast new classically fronted reading hall that Mudie's had been forced to build to meet demand at its premises in New Oxford Street. Having agreed to attend, Wilkie uncharacteristically failed to do so, offering a feeble excuse that he had been delayed by a dinner engagement in Sydenham. Charles Mudie, the owner, was not put out at all, however, and invited the author of perhaps his most sought-after book of the moment to visit the following day.

Wilkie suffered a temporary setback at the end of October when *The Times* review finally appeared. Written by the respected critic E.S. Dallas (though it appeared anonymously), its tone was generally favourable but it reiterated the often made point about the preponderance of plot over characterisaton. It added that for plots to work, their internal chronology must hold together, which was not the case with crucial details (duly spelled out) of Laura Glyde's visit to London. Wilkie was mortified by his mistake, and wrote immediately to Edward Marston, his editor at Sampson Low, asking him not to print any further editions until he could rectify the error.

He also had news of a personal tragedy to digest – the suicide of his old family friend George Agar Thompson. Seven years earlier Thompson had abandoned his wife and children and emigrated to Australia, hoping to make his fortune from the boom in gold. His journey had not started promisingly: from the Cape Verde islands off the west coast of Africa, he had written Charles Ward 'a journal of misfortunes'. But he seemed to have found his feet in the Antipodes and, if he did not prosper hugely, his organisational talents were recognised, for in 1858 he was appointed a police magistrate and warden of the gold fields at a salary of £750 per annum.

However, the pressure and the loneliness, exacerbated by a severe drink problem, got to him, and in July 1860 took his own life. Wilkie informed his mother, 'He has died at Melbourne (or near it) by <u>his own hand</u>. The fatal drinking-mania brought on delirium tremens – he was left with a razor within reach for a few minutes only and he cut his throat. The act was not immediately fatal – but his constitution was gone, and the doctors could not save him. He recovered his senses at the last, and died penitently and resignedly.'

Within days of returning from his holiday in Paris with Caroline, Wilkie was off again on a quick tour of Devon and Cornwall with Dickens, ostensibly to research the background to 'A Message from the Sea' for the Christmas issue of *All the Year Round*. By then Dickens had almost finished *Great Expectations*, which began serialisation on 1 December, pushing Charles Lever's story from the front page. Written mainly by Dickens and Wilkie (but also by others, including Charley Collins), the Christmas offering was a light detective tale about the search for the rightful owner of £500 mentioned in a message found in a bottle at sea. Set in the village of Steepways (based on Clovelly), it featured an American sailor, Captain Silas Jonas Jorgan, as an amateur sleuth.

While on this trip, Wilkie and Dickens are likely to have discussed the efforts of another detective, Inspector Jonathan Whicher, to discover the brutal murderer of a four-year-old boy in Road Hill House near Frome in Wiltshire in June. This case inspired widespread interest, not least in Dickens, who had written about Whicher in his earlier articles on the Detective Branch. Whicher was convinced that the child had been killed by his sister, Constance, but Dickens believed, as he had already written to Wilkie, that young Samuel had woken up to find his father in flagrante with his nursemaid. Wilkie took note and returned to this story when he wrote *The Moonstone* at the end of the decade.

Now that Charley was away from Clarence Terrace, Harriet Collins seemed at a loss. There was a vague plan for the newly-weds to take over the house on their return. But what was she to do in the meantime? She talked of going to look after the Bullars at Bassett Wood near Southampton – a notably male-dominated household – and perhaps returning to London for one or two days of the week. But was this for altruistic, practical or simply parsimonious reasons? Around Christmas time, Katey, back in Paris with her husband, was furious to hear that Harriet was trying to cut costs by vacating the main upstairs room in Clarence Terrace. 'Unless you immediately have that carpet put down, and unless you have a fire in that room, and go and sit there I shall never write to you again,' she thundered in a letter in which she called herself Katinka, her family nickname. 'I am in earnest when I tell you that Charlie [*sic*] and I are made <u>unhappy</u> if we think you are making yourself in the least degree uncomfortable.' After Christmas, Charley took up the matter of the move to the Bullars. 'It seems to me such an undertaking for you with so little strength to have the care and responsibility of all the Bullar family resting on you. Do tell me <u>why</u> you undertake it?' Katey added her trenchant voice in an addition to the same letter: 'Do leave the Bullar family to take care of itself and you take care of yourself.'

In these circumstances it is not clear where Wilkie spent Christmas. On New Year's Day 1861, he was back in Harley Street telling Henrietta Ward he had been in the country. With his liking for light entertainment, he accompanied Dickens that evening to St James's Hall, where Buckley's Serenaders were performing a variety of popular songs, including some for which they blacked-up as negro minstrels. A week later he and Dickens were up in arms against the Britannia Theatre for putting on an unauthorised production of 'A Message from the Sea'. They had written their own adaptation and lodged it with the Lord Chamberlain's Office, as much to forestall other productions as anything else. Being even more militant than Wilkie on the issue of piracy, Dickens wrote to *The Times* relating how his prompt action had forced the theatre's owner to withdraw the show. The pair of them later relented and, on payment of a stiff fee, allowed the rogue production to go ahead.

Wilkie had domestic duties to attend to in early January when Harriet was back from school. He had to decline an invitation from the (Edward) Wards because one of their children had measles, a disease Caroline's daughter had yet to catch. A couple of months later Charley and Katey returned from their extended honeymoon and were staying at Clarence Terrace. However, the prognostications for their future happiness were not particularly good. Commenting on Charley's ambition to write, Dickens stated bluntly that he would rather he painted. He added, perhaps sensing an element of sexual frustration in the marriage, that there were 'no "Great Expectations" of perspective [*sic*] Collinses', and admitted *sotto voce* that he thought this 'a blessed thing'.

True to form, Dickens was no more confident about the future of Wilkie's domestic arrangements. He allowed that his close friend had made his house in Harley Street 'very handsome and comfortable'. However, he told a correspondent, 'We never

speak of the (female) skeleton in that house, and I therefore
have not the least idea of the state of his mind on that subject.
I hope it does not run in any matrimonial groove. I can imagine
similar cases in which that end is well and wisely put to the
difficulty. But I can not imagine any good coming of such an
end in this instance.' To complete his baleful picture of the
Collins family, Dickens referred to a dinner attended by Harriet
Collins, who 'contradicted everybody upon every subject for five
hours and a half, and was invariably Pig-headed and wrong. So
I was very glad when she tied her head up in a bundle and took
it home.'

Nevertheless, the mood at 12 Harley Street remained positive. When the census was taken on 7 April 1861, Caroline, the
'skeleton in that house', appeared on the returns as Harriet
Collins, 'author's wife'. As well as this little fabrication, she, or
perhaps Wilkie, lopped a full five years from her age, which was
given as twenty-six.

Around this time came the first inklings that Wilkie was
contemplating a new novel, which would later be called *No
Name*. In May, he told his mother he was 'building up the
scaffolding of a new book', a phrase he repeated the following
month to Charles Reade, a fellow novelist and social campaigner,
whose book *Hard Cash*, published in 1863, would address the
issue of private lunatic asylums even more directly than Wilkie
had.

Over the next few months Wilkie continued to revel in
plaudits and honours, including his election to the Athenaeum
Club by the fast track Rule II which favoured men of 'distinguished eminence', and his chairing a meeting of the News-
vendors' Benevolent Institution, which tickled him as this role

was a new departure for him and he felt he did it creditably. *The Woman in White* was now being translated into French and German. In May it was also published by Sampson Low in a cheap one-volume edition, complete with a pasted-in photograph of the author (a publishing first), which he estimated would result in at least 50,000 extra sales.

Buoyed by his success, Wilkie was happy to accept an offer from Smith, Elder for *Armadale*, which would follow his ongoing project, *No Name*. Still chastened by his failure to bid sufficiently on *The Woman in White*, the eponymous George Smith offered £5,000 (£366,000 in 2013 money) for both serial and volume rights, which had Wilkie whooping for joy and telling his mother that no one but Dickens had ever been paid so much: 'if I live & keep my brains in good working order, I shall have got to the top of the tree, after all, before forty.'

Smith's commercial acumen had been sharpened by his entry into the increasingly competitive periodicals market. In January 1860, he had launched the *Cornhill*, which, although a monthly selling at a shilling, was aimed directly at the growing middle-class readership targeted by *All the Year Round*. It even boasted a similarly well-known author, Thackeray, as its editor. Two other publications launched around this time (*Macmillan's Magazine* in late 1859, and *Temple Bar* the following year) attested to the attractions of this field.

Smith had been itching to lure Wilkie back. On 31 October 1860, he wrote to Thackeray, 'At present we are badly off for matter for the December number . . . I am going to try Wilkie Collins for a story, but I am not very sanguine of success – and I don't know where else to look for that bit of fiction we want for [issue] No 12.'

If he did not succeed then, he did nine months later. But since anything Wilkie wrote for Smith would be serialised in the *Cornhill*, it created a potential conflict of interest with *All the Year Round*, where *The Woman in White* had recently proved so successful. However, Dickens realised it was an offer Wilkie could not refuse and generously agreed not to stand in the way. By the time Wilkie's story appeared in the *Cornhill*, his two-year contract with *All the Year Round* would have ended anyway.

The only thing holding him back was an 'old enemy whose name is Liver', an affliction which took him, together with Caroline and her daughter, back to Broadstairs, this time to the Albion Hotel for a couple of weeks in July. The following month he and Caroline went to Whitby in Yorkshire, a very different stretch of English coast – on the North (German, as it was called) Sea, facing Scandinavia.

Despite the noise of fellow holiday-makers in the Royal Hotel, Wilkie loved it there: 'everything in and about this place is on the grandest scale,' he told his mother. 'It is like journeying into another world, after the spick-and-span prettiness of the Southern watering places.' He was happy that she should continue to flit between her regular hosts – the Combes in Oxford, the Langtons in Slough, the Bullars in Southampton – a list to which she had recently added the Armytages in Tunbridge Wells, who were relations of Henry Brandling, the artist who had accompanied Wilkie on *Rambles Beyond Railways*. After several false starts, Wilkie even managed to write some of his new as yet unnamed novel, in which the resorts of the east coast featured heavily. In this context, he also visited York, Huntingdon, Cambridge, Ipswich and Aldeburgh, before returning to London.

Once settled back in the more peaceful surrounds of Harley Street, he began seriously to put pen to paper, though without feeling under any great pressure, since Bulwer-Lytton was already signed up to write the next serial in *All the Year Round*, once *Great Expectations* finished in August.

Wilkie's new offering featured the contrasting fortunes of

twin sisters, Norah and the more lively, minxlike Magdalen (names which had come to him in Whitby from where he had implored his chatterbox mother not to divulge them to anyone). It started with a pleasing evocation of settled family life in a Somerset house, not unlike Pigott's, where the main recreation was amateur dramatics, along the lines of those once staged by the Collinses. Indeed the book focuses on a production of Sheridan's *The Rivals*, which was one of the plays staged more than a decade earlier at their Theatre Royal, Back Drawing Room, in Blandford Square.

The Vanstone girls' futures seem assured, until their parents die in quick succession and it is revealed that they were never properly married; thus the girls are not only illegitimate but unable to inherit the family home. Owing to a legal loophole, they are left as 'nobody's children', forced to make their way in the world with 'no name'.

They deal with this calamity in different ways, according to their temperaments. Norah opts for the quiet life by becoming a governess, while the adventurous Magdalen, who has been the star of the theatricals, uses her sexual and other wiles to seek to regain her rightful property and name. To this end, she becomes an actress, which allows Wilkie to digress on the state of the theatre, particularly in the provinces. The book's underlying motif is role-playing, developed in a series of scenes, as if on the stage, with a series of personal letters inserted between the acts to help explain some of the detail. Gone is the suggestion found in *The Woman in White* that evidence is being presented as if in a court of law. Here the law is evidently an ass, and those involved even more so, prey as they are to the 'latent distrust which is a lawyer's second nature'.

One of Magdalen's ruses involves her marrying a cousin, Noel Vanstone, whom she despises. Much reduced in circumstance, she later concocts a scheme to change places with her maid Louisa. In this manner, Wilkie reinforces the idea that social and even moral differences can be mutable. In *No Name* the two women bond when Magdalen realises that her current situation is little different from Louisa's, who has been forced to give up an illegitimate child. Both Magdalen and Louisa are in their different ways victims of marriage laws that discriminate against women. And there is an added, more personal, dimension: Wilkie clearly regards Magdalen's marital status as legitimised prostitution, while Louisa, with her baby born out of wedlock, is the purer woman of the two. The similarities between Louisa's and Caroline Graves's situations are not hard to discern.

Given Wilkie's personal inclinations, it is again strange to discover that Magdalen is later saved from her unhappy fate by marriage to Captain Kirke, 'a man to be relied on', who has returned from the colonies on a merchantman called *Deliverance*. Not to read too much into this, Wilkie must have realised that he could push his readers only so far with his explorations into identity and legitimacy and that they required a happy ending after forty-four episodes in *All the Year Round*.

The story is sometimes silly, with its melodramatic ebbs and flows. It suggests that Victorians had an unhealthy obsession with wills and heredity, as if these were almost the only engines of social mobility. But the finished product was exciting and very readable, as Dickens acknowledged after poring over the first scenes 'with strong interest and great admiration'.

Because of this commitment, Wilkie produced very little for *All the Year Round* during 1861, aside from a couple of stories based on French archival records (a stop-gap when he was pressed for time), plus the usual tale for the Christmas number. Having met his first deadline for his new serial in March 1862, he went to Broadstairs with Caroline the following month to look for a place where he could finish the book over the course of a leisurely summer. He decided on Fort House, a spacious, turreted mansion on the cliffs overlooking the sea, which Dickens had often happily used for holidays. Having contracted to rent it for four months starting at the end of June, Wilkie ensured it was provisioned with all the latest creature comforts, including an icebox, while he made plans to play host to a stream of friends, including Charles Ward, Edward Pigott, Henry Bullar, Augustus Egg and Dickens. He was feeling more prosperous than ever after Sampson Low offered £3,000 in July for the rights to publish *No Name* in book form (a total of £4,600, he told his mother, when American and other receipts were included).

However, it was soon clear that all was not well, and he was having difficulty finishing *No Name*. In London, he had talked about 'the slashing battle (still undecided) of Collins against the printer'. Once he was settled at Fort House, his hopes of steady progress were dashed by another worry, his health, particularly problems with his liver, his joints and his dreaded gout.

He called on the ministrations of his new doctor, Frank Carr Beard, who lived in apparent style in Welbeck Street in the heart of Marylebone, with his American-born wife, Louisa, four children and three servants. Beard came from a rich and well-connected Sussex brewing family. His maternal grandfather Sir Thomas Carr had been high sheriff of the county and his brother Thomas was one of Dickens's oldest friends – a journalist who had worked with him on the *Morning Chronicle* and acted as his best man.

As often the case with Wilkie, there was rather more to the story. Beard was intellectually curious, unconventional and public-spirited: after taking a degree at University College, London, he dabbled in alternative therapies and was employed as a lowly surgeon at the subscription-based Hospital for Consumption and Diseases of the Chest in Margaret Street, around the corner from Welbeck Street. In 1854 he participated with Dickens's friend Dr John Elliotson in a mastectomy that was carried out solely under the influence of mesmerism.

However, he was plagued by debts, leading to bankruptcy in 1855 and two years later he was struggling to pay back his creditors at a rate of five pence in the pound.

Dickens first started using Beard's professional services around 1859, when he greatly appreciated the considerate manner in which his venereal symptoms were dealt with. The doctor was engaging and knowledgeable, yet he did not ask too many questions – qualities which doubtless endeared him to Wilkie, who took him on a couple of years later. After being recommended 'some wonderful Turkish Baths, with excellent shampoos and great care in the attendance' by Beard, Wilkie was soon enthusing about his new medical practitioner. (The word shampoo, of Hindi extraction, meant massage at the time.)

An added attraction was that Beard used opiates as a regular part of his pharmacopoeia. Wilkie now had a doctor who was prepared to indulge his habit for laudanum. On 10 October, Wilkie pleaded to Beard, 'Is there any hope of you being able to come here tomorrow? . . . for my stomach and nerves are terribly out of order again. Yesterday at 1 o'clock P.M. I had to give up work with deadly "all-overish" faintness which sent me to the brandy bottle.' He proceeded to relate his symptoms, which included sleeplessness. He added, 'My stomach wants tone, and my nerves want <u>soothing</u> and <u>fortifying</u> at the same time. If you are too much engaged to come tomorrow, will these particulars enable you to send me a prescription?'

Because he feared the 'possibility of breaking down at the close of my book', Wilkie returned to London a week later to be nearer his doctor. Beard was worried enough to contact Dickens who, in the latest of a series of encouraging letters, offered to write the closing sections of *No Name*, if he was provided with the necessary notes and a brief explanation. 'If you should want help, I am as safe as the Bank,' he stated supportively.

But Wilkie was too much of a professional not to finish what he had promised. When he needed precise information he corralled his friends for details. Charles Ward, in particular, was asked to find out how long letters took to travel between Zurich and England (ten days) and how much notice was required in order to obtain permission to marry by licence (a fortnight). Wilkie's experience with laudanum no doubt helped him when Magdalen, at a low ebb in her journey, acquired a bottle of the drug and considered using it to help her commit suicide.

On Christmas Eve, Wilkie was finally able to tell Beard, 'You will be almost as glad as I am to hear that I have Done! – for you have had no small share in the finishing of the book. I ended at two o'Clock this morning.' The word 'Done!' was written on its own in large letters on one line. He wanted to ask Beard, the source of his pharmacological support, to a cele-bratory dinner at Verrey's restaurant in Regent Street at 6 p.m. the following day. However, he was sensitive to the fact that Beard would be required at home. 'As you are a "family man" I dare not say – "come too!"' Once again, the domestic politics of his own situation were hazy: he did not stipulate the other members of his Christmas Day party, except to refer to 'we' and say that Pigott would be 'with us'. This suggests that he was taking Caroline and Harriet. But was his mother, the scourge of Wilkie's mistress, also there? The record is unclear. One thing was evident, however: Wilkie was extraordinarily grateful to Beard for helping him through his ordeal. When *No Name* was published in three volumes by Sampson Low on 31 December 1862, it was dedicated with feeling 'To Francis Carr Beard (Fellow of the Royal College of Surgeons of England); In Remembrance of the Time when the closing scenes of the story were written.'

12

MID-VICTORIAN SENSATION

WILKIE WAS ONLY dimly aware of it in 1862, but *The Woman in White* and now *No Name* had, in the manner of their carefully wrought, reader-friendly mysteries, pioneered a popular literary genre that would endure through the 1860s and come to epitomise a decade of great social and political change.

The genre was dubbed the sensation novel. No one can determine exactly where the term was first used – probably in the United States in the previous decade to describe a rather more downmarket type of fiction. But by the end of 1861 a writer in the *Spectator* was observing, 'We are threatened with a new variety of the sensation novel, a host of cleverly compli-cated stories, the whole interest of which consists in the gradual unravelling of some carefully prepared enigma. Mr Wilkie Collins set the fashion, and now every novel writer who can construct a plot, thinks if he only makes it a little more mysterious and unnatural, he may obtain a success rivalling that of *The Woman in White*.'

The use of the masculine pronoun belies the fact that many of the most successful practitioners of this new approach were women, such as Mrs Henry Wood, author of the best-selling *East Lynne* in September 1861 and the prolific Mary Elizabeth

Braddon, often described as the queen of the genre, whose *Lady Audley's Secret* appeared the following year.

Sensation fiction ranged over the themes Wilkie had made his own – mystery, crime, secrets, duplicity and identity. Not that there was anything particularly new in these topics. Gothic novels, the *Newgate Calendar* and penny dreadfuls had used them to keep their readers on the edge of their seats. Charlotte Brontë's *Jane Eyre* bore many of the hallmarks, as did several of Dickens's works.

What made sensation novels innovative was that they took excitement into ordinary homes. No longer was the drama situated in some far-off castle, as in gothic romances, or even a thieves' kitchen, as in *Oliver Twist*. As Wilkie's output, stretching back to *Basil*, demonstrated, it could all take place in one's back room. And the villain plotting murder and mayhem could, like Count Fosco, be the charmer next door.

In this manner, readers were seduced into sensation novels. Their involvement was often further encouraged by introducing a detective element into the plot. They could feel engaged in the unravelling of the mystery. Their participation was also encouraged by making the narrative up to date, through topical details such as the 'lunacy panic' in *The Woman in White*.

In keeping with their domestic settings, sensation novels went where their predecessors had feared to tread. In particular, they dealt with the secrets of marriage. Adultery and bigamy (the theme of *Lady Audley's Secret*) became accepted literary fare. The tribulations of passionate women, oppressed by matrimony, law and other social conventions, took centre stage. Once again, Wilkie led the way.

The critics realised that something unusual was happening, and did their best to explain it. One of the first was the Scottish novelist Mrs (Margaret) Oliphant who, writing specifically on 'Sensation Novels' in *Blackwood's Magazine* in May 1862, identified that, so far as Wilkie was concerned, his success came not from his outrageousness, but from his restraint. He was sparing in his use of blatant spine-chilling techniques, such as the occult or bloody murder. 'His effects are produced by common human acts, performed by recognisable human agents, whose motives are never inscrutable, and whose line of conduct is always more or less consistent. The moderation and reserve which he exhibits; his avoidance of extremes; his determination, in conducting the mysterious struggle, to trust to the reasonable resources of the combatants, who have consciously set all upon the stake for which they play, but whom he assists with no weapons save those of quick wit, craft, courage, patience, and villainy – tools common to all men – make the lights and shadows of the picture doubly effective.'

Mrs Oliphant was clear that the action-filled plots favoured by Wilkie and his co-writers were a direct reflection of the fast-changing world they inhabited. 'It is only natural, in an age that has turned out to be one of event, that art and literature should attempt a kindred depth of effect and shock of incident.' She argued that these developments were encouraged by a growing market, with readers in libraries and railway bookstalls demanding new literary experiences. In particular, she pointed to 'the violent stimulus of serial publication – of weekly publication – with its necessity for frequent and rapid recurrence of piquant incident and startling situation'. Wilkie's 'unknown public' was having its say.

These points were taken up by no less a figure than H.L. (Henry) Mansel, professor of Moral and Metaphysical Philosophy at Oxford University (and later Dean of St Paul's), when he reviewed a batch of twenty-four sensation novels in a seminal article in the *Quarterly Review* in April 1863. He took a harder line, railing against a genre in which 'excitement, and excitement alone, seems to be the great end at which they aim.' The result was a debasement of literature that now lacked any higher ideal; instead, 'a commercial atmosphere hangs around works of this class, redolent of the manufactory or the shop.' And he too placed the blame on those three same phenomena, 'periodicals, circulating libraries, and railway bookstalls'.

This charge of trivialisation became the main line of attack from high-minded critics, who argued that it undermined the advances made by literature towards respectability over the past century. Another widespread objection was that sensation novels were not only populated by, but designed to appeal directly to, women, and they were not the kind of books that should be doing this. The acerbic critic (and friend of the Lehmanns), Henry Chorley, adopted this approach in an article in which he voiced his uneasiness that 'the ideas of women on points of morals and ethics seem in a state of transition, and consequently of confusion.'

A related worry was that female characters in sensation novels, particularly Wilkie's, were unduly assertive. In the manner in which they sought to take control of their lives, they often displayed masculine characteristics. As Mrs Oliphant bemoaned, they provided 'a very fleshly and unlovely record' of femininity. And this raised the most significant, but as yet barely articulated, concern about sensation novels – that they blurred accepted social distinctions, crossed hitherto firmly demarcated limits and entered taboo areas. In the jargon of modern critics, they were liminal and transgressive.

Few people doubted Wilkie's role as the main progenitor. As Miss Braddon declared in a later interview, 'I always say that I owe *Lady Audley's Secret* to *The Woman in White*. Wilkie Collins is assuredly my literary father.' Her admiration was evident from the amateur sleuth Robert Audley's remark in her most popular novel: 'I haven't read Alexandre Dumas and Wilkie Collins for nothing. I'm up to their tricks, sneaking in at doors behind a fellow's back, and flattening their white faces against window panes, and making themselves all eyes in the twilight.'

Like Wilkie and many of his friends, she also enjoyed an unconventional love life, having struck up a relationship with John Maxwell, the publisher of the short-lived magazine *Robin Goodfellow*, which had first serialised *Lady Audley's Secret*. He was married with five children, but his Irish wife was in a lunatic asylum. Braddon moved in with him, and their joint earnings from sensation ventures enabled them to live grandly in Lichfield House in Richmond and have five children of their own. Inevitably her lifestyle intensified and personalised the criticism from her opponents. She and Maxwell were married only in 1874, after the death of his first wife.

Wilkie was fortunate to live in the heart of London's medical district, since the atmosphere at his house in Harley Street during the first few months of 1863 again resembled a convalescent home. No sooner had he finished *No Name* than his gout flared up. With more time on his hands to indulge his illness, he adopted increasingly unorthodox palliative measures, such as draping troubled parts of his body with 'a simple poultice of cabbage leaves covered with oiled silk'.

When his gout spread to both feet and he could no longer climb the stairs to his bedroom, he called in Dr John Elliotson, since Frank Beard was incapacitated with an attack of erysipelas, a severe reddening of the skin. Wilkie had a high regard for Elliotson, who he would refer to as 'one of the greatest of English physiologists' in *The Moonstone* later in the decade. As stand-in general practitioner, Elliotson prescribed a tonic of wormwood, together with a course of his trademark mesmerism, which would be carried out by Caroline, with the aim of anaesthetising

Wilkie's feet and helping him to sleep without opium. But this regime was undermined a few days later when Caroline herself was laid low by what Wilkie described to Beard as 'another nervous-hysterical attack. She was up all last night with the "palpitations".' As a result, she now had to be sedated with opium herself.

To add to the catalogue of woes, Harriet Collins was seriously ill in Oxford. Wilkie told Charles Ward that, although she was improving, she was 'still too weak to leave her bed – except when . . . carried for a little while, wrapped in blankets, to the fire.' He was frustrated that his own maladies meant that he could not visit her, nor attend the wedding in February of the daughter of Frances Dickinson – a lavish affair at the latter's family house, Queen's Charlton, near Bristol. Frances had recently cut back her Italian sorties, as she was looking forward to her own solid, status-defining marriage later in the year to Gilbert Elliot, the Dean of Bristol – an unlikely alliance that amused Wilkie and Dickens, since the groom was prim and puritanical, while the bride had a notably rackety past.

Caroline's hysterical episodes were clearly not unprecedented but, in the absence of obvious clinical illness, their cause remains a matter of speculation. It seems that even now, several years after meeting Wilkie, she was still nervous about her position in their relationship and in the wider world. Her illegitimacy made her particularly sensitive on the subject of marriage which, it later became clear, was something she wanted for herself. But Wilkie had other ideas and her resentment built up.

One way or another, Harley Street was proving a useful test bed for sensation novels. The heroines in this genre, whether depicted by the pens of Miss Braddon, Mrs Wood or Wilkie himself, were often women of heightened awareness, battling against the restrictions of modern society. They did not have to be dour: like Magdalen Vanstone in *No Name*, they tended to be

spirited and keen for new experiences (or sensations). Their
adventures made good copy, but so did their reverses and the often
inevitable consequences. Buffeted and hemmed in by circumstances,
they sometimes became hysterical or mad – a diagnosis reinforced
by men threatened by their assertiveness.

This is not to say that the Collins household followed this
model, but Caroline was obviously feeling the strain of living
with Wilkie. Her 'nervous-hysterical' behaviour was similar to
that of the jumpy, intelligent women in his fiction, who felt
frustrated in their desire for a fulfilled life. With her history of
illegitimacy and struggle to bring up her fatherless daughter,
she was more of a model for Wilkie's quirky, assured heroines
than has generally been supposed. (He, in sick mode, clutching
at poultices of cabbage leaves, acted out another trope of sensation fiction – the ineffectual, valetudinarian man.)

As was evident in *No Name*, Wilkie had little compunction
about portraying the less edifying characteristics of these
modern sensation-seeking women, even if they emerged as
manipulative, greedy and immoral. The critics tended to prefer
heroines who were fair of complexion and pure in heart. Henry
Chorley set the tone when he suggested in the *Athenaeum* that
Magdalen had been 'let off with a punishment gentle in proportion to the unscrupulous selfishness of her character'. Women
in Victorian England were not supposed to behave as she did
– brazenly swindling others and entering loveless marriages –
and expect to get away with it. Alexander Smith, in the *North
British Review*, believed he had located the problem: 'Everything
in these books is feverish and excited; the reader is continually
as if treading on bombshells, which may explode at any moment.'
But these intense effects were exactly what sensation novelists
were seeking.

Margaret Oliphant provided the textbook version of this
shocked reaction when she lambasted Wilkie in *Blackwood's*

Magazine for throwing his leading lady 'into a career of vulgar and aimless trickery and wickedness, with which it is impossible to have a shadow of sympathy', and then having the audacity to allow her to emerge from all her 'pollutions . . . at the cheap cost of fever, as pure, as high-minded, and as spotless as the most dazzling white of heroines'.

One result of this cool critical response was that sales of *No Name* fell sharply, after a spectacular start that saw most of the initial 4,000-copy print run sold on the first day. The combination of this widespread antipathy and his own physical pain made Wilkie unusually irritable. When his mother contemplated staying as a paying guest in Slough, he spluttered, for no apparent reason, 'Ladies who take in boarders, under the pretence of "their homes being too large for them", are bores I don't believe in.'

By early March he was feeling better and able to go out. Every afternoon, from two to six, friends would find that he was incommunicado as he took his regular drive in a carriage, followed by a visit to the London Medical Electrical Institution in York Place at the top of Baker Street, where he would immerse himself in 'Dr Caplin's Electro-Chemical Bath', designed to draw out the impurities in the body.

Wilkie's mood was not helped by news of the death in Algiers in late March of Augustus Egg, aged forty-six. Ever since the two of them had travelled with Dickens around Europe a decade earlier, Wilkie had kept up with Egg, a fellow Garrick Club member, who was close to several of his artist friends, such as Ned Ward, Holman Hunt and Frith. Wilkie's multi-perspective narrative style (epitomised in *The Woman in White*) owed something to Egg's artistic techniques, particularly to his 1858 triptych painting *Past and Present*, which showed the disintegration of a marriage from three points of view. At one stage Egg had been a spurned suitor for the hand of Georgina Hogarth. In April 1860, around the time he became ill and began wintering in Algiers, he married Esther Brown, a low-born East End girl whom his friends hardly knew or saw. Like Wilkie, Egg kept a woman out of public view, but, unlike him, he solemnised their relationship.

As Wilkie gradually regained his strength, he decided to treat himself to further recuperation in the German spa town of Aachen (which, as a Francophile, he insisted on calling Aix-la-Chapelle). Situated on the Rhine, it was easy to reach by train, but Wilkie grumbled about the prospect of 'hateful railway travelling, which disgusts and depresses me even when I am in health'. This was ironic, since the railways were an essential device in sensation fiction, giving the impression of speed and modernity.

Having decided to employ a Swiss guide-cum-courier who was offered courtesy of Coutts Bank, he overcame this phobia and by the end of April he was established in the Nuellens Hotel in Aachen, close to the Cathedral where Charlemagne was buried. Every morning before breakfast, he was required to drink a glass of 'steaming hot [spring water], perfectly bright and clear, and in taste like the worst London egg you ever had for breakfast in your life.' But he found that this foul-smelling brew only whetted his appetite, which seemed to take precedence over his daily regime of baths. The hotel employed a Parisian chef who, he admitted, encouraged his 'natural gluttony' by serving 'a continuous succession of entrées which are to be eaten but not described', while its cellar stocked the best hock and Moselle wines he had ever tasted.

When, unsurprisingly, his gout did not improve, he continued south to the Hotel de l'Ours in Wildbad, a cosier, self-contained but cosmopolitan spa town in the Black Forest, where he was relieved to find that the water did not have the off-putting sulphurous smell of Aachen. As he underwent a course of twenty-four often painful treatments in the splendid town baths, he began developing an idea for the new novel he had promised George Smith. It would be called *Armadale* and, showing no retreat from his sensation style, it would open with a gripping deathbed scene in Wildbad.

When he returned to London at the end of June, he had been away for two months and needed to attend to business affairs. With Sampson Low wanting to publish a one-volume edition of *No Name*, Wilkie prevailed on Millais to produce a frontispiece illuminating the scene in which Magdalen Vanstone contemplates using laudanum to commit suicide. Sampson Low also made plans to publish a collection of Wilkie's articles as *My Miscellanies*. However, he was forced to turn down an offer from John Hollingshead to edit a new literary journal underwritten by the Scottish publisher Alexander Strahan. He felt that, having just left Dickens and *All the Year Round* to join Smith and the *Cornhill*, it would be wrong to link himself to a rival, which turned out to be the magazine *Argosy*.

He thought that a cruise with Pigott in August might help build on the treatments he had had in Germany, but he ended up feeling worse, with a bad back to boot. So he decided to take Caroline and Harriet to the Isle of Man, on the pretext of finding some background detail for his new novel. He complained about the island's capital, Douglas, where 'every third shop [was] a spirits shop, and every second inhabitant drunk.' But the research pickings proved promising.

His doctor at Wildbad had predicted that his gout would recur in 'the fall of the year', and so it turned out. Having resolved to spend the winter months in a better climate abroad, he retraced his teenage steps and returned to Italy. This meant removing Harriet from school and taking her and Caroline with him through France to Marseilles, where he decided it was too windy for the two-day voyage to Civitavecchia. Instead, they travelled by carriage to Genoa and from there down the coast by land and sea to Livorno, Rome and Naples.

Wilkie had developed the habit of calling young Harriet 'Carrie'. Conceivably it was used to differentiate and even distance the twelve-year-old girl from Wilkie's mother, who still showed no desire to acknowledge, let alone embrace, her son's little family. Friends were in the know, as was clear from Wilkie's remarks when the three travellers took an overnight boat from Livorno to Civitavecchia in conditions that were still extremely turbulent. 'The two Carolines suffered sea-martyrdom,' he reported to Charles Ward. 'Caroline Junior had a comparatively easy time of it, and fell asleep in the intervals of retching – but Caroline Senior was so ill that she could not be moved from the deck all night, and she has hardly got over the effect of the voyage yet. The sea (as usual) did _me_ good – but I have registered a vow to take my companions on no more night-voyages.'

The political situation in Italy had changed considerably since Wilkie's previous visits with his parents a quarter of century earlier and with Dickens and Egg in 1853. After a prolonged campaign by Garibaldi and other nationalists (the repercussions of which Wilkie had experienced among his friends in England), Italy was now a united kingdom in every place but one – Rome, which, in a compromise guaranteed by the French Emperor Napoleon III, was still nominally under the control of the Pope. Nevertheless, Wilkie found the city very familiar, though the public garden on the Pincian Hill was now better laid out. Comfortably established in a five-room apartment in their hotel, with a dedicated cook, he and his family had only one bugbear – the intrusive French military presence.

The same sense of familiarity greeted him in wet and thundery Naples, where the bankers, the Igguldens, continued to rule the British roost. From his rooms in the Hotel d'Angleterre overlooking the bay, Wilkie informed Pigott that he was still 'ruminating his story', which would include memorable Neapolitan scenes. Pigott passed on this intelligence to his friend G.H. Lewes, who had been helping to edit the *Cornhill* following the resignation of the original editor, Thackeray, in 1862. Thackeray continued to write for the magazine, but when he died on Christmas Eve 1863, Lewes feared that a gap in the schedule would open up and asked George Smith, the owner, if they should press Wilkie to start his promised new serial in April or May. Otherwise, he added, they might have to ask Trollope – whose Barchester novel *The Small House at Allington* was running at the time – to start immediately on something new. Such was the wealth of talent the magazine could call on at this juncture, when it was at the height of its influence and enjoyed a circulation of 100,000 a month. However, Smith had already read the runes and given Wilkie until the following December to produce the first number of his new story.

Having decided against taking the winter sun in Egypt, Wilkie returned with his family to Rome, where his mood soon perked up for his fortieth birthday, which he regarded as a significant milestone. As he contemplated his 'gray hairs springing fast, especially about the temples – rheumatism and gout familiar enemies for some time past – all the worst signs of middle-age sprouting out on me', he marvelled that 'in spite of it all, I don't <u>feel</u> old.' Indeed, he congratulated himself, 'I have no regular habits, no respectable prejudices, no tendency to go to sleep after dinner, no loss of appetite for public amuse-ments, none of the melancholy sobrieties of sentiment, in short, which are supposed to be proper to middle age. Surely, there is some mistake?'

He received birthday greetings from his brother, who was back in London with Katey and living temporarily at 5 Hyde Park Gate, since Harriet Collins had finally given up her lease on Clarence Terrace. Charley had been unusually productive and was looking forward to having two novels published in the summer – *The Bar Sinister*, under the Smith, Elder imprint, and *Strathcairn* from Sampson Low. Both were gentle sensational works: the first drew on Charley's time in France and dealt with the consequences of illegitimacy, while the second looked back to his experience of Scotland with Millais, while tackling the issue of hereditary madness and toying with the idea of how much one could rely on the evidence of one's eyes. Charley now claimed to be writing a farce based on the story he contributed to *Mrs Lirriper's Lodgings*, the latest Christmas number of *All the Year Round*. He said he was doing this at the request of Charles Fechter, the brilliant actor whom Wilkie had first seen in the Théâtre de Vaudeville in the Place de la Bourse in Paris in the 1850s. Belying Wilkie's dictum about the superiority of the French theatre, Fechter had quit the Paris stage and crossed the Channel to London where, having befriended Dickens and later Wilkie, he soon made a name for himself as a passionate interpreter of Shakespeare. Large and irascible, Fechter abjured the old-fashioned declamatory style of acting and developed a new, much appreciated realism. As the *Athenaeum* once remarked, Fechter 'is Hamlet'.

Charley kept his brother informed about their mother, who had found a more or less permanent berth in Tunbridge Wells. She had been going there since the end of 1860, when she began to tire of London. She could now no longer find refuge in her usual bolt-holes, since the Bullars and Langtons were now spending most of their time in the capital, and since, by her own admission, she had antagonised the Combes by behaving atrociously.

Her point of contact in Tunbridge Wells was Frances Brandling, sister of Wilkie's old friend Henry. A couple of years earlier Frances had married Henry Armytage, a former colonel in the Coldstream Guards, who lived at Broomhill Bank just outside the town, where the Regency atmosphere must have reminded Harriet of living by the Park in Marylebone. The elderly Colonel died soon afterwards, leaving his widow to find solace in the arms of Arthur Pott, a former high sheriff of the county, who lived at Bentham Hill, an equally grand house designed by Decimus Burton in Southborough. However, Harriet tended not to stay with the Potts but with two or three families in the vicinity who were grateful for her rent.

Determined to make progress with his book, Wilkie kept himself to himself while in Rome. The only people he saw were Joseph Severn, who was now the British Consul, and Frederick Lehmann's artist brother, Rudolf, who was in town with his wife. Occasionally he went to the opera, which he liked because, unlike in London, it was cheap and informal. He was not the first or last tourist to be confused by Italian currency rates – a consequence of the still fluid political situation where 'there is one price for the Pope's gold, and another for Victor Emmanuel's, and another for Louis Napoleon's and another for silver.' He opened an account at Freeborns, the local English bank, which gave him a chequebook. When his mother wrote fussing that he might need more money, he told her not to worry as he had a thousand guineas at Coutts and 'if I can only go on, as I am going on now, I shall soon make some thousands more. No fear at present of my being worried by want of "means".' Charles Ward had helped by posting a £500 letter of credit, as well as sending some snuff, which provided a point of contact when (in a repeat of a fleeting encounter a decade earlier) he passed the Pope in a narrow street in Trastevere. Having just taken a pinch of snuff, Wilkie was amused to see the Pontiff doing the same as he clattered past him in a carriage.

By now Caroline was beginning to fret about getting home. 'How like cats women are!' Wilkie joshed to Charles Ward, who was the closest of his friends to his mistress. (His comparison was benevolent since cats were undoubtedly his favourite domestic animals.) He added that Caroline was looking forward to pouring Ward a glass of dry sherry. She and her daughter had both been under the weather, but were recovering. Harriet (as she will continue to be called) was now managing to astonish the locals with the 'essentially British plumpness of her cheeks and calves'.

Back in London at the end of March 1864, Wilkie's intense preliminary planning had borne fruit and he was ready to begin *Armadale*. Rich and tightly plotted, this book incorporated all the themes of sensation fiction, but more interestingly and intelligently than in other authors' attempts. It centred on the relationship – part friendship, part rivalry – between two distant cousins, both called Allan Armadale, whose fathers had once clashed over ownership of property in Barbados. Because of this background, one of them has been specifically warned by his father not to have dealings with anyone with his name, which he changes to Ozias Midwinter. But this general advice is ignored when he meets his cousin and they become unlikely friends.

The one who retains the name Allan Armadale is a naïve, trusting soul who inherits an estate at Thorpe Ambrose in Norfolk where he falls in love with the steward's beautiful daughter, Eleanor (Neelie) Milroy. But Lydia Gwilt, a sexy, ambitious, red-headed widow with a treacherous past involving murder and bigamy, is familiar with the Armadale family background as a result of her former employment as a maid. She sees an opportunity to inveigle her way into Allan's life, marry him, and inherit his substantial demesne and fortune.

Along the way, the novel ranges across the full gamut of sensational themes – extraordinary coincidences, mistaken identities, confusing doubles, scheming individuals and warring generations, all leavened with a dose of the supernatural. It takes in more specific obsessions, such as poisoning, marriage, inheritance, race and drugs (Lydia Gwilt turns out to be addicted to laudanum). The action culminates in a dramatic scene in a Hampstead sanitorium when Lydia has to murder Allan Armadale with a deadly but undetectable gas, gets muddled between him and cousin Ozias (whom she has fallen in love with and genuinely wants to marry), and ends up killing herself with the same poison.

But underneath these now familiar devices, *Armadale* is about destiny, and whether it is possible for people to escape the grim determinism of their pasts (whether hereditary or otherwise) and so establish their individuality. And is this a matter of 'Fate or Chance?', as one of Wilkie's chapter headings has it? In this way, the book offers another, more sophisticated take on his favoured theme of identity.

The novel showed signs of Caroline's influence since the name Midwinter, used for Armadale's alter ego, was also that of a carpenter in Toddington. As her father had worked in the same profession, it is reasonable to imagine that she suggested it to Wilkie.

Stimulated by discussion with G.H. Lewes and others, Wilkie also drew on recent developments in two areas of science – epistemology and psychology. In each he found a dichotomy that neatly reflected the binary theme of his novel: in the first, between rational and irrational ways of experiencing the world and acquiring knowledge, and in the second, between the conscious and unconscious processes of the mind. In this context, Allan and Ozias provided two archetypal versions of the human psyche – one bluff, light-hearted and matter of fact, the other dark, thoughtful and intuitive, or, by extension, the masculine and the feminine. No great imaginative leap is needed to see a model of the opposing sides of Wilkie's own personality.

By mid-July, he felt he was making good progress. He told his mother he had completed three parts, including the 'hardest' chapter in the book, but needed to go to Norfolk to check some points for his next section. This suggests he had just finished the dramatic dream sequence off the Isle of Man, and was preparing to explore the Broads, the location of Allan's grand house at Thorpe Ambrose.

However, his need for local colour did not mean he should not enjoy himself. So he was joined on his trip to East Anglia by Edward Pigott and Charles Ward, two of his regular companions on this type of jaunt. They almost certainly travelled by train, availing themselves of the Great Eastern Railway's special excursion rates (20 shillings first-class return from London, and 15 shillings second class). It was the height of the holiday season, when flotillas of sailing boats took to the sea in regattas organised by their local yacht clubs – at Great Yarmouth on 2 August, Oulton Broads two days later, and Lowestoft the following week.

Wilkie loved this nautical display: to his mother's consternation he had recently, and unrealistically, talked of acquiring, perhaps even buying, his own yacht. Having established themselves at Yarmouth's most expensive hotel, the Victoria, he and his party mixed cruising on the sea with leisurely sightseeing in the Broads.

After ten days disporting himself on the east coast, Wilkie consulted his *Bradshaw's Guide* and made his way alone by train to stay once again with Richard Monckton Milnes, now Lord Houghton, at Fryston Hall in Yorkshire. On his return to London, he ploughed on with his novel, where his depiction of Norfolk had none of the frenzy of the regattas. Instead, Allan Armadale's house at Thorpe Ambrose is described in deceptively bland terms: 'nothing picturesque, nothing in the slightest degree suggestive of mystery and romance'. The surrounding landscape takes on a surreal feel as an old lifeboat carries Allan and his guests through the flat, lonely Broads – 'gliding slow and distant behind fringes of pollarded willows, the sails of invisible boats moving on invisible waters' – until they reach Hurle Mere, where the new governess, Miss Gwilt, appears, standing by an open pool in the sunset, the shadow of a woman, as predicted in a dream by Allan.

Hurle Mere seems to have been based on Horsey Mere, a freshwater lake five miles north of Yarmouth. The lake is approached by boat from the River Thurne. It features in John Betjeman's poem 'East Anglian Bathe', which contrasts the calm of the Mere with the swirling North Sea on the other side of the reeds.

Wilkie later boasted about the 'personal investigation' he had made to ensure that the details of the Broads were correct. In his quest for authenticity, he also drew on his recent excursions to Wildbad, the Isle of Man and Naples. An important early location in the novel was Somerset, a county he knew well through Pigott, whose cousin was a parson near Taunton, like the Reverend Decimus Brock who befriends both Allan and Ozias in the book. Wilkie had never been to the West Indies, scene of the opening chapters, but one source might have been his cousin, Edward Carpenter, who worked in a bank in Jamaica. Or more likely, he called on Frances Elliot, whose Dickinson fortune originated in the trade in sugar and slavery in Barbados.

This geographical range allowed him to indulge his love of the sea as he conjured up a variety of boats in different waters – a 300-ton schooner-rigged ship in the Atlantic, a 35-ton yacht off the coast of Wales, the wreck of a merchantman off the Isle of Man, another yacht (affiliated to the Royal Yacht Squadron) off Naples, as well as assorted craft in the Broads.

He was not afraid to seek information when it was required. 'Wherever the story touches on questions connected with Law, Medicine, or Chemistry,' he claimed in an appendix, 'it has been submitted before publication to the experience of professional men.' He made enquiries of Dickens's solicitor Frederic

Ouvry who had been married by licence rather than traditional banns. This way he confirmed a crucial piece of information for his plot – that a licence could be obtained after three weeks' residence in one place and, significantly for the tortuous wedding plans of Lydia and Ozias, did not need to include any information about where the bridegroom had lived before that period.

He later checked further legal details with his own solicitor Ebenezer Benham. And when he came to his final section, where Lydia Gwilt attempts to gas Allan Armadale, he found himself held up by 'difficulties in reconciling necessary chemical facts with the incidents of the story'. So he approached Thomas Hyde Hills, who ran the Wigmore Street pharmacy John Bell (later John Bell & Croyden), which he often used. Hills would go on to become President of the Royal Pharmaceutical Society, in which role he was painted by Millais.

After returning from Norfolk in August 1864, Wilkie took steps to put Harriet back into school. The teenager had had no formal education since leaving Miss Milne's academy the previous summer, prior to the family's trip to Italy. If Wilkie's bank accounts are to be correctly interpreted, she was now sent to an establishment run by a Miss Cresswell, though its whereabouts are unknown.

The beneficial effects of his Norfolk holiday did not last long. By the end of September Wilkie was complaining that his gout had returned, and with a vengeance, since he now felt it was attacking his brain (a medical impossibility, but clearly Wilkie's health was poor). Frank Beard was not particularly concerned, but forbade his patient from working. Wilkie was put out because the first instalment of *Armadale* was due to appear in the *Cornhill* in November and he knew the issue would shortly be made up by the printers and he would need to look at the proofs at a time when George Smith was away and he himself was indisposed. He impressed on Pigott not to say anything to his mother about his relapse. 'For the present, keep all this a profound Secret, on the chance of my rallying back to my work,' he pleaded, in an unusual admission of the family pressure he'd always struggled under. 'If I can conceal my condition from my mother, I must. I have concealed it so far.' As ever, secrecy remained the watchword.

Within a month, Wilkie managed to find the time and energy to stay with Dickens and Georgina Hogarth at the Lord Warden Hotel in Dover, where his first proofs arrived. Between breezy walks and warm seawater baths, he was relieved to find that both Dickens and Georgina liked the excerpt, while, unusually and particularly gratifyingly, even the printers had expressed an interest in it.

This proved one of the few bright spots of the autumn, as his health continued to trouble him. When he felt giddy in December, Beard referred him to Dr Charles Radcliffe, Britain's foremost specialist in diseases of the nervous system, who again reported no cause for alarm, but put Wilkie on a light diet (though claret and hock were allowed) and counselled him against 'exciting [him]self with "Society" and dinner parties'.

Wilkie still took laudanum to ward against pain. But now, for the first time, his intake seems to have affected his writing which, while never hallucinogenic, does reflect thought patterns associated with opiates (in its emphasis on shadows and doubles, for example). He undoubtedly empathised with Lydia Gwilt's rhetorical outburst: 'Who was the man who invented laudanum? I thank him from the bottom of my heart whoever he was. If all the miserable wretches in pain of body and mind, whose comforter he has been, could meet together to sing his praises, what a chorus it would be! I have had six delicious hours of oblivion; I have woke up with my mind composed . . . "Drops," you are a darling! If I love nothing else, I love *you*.'

For months he had been muttering about the noise he was having to endure at Harley Street – 'nothing but pianos at the back of the house and organs, bagpipes, bands and Punches in front'. He raised the possibility of moving to the country (by which he probably meant somewhere like the fringes of Hampstead or Highgate, where the Lehmanns had a house), and at one stage he thought there was 'nothing for it but the Temple', the area of London frequented by lawyers, where at least he could find some cloistered peace. But the attractions of the area where he had been born and lived for so long proved too strong, and after Christmas he performed another typical Collins shuffle across the Marylebone Road to 9 Melcombe Place, a short-lease property off Dorset Square.

He was accompanied by his little family, and ensured that Caroline Graves was the name on the ratebook. It was a significant move, one 'in the right direction', Charley told his mother elliptically, adding, 'I hope he will get safe through his hard work, poor fellow.' (Charley and Katey had returned to the Continent, partly for health reasons and partly so he could make headway with another novel, *At the Bar*.)

By now the first instalments of *Armadale* had been published and Wilkie could begin to relax. After settling into his new house, he suddenly found that his work was not too pressing and his illnesses not too debilitating: what he needed was a holiday. On 25 February 1865, he cashed a cheque for £40 and left on a ten-day trip to Paris. In his usual bland letter to his mother he reported the city as busy as usual, requiring him and his companion, probably Lehmann, to book their nightly visits to the theatre well in advance. The good thing was that 'my book is as entirely off my mind here, as if my book was done.'

On his return to London, he found himself 'over head and ears in arrears of letters, "club"-difficulties (the eternal "Garrick" again), and all the other small worries which accumulate in one's absence'. His problems with the Garrick had been brewing over the previous two years, following his election to the Club's general committee, where his fellow members included Sir George Armytage, nephew of the Tunbridge Wells squire who had taken his mother under his wing. Wilkie was proud of such peer recognition, but found being a committee member a frustrating experience. His only recorded committee attendance was in May 1864, when the Club got into bureaucratic difficulties over its proposed move from 35 King Street to new premises in what, after being carved out of the stews of Covent Garden, would be called Garrick Street. (There was controversy over the name: the Club committee had originally wanted it called Shakespeare Street, the Metropolitan Board of Works countered with New King Street, and they compromised on Garrick Street.) Wilkie vented his anger to another member, his friend George Russell, to whom he wrote, 'I leave the little puddle in King Street to stink without any further stirring on my part.'

His association with the Club came to an abrupt end the following February when Dickens's colleague Wills was blackballed. Wilkie promptly resigned in protest and Dickens followed suit. Wilkie had experienced a similar rebuff after he claimed to have put up Frederick Lehmann (though there was some confusion as he somehow failed to sign his friend's page in the candidate's book).

His summer schedule in 1865 was disturbed by the demands of his mother, who had moved into a house in Tunbridge Wells where she could be more independent and keep a room for her son. He was able to work there, as he told Wills in July; indeed, he informed another correspondent that he was hardly ever in London. It seems to have been a time of domestic turbulence all round – a supposition given credence by the lack of any overt (or at least extant) communication between him and his great friend Dickens. On 9 June the latter was involved in a horrific rail accident at Staplehurst in Kent. He was travelling on the boat train on his way back from France, accompanied by Nelly Ternan and her mother. Ten people were killed and forty injured in the crash, which left several carriages dangling from a bridge over the River Beult. Dickens tended the casualties, but was left very shaken. His biographer Clare Tomalin has suggested that he had recently (and frequently) accompanied his mistress to France, where Nelly had had a baby who died there. However, neither the crash nor its circumstances is mentioned in any letter between Wilkie and Dickens. This indicates another example of the code of silence these two men adopted when it suited them. The logical conclusion is that their correspondence from this time has been destroyed. In this case, it seems that Wilkie was just as eager for the record to be interrupted, since he was experiencing unprecedented difficulties in his relationship with Caroline.

It was left to Charley, who had returned from the Continent, to make the only comment by one of the Collinses on the Staplehurst crash. Since Katey had wanted to check that her father was all right, they went to Gad's Hill to find him 'look(ing) something the worse' for his accident. Charley enjoyed working in Dickens's new Swiss chalet, a gift from Fechter, which had been erected in the grounds, providing magnificent views of the Thames from its second floor. Interestingly, Katey was the only member of the Dickens family, aside from her brother Henry, who was prepared to admit that Nelly had experienced the personal tragedy of losing a child.

Wilkie hoped to relax on a sailing holiday with Pigott in July. 'I want the sea badly – to freshen me after my work,' he told his mother. However, his regular nautical companion was now the political correspondent of the *Daily News* and was required to report on the general election that month. (Earlier in the decade, Pigott, like Ozias Midwinter, had spent time in Italy as a journalist.) The paper, which had been founded and briefly edited by Dickens, strongly supported the Liberal Party, which, under Lord Palmerston, was duly returned to government with an increased majority.

A disappointed Wilkie had to content himself instead with another of his trails around the comfortable country houses of Frances Elliot and the Lehmanns. He did, however, travel to Lowestoft at the beginning of August and it is a fair bet that he also went to Yarmouth for the regatta. But he does not seem to have been accompanied by any of his regular companions, nor indeed by Caroline and Harriet, for, after returning to London, he told Charles Ward in strangely disengaged tones, 'C. & the child have come back, both languid & dismal. I am myself far from well.' This suggests they had been on a separate holiday, perhaps with Caroline's mother-in-law, who had been notably absent from the scene of late.

In previous summers, Wilkie had often railed against the oppressive heat, dirt and noise of London. He now found himself appreciating a capital that was 'wonderfully quiet . . . I roam the empty streets, and inhale the delightful London air (so much healthier than those pretentious humbugs the seaside breezes!), and meet nobody, and come back with the blessed conviction that I have not got to "dress" and go out to dinner, and feel that London in August is London under a most attractive aspect.'

With his novel's end in sight, he found life strangely imitating art when, in November, he learned that three men had died from gas poisoning after sleeping on board a ship called the *Armadale* in Liverpool's Huskisson Dock. He took pains to explain in the appendix to his book that he had set down the details of the attempted asphyxiation in a Hampstead sanatorium a year and a half earlier. However, it was a coincidence to be savoured.

As he struggled to complete the last chapters in early 1866, Beard put him on a loathsome-sounding mixture which Wilkie described as 'a fortifying compound of drugs, Quinine, Acid, and Dandelion'. Luckily, he felt it did him 'infinite good' and, as a result, he was eager to accompany Frederick Lehmann to Paris in March, though the trip had to be postponed when Nina fell ill. Instead, he visited the Ned Wards, who both continued successfully to plough a traditional artistic path, with their aristocratic and royal clients. Wilkie was especially impressed by a recent historical portrait by Henrietta of Bernard Palissy, the French Huguenot potter who struggled in vain to reproduce the qualities of Chinese porcelain.

Finally, on 12 April, he finished his toils, signalling his relief to his mother with his customary epistolary flourish, 'I Have Done'. Now he could celebrate with his delayed trip to Paris. Ten days later, he and Lehmann were staying in the Hotel du Helder, near the Opéra, where, as they made the rounds of concerts, theatres and races in the spring sunshine, Wilkie delighted in having cast off 'a heavy responsibility' and was feeling 'content to idle about in the open air, without going anywhere or seeing anything in particular. And yet, such is the perversity of mankind, I am half sorry too to have parted from my poor dear book.'

FOURTH EPOCH

13

MARTHA ARRIVES

CAROLINE MAY HAVE contributed the name Midwinter to *Armadale* but she was otherwise strangely absent from Wilkie's life at this time. A few years earlier, at the turn of the decade, she had played a modest but nevertheless defined role at his side. She rarely went out with him, but she kept house and was known with varying degrees of affection to his close friends. In 1860, her support had been recognised when Wilkie took her on an expensive holiday to Paris, and in October 1863, she and Harriet accompanied him on a six-month-long tour of Italy. But following this journey, mother and daughter faded from view.

After Harriet was bundled back to school in the autumn of 1864, Caroline featured only twice in some five hundred letters over the next seven years. In the summer of 1865, Wilkie referred distractedly to 'C & the child' returning from their holiday. Then a year or so later he thanked Charles Reade for a copy of the proofs of Reade's sexually explicit novel *Griffith Gaunt: or Jealousy*, and sent him 'Mrs Graves' thanks' as well. Reade lived openly with a colourful actress called Laura Seymour whom Wilkie liked. She had also been married, so the two couples often spent evenings together, free from the moralising brickbats of society. Wilkie had clearly asked Reade's opinion about a proposed revival of his play *The Frozen Deep* and told him that if he needed any more copies, he had 'only to let Mrs Graves know it, and you can have them.' This suggests Caroline's role was now little more than functionary, as was confirmed when she next cropped up as his amanuensis in February 1868, following the death of his mother.

During the period between the two earlier letters – August 1865 and October 1866 – Wilkie might even have stopped giving Caroline money. At the start of that August, he made over three small amounts, presumably for her holiday, and then paid her nothing for over a year, until October 1866, when she received £80, a substantial sum, and considerably more than she received either before or in the immediate aftermath. It is wrong to make too much of this, as not only were his payments to her irregular, but he also paid over money for the house in Melcombe Place. However, the evidence of his correspondence and his bank account suggests that Caroline had been relegated to a minor role.

One does not have to look far for a reason: Wilkie had added another, equally mysterious, woman to his life. At some stage in the mid-1860s he became friendly with Martha Rudd, an agricultural labourer's daughter, who worked in a pub in Great Yarmouth. They almost certainly met when he was visiting the town with Pigott and Ward during the 1864 regatta season. Martha, then nineteen, was working in the Vauxhall Tavern in Runham.

She was a buxom wench with the physicality of the girl in Manet's painting *A Bar at the Folies-Bergères*. Caroline was more petite and conventionally pretty, with a love of fine clothes, which reflected her social ambitions. Martha had no such pretensions. Behind her distracted gaze, she was as near as Wilkie could reasonably get to his ideal of the broad-buttocked Italian woman, the *Venus Callipyge*. She was his literary approximation to the conventional Pre-Raphaelite stunner.

Martha's family came from the village of Winterton, on the coast, eight miles north of Yarmouth and three miles south-east of Horsey Mere, which featured in *Armadale*. It looked out on the Yarmouth Roads, a stretch of sea with the highest density of traffic in the world, as colliers and other vessels ploughed down from the north-east to London and back again. When the winds blew up, these waters were also among the most treacherous. Winterton 'beachmen' were often called out to rescue capsized or stranded ships – a dangerous, if lucrative, occupation.

Although most male inhabitants were involved with the sea, either as fishermen or sailors, Martha's father, James, was unusual in that he worked on the land as a shepherd. Such 'greenhands' were second-class citizens in a moderately prosperous village, which explains why many, like James, came from out of Winterton. He was born at Sparham on the other side of Norwich. He and his wife Mary were almost certainly illiterate, though Martha is likely to have received a basic education at Winterton's national school, established in 1845.

At the start of the 1860s, Martha had joined her elder sister Alice working at the Vauxhall Tavern. Nothing is known about how Wilkie met or courted her. He may have stopped off at the Tavern on arriving in Yarmouth by train. More likely, while staying at the Victoria Hotel, he strolled over the new bridge to the Vauxhall Gardens and had a drink at the pub. Perhaps he was with Pigott or Ward and they thought that, as in London, the Gardens were a place to pick up a young woman.

Significantly, Wilkie returned to Lowestoft the following summer when Caroline and Harriet were elsewhere. He almost certainly continued to Yarmouth and reacquainted himself with Martha. By April 1868, she had moved to London and was living in Marylebone, among the artisans of Bolsover Street, in lodgings paid for by Wilkie. It was a street he knew well, in the heart of the Portland estate, just around the corner from his own former home in New Cavendish Street. In his more impecunious days, his godfather David Wilkie had lived there too. As Martha settled into her new life, her presence must have exacerbated Wilkie's difficulties, particularly with Caroline.

In this context certain events need to be reassessed. The fault lines in Wilkie's relationship with Caroline emerged almost as soon as he returned from meeting Martha in Norfolk in the summer of 1864. As a result, Harriet was sent back to school that autumn. Wilkie's move a few months later to Melcombe Place can also be seen in a new light, especially since he chose to put Caroline's name on the list of ratepayers. Either he wanted to appease her by showing her she still had a role at his side or, as was mooted, he really did intend spending more time with his mother in Tunbridge Wells.

He certainly kept a room at Harriet Collins's place, as she wrote a chatty letter to Holman Hunt in July 1866, telling him that she had been visited by Frances Elliot (née Dickinson), who was 'as droll as ever, thinner but youthful still', and 'Wilkie gave up his room to her & slept at the nice little hotel opposite'. Hunt had recently married Fanny Waugh, and, to Harriet's evident displeasure, was about to depart on a painting tour of the Middle East. She complained that she would never live to see him come back, and added, suggesting her close relationship with the Pre-Raphaelites – maternal yet flirtatious – 'I always told you that you would at last find a Miss Right that would supersede the poor old Harriet, but I shall go on loving you for all that. You are now off my hands in that way & my most serious affairs are Henry Bullar & Henry Brandling . . . I send you a pho. of me. I look like an old [indecipherable] nurse who has had a snug glass of hot & strong gin & water.'

Meanwhile, what did Martha do with herself? Much as she liked Wilkie, she is unlikely to have left her family in Norfolk for London and a future that held little except as an alternative mistress to a successful but nevertheless jobbing writer. In the wake of Wilkie's death in 1889, a story was published suggesting that she had worked as a maid for his mother. It is possible (though no evidence has been found to substantiate it) that, having fallen for Martha in 1864, Wilkie made his second trip to Lowestoft and Yarmouth the following year to tell her that he had found a position for her in London and to negotiate the terms of her move. It is doubtful that Martha was employed by Harriet Collins, who was already at a peripatetic stage of her life, but, as later happened with her sister Alice, Wilkie could well have found her a position as a domestic servant in the house of one of his professional friends in Marylebone. However, it was not until 20 April 1868, when Wilkie made his first payment to Mrs Wells, Martha's landlady at 33 Bolsover Street, that it can be said with certainty that the Yarmouth barmaid was established in London.

Such a job might have enhanced her appeal, for a feature of mid-Victorian sexuality was that men were often aroused by women in socially inferior positions. The best-known of such fetishists was Arthur Munby, a lawyer turned civil servant who spent his leisure time sketching and collecting information about working girls. Munby kept a detailed diary of his life, from fashionable soirées to trails round the streets in search of women to document. On 23 November 1866, he went to dinner with the Thackeray sisters in Onslow Gardens, where his fellow guests included Charley Collins and his wife Katey, whom Munby found 'a lively pretty little creature, piquante & clever'. Wilkie does not feature in the diary, but Munby is likely to have met him through Charley.

The country was in the middle of a twin crisis by the time Smith, Elder published *Armadale* in two volumes on 18 May 1866. The political world was in turmoil after the introduction of the second

Reform Bill in March. When the government failed to get it through Parliament in June, its leader Lord John Russell resigned. It took one of the most dramatic volte-faces in British politics for the new Conservative Prime Minister, Benjamin Disraeli, to force the measure through fourteen months later. But he could not hold the confidence of the country either, and himself resigned in December 1868.

This mid-century political wobble was reflected in a parallel economic crash. On 'Black Friday', exactly a week before *Armadale* was published, Overend and Gurney, a leading City of London bank, collapsed, causing a knock-on effect that sent interest rates soaring, businesses folding and investors running for cover. Wilkie had a front seat on these events since his new friend Charles Oppenheim was a leading creditor of the bank.

Before the end of the month Wilkie was invited to dinner with the Oppenheims at their grand house in Upper Hamilton Terrace, St John's Wood. His entrée was Charles Oppenheim's wife, Isabelle, the daughter of his artist friend, William Powell Frith. Over the years he had kept in touch with Frith, another Victorian with a complex domestic life. Not satisfied with the seven sons and five daughters produced by his first wife, also called Isabelle, the artist had taken a mistress, Mary Alford, by whom he had seven further children. Frith's second family was greatly resented by his first, causing friends to have to choose between them. Wilkie opted for the first, and, having known them from infancy, kept in touch with the children, including Isabelle, who had married Oppenheim in October 1864.

Oppenheim was a member of an influential international banking family, originally from Frankfurt. An uncle was financier to the Khedive of Egypt, a brother went on to own the *Daily News*, where Pigott worked. In the wake of the Overend and Gurney crash, Charles had emerged as the frontman acting on behalf of the bank's creditors.

A couple of years later, he consolidated his reputation as a safe pair of hands when he proposed the construction of a statue of the late Prince Consort, subsequently erected in Holborn Circus and known as 'the Politest Statue in London' because it showed the Prince doffing his hat. He then went surprisingly quiet: nothing was heard of him after the mid-1870s, and his wife Isabelle was left to bring up their two daughters and present them at court. Wilkie probably got a sense of irregularities at the firm, which he parodies in his 1871 novella *Miss or Mrs?* as the troubled Levantine trading house Pizzituti, Turlington & Branca. Not surprisingly, his social dealings with the Oppenheims did not last into the new decade.

In the middle of these political and economic problems in the summer of 1866, the first reviews of *Armadale* came in, offering the usual range of opinions, with Henry Chorley, Wilkie's old sparring partner on the *Athenaeum*, lambasting a 'most perverse novel'. Wilkie took comfort from the more sympathetic comments of Dickens and Forster on his final chapter, which he had finished in mid-April. Referring to the demise of the scheming Miss Gwilt, the area that caused critics most problems, Forster, the book's dedicatee, called it 'a masterpiece of Art which few indeed have equalled to bring even pity and pathos to the end of such a career as hers.'

In no hurry to start a new book, Wilkie's next project was to produce a theatrical version of *Armadale*, which, as customary, was necessary to deter pirates. Twenty-five copies of the play were published in pink wrappers by Smith, Elder, and there were vague plans to stage the work later in the year. When these were not realised, Wilkie, still eager for renewed theatrical success, took up an offer from Horace Wigan to provide a West End premiere of *The Frozen Deep*, his play originally performed at Tavistock House in January 1857. Horace was the younger brother of Alfred Wigan, Dickens's actor-manager friend who had first recommended that the Ternan family should act in the play when it went on tour in 1857. As far back as 1855, Wilkie had tried to interest him in producing commercial versions of *The Lighthouse* and another of his books (probably the stage-orientated *Basil*) at the Olympic Theatre. Neither idea had come off, but now Horace gathered some financial backers and was also trying his hand as a producer. To this end he had himself taken a lease on the Olympic, where he was keen to put on *The Frozen Deep*, with himself in the part of Lieutenant Crayford. He hoped that the play would come on before Christmas, following the run of *The Whiteboy*, the latest offering from Wilkie's friend, the popular playwright Tom Taylor, whose *The Ticket-of-Leave Man* (1863) had provided Horace Wigan with his most successful role as Inspector Hawkshaw, an early example of the detective story on the stage.

With his gout playing up and making him feel depressed, Wilkie let these business matters run their course, while he got out of town as much as possible in the late summer, visiting his mother, Dickens, Frances Elliot and the Goldsmids, as well as embarking on two sailing trips around the Isle of Wight with Pigott.

As it happened, Taylor's play at the Olympic enjoyed a shorter run than expected, so the production *The Frozen Deep* was brought forward to open there towards the end of October. Still in relaxed post-novel mood, Wilkie was loath to put off a further planned holiday with Pigott on the Continent. So he left Dickens to attend the dress rehearsal and Charles Ward to deal with his business affairs, which included fielding any potential interest in the play from the provinces.

He arranged to spend a day in Paris with Dickens's old friend, François Regnier of the Comédie-Française, who was eager to work with him on a revision of *Armadale* for the French theatre. He and Pigott then proceeded through Switzerland to

Rome. En route they had hoped to stay in Florence with Thomas Trollope, the good-natured brother of the novelist Anthony. But he was unable to receive them at Villa Ricorboli, his rambling house just outside the city, since he was marrying Fanny Ternan, the sister of Dickens's mistress Nelly, in Paris that week.

Wilkie took this alteration to his travel arrangements in his stride, telling Nina Lehmann, the correspondent with whom he tended to be most chatty, 'A woman has got in the way . . . and so, there is an end of the Florence scheme.' He added, 'I don't complain – I am all for Love myself – and this sort of thing speaks volumes for women, for surely a man at a mature age, with a growing daughter, doesn't marry again without knowing what he is about and without remembrances of Mrs. Number One, which surround as with a halo Mrs. Number Two? But this is mere speculation.'

This comment is hard to interpret, given the ups and downs of Wilkie's own romantic life. It suggests that men invest their second wives with an aura related to their predecessors, but whether these are good or bad memories is not clear. Was the spectre of Caroline hanging over his more recent affair with Martha, and forcing him, perhaps, to seek solace abroad? He tried to leave behind such concerns by attending a public ball in Milan, but was disappointed to find it was held in a seedy hall, attended by only a handful of people, including (a feature he disliked) a couple of women smoking cigars. He was more comfortable when he and Pigott reached Rome, and he took his companion to see 'the illustrious' Shelley's grave at the Protestant cemetery. However, his attention was engaged not so much by the ghosts of dead poets but by a black tomcat, which disported itself seductively in the sun and, as told Nina Lehmann, proceeded to pronounce 'in the language of cats: – "Shelley be hanged! Come and tickle me!" I stooped, and tickled him. We were both profoundly affected.'

On his return journey Wilkie had hoped to visit Nina in Pau in south-west France, where, plagued with health problems, she had taken a house for the winter. But again he had to revise his plans, opting to go back to London, after learning that Wigan's production of *The Frozen Deep* had flopped. Although it was still only October, he had already counselled Nina to wrap up well against the cold and not to be afraid to wear thick boots. It was wrong to think that women could not look attractive in such footwear, he declared with an air of authority, adding that men understood such matters, as was evident from the influence of British-born couturier Charles Worth on French fashion. Forced to exclude Pau from his itinerary, he returned home, via Paris, where he snatched a few more hours discussing his new version of *Armadale* with Regnier.

Back in London before Christmas, he was disappointed to find that *The Frozen Deep* had already closed. The reason might have had something to do with the timing: the play had been forced onto the stage at the Olympic in October, rather than taking its turn, as planned, a little later, when it would have benefited from the Christmas market. Another factor was the depressed economy following the business failures associated with Overend and Gurney. Wilkie also blamed his refusal to pander to the masses in the content of the play, while the critics seemed to think it was simply a poor production.

Dickens's old paper, the *Daily News*, frowned on a comment in the playbill reminding the audience that *The Frozen Deep* had originally been performed 'by royal command' before the Queen and the Prince Consort in July 1857. It added, 'Royal commands will not make a successful piece, any more than a Lord Chamberlain's licence will make a well-managed theatre and a moral drama.' This was a political point about the censorship laws, which were being examined by George Goschen's Parliamentary committee for the first time since being tightened in 1843. An irony was that the

Daily News employed Edward Smyth Pigott, who would later become the Censor of Plays.

At this stage in his career, Wilkie might have felt peeved at his lack of theatrical success. But he was not the sort of person to appear downhearted. 'Is my tail put down?' he asked Nina. 'No – a thousand times, No! I am at work on the dramatic "Armadale" – and I will take John Bull by the scruff of the neck, and force him into the theatre to see it – before or after it has been played in French, I don't know which – but into the theatre John Bull shall go.'

He spent Christmas with his mother in Southborough, where he attended a party at his friends', the Salomons. The fact that he was not with Caroline is again indicative of an impasse in their relationship. His family problems continued, as neither his brother nor his sister-in-law Katey was in good health. And if he had hoped that the New Year would bring a boost to his literary fortunes, he received a setback when Smith, Elder declined to renew its six-year licence to carry on publishing six of his earlier novels. Smith, Elder still had the rights to *Armadale*, whose sales had slowed down after a promising start. But the other books, including *The Woman in White*, had not taken off in Smith, Elder's cheap editions. Wilkie good-naturedly declined to blame George Smith, suspecting that Sampson Low, the previous licensee of the copyrights, had flooded the market with its own editions, before selling the licence to Smith, Elder in mysterious circumstances in 1865.

With his instinct for popularisation, Wilkie decided to deal with this rebuff by taking his product downmarket. Stung by suggestions that the dramatised *Frozen Deep* had been too 'slow', he contemplated extending *A Rogue's Life* to make it into a 'lively' two-volume novel that would astonish the 'ideotic [*sic*] British Reader'. He also toyed with turning to the penny journals sold at railway bookstalls to republish some of the books that Smith,

Elder had turned down. He would start with *The Woman in White* and, if that took off, he would boil down *The Lighthouse*, *The Frozen Deep* and *The Red Vial* into one sensational volume for this market. And, as always, he retained his optimism, telling his mother he was full of ideas for new books and plays, and adding (unnecessarily), 'I have got my name and my brains – and I will make a new start, with a new public!'

For the time being he was preoccupied with revising *Armadale* (the play) with Regnier. He was still not sure if the finished product (now running to five acts) would appear in English or French. However, with the Frenchman also keen to collaborate on *The Woman in White*, he inclined to the latter, echoing his earlier articles on the French theatre when he told his mother from Paris, 'Successful play-writing means making a fortune <u>here</u> – and there is no really great French writer now in our way.'

This foolhardy boast meant putting his own immediate literary goals to one side. He was adamant that 'everything that <u>can</u> be sacrificed to the play, <u>must</u> be sacrificed to it. A great chance is open to me – and I must make the best possible use of it.' He made regular sorties to Paris to continue his work with Regnier. Did he, like Dickens, also take his mistress to France? There is no record of such a romantic journey. However, he certainly indulged his physical appetites. One morning in February 1867 he reported that he had breakfasted on 'eggs and black butter, and pigs' feet a la Sainte Ménèhould! Digestion perfect.' For some reason he thought this rich fare might be good for his ailing brother: as he told his mother, with no particular factual basis, 'St Ménèhould lived to extreme old age on nothing but pigs' trotters.' (The reference to the saint was to a rich style of cooking in breadcrumbs practised in a town called after him in the Champagne region.) Charley heard independently about this epicurean existence and concluded that his brother was again suffering from gout. Wilkie told him this was not the case and not to worry. Rather he was enjoying himself – participating in the carnival, meeting writers, and visiting the theatre – and would be unlikely to be back in London in time for his friend George Russell's wedding to Constance Lennox on 5 March 1867.

When he did reappear in Britain a few days later, he was bearing his customary gift for his mother – two pairs of boots, with fashionably high heels, which he reassured her she could shave down. Now it really was time for him to to stop playing the flâneur and begin thinking about his next novel. It was clear from an early stage that his honeymoon with Smith, Elder was over and he would be returning to Dickens's fold, at least to *All the Year Round* for his serial publication. This was more or less set in stone in May when he agreed to collaborate with Dickens on a Christmas number, his first for six years, to be called *No Thoroughfare*.

Before the month was out, he was discussing terms with Dickens and Wills for another project, a new novel, which he was determined would be shorter than the forty-five instalments of *No Name*. The process of serial publication would inevitably be quicker than *Armadale*, since *All the Year Round* was a weekly journal, rather than a monthly like the *Cornhill*. If the first episode appeared in January of the following year, he would expect to be finished by the late summer.

Dickens quickly got the point of *The Moonstone*, as the book would be called. After reading the first three episodes he described it to Wills as 'a very curious story – wild, and yet domestic'. He pinpointed the story's appeal: it again brought the mystery and excitement of the sensation novel into the home – and so helped establish the tradition of English crime novels for years to come. As a result, *All the Year Round* offered £750 for the serialisation rights, with a similar sum to come from *Harper's* in the United States.

Now that professional matters were more or less under control, Wilkie could turn his attention to personal affairs. His mother was not a particular concern as she was settled in Tunbridge Wells. But Charley continued to worry him. Dickens tried his best to look after him – publishing his work, allowing him and Katey to stay at Gad's Hill, and even making an additional marriage settlement on the couple in May. But Charley was still financially strapped. In order to raise money for his brother, Wilkie offered to share their father's remaining paintings between them (the idea being that Charley could sell those he did not want). After tossing a coin to ensure fairness, Charley chose first, but Wilkie was still very satisfied with his pickings, which included a seascape at Sorrento, a study of trees at Pond Street in Hampstead, and a portrait of his grandmother. His friend Frith subsequently came round to make a valuation of the works.

Before Wilkie could relax and go sailing around the Isle of Wight with Pigott and Charles Ward, he had two other domestic matters to attend to. One was the vexed issue of his relationships with Caroline and Martha. But, raddled by his opium consumption, he either proved unable or chose not to deal with it. The other was more practical since the lease on Melcombe Place was shortly due to run out. He had had his eye on somewhere in Cornwall Terrace, but in the end he opted for a large five-storey house at 90 Gloucester Place, which led northwards from Oxford Street to Regent's Park skirting his native Marylebone. Since it was a fairly busy road, it was a surprising choice for a man so fastidious about noise, which bothered him even in secluded Melcombe Place. But by the end of August, he had paid £800 to buy the lease, and hired a crew of workmen. And by then he was at last making good progress on his new novel.

14

DETECTION AND ALL CHANGE

DETECTIVE STORIES HAD a history. Some commentators look back to Voltaire's *Zadig* or even the Biblical Book of Daniel, but, leaving aside the true-life crime that appeared in the *Newgate Calendar* and fuelled the penny press, a good starting date for the modern fictional version was 1841, when Edgar Allan Poe's *The Murders in the Rue Morgue* established many of the features of the genre – the closed environment (the forerunner of the 'locked room' beloved of Agatha Christie's Miss Marple), the brilliant if eccentric sleuth, the bumbling constabulary, and the overall account given by a friend.

During the 1860s such stories proliferated, in parallel with the growth of the popular press and its appetite for accounts of murder. They slotted into the publishing catalogue as a well-defined branch of sensation fiction, with Mary Elizabeth Braddon again leading the way with *The Trail of the Serpent* in 1860. They invaded the theatre in plays such as Tom Taylor's *The Ticket-of-Leave Man*. Wilkie, with his keen cultural antennae, was already ahead of the game and had made detection an important part of the plot in several works of fiction, including *The Woman in White* and *Armadale*. Only in September 1867 he had sent his mother a copy of *The Female Detective* by Andrew Forrester, which featured a woman sleuth.

By now, the detective story, like sensation fiction in general, had become popular enough to provoke a backlash. In a petulant essay in the conservative *Saturday Review* in 1864, James Fitzjames Stephen argued that 'this detective-worship appears one of the silliest superstitions that ever were concocted by ingenious writers.' He was unhappy about the way fictional detectives assumed almost godlike powers that enabled them to visualise a whole sequence of events from a single clue. He felt it was more like guesswork than the proper sifting of evidence that went on in an established court of law.

Such polemics provided Wilkie with the spur to enter the fray with a full-scale detective novel, since Fitzjames Stephen was engaging with the ongoing debate about the nature of evidence, which provided much of the theoretical underpinning for Wilkie's work. As his father's son, he had observed painters trying to represent different aspects of reality. As a writer, he transferred this concern to the page as he struggled to find ways to express the truth of an event. Did it emerge by consensus, something teased out from different points of view, as in a court of law – the premise of *The Woman in White*? And how much could any observation, let alone an account, of an incident be relied on?

These questions went to the heart of nineteenth-century ideas about observation and knowledge. By the 1860s, scientists and philosophers were suggesting that the eye was not necessarily a trustworthy instrument. Their old model for sight, derived from Locke, suggested the eye was a tabula rasa that directly absorbed sensory data reaching the retina. But this had been superseded by a reinterpretation of the ideas of George Berkeley and Kant, which put the observer (not the mechanical eye) at the centre of the process. According to this approach, one does not actually see an object; instead one's mind infers what it is on the basis of previous experience and other inputs.

This introduces an element of uncertainty Wilkie was quick to latch onto for his literary purposes.

This way of looking at the world had ramifications for other aspects of his output, such as ghost stories. Earlier commentators, including Walter Scott, had regarded sightings of ghosts as optical illusions, which could be explained as manifestations of the eye not working correctly. But, in line with the latest 'associationist' theories of cognition, Wilkie's friend G.H. Lewes now argued, 'When a man avers that he has "seen a ghost", he is passing far beyond the limits of visible fact, into that of inference. He saw *something* which he *supposed* to be a ghost.' Similarly, madness was being reinterpreted: once regarded as the failure of a fevered mind to process outside stimuli, its causes were now seen as much more subjective.

Reflecting the way that man, rather than God, was taking centre stage in cosmology and history, the individual was now the master of his universe in matters of cognition. But this brought uncertainties. As John Stuart Mill, the archetypal Victorian philosopher, put it, 'What we are said to perceive is usually a compound result, of which one tenth may be observation, and the remaining 9/10ths inference.'

All this was exciting for a writer of detective stories – and particularly a clever one like Wilkie – willing to play with and gently subvert the genre. One consequence of the associationist approach was to give weight to the interpretation of events. And, as would become clearer later in the century, notably with Arthur Conan Doyle's Sherlock Holmes, the detective's business was to discover the true course of events by interpreting signs or clues. Another result of associationism, one that affected the man in the street as much as the detective, was that everyone's interpretation could be questioned. There was no absolute truth, for, as Lewes would later put it, 'With inference begins error.' The concept of inference, which was virtually interchangeable with interpretation, added to the uncertainty, since it bordered on intuition, and from there it was but a small step to telepathy and even spiritualism. Such was the direction of psychology and philosophy, always well monitored by Dickens and Wilkie in the pages of *All the Year Round*.

The Moonstone is basically a locked-room mystery about the theft of a much-revered Indian gem from an English country house. However, nothing is that simple in a Wilkie Collins novel. There was an earlier theft: the jewel had originally been looted by British forces at the siege of Seringapatam in 1799. The search for its whereabouts by three Brahmins continues in parallel to the mid-Victorian detective story, giving it an aura of exoticism. The Indian holy men's techniques of clairvoyance add a para-normal dimension to Wilkie's exploration of knowledge, while their ritual retribution brings a karmic frisson to another theme that plays throughout Wilkie's work – the nature of revenge and punishment.

The magnificent yellow gem is bequeathed by the looter to his niece, Rachel Verinder, on her eighteenth birthday, and brought to her family's sumptuous country house in Yorkshire by her cousin Franklin Blake. However, on the night of her birthday, her new present goes missing from her bedroom cabinet. The local police superintendent does little to advance the case, except by establishing an enduring trope for such stories with his bungling inquiries. Her mother calls in Inspector Cuff from Scotland Yard, who conducts an investigation along modern professional lines. He inspires everyone with 'detective fever' as he sets about his business. When a smear on the paint of Rachel's bedroom door is discovered, the local man dismisses it as a 'trifle', causing Cuff to respond dismissively, 'In all my experience . . . I have never met with such a thing as a trifle yet.' He resolves to find the piece of clothing that shows evidence of brushing the door and creating the smear. Initially, the suspicion falls on the troupe of mysterious Indian jugglers (the three Brahmins in search of the gem) who have been in the vicinity. But when Rachel's maid, Rosanna, a hunchback with a criminal past, is found to have taken a garment for laundering in the nearby village, the finger points to her.

The investigation only progresses when Franklin Blake returns to the scene of the crime (Frizinghall, based on Monckton Milnes's house Fryston Hall in Yorkshire) and discovers that Rosanna has hidden the tell-tale garment in quicksand on the coast. But when he alights on this vital item of clothing, he realises that it is his own night-shirt and thus, by deduction, he must be the culprit. Rachel then confirms that she had indeed observed him taking the diamond, and, since she (like Rosanna) is in love with Blake, this explains her earlier reluctance to co-operate with Cuff.

Among several well-realised subsidiary characters is Mr Candy, a doctor, who attended the house party celebrating Rachel's birthday, where he argued with Blake about the powers of modern medicine – he advocating the latest procedures and drugs, and Blake provocatively dismissing them all as hocus-pocus. However, after Blake admitted suffering from insomnia, Candy, wanting to prove his point, slipped some laudanum into the young visitor's drink. (This was later ascertained at the medical man's deathbed, in a hazy statement taken down by his assistant, Ezra Jennings.)

The drug proves the vital ingredient in unravelling the mystery. With 'his gipsy-complexion', 'dreamy eyes' and murky past, Jennings is very much the outsider in such social situations. It turns out that he himself is an opium addict, which allows him to suggest an alternative way of solving the fate of the

Moonstone. If Blake were to recreate the circumstances of the night of the theft by taking laudanum, he might go through his exact motions again and so reveal what had happened. As a learned, if unorthodox, practitioner, he quotes the associationist physiologists, Drs John Elliotson and William Carpenter, in his support. Elliotson, who had treated Wilkie earlier in the decade, had written of an Irish porter who could only remember his actions when drunk by becoming drunk again. Carpenter, more theoretically, had reported, 'There seems much ground for the belief, that every sensory impression which has once been recognised by the perceptive consciousness, is registered (so to speak) in the brain, and may be reproduced at some subsequent time, although there may be no consciousness of its existence in the mind during the whole intermediate period.' So, under the influence of laudanum, Blake in *The Moonstone* relives the events of that fateful night. As a result, it becomes clear where he put the diamond for safe keeping, and that another guest, the apparently upright Godfrey Ablewhite, has stolen it to pay off his debts.

Wilkie was drawing on his own experience of the drug. He was also straying into a contentious area of psychology – the power of the unconscious mind, which can be both a wellspring of truth and a source of enough bizarre behaviour to wrong-foot the most rational detective. However, as Jennings shows, its secrets can, under the right conditions, be accessed and interpreted, even if it requires a process of inference.

Secrets were, of course, a favourite literary commodity of Wilkie's. In *The Moonstone* he sought to explore the inside of a well-ordered country house (whose occupants resented any intrusion), while throwing light on not only a robbery but the processes of the unconscious mind. He was reprising several other regular themes, such as the position of women. Rachel Verinder and her maid Rosanna enjoy an important relationship at the centre of his story – the former proving to be a vapid heiress who is weaker than her much disadvantaged maid. Looking back to the scene in *No Name* where Magdalen Vanstone swapped roles with her servant Louisa, this again hinted at the iniquities of a social system that excluded Caroline Graves and Martha Rudd.

In touching on class in Victorian society, the novel is generally caustic. Rosanna pines for Franklin Blake, but clearly cannot have him. After her death, when he is informed of her unrequited passion for him, he casually remarks, 'I never noticed her.' In this hierarchic world she simply did not exist. Little wonder that her friend, Limping Lucy, another outcast, predicts that 'the day is not far off when the poor will rise against the rich.'

While not advocating revolution, Wilkie was affirming his dislike of any form of oppression, as was also apparent in his representation of the colonial aspects of his story. Although the Moonstone serves as a symbol of upheaval – the 'cursed Diamond' which 'cast a blight on the whole company' – he, unlike Dickens, treats Indians and the Hindu religion with respect: the Brahmins behave with dignity as they go about finding the Moonstone in England, and it is fitting that the gem is eventually restored to its rightful place in the Indian holy city of Somnauth.

In this way, as in discovering what really happened in Rachel Verinder's room, the novel reaches a satisfactory conclusion. However, this resolution does not come through Inspector Cuff's conventional, rational, mid-Victorian sleuthing methods. The restitution of the Moonstone results from a religiously inspired quest, while the mystery of the theft is arrived at in an unorthodox manner, which involves tapping Blake's unconscious memory and reliving the incident. On the surface, the book's various narrators offer different perspectives on events, and so, as in a court of law, increase the possibilities of arriving at the truth. But it remains an elusive commodity. As Blake, who has picked up some of this intellectual background while studying in Germany, puts it, 'One interpretation is just as likely to be right as the other.' Wilkie orchestrates this debate on the nature of evidence with humour and verve. It is easy to see why *The Moonstone* has been claimed as a modernist (or proto-modernist) novel.

Wilkie did not need to do much research on the British aspects of the novel, but, as a writer who prided himself on the veracity of detail, he worked hard to ensure that the Indian side of his story was correct. He ended up taking even more pains than usual. With the help of the Athenaeum Club library, he consulted many books on precious stones, the Hindu religion and the history of India, as well as the eighth edition of the *Encyclopaedia Britannica*. When he took some of these volumes home, Caroline copied out relevant passages to act as aides-memoire.

With a nice sense of synchronicity, diamonds were in the news. New, potentially vast, deposits had recently been discovered in South Africa, from where the Eureka diamond was sent to the Paris Exhibition of 1867. Before long these sources would bring diamonds within the purchasing power of the well-off middle classes. In his preface to *The Moonstone*, Wilkie recorded how he based the eponymous jewel on the histories of two massive diamonds, both originally from India, that ended up in distant royal collections – the Orloff diamond, part of the Russian crown jewels, and the Koh-i-Noor, or Mountain of Light, which was presented to Queen Victoria following the defeat of the Sikh kingdom in the Punjab in 1849 and which was shown at the Great Exhibition a couple of years later.

Wilkie took his information where he could find it, and there was another source closer to home. In her book *Swallowfield and its Owners*, Lady Constance Russell suggested that his interest in precious stones might at least in part have derived from accounts of the extraordinary 410-carat Pitt Diamond that he heard of when visiting Swallowfield Park, the Berkshire estate of her husband, George Russell. This gem had been owned by Thomas 'Diamond' Pitt, an East India Company nabob (and great-grandfather of the Prime Minister, William Pitt) who lived at Swallowfield at the start of the eighteenth century, before the property passed in 1820 to Sir George's father, Sir Henry Russell, the former Chief Justice of Bengal, whom the Collinses had met in Italy.

This theory is entirely plausible since, only in September 1866, Wilkie had written to Lady Constance, under her maiden name of Miss Lennox, sending her photographs of himself (taken by Elliot and Fry) and signing off 'with kindest remembrances to all at Swallowfield'. (It was not until the following March that she married George Russell, Wilkie's barrister friend from the Garrick Club, who was often at Swallowfield, though he did not inherit it until the death of his bachelor brother Charles in 1883.)

Wilkie was in a mellow mood as he settled at his desk in his new house in Gloucester Place one evening in mid-September 1867. He had just returned from dining with Dickens at the Athenaeum, the temperature had been in the mid-sixties that day, and the smell of paint was still in the air. So the windows were open, allowing a kitten to stray into the drawing room and drape itself around him. He admitted that having it 'galloping over' his back and shoulders made 'writing difficult'. But, like the cat in the Protestant cemetery in Rome, animals tended to gravitate towards him, and he usually reciprocated. Before long a Scottish terrier called Tommy was added to the household.

By the end of the month the carpenters and painters had finished their work, the prints and paintings were on the walls, and Wilkie was enjoying the spaciousness of his new home. To ensure his creature comforts, he hired three new servants, two of them women, whom he provided with new 'gowns'. His centre of operations was a double drawing room, dominated by a large writing table with a smaller inlaid desk, similar to the one used by Dickens. There was a separate study and a large, airy bedroom. The building was constructed on dry soil, which Wilkie, like his father before him, seemed to think was good for his health. At the back was a stable which was surplus to requirements, so he was able to let it out at £40 a year.

Not everyone loved the result. Visiting some years later, the novelist Hall Caine found it 'large and rather dingy. The walls were panelled, the stairs were of stone, the hall was cold, and the whole house cheerless,' even if it was hung with 'pictures of the greatest interest'.

At the end of October, Wilkie gathered various friends for a dinner that was both a house warming and a farewell to Dickens, who was shortly embarking on a much-mooted speaking tour of North America. Because of this imminent departure, Wilkie was not able to spend much time on *The Moonstone*. Instead, the two friends were busily discussing their collaboration on *No Thoroughfare* for the Christmas number of *All the Year Round*. The plot of this new story resembled *The Frozen Deep* in that it centred on two rivals who confront each other in harsh foreign climes – in this case, an avalanche on the Simplon Pass into Switzerland (a route Wilkie had travelled in the past). Jules Obenreizer was the thieving London agent of a Swiss wine supplier; George Vendale, a new recruit to the firm, who had fallen in love with Obenreizer's niece. Add in issues about birth and legitimacy, and present the resulting melodrama in the form of an overture and three acts, and they had a cliffhanger (often literally) that would transfer easily to the stage. After the idea had been raised at their dinner at the Athenaeum in September, Wilkie regularly dashed to Gad's Hill to confer with Dickens on the story. His patient and reliable friend Charles Ward helped by copying each instalment for sending to Harper's in New York.

After the gathering at Wilkie's, Dickens was feted at further farewell dinners – one a grand event, chaired by Bulwer-Lytton (with Wilkie as a steward), for 450 people at the Freemason's Hall; another a more intimate occasion hosted by Frank Beard, whose wife Louisa had recently died. Even so, Dickens insisted that Wilkie accompany him and a small party to Liverpool to see him off on his transatlantic liner on 9 November.

Only two days later, Wilkie was invited to dinner by his friend's estranged wife Catherine in Gloucester Crescent, Camden Town. This was curious, as it gave the impression that their meeting had been held off until after Dickens's departure. However, Wilkie had always tried to stay on good terms with Catherine, not least because she was his brother's mother-in-law.

Wilkie was left with several responsibilities by Dickens. One was to help Wills with 'conducting' the magazine. Another was to work with the experienced actor-manager Benjamin Webster on adapting *No Thoroughfare* for the theatre in time for Christmas. The story had been written with this end in mind, with Charles Fechter slated for the lead role of Obenreizer. As soon as he and Webster completed each section, Wilkie would send it for comment and alteration to Dickens, who was enjoying extraordinary acclaim in America. At the end of November, Wilkie was juggling this responsibility with reading the first proofs of *The Moonstone*, which was due to start appearing in *All the Year Round* and *Harper's Weekly* on 4 January. At the same time he had to keep writing regular instalments of his novel, so as to ensure that he was always ahead of the printers. No wonder he told his mother that he had never worked so hard in his life.

Despite this punishing schedule he was able to snatch a couple of days off to spend Christmas with his ailing mother in Tunbridge Wells. He always brought her something to drink – some brandy or wine – and, as festive offerings, he added some eau de cologne and some chocolate that Charley had purchased in Paris. On Boxing Day he was back in London to see the first night of *No Thoroughfare* at the Adelphi Theatre in the Strand. Although it had now grown to six acts and ran for four hours, it was enthusiastically received. The consensus was that it was rather better than the published serial, which was too obviously written by two different hands. His capacity for self-promotion undiminished, Wilkie was soon writing to a producer in San Francisco offering him West Coast rights to the work.

On 3 January 1868, he was again in Southborough, where his mother had moved to Bentham Hill Cottage, closer to the Potts, so she could be better cared for. A couple of weeks later he was telling her that he was halfway through *The Moonstone*, but the following day he admitted to Holman Hunt that she was 'sinking' and he had to drop everything to return to her bedside. He called in Frank Beard to tend her and did his best to share caring duties with Charley, but he found he had to work in London, which came as something of a relief. 'I am (luckily) obliged to work,' he told Hunt, 'in other words obliged to resist the suspense and distress of this anxious time. All the leisure I can spare from my mother, must be devoted to my book.'

The relentless pressure got to him, and before long he was immobilised by an excruciatingly painful combination of rheumatism and gout. As a result he could not travel when, with cruel inevitability, his mother died on the morning of 19 March. Nor could he attend her funeral at Speldhurst on the 25th. He was gratified that Holman Hunt was able to represent him and support Charley, who made the arrangements.

This failure compounded his feeling of uselessness and exacerbated his pain. He described his mother's death to George Russell as the 'bitterest affliction of my life – and a pang has been added to that affliction by my miserable inability to follow her to the grave.' This did not mean he felt suicidal, but that he was mortified at being unable to see her laid to rest.

Back in Gloucester Place, his aggravated stress meant that he was unable to write and had to call on the services of an amanuensis, probably young Harriet Graves. As he recalled in a second preface to *The Moonstone* in 1871, 'At the time when my mother lay dying in her little cottage in the country, I was struck prostrate, in London – crippled in every limb by the torture of rheumatic gout.' But, always aware of his duty to his public and taking pride in the fact that he had never missed a deadline, he remembered, 'In the intervals of grief, in the occasional remissions of pain, I dictated from my bed that portion of *The Moonstone* which has since proved most successful in amusing the public – the "Narrative of Miss Clack."' (She was a hypocrite who went around distributing Bible tracts with titles such as 'Satan under the Tea Table'.)

Once again work proved a solace and helped him overcome his pain and grief, for he added, 'Of the physical sacrifice which the effort cost me I shall say nothing. I only look back now at the blessed relief which my occupation (forced as it was) brought to my mind. The Art which had been always the pride and the pleasure of my life became now more than ever "its own exceeding great reward".'

Wilkie struggled through the next couple of months and somehow finished the physical task of writing *The Moonstone* at the end of June. As Dickens was back from America, he was able to oversee *L'Abîme*, a French version of *No Thoroughfare* for the theatre, and he made no secret that he thought it was superior to Wilkie and Webster's English-language effort. The last instalment of *The Moonstone* appeared in *All the Year Round* and *Harper's Weekly* on 8 August, by which time the book had been published in a three-volume edition by Tinsley Brothers, a specialist in sensation novels, who had enjoyed great success earlier in the decade with Mary Elizabeth Braddon's *Lady Audley's Secret*. Wilkie was probably drawn to the firm by a combination of this track record and his friendship with Edmund Yates, who had recently gone into partnership with the firm to edit *Tinsley's Magazine*, a self-professed 'illustrated monthly magazine of light literature' which was the latest challenger to the *Cornhill* magazine and *Temple Bar* for the bookish middle-class market.

After a couple of lukewarm reviews of *The Moonstone* in the *Athenaeum*, which referred to the 'sordid detective element', and the *Spectator*, which judged the book 'not worthy of Mr Wilkie Collins's reputation as a novelist', critical reaction, spurred by an anonymous notice in *The Times*, was generally positive, even if, to Wilkie's disgust, Mudie's took only five hundred copies, a drop of 75 per cent on *Armadale*. As it was, the first edition of 1,500 copies quickly sold out. William Tinsley, the publisher, recorded how 'even the porters and boys were interested in the story, and read the new number in sly corners, and often with their packs on their backs,' whereas *The Woman in White* had rather gone over their heads.

A second edition of 500 soon followed. By then, however, relations between publisher and author had broken down over money. Wilkie even tried to acquire Tinsley's blocks of type and have this edition published elsewhere. His concerns were not unreasonable since Tinsley Brothers had a reputation for sharp practice. Indeed, when they ran into financial difficulties, Yates soon moved on, and Wilkie never returned to them after this book. It is surprising that a man with his knowledge of the book business should have entered what from all accounts was a flimsy agreement with this particular publisher at this stage of his career. One reason might have been that, as would soon become apparent, he was now estranged from his solicitor, Ebenezer Benham, who had overseen the negotiations with Tinsley, as well as other efforts to reach a wider market through, for example, a penny edition of *The Woman in White*.

Once the task of writing was over, Wilkie was able at last to catch up on other matters in his life. One of his first moves in early July was to book an appointment with his dentist, George Gregson, who was also his landlord when he lived in Harley Street. In a small notebook (which survives in the New York Public Library) he drew up a list of people to visit and those to receive copies of his book. It contains no real surprises: both Russell brothers (of Swallowfield) are there, as well as Mrs Elliot and a note to 'return Indian books' to Pigott.

Otherwise, the main interest was a note of items to collect, including a gold locket and watch key, for which he paid the South Audley Street jeweller Tessier £15 7s on 20 July. The locket was important because it was a memento of his mother, containing her portrait on one side and a lock of hair (presumably hers) on the other. He would later give it to Martha.

Wilkie's respite from work did not mean his problems were over. Charley continued to worry him. He was staying with his father-in-law at Gad's Hill, from where came news that he had been vomiting profusely and seemed on the point of death. Wilkie became so alarmed that he asked his brother's doctor, Henri de Mussy, if he and Beard could accompany him on his next visit to Gad's Hill.

Wilkie also had unusually pressing financial concerns, the catalyst being the Weston-super-Mare doctor Joseph Stringfield, who had contacted him a couple of years earlier at Harley Street. Since this address was by then already eighteen months out of date, they cannot have seen much of one another. Nevertheless, Wilkie replied positively, sending his 'kindest remembrances' to Mrs Stringfield and his 'love' to their daughter Florry.

Wilkie's good wishes were misplaced, as became clear when Stringfield's wife Mary sued him for divorce in December 1866, citing charges of drunkenness and cruelty towards her and their three children. The doctor's case was not helped when, the following June, he threatened to kill the solicitor conducting Mary's case. He seems to have been treated leniently on this score, perhaps because Wilkie stood bail on a surety of £250. The divorce court judge had no hesitation in granting Mary a judicial separation, with costs and custody of the children. But when Stringfield counter-sued, he got into financial difficulties and was unable to pay her what he owed. As a result, by June 1868, Wilkie became worried about his bail money and asked Benham for advice.

He does not seem to have paid anything out, and Stringfield died shortly afterwards. However, Wilkie had another financial matter to resolve with his solicitor. The previous summer, when he had needed to raise £800 to buy the lease on Gloucester Place, he had borrowed the money from a client of Benham's. Why he did this is unclear, since his Coutts account had a healthy surplus – £1,931 in April 1867 and £2,301 in January 1868. Nevertheless, for all his earning power, he was always worried about financial affairs. Only a few weeks before his mother died, he had asked her to sign a document which would ensure that, after her death, he and Charley would have no problems inheriting and passing on their half-shares in £5,000, which had been left by her aunt, Mary (Easton) Davis. Harriet did not make a will, since, as was enshrined in the law of the time, she had no assets of her own and no property; all her money coming from her interest in her late husband's estate.

Since 'Aunt Davis's' inheritance (or the prospect of it) had been used to guarantee Wilkie's loan for the house, his solicitor Benham did not wait long after Harriet's death before issuing a writ (or distringas) threatening to distrain this money. This seems to have been remarkably bad manners on his part, but Wilkie took it in his stride, resolving to settle the matter before going abroad in August. His bank records confirm that he paid Benham £800 on his return at the end of the following month.

Benham's precipitate action may have been caused by his own urgent need to raise money to save a business in which Dickens's son Charley was involved. That same August, the Kennet Paper Making Company was wound up in the High Court at the request of Edward (as he now liked to call himself instead of Ebenezer) Benham, of Isleworth, who was a creditor and shareholder (as was Charley Dickens). The managing director of the firm went bankrupt later in the year.

Wilkie seems to have been an entirely innocent party, but the incident soured his relations with Benham, whose partner William Tindell took over his affairs from around this date. It also affected his friendship with Dickens, who became appreciably cooler towards him. It was sad if, after all their shared experience, the two men fell out over money. But there were other factors. Perhaps feeling aggrieved, Dickens reversed his opinion of *The Moonstone*, describing it to Wills as 'wearisome beyond endurance' in construction, 'and there is a vein of obstinate conceit in it that makes enemies of readers'. He was also, perhaps unfairly, critical of what he considered Wilkie's blinkered approach to his brother Charley's physical well-being. As he told Wills, 'It is a part of the bump in Wilkie's forehead that he *will not* allow his brother to be very ill . . . The obstinacy of said

Wilkie is something perfectly inconceivable. His bodily condition is robust health, when compared with his mental.'

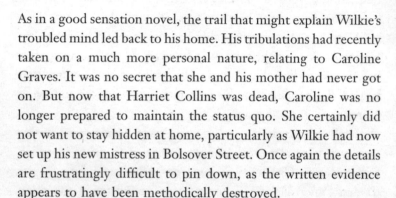

As in a good sensation novel, the trail that might explain Wilkie's troubled mind led back to his home. His tribulations had recently taken on a much more personal nature, relating to Caroline Graves. It was no secret that she and his mother had never got on. But now that Harriet Collins was dead, Caroline was no longer prepared to maintain the status quo. She certainly did not want to stay hidden at home, particularly as Wilkie had now set up his new mistress in Bolsover Street. Once again the details are frustratingly difficult to pin down, as the written evidence appears to have been methodically destroyed.

What is clear is that Caroline quit Gloucester Place, and on 29 October she surprised everyone by walking up the aisle at St Mary's parish church in Marylebone on the arm of Joseph Charles Clow – the son of a distiller's agent – who was aged twenty-three. She was thirty-seven and quite what she saw in this mere stripling is hard to determine.

She must have known her new husband for a while. He cannot have appeared out of the blue after Harriet Collins's death. He had probably been in the wings since Wilkie first took up with Martha four years earlier. But how had Caroline become friendly with him? His upwardly mobile family gives little clue. Having grown rich from selling liquor and then in property, the Clows now lived in some style on the north side of Regent's Park on Avenue Road, where the Collinses once had a house. Joseph Charles's London-born father, also called Joseph, first surfaced in the public records as a 'proprietor of houses', while visiting relations in the Leicestershire village of Great Easton in 1851. At the time, when newly married Caroline

Graves had just given birth to her first child, Joseph Charles was five and living with his mother in the family house in Kentish Town. By 1861 the Clows had moved to a better address in Kentish Town and the boy's father was working as a commercial traveller and distiller. Five years later they were ensconced at 2 Avenue Road.

However, the paterfamilias – and the probable reason for Caroline's knowing them – was Joseph's cousin Leonard, who lived and worked in Fitzrovia, close to where Caroline had lodged on her return to London in 1852. She had then been at Charlton Street, around the corner from Leonard Clow, a 'spirit and wine merchant' at 22 Grafton Street. He later moved to nearby Russell Place, and kept a number of off-licences, all within walking distance of Fitzroy Square.

After marrying the daughter of a Cheltenham music seller, Leonard became a respected member of the community. He was involved in local politics and, from the early 1860s, was secretary and treasurer of the Fitzroy Market ragged school – a thankless task since, until the introduction of state education in 1870, such establishments stood at the bottom of the pecking order after private, endowed, Church and national schools.

Caroline's relationship with Wilkie had been problematic for some time, and it had not been improved by the arrival of Martha. Dickens throws more light than anyone on Caroline's brittle character. Reading between the lines of his letters, she must at some stage have given Wilkie an ultimatum: he should either marry her or face the consequences. This could have happened at any time after 1864. But this year in particular he was in no frame of mind to be cajoled. By the summer she had decamped, leaving Wilkie to seek refuge with the Lehmanns in Highgate, before departing for Switzerland and Germany in August. Frederick Lehmann was to have accompanied him, but he was initially detained by business and was only able to join

Wilkie later in the Black Forest resort of Baden-Baden, where he had travelled with his son Rudolph. At one stage while they were together, Frederick Lehmann had to trail round four chemists in one town in order to obtain enough laudanum to satisfy Wilkie's habit (the limit that each outlet was allowed to prescribe not being enough).

By now, with his usual insouciance (aided by amnesiac qualities of opium in various forms), Wilkie's mind was onto other things. He was thinking of his next book, *Man and Wife*, which has been described as his first ostensibly didactic novel. Here, he again added his voice – surprisingly, given his situation – to the demand for reform of Britain's matrimonial laws. A new Liberal government under William Gladstone had been returned to power at the start of the year, and John Stuart Mill would publish his powerful treatise 'The Subjugation of Women' a few months later. One result was the Married Women's Property Act of 1870, which, for the first time, would allow women to own money and property.

Wilkie chose to focus on a couple of other anomalies in the matrimonial laws, which varied in England, Scotland and Ireland. By October, he was asking his solicitor Benham (they were still communicating) about the complexities of the ongoing Yelverton case, in which a Protestant Irish aristocrat exploited a century-old statute that nullified any marriage involving a member of his religion if the ceremony had been conducted by a Catholic priest. Major William Yelverton, later Viscount Avonmore, tried to use this legislation to revoke his marriage in Ireland to a Catholic woman, to justify not paying her any maintenance, and to seek to marry another woman. One of the endless legal actions in the dispute took place in an Edinburgh court, which, under Scottish law, allowed marriages to be solemnised on the declaration of the two participants without the need for intervention by any priest. This was not the case in England, a difference around which Wilkie would spin an important aspect of the plot of *Man and Wife*. This particular anomaly was also dealt with in the 1870 Marriage Act, so his novel did not lack for up-to-the-minute detail.

Wilkie now took a more relaxed attitude to Caroline's departure from his life. He attended her wedding to Clow in Marylebone parish church, and his friend and doctor, Francis Beard, was on hand to sign the register as a witness. As Harriet had recently finished her schooling (Wilkie signed the last cheque for £75 on 15 July 1868), she stayed on at Gloucester Place, swapping roles with her mother as Wilkie's secretary and housekeeper. In return, he helped Caroline get established in her new matrimonial home, paying her a small sum in December 1868, followed by a more substantial sum of £50 in June the following year.

Wilkie was no doubt relieved to have more time with Martha in Bolsover Street. In early October, a few weeks before Caroline's wedding, he impregnated his young mistress with his first child, who would be born the following July.

Dickens was not able to attend Caroline's wedding, since he was away on a reading tour. He clearly knew about it since, on 25 October, he wrote to Wills from the Adelphi Hotel, Liverpool, acknowledging his colleague's excited news about the forthcoming ceremony, and adding, 'Let me communicate another point of interest which may not have reached you – Frank Beard will give away the Ber-ri-i-ide!'

However, even Dickens's knowledge of the nuptials was limited. For, four days later, on the day of the marriage, Dickens wrote (still from Liverpool) to Georgina Hogarth, 'Wilkie's affairs defy all prediction. For any thing one knows, the whole matrimonial pretence may be a lie of that woman's, intended to make him marry her, and (contrary to her expectations) breaking down at last.' In other words, Caroline may have tried emotional blackmail on Wilkie, but failed. She was clearly not popular in the Dickens household. But, for all Wilkie's coolness at this stage, the tensions of the relationship must have taken a fearful toll on him when his mother was dying and he was working so hard on *The Moonstone*.

Years later, Dickens's daughter and Wilkie's former sister-in-law Katey put a different spin on events when she told her friend and biographer Mrs Storey, 'Wilkie had a mistress Caroline with whom he lived for twenty years & then she married & afterwards Collins said to her I suppose you could not marry a man who had ----- & she said "No".' Katey's statement, recorded thus in Mrs Storey's diary, with its tantalising omissions, suggests that Caroline precipitated the break-up, since there was something about him that prevented her marrying him. What could she have been referring to? She might simply have meant 'a mistress' or 'another woman', or, conceivably, a medical condition, perhaps a recurring venereal disease. Either way, it seems that she wanted a formalisation of their relationship, and he refused or she did not think he was up to it.

Wilkie typically stayed mum. If, as Dickens had detected, he had shown emotional obtuseness in his attitude towards his brother Charley, he was not now going to make a fuss about a breakdown in his sexual ménage. Instead he moved to draw a decisive line under the matter and, from November, as noted in the records of the parish of St Marylebone, it was he, rather than Caroline, who now paid the rates on the house in Gloucester Place.

15

BECOMING A FATHER

S INCE CAROLINE HAD played only a peripheral part in his life for some time, and since he generally preferred a bachelor existence, Wilkie's day-to-day schedule barely changed as a result of her wedding. He had a pregnant girlfriend living less than a mile away but he did not let this concern him too much. After publication of *The Moonstone*, he went through his usual round of literary housekeeping duties, such as arranging foreign translations. Although the book sold well in Britain, it did not prevent Tinsley from suffering financial problems, and Wilkie had to be tough about obtaining payments which were frequently late.

Following his mother's death, his bank balance was again looking healthier, as indeed was Charley's. The two brothers could now inherit under their father's will, which meant sharing some £16,000 in various securities, as well as just under £2,000 in further assets. With these investments to fall back on, Wilkie had, by the end of September, added to his portfolio with his own purchases of around £1,500 worth of Russian and US bonds, as well as Indian railway stocks. Casting aside his occasional frugality, he was again able to spend freely on clothes, drink and items such as the locket he commissioned in memory of his mother. With an amazing lack of rancour, he continued to subsidise both Caroline and her daughter, while Martha also began receiving modest sums towards the end of 1869.

He was now more reliant than ever on the Lehmanns for his social life. They had moved from Westbourne Terrace to an imposing town house in Berkeley Square, but they also liked to spend time at Woodlands in Muswell Hill. Still obsessed by the theatre, Wilkie invited the vivacious Nina Lehmann to join him at a pantomime at the start of 1869 at the revamped Marylebone Theatre (now named the Royal Alfred in honour of the Queen's second son). She had been hoping to employ his cook, but this proved not possible, as he had just sacked her. 'She has done all sorts of dreadful things,' he explained. 'Alas! such but too frequently is the fatal gift of Genius!' He offered his own services, in the absence of any obvious alternative, but warned that his style was expensive since he looked 'on meat simply as a material for sauces'.

The following month Wilkie accompanied Elizabeth Benzon (Frederick's sister) to a concert of Schumann's work at St James's Hall in Regent Street. He did not enjoy himself, bluntly informing his fellow guest, 'Herr Schumann's music, Madame Schumann's playing, and the atmosphere of St James's Hall, are three such afflictions as I never desire to feel again.'

He had reason to feel grumpy since he was trying to wean himself off laudanum, and believed he could do this by injecting himself with morphine. As he told Mrs Benzon, 'My doctor is trying to break me of the habit of drinking laudanum. I am stabbed every night at ten with a sharp-pointed syringe which injects morphia under my skin – and gets me a night's rest without any of the drawbacks of taking opium internally.' He believed that, if he persevered, he would be 'able, before long, gradually to diminish the quantity of morphia and the number of the nightly stabbings – and so emancipate myself from opium altogether.'

Morphine was a modern drug and injection the latest means of taking it. Its synthesis at the start of the century had been a triumph for rational scientific endeavour, and for organic chemistry in particular. It was a pure and consistent substance, unlike laudanum, which was unreliable and more of a vehicle for the dreams of poets. Morphine's delivery had been greatly improved by the development of the hypodermic needle in the 1850s. As a result, it was widely used for pain relief in both the Crimean War and the American Civil War. Like methadone in the twentieth century, it was supposed to wean users off their habit, but it was actually stronger and more addictive. And in Wilkie's case, it did not work. He was taking opiates to deaden the pain of his gout. As that did not go away, he became increasingly addicted to opium in one form or other.

This, in a strange way, made him more prosaic. Opium no longer opened the door to the romantic hallucinations of *The Woman in White* or even the eerie dreams of *The Moonstone*. It was now more of a painkiller than ever, and the evidence would show in Wilkie's writing, where sensationalism gave way to greater realism. Despite his artistic background and cerebral interests, he was out of tune with his contemporary Walter Pater's remark that 'All art constantly aspires towards the condition of music.' Wilkie wanted structure and content, which set him on a different path from the emerging aesthetic movement.

Although Wilkie had decided to write a new novel focusing on the marriage laws, he was initially more interested in further theatrical success. Since *No Thoroughfare* had been a commercial hit, particularly in the provinces, he hoped for a repeat of this with a new drama, written in conjunction with Fechter.

Black and White tackled the thorny issue of race, which was beginning to be discussed in the wake of Darwin. It told of Miss Milburn, an heiress in Trinidad in 1830, before the emancipation of slaves. Before marrying her fiancé, a local landowner called Stephen Westcraft, she goes to Paris where she meets the swarthy Count Maurice de Layrac. He pursues her back to the Caribbean, where he discovers he has mixed blood and is technically a slave. Miss Milburn initially baulks at the idea of marrying a man with this background, but later agrees, assisted on her way by a useful turn in the plot – the discovery of a letter proving that the Count has already been released from slavery.

Although the idea came from Fechter, who saw a good part for himself in the Count, the story was developed by Wilkie, with help from Frederick Lehmann's recollections of slavery in America. As a result of his business dealings in the United States, Lehmann had taken a strong stand against slavery, befriending Martha Griffith Browne, a poet and abolitionist from Kentucky. Her *Autobiography of a Female Slave*, written in 1856, was one of the first of a genre known as a pseudo-slave narrative. Through it she aimed to raise funds to emancipate her slaves and settle them in the free North. When she came to London in 1860, she visited the Lehmanns and almost certainly met Wilkie.

Fechter was reunited with Carlotta Leclercq, his leading lady from *No Thoroughfare*, when *Black and White* opened at the Adelphi Theatre on 29 March 1869. Dickens thought the first night went 'brilliantly . . . It was more like a fiftieth night than a first.' However, though the play won critical plaudits, it failed to attract audiences. The *Daily News* suggested it was too similar to Dion Boucicault's *The Octoroon*, which had run ten years earlier, as well as to Poe's classic story 'The Purloined Letter'. Wilkie seemed to accept this lack of novelty when he admitted that the British public had been exposed to too many adaptations of *Uncle Tom's Cabin*.

He also took his personal financial loss on the chin. This proved worse than expected since, over the past year, he had been lending regular sums of money to Fechter, who was notorious for getting into debt. At one stage, after Wilkie had given the actor a cheque for £100, Lehmann became concerned that his friend was over-extending himself. Wilkie assured him that there was nothing to worry about, but was touched by this cultivated businessman's solicitude. 'Thank you, from the bottom of my heart, for your kind letter,' he wrote. 'No man – whatever his disappointments may be – can consider himself other than a fortunate man, when he has got such a friend as you are.'

Wilkie was solvent enough to spend £60 on having two hundred copies of the play printed by Charles Whiting. He then methodically set about finding an outlet for *Man and Wife*, his book about the marriage laws. He skilfully used an offer from *Cassell's Magazine* for weekly serial rights, starting in November, to negotiate with various American publishers, including Putnam's and Appleton. Eventually he went back to Harper and Brothers, though for their £750 fee they required an assurance that the publication of the Cassell's book would not appear in America before their own serial. As often before, Wilkie was plagued by the complexities of copyright in the United States, where piracy was still rife since it had yet to sign any international agreement on the matter.

Not that the situation was much better in Europe, as became clear when he was approached by the Dutch publisher Belinfante Brothers. He dealt elegantly enough with their effrontery in addressing him as Madame Wilkie Collins. 'I am not the charming person whom you suppose me to be,' he replied. 'I wear trowsers; I have a vote for Parliament; I possess a beard; in two dreadful words, I am – a Man.' But he was incensed at their offer to pay him with a single copy of their Dutch-language *Stuivers Magazijn*. At least he now had Benham's partner William

Tindell to provide solid advice on contract and copyright matters.

He did not take his usual summer holiday that year, largely because on 4 July Martha gave birth to his (and their) first child, a daughter called Marian. The baby's arrival was not officially registered, so it almost certainly took place in the hurly-burly of Bolsover Street, and the news was kept quiet. Wilkie, predictably, made no comment about the new arrival, though it is noticeable that she carried the first name of his best-known heroine, Marian Halcombe. *The Woman in White* also provided a surname for Martha, who was now known as Mrs Dawson, after the doctor who tended Marian in the novel. It is surprising that history has tended to associate *The Woman in White* with Caroline, when it has more enduring links to Martha.

Wilkie was thrilled by this addition to his extended family. Before the end of the year he took steps to include all his dependants – Martha, Marian, Caroline and Harriet – in a new will. He showed further evidence of his earnest in October when his payments to Martha became regular – £20 per month, rising to £25 per month in September 1871.

Without any travels to occupy him, Wilkie was now, in the latter half of 1869, free to concentrate on writing *Man and Wife*. The result was the last of his meandering plot-driven sagas. His subsequent books would be shorter, showing something of the new realism he also hoped to bring to his efforts for the stage.

Man and Wife opens in the comfortable Hampstead villa of Mr Vanborough, a gentleman with Parliamentary ambitions, who is tired of his wife, Anne, a former actress, and wants a younger, better-class replacement. He is helped by the judgement of a slick lawyer called Delamayn, who tells him that his marriage is in fact null since his wife is a Roman Catholic and, as in the Yelverton case, their original ceremony had been conducted by a Catholic priest. The lawyer goes on to become Attorney General and is ennobled; Anne wastes away and on her deathbed has only one request of her best friend Blanche – that her daughter, also called Anne, become a governess. Otherwise, she plaintively asks, 'Will she end like me?'

Twelve years later Delamayn's smooth, Oxford-educated son, Geoffrey, enters a relationship with this younger Anne, without either of them knowing this back story. Anne has duly become the governess to Blanche, the daughter of her mother's best friend. While she and Geoffrey are both at the house of Lady Lundie, the younger Blanche's stepmother in Scotland, Anne becomes worried that she is destined to follow her mother's fate and threatens suicide if he does not marry her. Since they are in Perthshire, he suggests a 'private marriage', or a Scottish wedding ceremony, requiring nothing more than their assent. They arrange to meet at a nearby hotel to go through with this. But he has been wavering and, when he is recalled to London because his father is ill, he fools his friend Arnold Brinkworth into going to the hotel, in his guise, to explain the situation to Anne.

Once there, the decent-minded Arnold, who is eager to save Anne embarrassment, goes through the charade of being her husband, since this is what the hotel was expecting. He even spends the night in her room. As a result, everyone there is prepared to say they were married, though Delamayn's letter explaining the real situation to Anne has been stolen by one of the staff. Delamayn later seizes on these circumstances to inform Anne that they cannot go through with their nuptials since, under Scottish law, she is now married to Arnold. By then his family has a well-heeled young widow, Mrs Glenarm, lined up as a wife for him.

In her efforts to prove this has all been a mistake, Anne is helped by Blanche's uncle, the charming and sophisticated Sir Patrick Lundie, who joins her as a quasi-detective – a now almost obligatory role in much of Wilkie's fiction.

In presenting his usual mixture of mistaken identities, villainous behaviour and revenge, Wilkie's general aversion to matrimony is never in doubt: it is a functional institution. 'Done, in the name of Morality. Done, in the interests of Virtue. Done, in an age of progress, and under the most perfect government on the face of the earth.' At one stage, he satirises an actual marriage ceremony: 'There was the proper and pitiless staring of all the female spectators when the bride was led to the altar. There was the clergyman's preliminary look at the licence – which meant official caution. And there was the clerk's preliminary look at the bridegroom – which meant official fees. All the women appeared to be in their natural element; and all the men appeared to be out of it. Then the service began – rightly-considered, the most terrible, surely, of all mortal ceremonies – the service which binds two human beings, who know next to nothing of each other's natures, to risk the tremendous experiment of living together till death parts them – the service which says, in effect if not in words, Take your leap in the dark: we sanctify, but we don't insure, it!'

While his obvious target, as set out in his preface, was Britain's marriage laws, which deprived women of their property and condemned them to servitude, he was also tilting at the coarsening of British culture, which he held at least partly responsible for this situation. As his preface also stated, he was concerned about the 'spread of grossness and brutality among certain classes of the English population'. Echoing Matthew Arnold's reference to Barbarians and Philistines in his recent polemic 'Culture and Anarchy', Wilkie noted the offensive presence of 'Roughs' in all areas of society, including medicine, the City and the universities (where riots at Oxford had been followed by the sacking of Christ Church Library). He equated these 'hearties' with the rise of Muscular Christianity, which emphasised the development of the body at the expense of the mind. And no one epitomised this uncivilising trend more obviously than the smarmy, insensitive lawyer Geoffrey Delamayn, who had rowed for Oxford and competed in a national road race that killed him.

Wilkie was also interested in the contemporary theme of destiny and free will. The publication of Darwin's *On the Origin of Species* a decade earlier had highlighted the extent to which people's lives were dictated by outside forces. The cult of athletics was related to this, since physical fitness was regarded as a way of enhancing one's chances in a world ruled by natural selection. Wilkie ridicules this idea by suggesting that running could actually be harmful to one's health.

Like all Wilkie's books, *Man and Wife* is littered with his prejudices. There is no mistaking his disdain for the law and, particularly, its attitude to women. His mildly progressive views about the opposite sex's role in society filter through, as when the indolent Blanche is told that she suffers from a malady common to English young ladies 'and the name of it is Nothing-to-Do'. However, Wilkie can also be more conventional, as when he editorialises that 'the natural condition of a woman is to find her master in a man. Look in the face of any woman who is in no direct way dependent on a man – and, as certainly as you see the sun in a cloudless sky, you see a woman who is not happy.'

In such contexts, he is often being mildly satirical, as when he describes the main attractions of English women as 'youth, health, plumpness'. His own preferences are apparent in his portrayal of the younger Anne, who, although no beauty and indeed suffering from physical defects, was nevertheless 'one of those women – the formidable few – who have the hearts of men and the peace of families at their mercy. She moved – and there was some subtle charm, Sir, in the movement, that made you look back, and suspend your conversation with your friend, and watch her silently while she walked. She sat by you and talked to you – and behold, a sensitive something passed into that little twist at the corner of the mouth, and into that nervous uncertainty in the soft gray eye, which turned defect into beauty – which enchained your senses – which made your nerves thrill if she touched you by accident, and set your heart beating if you looked at the same book with her, and felt her breath on your face. All this, let it be well understood, only happened if you were a man.' In this he was conveying his idealised appreciation of Martha Rudd's sex appeal.

Wilkie had already researched the Yelverton case and other legal precedents for his story. For guidance on athleticism, a little-known area for him, he contacted J.C. Parkinson, a crusading journalist (and prominent Freemason), who had worked on *Household Words* and was now at the *Daily News*, who supplied him with details about rowing and running. This was ironic since the book was dedicated to the Lehmanns, whose son Rudolph would become one of the leading oarsmen of his generation at Cambridge. However, his friends were in on the joke since much of the book was written at their house, Woodlands, and their name clearly resonated in that of Delamayn.

When he was abroad on business, Frederick Lehmann often sent Wilkie a gift from wherever he was visiting. His present from the United States in October 1869 was a box of Stoughton's Bitters, a sought-after 'mixer' of the time. Wilkie thanked him profusely: 'I suspended an immortal work of fiction, by going down-stairs, and tasting a second bottle, properly combined with Gin. Result delicious! Thank you a thousand times!' But in his letter, sent just three months after the birth of his daughter, he never mentioned his domestic situation. Instead, he stated categorically that he had little news. 'I sit here all day, attacking English Institutions – battering down the marriage laws of Scotland and Ireland, and reviling athletic sports – in short writing an <u>un</u>popular book, which may possibly make a hit, from the mere oddity of a modern writer running full tilt against the popular sentiment, instead of clinging to it.'

As Wilkie worked his way through the instalments of his novel, he found *Cassell's* as demanding as any other publisher: although he had negotiated that he would have the final say on what went into the magazine, they asked him to remove the words 'damn it' from his copy. He reluctantly agreed, but asked that this should not be regarded as a precedent: 'Readers who object to expletives in books, are – as to my experience – readers who object to a great many other things in books, which they are too stupid to understand.'

Aside from this, his progress went smoothly, and by early the following June he had finished all thirty-seven instalments. On the very day (the 9th) that he completed his task, he fell asleep from exhaustion and awoke to learn that Dickens had died that morning at Gad's Hill, following a stroke.

Their relationship had been clouded for the last year or so. Wilkie had benefited from his old friend's generosity in January 1870 when he had asked for (and received) a formal letter confirming that, as the author, he held the copyright on everything that he had written for *Household Words* and *All the Year Round*. But underlying problems persisted, one being Charley Collins and what Dickens felt was Wilkie's ineffectual response to his brother's plight. Although Charley was solvent, following the death of his mother, he seldom had much ready cash. Katey, his prima donna-ish wife, who had been modelling for various artists, even discussed a possible acting career with the impresario Horace Wigan. Dickens tried to help by offering Charley a chance to draw the illustrations for what would be his last (unfinished) novel *The Mystery of Edwin Drood*. Although he wanted to return to painting, Charley was unable to complete more than the cover, so the main task passed to the young Luke Fildes, who was also on hand to execute an evocative watercolour of Dickens's library, with its now empty chair, on the day of the master novelist's death.

Another bone of contention was *Edwin Drood*. Perhaps Wilkie felt that this story, which places opium at its centre, drew too much on *The Moonstone*. He was certainly not kind in his description of it as 'Dickens's last laboured effort, the melancholy work of a worn-out brain'.

Wilkie attended Dickens's funeral in Westminster Abbey on 14 June, but showed little overt emotion. He seemed more interested in ensuring that *The Times* had a list of the mourners, on which point he wrote to William Stebbing, a fellow member of the Athenaeum Club, who was chief leader writer. The paper reported the following day that fourteen people had attended the funeral, but listed only thirteen, which has led to speculation that Nelly Ternan's name was omitted. If so, this would have provided a fitting finale to the long-running farce in which the two friends colluded (rather successfully) to ensure that no evidence of their dalliances seeped out.

When Wilkie told William Tindell that 'the day of Dickens's Funeral was a lost day to me', he was thinking how it had kept him from preparing proofs for the next stage of his story's development – its appearance at the end of the month in three volumes under the imprint of F.S. Ellis, a smallish firm with origins in the bookselling trade, whose main claim to fame was as the publisher of Dante Gabriel Rossetti.

By then, the combined effect of Dickens's death and his own exertions on his book had set him back physically. He dragged himself to Antwerp with Frank Beard, more for the air of the cross-Channel voyage than anything else, but reported that he was so weak he could 'hardly write even a note'. The widowed Beard was in many respects worse than he, and in July Wilkie showed his capacity for friendship when he took off a further week to tend to his doctor, who 'stands in some need, poor fellow, of rest and peace, and of the help and company of a friend'.

Wilkie was never out of action for long. Although the first 1,000-copy edition of *Man and Wife* sold out immediately, he was soon complaining about the lacklustre way in which F.S. Ellis had gone about selling his book. He was particularly incensed by the failure to advertise in either *The Times* or the *Daily Telegraph*. Perhaps his chivvying was effective, or perhaps the publisher had done the right thing in the first place, for the book quickly went into a second and third edition (even if copies were remaindered four years later). It was helped by a clutch of positive notices, as in the *Saturday Review*, which found it 'exceedingly entertaining'. The main criticism was that it was too didactic, though Mrs Oliphant in *Blackwood's Magazine* had changed her tune, describing it as 'one of the cleverest of recent works of fiction'.

Before the end of August, Wilkie completed a four-act stage adaptation of the book, the usual preventative measure he took to ward off piracy. When he discovered his works were still being illegally published in Canada, he found himself a publisher in Toronto, the rapidly expanding firm of Hunter, Rose. He deftly achieved this feat without alienating Harper and Brothers, his main outlet in the United States, which tended to look on its northern neighbour as a captive subsidiary market.

In this, as in other areas of his life, Wilkie had learned to compromise. Although he was annoyed when the New York manager Augustin Daly put on *Man and Wife* at his Fifth Avenue Theatre, purporting that it was the author's original text, he reached an agreement with the influential Daly, who before long was presenting Wilkie's official renderings of not only *Man and Wife* but *No Name*. For a while their relationship remained rocky: when Daly sent him $1,000 'purely out of courtesy' at the end of *Man and Wife*'s run, Wilkie made clear that he regarded this approach as offensive since their dealings were entirely commercial, but nevertheless he accepted the money and a friendship soon developed. In this accommodating mood, Wilkie even signed a contract with Belinfante Brothers, who later paid him one hundred guilders (under £9) for the privilege of printing *Man and Wife*. He considered this a triumph, since they had 'never hitherto paid sixpence to any author (not a Dutchman) in the civilised universe', and he agreed to let them publish his next book, which would be *Poor Miss Finch*.

Wilkie's readership was international, which explained his muddled concerns about the repercussions of the Franco-Prussian War during the autumn of 1870. On the one hand, he wrote to his translator Emil Lehmann telling him that, 'like the rest of my countrymen', he was 'heartily on the German side in the War'. On the other, as the German armies converged on Paris, he tried to help his old friend François Regnier, who was holed up there, offering him not only a bed, but also the use of his banking services at Coutts. He was ridiculed at the Athenaeum Club when he told fellow members that he expected fierce French resistance. They told him to return to his fiction and not trifle with politics. But he felt strongly about the issue, telling Regnier of the rousing support for the French cause he had witnessed at the Alhambra before Christmas. By then Regnier had quit Paris and was living out of harm's way in Boulogne.

Wilkie's attitude arose from a deep-felt pacifism that despaired of nations being 'still ready to slaughter each other, at the command of one miserable wretch whose interest it is to set them fighting! Is this the nineteenth century? or the ninth?' He became an early advocate of the theory of Mutually Assured Destruction when he mused, 'I begin to believe in only one civilising influence – the discovery one of these days, of a destructive agent so terrible that War shall mean <u>annihilation</u>, and men's fears shall force them to keep the peace.'

Early in 1871, Wilkie was to be found playing the genial host at a 'pic-nic dinner' at Gloucester Place. This was his way of describing an informal gathering of his closest friends – Lehmann, Frith, Charles Reade and his mistress Mrs Seymour, his brother Charley, and 'another woman', as he coyly put it to the final invitee, his doctor Frank Beard. (Of his usual coterie only Charles Ward and Pigott were missing.) In the absence of other evidence, we can only speculate on the identity of this mystery lady, but she was almost certainly Caroline Clow (formerly Graves), who had returned to base after a brief experiment in matrimony.

She was definitely at Gloucester Place two months later, when she was listed as a resident (albeit as housekeeper and domestic servant) in the 1871 census taken on 2 April. Caroline's marriage had probably ended rather earlier, for in January 1870 there was a record of a J. Clow arriving in Brisbane, Australia, on the *Melmerby*, a 1,500-ton sailing ship registered in Liverpool. The man's age was given as twenty-five, near enough to Caroline's husband's, and he was not listed in the 1871 English census.

Caroline's husband, as he remained until her death, certainly went to Australia, where he worked as a mining engineer and maintained a pattern of relationships with the opposite sex that was every bit as complex as it had been in Britain.

If Caroline's marriage was over by 1870, she may have accompanied Wilkie on his most recent visit to the Kentish coast in September that year. Broadstairs now held too many ghosts for him. Instead he went to Ramsgate, a childhood haunt, which was now enjoying a mid-Victorian renaissance. He stayed at the Granville Hotel, designed by Edward Welby Pugin, son of the Gothic architect, A.W.N. Pugin, who had lived locally. The hotel was in St Lawrence on Sea, an up-market development on the east side of the town, which was intended to cash in on the popularity of the main resort. Although magnificently appointed, the hotel, adjacent to the estate of the Jewish financier and philanthropist Sir Moses Montefiore, never caught on. Within a few years it was in financial difficulties and is described in Pevsner's *Buildings of England* as 'a monstrosity'. But Wilkie liked such lavish hotels and, thinking back to the Meurice in Paris, may have considered it a good place to resurrect his relationship with Caroline.

Her reappearance in Gloucester Place must have made life more difficult, and more lonely, for Martha and her young daughter in Bolsover Street. This was especially true because Martha was pregnant again. At least she had the company of her sister Alice, who had been working with her in the Vauxhall Tavern in Great Yarmouth when she met Wilkie. Alice was now living around the corner from her in Harley Street, where she cooked for a well-known doctor, John Hall Davis. She later acted as housekeeper for her sister and Wilkie's growing family.

On the work front, Wilkie was increasingly disillusioned by the state of British publishing. As he complained to Harper and Brothers in New York, their transatlantic counterparts remained in thrall to Mudie's, which continued to dictate public taste and purchases. As a result, they were totally uncommercial and he was 'seriously contemplating turning to dramatic writing for the future instead of novel-writing. The publishers here who have money, have no enterprise. The publishers with enterprise have no money. The small booksellers are being ruined. The public is as badly supplied as possible. And all for want of the courage, among English publishers, to issue a book, as you do, at a price which the reader can pay.' He claimed to have put forward ideas for improving the situation, but British publishers were averse to risk – 'in other words they object to that bold speculation on the public taste which is the essence of a publishers business!'

This meant that Wilkie was even more eager for success in the theatre. At this stage he was juggling dramatic versions of three books – *Man and Wife*, *No Name* and *The Woman in White*. But before he could allow himself licence to pursue these interests, he had two new print projects to complete. His novel *Poor Miss Finch* returned to the subject of disability, which he had explored most recently in *Man and Wife*. This time, he offered an original twist: although the heroine Lucilla Finch was blind, she preferred this condition to full sightedness, which for her was fraught with unhappiness.

The book is another typical Wilkie Collins concoction involving doubles and confusion about identity. A synopsis makes it sound more than faintly ridiculous. Lucilla, the daughter of the rector of Dimchurch, near Lewes in Sussex, falls in love with Oscar Dubourg, who is later struck down with epilepsy after being hit on the head. Their wedding is postponed while he goes away in search of a treatment, which turns his skin a blackish shade of blue since it is based on silver nitrate. She is not aware of this until Oscar's twin brother Nugent, who is also in love with her, suggests that she should seek a cure for her cataracts from a well-known ophthalmologist. Previously she had only known Oscar by his feel; she had no idea what he looks like. This gives the malevolent Nugent an opportunity to pass himself off as his brother. When she goes to Ramsgate to recuperate from her eye operation, he follows and presses her to marry him. He goes so far as to obtain a marriage licence in his absent brother's name. But Lucilla now senses that something is wrong, and, under the stress, her sight deteriorates. When Oscar comes back from abroad, she, partially sighted again, immediately recognises him by his 'delicious tingle'. Nugent confesses and offers the couple his fraudulent licence for a wedding in Sydenham two days later. Once again a complex saga ends in marriage – this time, a happy one.

However, the book's overall theme was one Wilkie had often chewed at – the nature of perception. Since the seventeenth century, philosophers had pondered what blind people might experience if their sight were restored. Was an ability to interpret the world through one's eyes an innate gift or a learned skill? The surgeon William Cheselden had subsequently written about how patients experience the world after the removal of cataracts. Wilkie's own ophthalmologist George Critchett, based in Harley Street, was perhaps the most distinguished practitioner in his field, having recently been elected to the Council of the Royal College of Surgeons. Drawing on these sources, Wilkie showed empathy in understanding not only the bewilderment Lucilla might feel when her sight was restored, but how, in her state of blindness, she might have developed other sensitivities, or equally valid ways of reading the world.

This raised another aspect of the 'nature versus nurture' debate. When the (male) Dubourg twins first appear in Dimchurch, they are seen doing something 'worse than crying':

they kiss one another on the cheek. As Lucilla's old nurse comments disgustedly, 'Two men! Foreigners, of course.' Wilkie was poking fun at British reserve. Having no such inhibitions himself, he regularly kissed his male friends, particularly the effusive Fechter. In his story, he notes how Lucilla, despite her blindness, is remarkably outgoing. This leads her carer (as she would now be called) to observe that 'modesty is essentially the growth of our own consciousness of the eyes of others judging us'. Without this pressure from society, Lucilla had grown up with the passions of a woman but 'the fearless and primitive innocence of a child'.

The prominence of children in this book reflected Wilkie's new role as a parent. His second daughter, Harriet, was born in May, just as he was finishing the first chapters. Her elder sister, Marian, was a possible model for Lucilla's half-sister, the gypsyish three-year-old Jicks. However, Wilkie hedged his bets: Lucilla's stepmother is a slovenly breast-feeding machine surrounded by a vast brood. This suggests he still had mixed feelings about having his own demanding daughters around him. He no doubt preferred them to let off steam in Bolsover Street, leaving Gloucester Place a haven of peace for himself.

While working on *Poor Miss Finch*, Wilkie was also thinking about his other main literary commitment – a tale for the Christmas edition of the *Graphic*, the latest challenger in the picture newspaper market dominated by the *Illustrated London News*. *Miss or Mrs?* tells of a respected City trader who, having fallen on hard times, thinks he can resurrect his fortunes by marrying the daughter of a rich friend. She has other ideas since she is in love with her cousin and they arrange to marry, but keep their plans secret since she is fifteen and technically underage. When the trader discovers this, he plots to murder her father.

Aside from its sensationalist themes of deception and murder, the story showed several personal touches. Its depiction of sailing owed much to Wilkie's yachting with Pigott, the City background drew on his friends Charles Oppenheim and Frederick Lehmann, while the underage marriage looked back to Ned and Henrietta Ward. Since such subject matter was potentially actionable, he consulted his new solicitor, Tindell, about the relevant law.

With these work commitments and a growing family, there was no question of his sailing or taking the waters in Europe this summer. The farthest he would go was the unlikely spot of Upper Norwood in Surrey, where he spent a week in August at the fashionable Queen's Hotel, which, because of its elevated position close to the Crystal Palace, was promoted as a healthy alternative to the heat and grime of central London. Wilkie agreed, describing how 'drunk' he was with 'this fine air', and the 'good and dry' champagne no doubt helped.

Wilkie returned to London feeling better for his time away. His gout had subsided and he was able to climb the stairs at Gloucester Place, even if, by the time the first episode of *Poor Miss Finch* appeared in the September issue of *Cassell's* magazine, his medical regime had been extended to include regular enemas and doses of quinine, as well as his usual laudanum.

However, Wilkie was determined to enjoy living at Gloucester Place. The domestic upheavals of the last three years seemed a distant memory when, the following month, he invited Charles Reade to dinner, promising that 'a new stock of Moselle is at this moment being put into the cellar.' He admitted he was 'all in arrear with "Poor Miss F."', and emphasised that 'the two Carolines send you their love, and join in asking you not to forget No 90' (his house at 90 Gloucester Place). The two Carolines were of course Mrs Graves (a name she quickly re-assumed) and her daughter Harriet.

He had further reason to feel cheerful because, in early October, a cherished theatrical project, a new version of *The*

Woman in White, had come to fruition. After the extravagances of *Black and White*, he had taken pains to make this one less melodramatic. He stripped the novel back to basics, eschewing several of its most obviously theatrical scenes, including Walter Hartright's initial encounter with Anne Catherick. Peripheral characters were dropped and, rather than disappearing to Central America, Hartright was involved throughout.

Wilkie found a home for it at the Olympic Theatre, which had staged *The Frozen Deep* five years earlier. The play opened on 9 October and proved a huge success, running over an extended Christmas season until 24 February 1872. Wilkie was delighted at the financial returns, which flowed regularly into his bank account – £47 10s after the opening week, £56 2s 9d after the second. The only problem was that, although the critics were positive, they did not like the new Fosco, who, now that Fechter was in America, was played by the experienced George Vining. The *Daily Telegraph* stated dismissively that he was 'not Fosco', an opinion that pushed Wilkie to respond with a letter in the actor's defence. However, he was sympathetic to this view for, when the production later toured, the part of Fosco was taken by Wybert Reeve, the original Walter Hartright in the London production, whom Wilkie much preferred in the role.

The production played an interesting part in the development of the illustrated poster. Wilkie had originally asked Frederick Walker, a dapper artist in his early thirties who had been born and raised in the same streets of Marylebone, to see what he could produce. Walker's dramatic, swirling rendition of a woman looking over her shoulder as she passed through a door was done in the week before the play's opening at Charley Collins's small house in Thurloe Place, South Kensington. The model may well have been Katey. (This is the suggestion of her biographer Lucinda Hawksley, who adds that Walker was greatly attracted to her.) Once the image was deemed suitable, Walker enlisted his friend W.H. Hooper, a pupil of Ruskin and later the engraver at William Morris's Kelmscott Press, to do a 'vigorous wood-cut' four feet six inches to five feet high. Walker was 'warmly' thanked by Wilkie, encouraging him to think that such posters could 'develop into a most important branch of art'.

Shortly after *The Woman in White* opened, Wilkie was at his brother's home in South Kensington when Luke Fildes, another admirer of Katey, was also present. By then Wilkie was thinking about *Miss or Mrs?*, his forthcoming story in the *Graphic*, and asked young Fildes, who had successfully completed his work on *The Mystery of Edwin Drood*, to do the drawings. Fildes was happy to oblige, but could not engrave them. So Charley contacted Fred Walker, who again called on W.H. Hooper, who was paid £9 17s by Wilkie on 13 October (whether for this latest or for both commissions, is not clear).

Wilkie's behind the scenes activity did not save him from Arthur Locker, editor of the *Graphic*, who refused to print some light swear words in *Miss or Mrs?*, claiming they could be harmful to children. Wilkie objected strongly to such censorship. 'My story is not addressed to young people exclusively – it is addressed to readers in general,' he told Locker. 'I do not accept young people as the ultimate court of appeal in English literature. Mr Turlington must talk like Mr Turlington – even though the terrible consequence may be that a boy or two may cry "Damn" in imitation of him.' Despite quoting the works of Scott and Dickens in his support, Wilkie failed to impress Locker, who proceeded with his bowdlerisation.

At the same time, *Poor Miss Finch* was coming together. Wilkie was approached by Samuel Tinsley, a bookseller unknown to him, but apparently a brother of William, who had put out *The Moonstone*, and a man who was now keen to develop a publishing business of his own. This new Tinsley came up with the sort of competitive proposal Wilkie liked – a potentially lucrative package that included putting the book out as a one-volume hardback. But after asking advice from Tindell, taking up references and meeting Tinsley, Wilkie opted for caution and declined. He was put off by Tinsley's inability to look him in the eye. Nevertheless, this unsolicited approach encouraged him to tell Cassell's that he had been 'pressed by so many proposals for republication' that he was now asking £1,500 for a three-year licence to print the hardback of *Poor Miss Finch*.

When this opportunistic negotiating gambit was politely rebuffed, Wilkie took up an offer from George Bentley, who had been waiting on the sidelines since publishing *Hide and Seek* in 1864. Bentley had recently asked him to intercede with John Forster, whom he feared would traduce his late father's name in his life of Dickens. Wilkie was unable to do anything, and Bentley was outraged when Forster's account of his father's quarrel with Dickens was included in the biography. However, Bentley was now solvent and agreed to pay £750 for the rights to publish 2,000 copies of a three-volume edition of *Poor Miss Finch*, which duly appeared, with a dedication to Frances Elliot, at the end of January 1872.

The reaction was unenthusiastic, suggesting that Wilkie might have misread the public's taste. Normally, he was astute at striking the right balance between heightened drama and acceptability. But on this occasion he seemed caught between the two conflicting poles. On the one hand, the implausibility of his plot failed to please the *Nation*, which declared, 'Whatever may be said against the vanity of existence, it is not all a combination of missing trains, listening behind doors, and mysterious meetings.' On the other, he was taken to task for being too tame and sentimental, leading even the usually conservative *Athenaeum* to dismiss his book as 'Sunday reading' which could 'be confidently recommended to the notice of parents and guardians'. In particular, the magazine's critic bemoaned the lack of staple

sensational characters, such as 'red-headed Messalinas, aged
Jezebels, rascally doctors, or spurious baronets', and attributed
this 'sanctifying influence' to *Cassell's Magazine*'s cowed response
to widespread criticism of the salaciousness of its recent offering
A Terrible Temptation by Charles Reade. Wilkie might have countered that the experience of blindness was by definition sensational. Nevertheless, although *Poor Miss Finch* was a typical
page-turner, it did lack some of the visceral excitement of his
novels of the previous decade. Perhaps his sensibilities had been
affected by having a family. Perhaps he was feeling the loss of
Dickens. Or perhaps he was aware that public morality was
changing. After a relatively liberal period, which had allowed
the sensational school to flourish, a puritanical reaction was
setting in, leading to the introduction of new licensing laws, the
banning of prostitutes in public houses and the formation of the
Social Purity Alliance in 1873.

At this stage, Wilkie had had enough. He told a correspondent he was 'going away soon to get a little rest and change
after a year's hard work'. He took the South Eastern Railway to
Ramsgate, but after a few days at the Granville Hotel, the sea
air failed to work its usual magic, and he returned to London
still feeling exhausted.

Wilkie had at least had the opportunity to contemplate his
future. Ever since Dickens's tour of the United States five years
earlier, Wilkie had harboured a desire to follow him on the
lecture circuit there. Now, in answer to a query from an enquiring
American journalist, he said that he could not envisage crossing
the Atlantic in the next few months. However, he had 'positively
resolved not to saddle' himself with 'the heavy strain of another
long story, for a year to come at least.' That way he hoped he
could 'train' himself for a visit to the United States.

FIFTH EPOCH

16

THE NEW MAGDALEN

Now that he was nearing fifty, Wilkie was showing his age. At around this time he was recalled by the actor Wybert Reeve as 'a short, moderately thick-set man, with beard, moustache, and whiskers slightly tinged with white; a bent figure, caused by suffering'. However, nothing could disguise his mental energy, with his 'full, massive, very clever head and forehead; and bright, intellectual eyes, looking out of strong eye-glasses mounted in gold'. This engaging, contradictory impression was reinforced when he was caricatured by the talented Italian Adriano Cecioni in the 3 February 1872 issue of *Vanity Fair*. Cecioni was one of several artists employed by the publication before Ned Ward's Etonian son Leslie made the 'Men of Today' slot his own with his 'Spy' cartoons. Wilkie was pictured sitting down, full bearded and alert. His image was captioned 'The Novelist who invented Sensation', and the accompanying blurb quoted him saying that the best things about his stories were 'the interest of curiosity and the excitement of surprise'. There was a valedictory tone in its verdict that his finest work was *Armadale*, from the height of his sensation period. The literary caravan was moving on, though no one could fault its opinion that 'his special merit is that he treats a labyrinthine story in an apparently simple manner, and that the language in which he writes is plain English.'

Predictably, Wilkie did little to cut back his workload in 1872. He suggested that his next book, *The New Magdalen*, would be 'a trifling literary project'. But what was originally a short story and then a modest serial grew over the course of a year into a major 100,000-word novel published in Britain by Bentley the following May (after serialisation in the publisher's in-house *Temple Bar* magazine) and in the United States by Harper's and its eponymous monthly magazine.

After suffering brickbats for *Poor Miss Finch*, Wilkie was determined to rebut his critics with a hard-hitting storyline. Over the years he had written about fallen women in various guises, but this time there would be no ambiguity about his main character, a reformed prostitute. His plot centres on Mercy Merrick who, after being tricked into a life on the streets, seeks rehabilitation as a nurse in the Franco-Prussian War, where she is inspired by a sermon given by a charismatic young priest, Julian Gray. When the respectable Grace Roseberry appears to have been killed by a German shell, Mercy sees an opportunity to escape her past by assuming her colleague's identity. She steals a letter of introduction to Grace's distant relation Lady Janet Roy, who adopts her as a companion. At this stage Grace reappears, having been restored to health by a German surgeon (a breed in which Wilkie had inordinate faith). Mercy is inclined to come clean and admit that she is an impostor, until she is put off this course of action by Grace's high-handedness. As a result, no one believes Grace and she is confined to an asylum. In the meantime, Mercy, who was set to marry a war correspondent, has been reintroduced to Julian Gray, who turns out to be Lady Janet's nephew. The two of them fall in love, but at first she refuses to marry him because she fears he will be socially ruined when the truth of her origins are known. Instead, she insists on returning (as a nurse) to a Urania Cottage-like refuge where she had once stayed, seeking respite from sexual abuse by her employer and, later, from life as a prostitute. However, when Julian becomes ill, she relents and the novel finishes with them making their way to the New World to rebuild their lives beyond the bounds of conventional society.

The result is a curious mish-mash. Wilkie reprises several sensational tropes, such as the confusion of identities between Mercy, the tart with a heart (one of his old-style strong women) and goody-two-shoes Grace Roseberry, who is a nasty piece of work. He is vehement about a world that can find no place for penitent prostitutes, except in a stigmatised refuge. His account of Lady Janet's ball for the newly-married Mercy and Julian is great satire: the privileged matrons attend, but unaccompanied by their unmarried daughters, as a form of protest against Mercy and her origins. So scathing are Wilkie's observations that he seems to be getting back at society for all the slights heaped on Caroline and Martha over the years.

However, the book is more than mockery, as is apparent from its depiction of Julian Gray. Wilkie is determined to defy convention by having a clergyman marry a fallen woman. But Gray is almost too perfect; in earlier novels he might have served as a vehicle to attack the hypocrisy of religion. But, as he neared his sixth decade, Wilkie turns his parson into a virtual saint.

A clue to his thinking comes in the final scene when Julian and Mercy flee Britain. This is reminiscent of the would-be emigrants in Ford Madox Brown's 1855 painting *The Last of England*. Indeed, the whole of *The New Magdalen* reprises the Pre-Raphaelitism of Wilkie's youth. Its theme of the fallen woman harks back to the experiences of the Pre-Raphaelites as they fumbled towards an understanding of female sexuality that moved beyond the stereotypes of the whore and the angel in the house.

Wilkie's renewed interest in this topic was influenced by Holman Hunt's recent return from Jerusalem. He found his old friend 'the same sweet fellow as ever, and' (unlike himself) 'without a grey hair on him'. Hunt was a past master at depicting fallen women in his art. He had anticipated Wilkie and Martha when he plucked his former girlfriend and muse Annie Miller from a bar. He subsequently married another woman and had a son, but his love life continued to be fraught and unconventional. After his wife Fanny died in late 1866, a year after their wedding, he fell in love with her sister Edith – an action proscribed in English law. The couple's subsequent estrangement from their families (their equivalent of Mercy being cast out by society) would force them to Switzerland for a legal marriage in 1875.

Hunt's impact was apparent in other ways. His simple Christianity seems to have encouraged Wilkie in his own undemonstrative, non-denominational faith and led him to experiment with a new approach to sensation fiction, which had more or less run its course after its successes in the 1860s. When it came down to it, he really had little sympathy with the alternative model for the novel – the realism of George Eliot, whose *Middlemarch* had been appearing since December 1871 in a special eight-part edition published by Blackwood. He was temperamentally more attuned to an allusive, even allegorical style – a literary equivalent of the Pre-Raphaelites' paintings. He gave his book a Biblical title (Mary Magdalen was the former prostitute who became a disciple of Jesus) and developed it as a religious fable. Julian Gray became an idealised Christlike figure who, in contrast to the unforgiving snobs around Lady Janet, offers real redemption to the once sinful Mercy. Hunt was not Wilkie's only inspiration here, but also his pious brother

Charley, to whom the work was dedicated and who also played an influential role.

Once again marriage is presented as the fitting conclusion to Mercy's troubles. In the context of *The New Magdalen* it takes on a sacramental significance, which may have been at the back of Wilkie's mind whenever he wrote about the subject. As far back as *No Name*, Magdalen (that religiously charged name again) atones for her former sinful ways by becoming the lawful wife of the virtuous Captain Kirke. In *The New Magdalen*, the fallen Mercy finds similar redemption at the side of Julian Gray, though the material world is still not satisfied and forces them abroad. Wilkie's attitude makes his dealings with Caroline and Martha all the more curious. No wonder he found the writing difficult. As he explained to Frederick Lehmann, 'The principle [*sic*] female character this time is a reclaimed woman from the streets – a glorious creature who requires constant attentions. She is matched by a remarkable clergyman, who declines entirely to run in the ordinary clerical grooves, and who gives me nearly as much trouble as my beautiful reclaimed woman.' He might almost have been referring to Caroline herself.

During the summer of 1872 Wilkie was distracted by other matters, including a flying visit by Fechter from the United States, which required him to lend his actor friend a further £100. To his relief, he finally resolved the long-running problem of the stable at the back of his property. His former tenant had always been slow in paying, but now he had a new one who did not baulk at the rent of £40 a year. The actual cash was not important, but it provided welcome pocket money for Caroline and her daughter.

As so often before, he was agitated about copyrights – this

time, following a lengthy correspondence with an official at the Customs House about the need to register his works so as to prevent the importation of foreign editions. This was the kind of bureaucratic procedure he abhorred and which made him increasingly fed up with the book trade. Another example was the unilateral demand by Canadian publishers to be able to print any book they wanted by simply paying a royalty of 12.5 per cent. He described this as 'a flat denial of the right of property in the production of a man's brains to publish that man's book without his leave, on any conditions and under any circumstances whatever.' Wilkie's anger led him to join the Copyright Association, which had recently been set up to fight this and other matters of authors' rights. He would later work closely with the Society of Authors, which succeeded it.

His attitude towards the British book business was not improved by the opportunistic unilateral decision by W.H. Smith's Railway Circulating Library to bind together the extracts from *Cassell Magazine's* version of *Poor Miss Finch* and sell four hundred copies directly to its customers. Wilkie was upset on behalf of Bentley, who had purchased the volume rights to the book and stood to make not a penny. He was also furious that he himself had lost four hundred good sales, which would have resulted in the Bentley edition selling out.

But while Wilkie was the most professional of writers, he now had other things to think about – in particular, the well-being of his young family. During the summer he had a worrying time when his elder daughter Marian broke her leg. Frank Beard put it in plaster and looked after her, before her mother took her 'to the seaside', which probably meant Norfolk. Fred Lehmann did his bit by offering the young invalid a new pram, but Wilkie declined, saying, in effect, that he preferred the sentimental associations of the old one.

Wilkie also had his brother to consider. Charley had 'a

horrible sore on his leg' and 'a red swelling' on his ankle (apparently gout), when Wilkie visited him in August. He was 'very gloomy about himself and about human destiny generally', so Wilkie irreverently tried to cheer him by suggesting he adopt a Gnostic approach to life's problems, which essentially meant seeing them as illusions, though Wilkie's later synopsis of this creed in a letter to Lehmann suggested he had only a cursory understanding of it.

As Lehmann was in Germany in August, he invited Wilkie to join him. But Wilkie could not face the journey as his rheumatism was playing up. His cure was to dissolve three pounds of powdered alum, and lie in the bath soaking in 'something which feels like liquid velvet'. The result was 'an untied back and a straight left arm (for the time being)'. But he then spoiled the effect by eating a grouse and drinking a bottle of Schartzhofberger: 'Just like Germany, without the trouble of going there, and the horrid necessity of speaking the language, or of communicating in serious pantomimes with the people about me.'

Instead, he settled for the summer breezes of Ramsgate, which Frank Beard never failed to recommend for health reasons. This time, rather than stay at the Granville Hotel, he took a house in Nelson Crescent, in the centre of town, overlooking the sea. His landlady at number 14, an elegant, brick-fronted house dating back to Ramsgate's earlier heyday as a Regency resort, was Catherine Shrive, the daughter of a licensed victualler from Northamptonshire. As he began to relax, he asked Charley to stay, and also invited Tindell, telling him, 'I am comfortably established here with my womankind.' This seigneurial term referred to Caroline, her daughter and possibly her mother-in-law, Mary Ann. On this occasion, in late September, Martha and her two daughters were elsewhere, having been to the seaside the previous month.

By the time Wilkie returned to London, the serialisation of
The New Magdalen had started in *Temple Bar*, and he was able
to turn his attention to a new theatrical project – the dramatisation of *Man and Wife*, his complex novel about the marriage
laws. His frustrations with the book business made him more
eager than ever to succeed on the stage, which he thought was
much more professionally run than publishing. No one epitomised this commercial approach more than the actor-manager
Squire Bancroft who, with his actress wife Marie Wilton, had
transformed the Prince of Wales Theatre, off down-at-heel
Tottenham Court Road, into a fashionable venue. The Bancrofts
had done this by revamping their auditorium, replacing the
cheap benches near the stage with comfortable seats, restricting
their bills to one play, and serving up a dish of light realism
known as 'cup and saucer drama'.

Wilkie again made changes from his novel, such as cutting
out the character of the mute Hester Dethridge and any
mention of her involvement in murder – all designed to make
the play more realistic. When he came to read *Man and Wife*
to the cast in December, Bancroft thought he did it 'with great
effect and nervous force, giving all concerned a clear insight
into his view of the characters'. The opening night a couple
of months later showed how competitive the London theatre
scene had become. The Prince of Wales had taken a risk by
departing from its recent crowd-pleasing repertoire, and it was
packed with theatregoers eager to see if the Bancrofts had
managed to pull off this trick. Wilkie had no illusions about
what this meant and handed out tickets to anyone he could,
including Tindell, Ned and Henrietta Ward, and his brother
Charley, who came with his wife Katey and Holman Hunt.
Even so, he was disappointed to count only thirty friends in
the house to match against a picked band of the "lower orders"
of literature and the drama assembled at the back of the dress

circle to hiss and laugh at the first chance'. As a result, he sat in Bancroft's dressing room for most of the performance 'in a state of nervous terror painful to see'. He need not have worried; the audience's reaction was enthusiastic, and he was glad to find that 'the services of my friends were not required. The public never gave the "opposition" a chance all through the evening.'

This proved to be Charley Collins's last appearance in public. Shortly afterwards, his health deteriorated and his stomach ulcers were diagnosed as an advanced case of cancer. Two of Britain's most illustrious surgeons, Sir James Paget and Sir William Jenner, were called in, but they could do nothing to arrest or even mitigate the painful disease, which led to Charley's death on 9 April 1873, aged forty-five.

On a mild Monday morning, five days later, his funeral took place at the Government cemetery in Brompton. Wilkie was there with members of the Dickens family, as well as a smattering of artists, including Holman Hunt, Millais, Frederick Walker and Leighton. Hunt, who had just sold two versions of his painting *The Shadow of Death* to Agnew's for the massive sum of ten thousand guineas, had been at Charley's bedside, where he had drawn a sketch of him finally at peace. This he gave to Wilkie, with a request that he should return it after his own death. Wilkie instructed his solicitor to arrange this, once 'life's idle business has ended for me'.

Following Charley's death, Katey wasted little time in moving out of their little house and going to live with her siblings, Mamie and Henry, and their aunt Georgina Hogarth, at 81 Gloucester Terrace in Bayswater. Wilkie had to liaise with Millais, who was the somewhat reluctant executor of Charley's will. For all his financial problems during his life, Charley died comfortably off. His estate was worth over £10,000, which included the leases on two houses.

Charley's death drew a further line under the past. Aside from the regular small sums Wilkie paid under the terms of his father's will to relations such as his cousin William Jones in Ireland, he now had no more financial involvement with his parents' families. Even his aunt Margaret Carpenter, a remarkable example of a successful, self-motivated Victorian woman, had died the previous November. Wilkie's responsibilities were now limited to the two women in his life, Caroline and Martha, and their respective families.

He delivered the last instalment of *The New Magdalen* to the printers on 7 April, two days before Charley's death. By then he was already working on a dramatic adaptation of the text and hoped to stage it at a venue he knew well, the Olympic Theatre, which was also enjoying a renaissance after being revamped under the management of Ada Cavendish, a favourite actress of Wilkie's who had made her name in burlesque. He was keen to take more of an initiative in the business side of such proceedings, so, with Tindell's help, he acted as an impresario, hiring an agent, Stefan Poles, to represent him in negotiations. Mindful of his problems with George Vining over *The Woman in White*, he also drew up a detailed agreement with Miss Cavendish, stipulating that he was responsible for half the costs of the production and would reap half the profits. (His care was sadly misplaced as Poles turned out to be a confidence trickster.)

The New Magdalen opened at the Olympic on 19 May, the very day Bentley published the book version. There was a last-minute hiccough when Mudie's objected to the title, because of its connotations of prostitution. Wilkie, who had generally tried to maintain amicable relations with the largest lending library in Britain, could no longer contain himself. 'Nothing would induce me to modify the title,' he fulminated to his publisher. Then, referring to the firm's owner, Charles Mudie, he added,

Caroline Graves, one of Wilkie's two mistresses, in the early 1870s.

Entry in the register of baptisms from Toddington parish church, Gloucestershire, which records the illegitimate birth of Elizabeth Compton, later Caroline Graves, in November 1829.

"HE WROTE 'THE WOMAN IN WHITE.'"

Cartoon portrait of Wilkie Collins by Frederick Waddy from 1873. It shows Wilkie in front of Frederick Walker's famous poster for the production of *The Woman in White*, which ran at the Olympic Theatre in London from October 1871 to February 1872.

Front cover to 'The Fosco Galop', music inspired by *The Woman in White* and composed by G. Richardson in 1871.

Christmas message from the early 1870s by the English versifier Reverend Frederick Langbridge, which playfully draws on the titles of some of Wilkie's novels.

Frontispiece by John Everett Millais to Sampson, Low's single volume edition of *No Name* from 1864. Wilkie's novel was originally published in three volumes in 1862.

Wilkie Collins and the other of his two mistresses, Martha Rudd. It is unusual to see Wilkie photographed without glasses.

Martha Rudd in a studio portrait.

Martha Rudd in older age.

ABOVE: Frederick and Nina Lehmann, two of Wilkie's closest friends.

RIGHT: Mrs Katey Collins, Dickens's daughter, became the wife of Wilkie's brother Charley in 1860. After Charley's death in 1873, she married the artist Carlo Perugini.

ABOVE: Edward Smyth Pigott, Examiner of Plays, pictured in a cartoon by Pal for *Vanity Fair*, 11 January 1890.

Wilkie's close friend, the history artist Edward M. (Ned) Ward.

Harriet Ward, Ned Ward's wife, also a painter.

ABOVE: Locket commissioned from Tessier by Wilkie in 1868: a photographic portrait of his mother adorns one half and a curl of her hair the other. The locket was later gifted to Martha Rudd.

RIGHT: Mary Anderson, an American actress who became a good friend of Wilkie's in the 1880s.

Thursday 20 Sept 1886

This, dearest missus is Me.
You have heard of "the tortures
of the D———d" I am just
able to announce that the
Gout attacked my eye in

Letter dated 20 September 1886 from Wilkie to his young friend 'Nannie' Wynne. Note his sketch of the patch he wore when suffering from gout.

ABOVE LEFT: Harriet Graves, Caroline's daughter, on her wedding day, 12 March 1878.

ABOVE: Doris Beresford (née Bartley) the actress grand-daughter of Caroline Graves.

90, GLOUCESTER PLACE.
MARDI 12 MARS, 1878.
—:o:—
MENU DU DÉJEUNER.
—:o:—

Chauds.

Cotelettes d'Homard.   Ris de veau aux Truffes.
Cotelettes d'Agneau aux petit pois.

Froids.

Saumon Mayonaise.
Gallentine de Dinde aux truffes et pistach.
Gros Pates de Volaille.   Langues des Bœuf.
Aspecs des Homards.   Petit patés à la reine.
Croquette d'Artois.   Salades d'Homard.
Poulards rotis et Jambon.
Mayonaise de Volaille.
Gateaux de Genoise.   Gateau de Vin.
Gelée de vin et noyau et des Oranges.
Crêmes des Fraises et d'Ananas.
Chartreuse des Oranges.   Chartreuse des raisins.
Compôte des Abricot.   Compôte des Oranges.
Gateaux Marangue à la Vanille.
Petit choux à la Crême.   Patisserie.
Fruits et Deserts.

BRIDE CAKE.

Glaces.

Crême des Bisquetts.
L'eau des Fraises.
Goffes.

LEFT: Menu from the extravagant dinner at Wilkie's home, 90 Gloucester Place, after the wedding of Harriet to Harry Bartley.

Martha Rudd and her family, most likely photographed during the First World War. From left to right: (*top row*) Harriet Dawson, Florence Dawson (née Sugg) and Marian Dawson; (*bottom row*) 'Bobbie' Dawson, Lionel Dawson (both children of William) and Martha Rudd.

Martha Rudd's and Wilkie Collins's son, William Charles Collins Dawson, in uniform.

BIRTHS in the District of *Christ Church*				in the County of *Middlesex*.					
Born.	Name, if any	Sex	Name and Surname of Father.	Name and Maiden Surname of Mother.	Rank or Profession of Father.	Signature, Description, and Residence of Informant.	When Registered	Signature of Registrar	Baptismal Name, if added after Registration of Birth.
19 [...] ember [...] 74 [...] ston [...] ace	*William Charles Collins*	*Boy*	*William Dawson*	*Martha Dawson formerly Rudd*	*Barrister at Law*	*Martha Dawson Mother 10 Taunton Place Marylebone*	*First February 1875*	*Frank Nokes Registrar*	—

Birth certificate of William Charles Collins Dawson, with the only known example of the handwriting of Martha Rudd: her signature.

LEFT: Wilkie Collins in a painting attributed to Henry Gray, from a photograph by Napoleon Sarony, New York, *c.* 1873/4.

No. 170.   MEN OF THE DAY, No. 39.
"The Novelist who invented Sensation."

ABOVE: Wilkie Collins in a caricature by Adriano Cecciano for *Vanity Fair*, 3 February 1872.

LEFT: Wilkie Collins by photographe Alexander Bassano, *c.*1880.

'His proposal would be an impertinence if he was not an old fool . . . But the serious side of this affair is that this ignorant fanatic holds my circulation in his pious hands.'

When the theatre production proved an immediate success, Wilkie crowed, 'That fanatical old fool Mudie will be obliged to increase his order.' However, despite translations into several foreign languages, including Russian, sales of Bentley's edition were modest. At least the play was widely hailed, with the *Sunday Times* leading the way in describing it as 'one of the most signal triumphs of modern days'. The paper did have reservations about the ending, adopting a moralistic stance to argue that, although Mercy's penitence was commendable, it was dangerous 'that she should be extolled at the expense of those who have not erred, and that the soul that has just cleansed itself from dismal surroundings of sin and falsehood, should immediately be held up as a type of highest excellence'. Such criticism only reinforced the personal nature of Wilkie's project, since any rejection of the fallen woman by extension condemned Caroline and Martha, his own two imports from the fringes of society.

Wilkie was at last able to think seriously about his long imagined trip to the United States. Earlier in the year he had been approached by Charles S. Brelsford, of the American Literary Bureau in New York, who offered to arrange a programme of talks. Wilkie was not impressed by 'the Speculator who offers to buy me for the U.S.', but asked Tindell to liaise on his behalf, making sure not to commit him to more than ten performances so that he could go elsewhere if the relationship did not work out.

Wilkie was aware that he had little experience of the kind of presentation he would be required to give on such a tour. As practice, he arranged with Ada Cavendish to participate in a charity concert she was sponsoring at the Olympic Theatre on the afternoon of 28 June. The programme included music by the French composer Charles Gounod and his litigious lover Georgina Weldon, as well as Cavendish's rendering of Tennyson's 'The Charge of the Light Brigade', and Wilkie's reading of 'A Terribly Strange Bed', his twenty-year-old story about peculiar happenings in a French hostelry. His turn was not a great success: according to the *Pall Mall Gazette*, 'the audience sat it out, listening to words which were not very audible, smiling at jokes which were by no means laughable, and finally applauding a story which no-one could quite have understood who had not previously met with it in print . . . We should counsel Mr Wilkie Collins to adopt the tone and method of a lecturer, which anyone can acquire, rather than attempt those of an actor which lie beyond his reach.' Georgina Hogarth thought much the same, damning Wilkie with faint praise in a letter to her friend Annie Fields in Boston, 'I have heard he is to read but I cannot imagine his reading <u>well</u>. He seems to me to have no physical qualification for it . . . He is agreeable and easy to get on with – and he has many fine qualities but he has an unusual amount of conceit and self-satisfaction – and I do not think any one can think Wilkie Collins a greater man than Wilkie Collins thinks himself.'

He could afford to be chirpy as he had two successful plays running in London. The Prince of Wales had seen *Man and Wife* twice, on one occasion accompanied by the Tsarevich and Tsarevna of Russia. Wilkie had only to beware of falling between two competing managements. One can imagine the aggrieved enquiry that led him to tell Squire Bancroft in July, 'The least I can do, if all goes well, is to write for the Prince of Wales's Theatre again, and next time to give you and Mrs. Bancroft parts that will be a little more worthy of you.'

Before proceeding any further, and certainly before embarking for the United States, Wilkie was determined to make lasting arrangements for his two families. Caroline had been back at Gloucester Place for at least two years, and Harriet had resumed her role as his amanuensis. Martha continued to lead a more unsettled existence. She and her children were now living at 55 Marylebone Road, a few hundred yards from her previous lodgings in Bolsover Street. It is not clear when they moved – probably in January 1873 when Wilkie made his last payment of £25 to her landlady, Mrs Wells. On 1 February, Wilkie took Martha to Hewetson and Thexton, a furniture shop in Tottenham Court Road (conveniently close to the Prince of Wales Theatre, which was then rehearsing *Man and Wife*). They spent £100 on a range of goods, including a five-foot six-inch medieval sideboard and, the most expensive items, two black and gold chimney glasses, which together cost £15 10s. The invoice was made out to 'Dawson Esq', which showed Wilkie still living the hypocritical double life he so often ridiculed in his writings.

After discussing these matters with Tindell, Wilkie disappeared on a short holiday, which took him to the Hotel Granville in Ramsgate and, a week later, to Eastbourne. He decided on two locations, it may be assumed, because he wanted to spend time with his two families, first with Caroline and Harriet, and then with Martha and their children, in which capacity he doubtless signed the hotel register as Dawson. He subsequently went to Paris for a few days, almost certainly with a male friend, since he stayed at an old bachelor haunt, the Hotel du Helder.

On his return, he finalised details of yet another new will, this time specifically dividing his estate between Caroline and Martha (with their children as subsidiary beneficiaries). He asked Tindell to advise both families should they need it. He also asked him to attend to various domestic details such as the insurance of 'Mrs Dawson's furniture at 55 Marylebone Road', and ensuring that a character reference for his manservant Edward Grosvisier was in order. Then he was ready to take the train to Liverpool and board the Cunard liner, the SS *Algeria*, for the start of his voyage to the United States on 13 September. The actor Wybert Reeve was to have accompanied him, but he could not make it, so Wilkie crossed the Atlantic on his own, with only the prospect of composing a new Christmas story to distract him.

17

AMERICA AND AFTER

ASIDE FROM PROFESSIONAL aspects, Wilkie had never spent much time thinking about the United States. He had a vague sense of the Boston Brahmin intellectual establishment from his father's friendship with Washington Allston. He was familiar with literary representations of the frontier, as found in the work of James Fenimore Cooper, whom he surely drew on for his portrayal of the maverick Mat Marksman in *Hide and Seek*. He also knew something of the country's history and economic potential from Frederick Lehmann. But otherwise he had been surprisingly uninterested in transatlantic developments. He tended to regard the country as a huge market for his work, but a frustrating one, because it failed to protect the copyrights of foreign writers such as himself.

At least there was a friendly, florid face to meet him when he stepped off the *Algeria* at the Cunard pier on the eastside of Manhattan. Charles Fechter, who was now living in Pennsylvania, rescued him from the journalists, who made up a large proportion of the noisy crowd on the quayside, and took him to the Westminster Hotel on the corner of Irving Place and 16th Street, where Wilkie was given the suite Dickens had once occupied, with a private entrance and staircase to the street. Later in the day, Fechter introduced his fellow gastronome to the delights of American cuisine. At the end of the meal, he told Wilkie encouragingly, 'You will find friends here wherever you go', and added, 'Don't forget that I was the friend who introduced you to soft-shell crab.'

Wilkie was well known in the United States, albeit through the widespread pirated editions of his work. One publisher had reportedly sold 120,000 copies of *The Woman in White*, but, as Wilkie plaintively remarked, 'He never sent me sixpence.' His American readers were keen to find out more about the man touted as the new Dickens, and journalists and autograph-hunters pursued him throughout his trip. But they were never quite sure what they were getting and he refused to be typecast. With his thick beard, he was likened in appearance to the late Edwin M. Stanton, who had served as Lincoln's Secretary of War. But, as the *Boston Commonwealth* noted, he was 'not quite what is suggested by his portraits'. Perhaps he needed to be more demonstrative, more pantomime English.

Wybert Reeve told how, before departing on his trip, Wilkie bought himself a cheap ready-made suit at E. Moses and Son. Once in the United States, this tawdry piece of cloth became, in the eyes of a reporter at the *New York Herald*, a stylish suit 'of a fashionable cut, by which an Englishman of taste is known'. Reeve pompously suggested that this was 'a very good illustration of what housekeepers have to put up with in servants in that part of the world'. In fact, it emphasised how difficult Wilkie was to categorise.

On his second night in New York he plunged into the first of many calorie-rich dinners when he was the guest of honour at the Lotos Club, a gathering of authors and journalists, presided over by Whitelaw Reid, the editor of the *New York Tribune* who would later become American ambassador to both France and Britain. Wilkie amused his audience by telling them of his first experience of 'American kindness and hospitality' when he was in Sorrento, aged thirteen, and one of their countrymen lent him two novels, *The Sorrows of Young Werther* and *A Sentimental Journey*.

An early priority was a visit to his publishers Harper and Brothers, who had worked hard to promote his American tour, including running a feature on him in their monthly magazine. They were preparing a special 'Harper's Illustrated Library Edition' of his works, with each novel priced at $1.50 and containing a piece in Wilkie's hand (reproduced in facsimile) which read, 'I gratefully dedicate this collected edition of my works to The American People. Wilkie Collins September 1873.' He created a slight problem when he asked specifically for dry champagne at a dinner hosted by one of the partners, Joseph W. Harper Jr, on 22nd Street. He claimed he preferred it because it was better for his gout. However, his request was not easy to fulfil as Americans usually drank sweet champagne.

Before embarking on any reading, Wilkie travelled to Pennsylvania to spend a few days with Fechter on his 56-acre farm at Quakertown in Bucks County. As was only too clear, Fechter was now but a shadow of his former self. His theatrical ventures in the United States had flopped, and he was drinking heavily. He had been forced to deny persistent rumours of an affair with his long-term leading lady Carlotta Leclercq. More seriously, the newspapers were beginning to refer to his relationship with a married Philadelphia actress called Lizzie Price, whose husband was threatening legal action. However, Fechter was not the sort of person to let such matters obstruct him. He had recently knocked down the fences around his property, saying that a gentleman did not need them. After Price obtained a divorce the following year, Fechter would marry her bigamously. His problems were not helped by his being in greater financial difficulties than usual, a result not only of the mortgage he took out to buy his $10,000 property, but of the economic downturn that was beginning to hit the country following the recent collapse of the Jay Cooke banking house in Philadelphia only thirty miles south of Quakertown. Cooke had failed to raise enough capital to fund the expansion of the Northern Pacific Railway. As a result, the New York Stock Exchange was closed for over a week, and Wilkie now witnessed some of the ensuing panic.

In this uneasy atmosphere, he tried to relax before his first reading in Albany the following week. En route northwards from New York City, he stopped to see his friend John Bigelow, the former American ambassador to France, who lived at a grand house, The Squirrels, at Highland Falls on the Hudson River. While in Europe, Bigelow had lobbied France and Britain to support the Confederacy. Wilkie had met him in Paris and particularly liked his pretty wife Jane. On this occasion Wilkie sang for his supper with the latest literary gossip from England. He revealed that he still had many letters from Dickens, but had been unable to agree terms with Forster for their use in his biography. One of these letters apparently set out Dickens's reasons for leaving his wife. Bigelow recalled how 'Collins enjoyed his dinner, but his brandy after it, yet more so.'

Wilkie continued his journey to Albany by steamboat for the first leg of his tour. Despite advance publicity, his reception was generally modest, in sharp contrast to the regular standing ovations experienced by Dickens. His initial reading of 'The Dream Woman', a reworking of his creepy 1855 story 'The Ostler', went well enough, but the audience at the Opera House in nearby Troy a couple of days later was below expectations. The *Troy Daily Press* judged that Wilkie was 'no actor, and only the thrilling nature of the story redeemed his reading from dullness'. He found the same underwhelming response in Utica and Syracuse, where the local *Daily Courier* opined that he was 'unquestionably a failure' as a reader. Already it was clear that he was out of his depth, and he was not helped by the Amercan Literary Bureau, which was charging too much for his tickets. He decided to skip his scheduled appearance in Rochester and return to Manhattan. The official explanation was that he was suffering from 'nervous prostration and a severe cold', which were affecting his voice.

One bonus was that while in Troy he was given a pamphlet called 'The Trial, Confessions and Conviction of Jesse and Stephen Boorn', detailing a legal scandal in 1812 when a man who had apparently been murdered and disposed of was found alive and well. This gave Wilkie an idea for a story, which he worked on in idle moments during his travels. This grew into 'John Jago's Ghost', which told an identifiable version of this true tale through the eyes of an Englishman who was visiting America after being advised by his doctor to take some rest and enjoy the sea air of the Atlantic. It was ready for publication at the end of the year in the New York *Fireside Companion* and in Britain in the short-lived penny weekly *Home Journal*. It later appeared in book form in the United States with the deliberately chilling title of *The Dead Alive*, which also happened to be a chapter heading in *The New Magdalen*.

Undeterred by an inauspicious start to his tour, Wilkie decided to consolidate by spending most of the next two months in New York, with sorties to Philadelphia, Boston, Baltimore and Washington. Of these last two cities, Wilkie 'greatly preferred Baltimore. The prodigious streets and "avenues" at Washington depressed me indescribably – and I never could get over the idea that the enormous cupola of the Capitol was slowly squeezing the weak and attenuated building underneath into the earth from which it had feebly risen.' His attitude may have been coloured by the inebriated congressman in Washington who insisted on calling him 'Milky' and saying how much he liked his books, including *The Lay of the Last Minstrel*, which was by Walter Scott.

In Boston he was happy to renew his acquaintance with Frederick Lehmann's cousin, Sebastian Benzon Schlesinger, whom he had met in London at the start of the decade. Schlesinger was a cultivated composer who acted as the local German Consul and earned his living at the family firm, the Vickers affiliate Naylor and Co. Wilkie had taken advantage of this connection to arrange for his godson Frank Ward (Charles's son) to work there. When he asked if Frank could be spared to accompany him as his tour assistant, Schlesinger readily agreed.

Wilkie's main reason for remaining in New York was that *The New Magdalen* opened at Augustin Daly's Broadway Theatre on 10 November, with Carlotta Leclercq in the lead role of Mercy Merrick. He was keen to reinforce the idea that this was the official version of his text and anything else was pirated. The play, which had been touring the United States since before its London opening, went down well, even if some individuals still claimed to be outraged. A correspondent of the *Daily Graphic* in New York, for example, thought that 'the author of *The New Magdalen* has opened a recruiting office for prostitutes and has made a direct attack on virtue and honesty. In the whole range of English dramatic literature, there is not a drama so vicious in its teaching, so shameless in its infamous purpose as *The New Magdalen*.'

New Yorkers, suffering from the financial downturn, had little appetite for perceived salaciousness. After a relatively short run, the play was replaced before Christmas by *The Woman in White*, with Wybert Reeve now in New York and playing the role of Count Fosco. This standby received good notices, but it again failed to capture the popular imagination and was closed after running for only two weeks.

Meanwhile, Wilkie's readings continued to meet with a muted reaction. The *New York Herald* reported on his appearance at the

Association Hall, 'Some of the audience went to sleep, some rose and left the hall, and expressions of disappointment were numerous. Our opinion is that Mr Collins has made two mistakes. One consists in reading a piece of trash . . . and the other in having assumed that his vast and deserved success as a novelist was sufficient to waft him triumphantly through an enterprise demanding qualities of the very opposite to those he is universally admitted to possess.' At least there was a ready escape route: he decided not to renew his contract with Brelsford at the American Literary Bureau and instead put himself in the hands of the rival Boston Lyceum Bureau, headed by James Redpath, a former journalist from Scotland.

At some stage he sat for publicity pictures taken by the photographer Napoleon Sarony, who worked out of a studio on Broadway. The business arrangement is not clear since the flamboyant Sarony liked to pay a fee to his celebrity sitters and then recoup his costs by retaining and exploiting the copyright. He noticed that Wilkie adopted a particular expression when talking about his work, especially *The Woman in White*, and endeavoured to capture it. Finding they shared an interest in mildly pornographic pictures of women (one of Sarony's sidelines), the two men became firm friends. Until his death, Wilkie would regard Sarony's images of him looking thoughtful (sometimes wearing a fur coat) as the best ever taken of him.

Before Christmas, Wilkie left on the next lengthy stage of his tour, which took him (and Frank Ward) by rail to Canada and then, via various cities, westwards to Chicago. He was duly feted by his publishers Hunter, Rose in Toronto. In Buffalo on 6 January 1874, he sent an upbeat letter to the actor Frank Archer, who was keeping him informed about the London theatre scene, declaring that his readings were 'getting on famously', 'the one drawback' being that he could not fulfil enough engagements to make decent money, without putting his health at risk.

'Everywhere there is the same anxiety to see and hear me, but I cannot endure the double fatigue of railway travelling and reading on the same day. Thus three or four days a week are lost days (in the matter of money), but gained days (in the matter of health), and I have suffered enough to make health my first consideration.'

For the time being he struggled on. On 8 January, he celebrated his fiftieth birthday in Cleveland, on the southern shore of Lake Erie, but there is no record of any great festivities. After performances in Toledo and Detroit, he and Ward then made a gruelling overnight journey to Chicago, where they arrived on the morning of 16 January and stayed in the luxury Sherman Hotel. At his reading of 'The Dream Woman' in the brand-new Music Hall, only half the 1,700 seats were filled.

At this stage, as he told Fred Lehmann, he was still contemplating 'going "out West" from this – and I may get as far as the Mormons', a sect whose polygamous beliefs continued, for obvious personal reasons, to fascinate him. A few years earlier he had been a guest at a dinner party with the radical politician Sir Charles Wentworth Dilke, who had just published a book called *Greater Britain*, about his travels in America. This was partly a manifesto for the unity of the English-speaking peoples, but also a creditable account of the places he had visited, including Salt Lake City, the Mormon headquarters in Utah, a topic he discussed with Wilkie. Dilke had travelled there with Wilkie's friend William Hepworth Dixon, editor of the *Athenaeum* magazine (which Dilke owned). Wilkie and Dixon did not always see eye to eye, since the latter advocated the cult of athleticism, which Wilkie had pilloried in *Man and Wife*. But they generally got on well, and Dixon had called round at Gloucester Place as recently as late June. Dixon had written *New America*, a book about the journey he shared with Dilke, in which he focused more directly on the Mormons and their taste for polygamy.

He had subsequently visited Oneida, a community in Connecticut, which practised pantagamy, where everyone was married to each other. Dixon had explored this topic further in his 1868 book *Spiritual Wives*, which examined the spiritual and sexual practices of the Somerset-based sect, the Abode of Love or the Agapemone.

If Wilkie had continued west, he might even have reached California, the home of his globe-trotting cousin Alexander Gray, whose mother Catherine (Wilkie's aunt) still worked as an artist in London, though his father John Westcott Gray had long since decamped to Thun in Switzerland, where he was more interested in fundamentalist Christianity than painting.

But Wilkie felt exhausted by the hardships he had experienced in American trains rolling across landscapes 'as flat, as monotonous, and as uninteresting to the traveller, as any that the earth can show'. As he wrote to Sebastian Schlesinger from Chicago on 17 January, 'I feel the "sleeping car" in the "small of my back", and in the drums of my ears at this moment.'

He later recalled an incident on this trip when, 'after two days and a night's travelling, I was so utterly worn out that I asked the landlord of the hotel if he had any very dry champagne . . . I drank the whole of it, and informed him that although it was only noon, I was going at once to bed, and all visitors were to be told that I might possibly not get up for a week. I heard afterwards that after 24 hours some callers were allowed to come up and peep in the door, which I had not blocked; but all they saw was Mr Collins still fast asleep.'

Aside from a touch of rheumatism while at Niagara Falls, Wilkie's health held up well. He showed no signs of gout and, if he was taking opium, he kept quiet about it. But he was exhausted and needed to reassess his plans. If he was looking for an excuse to curtail his trip, he could point to the economic downturn, which had led to factory closures and was affecting his audiences. But at this point, a more personal matter arose:

Martha's landlord was preparing to vacate the house in Marylebone Road and was offering Wilkie an opportunity to buy the lease. He counselled his mistress to seek advice from Tindell, whom he took the trouble to remind, 'N.B. <u>You remember our name</u> – Mr and Mrs "Dawson".'

He had had high expectations of Chicago, a city which had captured his imagination when it was razed to the ground in the great fire of 1871 (after which he had contributed spontaneously to its rebuilding appeal). But he now told Jane Bigelow, 'Don't tell anybody – but the truth is I am not sorry to leave Chicago. The dull sameness of the great blocks of iron and brick overwhelms me. The whole city seems to be saying, "See how rich I am after the fire, and what a tremendous business I do!"'

Back in Boston at the end of January, he was happy to relax with Sebastian Schlesinger and his wife Berthe, who lived at 79 Marlborough Road, one-time home of Richard Dana Jr, who had corresponded with Wilkie back in the 1840s. Wearing his businessman's hat, Schlesinger arranged two $5,000 (or £1,000) life insurance policies (both underwritten by American companies) for his guest. Though Wilkie was required to pay a premium of over £70 per annum on each of them, he could at least reassure himself that Caroline and Martha, the ultimate recipients of the policies, would be financially secure if anything should happen to him.

The following month he was overwhelmed when the cream of New England's intelligentsia congregated at the St James Hotel in Boston for a dinner in his honour. Among those present were Henry Wadsworth Longfellow, Oliver Wendell Holmes and Samuel Langhorne Clemens (Mark Twain). Wilkie no doubt enjoyed hearing the literary critic Edwin Whipple proclaim that there was now a region of the imagination called 'Collins's land' and that 'one would as soon doubt of the reality and veracity of Robinson Crusoe as some of the beings' Wilkie had created.

The evening concluded with a toast in verse by Wendell Holmes, which played on the artist and poet commemorated in Wilkie's name:

> And so his double name comes true,
> They christened better than they knew,
> And Art proclaims him twice her son,
> Painter and poet, both in one!

Wilkie had made arrangements to return home on the Cunard steamship the *Parthia* out of Boston on 7 March. But first he travelled to New York to say his farewells (to Fechter among others) and to carry out a short journey that was important to him. Three days before his departure, he slipped away to visit a religious community at Wallingford in Connecticut. He had been hoping to follow Hepworth Dixon to Oneida, but that group had merged with the one at Wallingford. Known as Perfectionists, from their belief in the possibility of the perfect life on earth, the members of this communistic, polygamous, professedly Christian society continued to enjoy remarkable sexual freedom, with the elders encouraged to initiate young boys and girls into the pleasures of lovemaking. One member later wrote about Wilkie's three-hour visit: 'Mr Collins thought our system of communism the most perfect democracy in existence . . . He thought there is a great need of social reform in England, and said that underneath the surface of society there is a great deal of seething and fermentation which is sure to break out at last, in some form or other. He had no doubt that a Community such as ours would not be tolerated in England, and mentioned the Agapemone as a case in point.'

This not only confirms Wilkie's familiarity with the Agapemone but shows that, as a persistent critic of formal matrimony, he was fascinated by the practice of polygamy. At least his visit to Wallingford made up for his missing the chance to observe the practices of the Mormons in Utah. He would draw on it to describe Amelius Goldenheart's utopian community in his 1879 novel *The Fallen Leaves*.

Shortly after returning to London, Wilkie was walking in Hyde Park when he ran into Lucy Bethia Walford, a well-connected Scottish novelist who wrote the sort of frothy books that were popular with Mudie's library customers but are forgotten today. She and a friend had been visiting Holman Hunt and they invited Wilkie to dinner. He proved surprisingly eager to accept, insisting that they should make it that same evening since he was just back from America, had seen no one, and had nowhere else to go. Over dinner, he talked inconsequentially about having been the centre of journalistic attention and how his health had benefited from the dry climate, before concluding with a typical piece of polite obfuscation, 'A kinder, warmer-hearted set of people surely does not exist, only their ways *are* queer.'

One reason Wilkie had not seen anyone was that his immediate priority was to sort out accommodation for Martha and their two children. Any idea of buying the lease on the house in Marylebone Road had been abandoned. Instead, they moved a few hundred yards to 10 Taunton Place, tucked away off the northernmost end of Gloucester Place. He would describe a similarly situated house in *The Fallen Leaves* later in the decade – a cottage 'in a by-road, just outside' Regent's Park, where the do-gooding Amelius Goldenheart lived with Simple Sally, the teenage prostitute he found on the street.

Wilkie had earned £2,500 from his American trip, which was nothing like the £19,000 Dickens brought back from his venture across the Atlantic. It was, however, a tidy sum for six months' work, and he comforted himself with the thought that he could have made much more if he had been prepared to speak every night, but it would have been at the expense of his health. As it was, it did not take long for his old afflictions to creep back. Before a month was out, he was complaining, 'My native climate has already made me so "bilious" that I can hardly see. My eyes are yellow, and my head aches.'

As he eased himself back into London life, taking in the Bancrofts' production of a favourite play, Sheridan's *School for Scandal*, at the Prince of Wales Theatre, his solution for his constitutional problems was a well-tried one – a redoubling of his work effort. Over the next few months he packaged for Bentley a selection of his readings from America, including a lengthy new adaptation of *The Frozen Deep* that he had tried out on his audiences towards the end of his tour. He also channelled his energies into a new novel, *The Law and the Lady*, which indicated how difficult it was for him to wrench himself from his roots, since it bore many hallmarks from his earlier sensation fiction as it relentlessly set about unravelling secrets and allowing the truth about marriages, identities, madness and alleged murder to emerge.

Wilkie marked out his ground by starting his story with the words from the marriage service: 'For after this manner in the old time the holy women also who trusted in God adorned themselves, being in subjection unto their own husbands; even as Sarah obeyed Abraham, calling him lord; whose daughters ye are as long as ye do well, and are not afraid with any amazement.' This immediately set the book up as another variation on his fascination with the institution of matrimony, but this time as a vehicle to subvert the patriarchal nature of traditional marriage.

The wedding in question is ostensibly between Eustace and Valeria Woodville, but little about it is right; nobody seems to be who he or she is supposed to be. While on honeymoon in Ramsgate, Valeria discovers that her husband's surname is really Macallan. But she remains in the dark about the significance of this until, donning the mantle of a sleuth, she visits his old friend, the libidinous Major Fitz-David, who claims that he is honour-bound not to reveal anything, but allows her to search his rooms for further information. She finds a photograph of Eustace holding hands with another woman, inscribed to the Major from 'his friends S. and E. M.' She then alights on an account of a trial in which Eustace Macallan was accused of poisoning his first wife, Sara, with arsenic. He was set free, but only after the ambiguous Scottish verdict of 'not proven'. The tenacious Valeria then determines to overturn this judgement and prove her husband's innocence. She pursues various contradictory leads which take her *inter alios* to another of Eustace's friends, the comic-grotesque figure of Miserrimus Dexter, 'a mixture of a tiger and a monkey', who, though crippled, half-mad and confined to a wheel-chair, helps her solve the mystery.

Describing herself as 'capricious, idle, inquisitive', Valeria is another self-motivated sensation heroine, who refuses to play the subservient wife and turns herself into a detective. Her husband is ineffectual by comparison as she works to restore his good name and, by legitimising her marriage, her name too. Though the narrative moves sequentially, she often seems to operate in a hall of mirrors, emphasised by the recurring image of the looking glass. The book's dedication to Wilkie's French actor friend Regnier underlines the theatrical dimension. But the rendering takes it to another level, as if he is sharing a fantastical joke. In an enigmatic preface he asks his readers to 'bear in mind certain established truths', the first being 'that the actions of human beings are not invariably governed by the laws of pure reason'. In his world of illusions, an outsider, such as Ezra Jennings in *The Moonstone*, often possesses the psychic faculties to uncover the truth. Dexter is no Jennings, or rather his insights come from a different place in the spectrum of human experience (where eccentricity moves into madness), but Valeria admits that he 'openly expresses . . . thoughts and feelings which most of us are ashamed of as weaknesses, and which we keep to ourselves accordingly'.

Wilkie again drew on the trial of Madeleine Smith, the middle-class Glaswegian whose guilt was 'not proven' in 1857 when she was accused of using arsenic to poison her former lover. Wilkie asked Tindell for details of Smith's case, which he supplemented with information from his copy of John Hill Burton's *Narratives from Criminal Trials in Scotland*. While he continued to be exercised by the quirks of the legal system, his main target was the state of matrimony and its attendant hypocrisies.

In the process, he peppered his text with autobiographical snippets – the honeymoon in the 'favourite watering place' of Ramsgate, the disapproving mother-in-law, Fitz-David's address off Portman Square (around the corner from Wilkie's house), and Eustace himself is something of a self-portrait, with his slight impediment, and beard streaked with grey. The womanising Fitz-David shows another side of Wilkie, torn between the two types of women represented in fine brass reproductions in his house – the Venus de Milo and the Venus Callipyge, or the cool beauty of Caroline and the more overtly physical attractions of Martha. One of Fitz-David's girlfriends comes from the same background as Martha: 'Would you believe it,' he crows, 'I met with her at the railway station. She was behind the counter in a refreshment-room, poor innocent, rinsing wine-glasses, and singing over her work.'

In June 1874, Wilkie arranged for this promising new story to be serialised in the *Graphic*, but he was uncertain where and how it should be published in volume form. He remained as keen as ever for his books to circulate widely among 'the unknown public', the mass readership he had identified in his 1858 article for *Household Words*. But the books market was still dominated by Mudie's and the circulating libraries with their insatiable demand for expensive three-volume editions for their customers. Smith, Elder tried to steer him towards cheap two-shilling editions, at least after Mudie's had had their way. But George Bentley, who had a significant financial interest in Mudie's following its flotation in 1864, waged a subtle campaign to lure Wilkie from Smith's clutches. Focusing initially on *The Woman in White*, he argued that Wilkie would profit more from a six-shilling edition than from anything Smith could put out at a cheaper price, and to gild the lily he pointed to the phenomenal sales Mrs Henry Wood had enjoyed at that price. By the end of the decade, her most successful title, *East Lynne*, would have sold 85,000 copies in Bentley's six-shilling uniform edition. Wilkie was hugely impressed and not a little jealous to learn of the success of his female competitor, whom he often enlisted as an ally in his campaign on theatre copyright.

Matters took a new turn in August when he received an unsolicited offer for his new book from Andrew Chatto, who had recently taken the helm of a new publishing house, Chatto & Windus. Chatto proposed a sum of £1,000 for a seven-year licence on *The Law and the Lady*, with the copyright remaining with Wilkie. However, Chatto was not prepared to allow any edition under the price of two shillings and sixpence for the duration of that period. This was attractive since Smith aimed to price his cheap editions well below that figure. When the competitive Chatto returned with a further offer of £2,000 for a similar seven-year licence on all the back titles, plus a promise to bring them out in a uniform edition, Wilkie was hooked. George Bentley graciously ceded his corner. He and Wilkie remained on good terms, but Smith felt aggrieved and fought to keep control of *No Name*, *After Dark* and *Armadale*, as indeed was his right. Aside from the collection *The Frozen Deep and Other Stories* and *A Rogue's Life*, which were committed to Bentley, all Wilkie's titles, new and old, were published thereafter by Chatto & Windus. (Exceptions were the three titles retained by Smith, which went to Chatto in 1890 following Wilkie's death.) In the end, Chatto did not publish the six-shilling editions Wilkie wanted. At the request of the circulating libraries, his books were still first presented in three-volume editions retailing at a guinea and a half, followed by a series of editions at around two shillings.

In between these negotiations, Wilkie took time off to support Ted (as he now called him) Pigott's candidacy for the position of Examiner of Plays (effectively the official theatre censor under the Lord Chamberlain), following the retirement of William Bodham Donne. His friend had recently failed to land the job of Secretary of the Royal Academy, despite Wilkie lobbying Millais and others. So Pigott went to considerable lengths to produce a thirty-page booklet of testimonials, which he sent to interested parties. He included letters of support from influential friends such as Jean-Sylvain Van de Weyer, Belgium's well-read Minister (or Ambassador) to Britain, who was respected at Buckingham Palace, as well as from writers such as Anthony Trollope, G.H. Lewes and, of course, Wilkie. This time Pigott proved successful and was appointed to the highly important post.

In early September, Wilkie took a short holiday in another of his old haunts, Boulogne, before returning for *The Law and the Lady*'s first outing in serial form in the *Graphic* on 26 September. He wrote another story, 'A Fatal Fortune', which appeared in *All the Year Round* in October, tilting at two of his favourite targets – the marriage laws and private asylums. This joined 'The Dream Woman' and the title story in the composite volume *The Frozen Deep and Other Stories*, which appeared from Bentley in November.

There was drama in early October when the Avenue Road house of the Clows, Caroline's ex-parents-in-law, was badly damaged following a huge explosion on a barge passing through the Regent's Canal en route to the nearby Albany Street Barracks. This marked the start of a new round of terrorist alarm when the Fenians were wrongly blamed for the outrage and troops were called in to ensure the safety of the animals in the zoo. According to one newspaper report, the walls, windows and doors were all destroyed, but Mr and Mrs Clow 'scrambled, half dazed, but without injury, from the bed, and made their escape in the wind and rain in their night clothes to the stable'. Joseph Clow later sat on a committee looking into questions of liability relating to the accident.

Wilkie now had his own domestic drama to deal with. On Christmas Day 1874, Martha presented him with what he called 'a Christmas Box, in the shape of a big boy'. William Charles Collins Dawson was the first of his children to be officially registered, as was now required by law. The date of his birth suggests that he was conceived almost immediately after Wilkie returned from America. William's arrival raised a not unprecedented dilemma for Wilkie. Should he spend Christmas Day at the bedside of the mother of his first-born son? Or was his place with his *maîtresse-en-titre* in Gloucester Place? It is not known how he resolved this, but it seems extraordinary that he failed to mention this addition to his family when he wrote to his friend Jane Bigelow a few days later. Aside from the frost and the fog, he noted that 'there is really no news here'.

18

TWO HOUSES, TWO FAMILIES

AFTER YEARS OF rootlessness, Wilkie had, at the start of 1875, not one but two fixed points in his universe – Gloucester Place, where he lived with Caroline and Harriet, and, within easy walking distance, Taunton Place, the home of Martha and what he was starting to call his morganatic family. At the former, his *maîtresse-en-titre*, who was now in her mid-forties, presided over his domestic life with steely exactitude and maintained him in as good a state of health as possible. At her side was her daughter who, as Wilkie's acknowledged amanuensis, assisted with writing his letters and copying his manuscripts. Together they provided the support system any industrious writer might want. At Taunton Place, his buxom lover, who was not yet thirty, gave him children, sex and a different form of relaxation. It was an unequal set of relationships, given particular emphasis by the word 'morganatic', which implied social disparity between the parties. But somehow it worked, and the two women involved learned, albeit sometimes reluctantly, to live with each other's presence.

Wilkie also hoped for stability in his professional affairs, having recently alighted on Andrew Chatto, who would serve as his publisher for the rest of his life. As he had begun to experience, English literature was entering a difficult twenty-year hiatus between the passing of the great mid-Victorian masters, such as Dickens and Thackeray, and the emergence of a new generation of single-volume storytellers, including Stevenson and Kipling. The old, once thriving market for serials in magazines, such as the *Cornhill*, had melted away, and it would take a while before a new mass readership created by the Education Act of 1870 would take its place.

The 1870s were proving to be a period of global economic downturn that led to renewed workers' agitation, followed by an inevitable conservative reaction. On cue, in April 1874, Gladstone's reforming Liberal Government was thrown out of office and Disraeli returned to power, keen to divert attention from domestic problems by expanding the Empire abroad.

As so often, Wilkie could see the ramifications for his profession. As he told George Smith at the start of the decade, 'My own impression is that a very few years more will see a revolution in the publishing trade for which most of the publishers are unprepared . . . I don't believe in the gigantic monopolies, which cripple free trade, lasting much longer. The Mudie monopoly and the W.H. Smith monopoly are anomalies in a commercial country.'

At the time, Wilkie had been reassuring George Smith that he wanted to retain him as his publisher. But now he felt differently. Unlike Smith and Bentley, both second-generation bookmen, Andrew Chatto was an entrepreneurial one-man operator, whose favourite pastime was yachting, which endeared him to Wilkie. After the death of his former employer John Camden Hotten, a small publisher in Piccadilly, he teamed up with William E. Windus, a rich poet willing to act as sleeping partner in their new firm, Chatto & Windus. Chatto had recently shown his commercial instincts by issuing *Thackerayana*, a book of notes and sketches by the late William Makepeace Thackeray, which George Smith, of Smith, Elder, then went to court to prove it infringed his copyright. Chatto had to withdraw the book, which did nothing to improve relations, already soured by Wilkie's defection, between the two publishers.

Meanwhile, Wilkie could enjoy a bird's eye view of the wider domestic political scene. The 1874 general election had seen Frederick Lehmann wanting to give something back to society and so he had stood as a Liberal candidate for Middlesex, where he was defeated. Undeterred, he returned to the hustings three years later in Waterford in Ireland, where *The Times* described him as on the 'left wing' of his party and eager 'to assist as far as possible in getting everything done a Munster peasant can desire'. Wilkie told Sebastian Schlesinger, 'He seems to have a good chance of getting into Parliament this time, so far as I can learn.' But Lehmann again failed to win election. He was eventually returned to Parliament as MP for Evesham in a by-election in 1880. But his majority of just two votes was challenged and overturned. While Wilkie did not follow his friend in all his policies, such as in promoting denominational schools in Ireland, he shared his basic liberal instincts.

Wilkie started 1875 on the wrong foot when he became involved in a spat with the *Graphic*, which was serialising *The Law and the Lady*. He was annoyed that the paper's editor, Arthur Locker, had seen fit to bowdlerise a section of his story where Miserrimus Dexter forcibly tried to kiss Valeria. A sign of uncertain times in publishing, Locker declared that he and his directors regarded this incident as an attempted rape (his word was 'violation') and, as such, unfit to appear in a family paper. When he added that they were also concerned to discover that Valeria was pregnant, it became clear that this was Wilkie's real offence – to have suggested such an ordeal for a woman with child. After Locker tried to justify his censorship in a later issue of the *Graphic*,

Wilkie enlisted the help of his friend Edmund Yates, who was now editing the gossipy weekly *The World*, to run an editorial piece detailing what had happened and then allow Wilkie to vent his spleen in a letter to the editor, which poked fun at Locker and his fellow directors 'all simmering together in a moral miasma of their own dirty raising'. This revealed that the *Graphic* had reneged on an agreement Wilkie had cannily inserted in his contract, giving him ultimate copy approval for anything that went into the paper under his name.

Following the book's publication by Chatto & Windus in February, the reviews were poor. While praising Wilkie for his readability, the *Observer* declared, 'Anything less literary, in any sense of the word, it would be impossible to conceive than this novel. There is no attempt at any sort of style, unless it be the style of studied baldness.' The *Pall Mall Gazette* could not cope with the surrealism of the characters of Miserrimus Dexter and his female sidekick Ariel: 'If a man has the misfortune to be visited by such dreams the best thing he can do is to try and forget them as soon as possible afterwards.'

Since he liked to share his experiences of publishers with writer friends, Wilkie warned Charles Reade to steer clear of the *Graphic*. As professional authors, both men had a similar approach to the literary world, fighting their corners against publishers (Reade was particularly active in the struggle for international copyright), and working hard to ensure their novels were topical and well-researched. They certainly had a mutual respect for one another. On one of Wilkie's letters to him, Reade scribbled approvingly, 'For literary ingenuity in building up a plot and investing it with mystery, give me dear old Wilkie Collins against the world.' On a personal level, their relationship flourished owing to the similarity of their domestic situations. Reade's mistress, Mrs Seymour, was known as his 'housekeeper', which was also Caroline's official designation. Reade had a son from a previous liaison, who was described as his 'godson', in the same way that Harriet would call Wilkie her 'godfather'.

Having finished *The Law and the Lady* in March, Wilkie treated himself to a short restorative break in Paris. On his return, he contentedly described himself as 'the idlest man living'. But he was not the sort of person to stand still for long. He had been contemplating a pared down version of *Armadale*, which would be staged as *Miss Gwilt* at the Alexandra Theatre in Liverpool in December. Ada Cavendish took the title role, which had been restructured to make the scheming minx of the book into a more sympathetic character and her accomplice Dr Downward, played by Arthur Cecil, as the unmitigated villain.

As for stories, he told the forgiving George Bentley that he was considering a serial for his magazine *Temple Bar*. He gave a hint of his intended subject matter in 'The Clergyman's Confession', an interim tale that appeared in *The World* in August. Sometimes described as a ghost story, it was really about the power of second sight, chronicling the inexorable course of events leading to the murder of a sweet-natured Frenchwoman.

Inspiration for his *Temple Bar* piece struck the following month when, as he put it to Bentley, he holed up in Lowestoft, after 'wandering about the Eastern coast'. This was Wilkie's way of saying (or, true to fashion, not saying) that he had been spending time with Martha and her family at nearby Winterton. This year there was an added reason for his being there since Alice Rudd, who had been working for her sister Martha in London, had followed her in another way and had become pregnant out of wedlock. The conception of Alice's illegitimate daughter Anne is impossible to date since the baby has no birth certificate. It may have occurred in the previous few months, providing a reason for this trip. Or it may have taken place during this holiday. (Anne's given age in subsequent censuses suggests that she was born in 1875 or 1876.)

Her father was James Spooner, an agricultural labourer in Winterton. However, Alice did not hang around to bring up her daughter. She left Anne with her grandparents, James and Mary Rudd, and returned to London to help her sister Martha. Since Wilkie supported the Taunton Place household, she was doubtless able to make more money to support her child there as the housekeeper (as she was described in the 1881 census) than in Norfolk. While she was away, her daughter and James Spooner lodged with her parents in Winterton. It was not until 1891, after Wilkie's death, that Alice was definitely back in Winterton, living in Beach Road with her daughter and her husband. No marriage is recorded, but she is described in the census of that year as Alice Spooner, James's wife. Living with them also was her daughter Anne, as well as her (and Martha's) doughty eighty-four-year-old father. Her mother Mary had died three years earlier in 1888.

After his trip to the east coast, Wilkie was to have joined George Bentley on a climbing trip in Wales, but something, either in his relationships or his own health, had gone wrong, and he did not feel up to it. However, he cheerfully told the publisher that he had 'got an idea of another new story (of the fanciful kind with a touch of the supernatural in it) – but it would occupy four or five numbers at least.'

This was *The Two Destinies*, which drew on his Suffolk surroundings to tell of George and Mary, two childhood sweethearts who for a long time defy and then finally fulfil her grandmother's prophecy that their lives are inextricably linked. In the meantime, George goes to America and returns as the heir to the considerable Germaine fortune, while Mary suffers a serious illness that results in a complete change in her looks. They subsequently bump into each other without any spark of recognition. George is attracted to her but she is now the wife of a bigamous Dutchman. George and Mary develop a powerful telepathic communication, which leads to his being summoned to her side on three occasions. At the last of these encounters, in Holland, they finally recognise each other and resolve to marry. However, the whiff of scandal attached to her past means that, like Mercy and Julian in *The New Magdalen*, they are ostracised by English society. In a scene reminiscent of Lady Janet's ball in that story, the newly-wed Germaines hold a dinner party to which none of the men (apart from a visiting American) bring their wives. As a result, again like Mercy and Julian, but without the moral hand-wringing, they emigrate, this time to Naples.

Although its immediate inspiration was his trip to Suffolk, the story harks back to Wilkie's visit to Wallingford in Connecticut. That had sparked his interest not only in polygamy but in communal living, which led him to look into New Harmony, an atheist utopian society in Indiana started by the Scottish industrialist Robert Owen and continued by his son, Robert Dale Owen, a spiritualist who advocated radical causes such as divorce reform.

Wilkie would return later to the theme of communal living. For the time being he was interested in the younger Owen's spiritualism. Although he had no truck with this set of beliefs as a quasi-religion, he was fascinated by its exploration of extrasensory powers. Following his journalistic forays into mesmerism and animal magnetism in the early 1850s, his books often touched on the hidden psychic forces at play in everyday life.

The Two Destinies drew inspiration from Robert Dale Owen's book *Footfalls on the Boundary of Another World*, a brisk digest of paranormal experience through the ages. There was leavening too from Emanuel Swedenborg, the eighteenth-century Swedish spiritualist with a scientific bent, who had a strong following among writers, including Coleridge, Balzac and Julian Hawthorne, son of the author of the classic American novel *The Scarlet Letter*, who was then living in London.

Wilkie was still writing *The Two Destinies* when he visited Brussels with Caroline in October. Following the route his father had taken in 1828, they continued to Antwerp, where he paid homage to Rubens, and then on to The Hague, where he saw his now authorised Dutch publishers, Belinfante Brothers, and gathered local details about Holland for the end of this story.

After *Miss Gwilt*'s successful premiere, attended by Wilkie, in Liverpool in early December, the play had to wait until the following April before opening in London at the Globe Theatre. By then, *The Two Destinies* was running as a serial in *Temple Bar*, and would be published by Chatto & Windus in August, with a dedication to Charles Reade, 'my old friend and brother in the Art'. (As usual, it was published more or less simultaneously in serial and volume form by Harper's in America.)

Miss Gwilt received a mixed reception when it reached London. The consensus was that Wilkie had failed to boil down a complicated story into digestible theatrical fare, and that it was too long. He did not see the production himself because his rheumatic gout was playing up and badly affecting his eyes. He was consulting George Critchett, a leading Harley Street eye surgeon, who forbade him from public appearances. (Critchett was familiar with the theatre since his son Richard had just embarked on a career at Henry Irving's Lyceum under the stage name Claude Carton.) All a chastened Wilkie could do was 'work, walk, visit to my morganatic family – such is life'.

Once able to venture out with an eye patch, he took himself (and perhaps Martha and the children) to Worthing in July 1876. In his usual non-committal style he referred in a letter to 'wandering about the south coast', so he may also have travelled to Brighton to see a spoof version called *The Gwilty Governess and the Downey Doctor*. At the end of August, *The Two Destinies* was published, but the reaction was again disappointing. The *Observer* found it simply implausible and chastised Wilkie for failing to make clear whether he believed in the supernatural or not. The *Saturday Review* did not waste words in demolishing 'an amazingly silly book . . . almost silly enough to be amusing through its very absurdity.'

Within days of the novel's publication, Wilkie turned his back on this harsh competitive world and went to Paris and then Switzerland with Caroline and Harriet. Continental Europe was still his favoured destination when his spirits needed lifting. En route, his party travelled with Henry (known as Harry) Powell Bartley, a twenty-one-year-old trainee solicitor. Harry's late father had followed the same profession in a family firm in Portman Square, close to Wilkie in Gloucester Place. He had also enjoyed a significant side-line as a property developer in West London, but since his death his relations had been squabbling over his assets.

Wilkie and Caroline liked young Harry and identified him as a potential suitor for Harriet, who was now twenty-five and getting to the point when, if she did not marry soon, a lifetime of spinsterhood loomed. There was a sense of purpose in the way Wilkie wrote to Harry from the Hotel Westminster in Paris on 17 October, declaring, 'I am indeed sorry that the claims of business obliged you to leave us here. We all miss our travelling companion,' and concluding, 'I hope we shall meet in Gloucester Place.'

Paris still offered special attractions, for Wilkie returned there in February 1877 for a post-Christmas jaunt of the kind he used to enjoy with Dickens. For a variety of reasons, his health being the most obvious, he was having difficulty conceiving full-length novels and now fell back on his proven skills at producing short stories. Chatto made life easier for him by purchasing the monthly magazine *Belgravia* from John Maxwell, who had married Mary Elizabeth Braddon a couple of years earlier and wanted to concentrate on other things. *Belgravia* had been the house organ of sensationalism under the Maxwells, but Chatto, who now not only owned but edited it, aimed to steer it away from these roots.

Wilkie had no problem finding a home for 'The Captain's Last Love' in *Belgravia* in January. Before long he was working on 'Percy and the Prophet', which appeared in July in a special summer number of *All the Year Round*, which was now under the direction of Dickens's son Charley. He also completed two further stories for Christmas issues at the end of the year – 'My Lady's Money: An Episode in the Life of a Young Lady' for the *Illustrated London News* and 'The Duel in Herne Wood' for *Belgravia*. These were unremarkable potboilers, which offered a combination of exotic locations, romantic triangles, detection and the supernatural.

'My Lady's Money' was the most interesting because it picked up on the widespread dissatisfaction with the police force, and in particular with its detective branch. Echoing Count Fosco, a character observes, 'Every crime is more or less a mystery. You will see that the mysteries which the police discover are, almost without exception, mysteries made penetrable by the commonest capacity, through the extraordinary stupidity exhibited in the means taken to hide the crime. On the other hand, let the guilty man or woman be a resolute and intelligent person, capable of setting his (or her) wits fairly against the wits of the police – in other words, let the mystery really *be* a mystery – and cite me a case if you can (a really difficult and perplexing case) in which the criminal has not escaped.' So Lady Lydiard, the victim of a theft, is prevailed on to engage a retired sleuth, Old Sharon, who lives in run-down lodgings, smokes a pipe, wears a tattered flannel dressing gown and reads French novels (a version of Sherlock Holmes a decade *avant la lettre*). The story also includes an affectionate portrait of a Scottish terrier called Tommie, the subject also of an in-joke since Wilkie had a much-loved dog of that name, but spelled with a 'y', which the story suggests is more vulgar than the 'ie' of the text. Tommie even turns investigator and unearths evidence of the stolen £500 bank note, leading some commentators to dub him unconvincingly as the first canine detective.

Unable to make much progress in the current literary market, Wilkie was keener than ever to succeed in the theatre. His great hope now was his collaboration with the actor-manager Henry Neville on the first official dramatic version of *The Moonstone* at the Olympic Theatre. As with his previous adaptations, Wilkie worked hard to compress his meandering text into suitable theatrical form. Certain characters were killed off, the love interest between Franklin Blake and Rachel Verinder became the main focus, the Moonstone was now stolen in an alcoholic stupor rather than an opium-induced reverie, and the whole play took place over the course of twenty-four hours on a single set in the inner hall of the Verinder house.

Wilkie struggled through until the opening night on 17 September, and then departed with Caroline for 'a little rest and change' in Southern Germany and Northern Italy, including a trip to Venice. Caroline was due a holiday since her former mother-in-law Mary Ann Graves, had died four months earlier at the age of seventy-nine. Having played an important part in Harriet's early years, Mary Ann had lived latterly at nearby 21 Molyneux Street, which meant she was available if assistance was required. Her close liaison with Wilkie's household is attested by the fact that his cook, Sarah Masey, provided the authorities with the details of her death.

This time Harriet did not accompany her mother and Wilkie

but stayed in Gloucester Place, signing letters and performing odd jobs on his behalf. With her grandmother no longer around, she probably welcomed an opportunity to get to know her near neighbour, Harry Bartley, who had just qualified as a solicitor.

Wilkie's holiday got off to a bad start. He had been negotiating a New York transfer for *The Moonstone* with Augustin Daly, and was even prepared to change the title so his work could be protected from pirates. In this respect he put forward various alternatives, including *The Yellow Diamond* (his favourite), *Dreaming and Waking* and *False Appearances*. However, he got no further than Brussels when he read in *Galignani's Messenger*, the leading English newspaper on the Continent, that Daly was in serious financial difficulties. And by the time he reached Munich, three weeks after the play's opening in London, he learned that receipts there had plummeted. So he agreed with Henry Neville that the production should close on 17 November 1877.

Back home, a Christmas profile of Wilkie in the 'Celebrities at Home' slot in Edmund Yates's *The World* could disguise neither his own disappointment nor his physical decline. At the age of fifty-three, his hair was almost white and he was smoking incessantly, it reported. However, he was, as always, prepared to air his opinions. Joseph Addison was dismissed as 'a neat but trivial writer, not in the least vigorous or dramatic', so different from Byron whose letters displayed the best English he knew – 'perfectly simple and clear, bright and strong'. As the reporter noted, Wilkie demanded 'dramatic power and poetic insight' in his prose writers. Thus Goldsmith always scored over Fielding and Smollett. And it was 'the same on the great stage of the world', where Wilkie argued for the greatness of Napoleon, who had been debunked of late. 'But you cannot break the idol, for his deeds strike the imagination. He was a dramatic man.'

Despite the robust nature of these pronouncements, Wilkie's

low spirits were again evident when he sent end of year greetings
to Nina Lehmann and her family, who were enjoying winter cheer
in Cannes. He apologised for being unable to join them, since
there were 'all sorts of impediments – literary and personal – which
keep me in England at the most hateful of all English seasons (to
me), the season of Cant and Christmas.'

Wilkie still hoped to get stuck into a full-scale novel. He
had an idea for a major work, a further spin-off from his experience of communal life in the United States, but when the
complexity of his domestic life prevented him committing
himself, he marked time with *The Haunted Hotel*, a novella that
drew on his recent visit to Venice.

The restraints on his progress inevitably included his health.
As he told fellow author (and fellow gout sufferer) James Payn
in early February 1878, 'I am (say) half alive. While I was away
last year in the Tyrol and Italy, I was 25 years old. Towards the
end of [18]77, being obliged to return to my native damp and
changes, I became, by rheumatic reckoning, 95.'

He usually managed to overcome such afflictions, but the
event holding him back from any major initiative was Harriet's
imminent marriage to Harry Bartley. Although Wilkie was not
the type to spend much time in elaborate planning, he regarded
this as an important event. On 4 February he gave Harriet a
wedding gift of £50 (it was clearly thus because the sum differed
so greatly from the five or six guineas he usually paid her for
her secretarial duties).

Five weeks later, on 12 March, the ceremony took place at
St Mary's, Bryanston Square. Taking a leaf out of her mother's
book, Harriet managed to tell a couple of fibs when she signed
the register, claiming that she was twenty-four, when in fact she
was twenty-seven, and that she was the daughter of an army
captain, when her father had been nothing of the sort. Harry
correctly stated his age as twenty-three, and that he was living at

14 Upper Hamilton Terrace in Maida Vale, where the Bartleys had moved following the death of Harry's father. The service was conducted by Harry's uncle, the Reverend Henry Powell, who was also a trustee of his father's will, with help from the church's vicar, the high-minded Reverend the Honourable W.H. Fremantle, who had been a fellow of All Souls, Oxford. Wilkie signed the register as a witness, the first time he had done so since Joseph Stringfield's wedding twenty years earlier. After the ceremony, everyone filed back to Gloucester Place for an extravagant wedding dinner. The menu, all in French, offered *Cotelletes de homard*, *Ris de veau aux truffes* and *Cotelletes d'agneau aux petits pois*, as well as salmon, ham, chicken, pâté and innumerable puddings.

The newly-weds went to live in Alexandra Road, less than a quarter of a mile from Finchley Road, and just down from where Walter Hartright had first met the Woman in White. St John's Wood was expanding northwards into Swiss Cottage. From there Harry could take the omnibus to Baker Street and walk to his office. In 1879 South Hampstead railway station opened at the bottom of the Bartleys' garden, offering a quick connection to Euston.

One immediate consequence of the marriage was that Wilkie abruptly replaced the long-suffering Tindell with the neophyte Bartley as his solicitor. Doubtless there was some logic in this, perhaps it was even part of the marriage deal, but Bartley, while perfectly competent, had none of Tindell's specialist interest in contracts and copyright. As a result, Wilkie was on his own in May 1878 when he was approached by William Tillotson, a Bolton newspaper proprietor, who was trying to expand fiction coverage in his many print outlets in the north-west. As Wilkie was still trying to reach as much of his 'unknown public' as possible, he was happy to sign a contract to produce a novel, *Jezebel's Daughter*, for serialisation in Tillotson's papers the following autumn. In the same vein, he had recently made a deal with Leader and Son, a floundering Sheffield publisher, whose *Sheffield and Rotherham Independent* would serialise *The Black Robe* in 1880.

In the meantime, he persevered with *The Haunted Hotel*, a curious fusion of sensation and horror fiction, revolving around a murder and insurance fraud. Serialised in *Belgravia* over the latter half of 1878, it had genuinely macabre moments, as when a severed head floats around a Venice hotel room. But, despite some amusing travellers' tales, such as the Americans unable to endure the lack of heating in their freezing hotel, it failed to conjure up the special atmosphere of La Serenissima, found in his early story *Volpurno*.

As a diversion, particularly from the tribulations of gout, Wilkie enjoyed keeping up with his American contacts, above all those involved in the theatre. He carried on a flirtatious relationship with the feisty American writer and actress Kate Field, to whom he had been introduced by Trollope. He also struck up an epistolary friendship with William Winter, whose regular slot at the *New York Tribune* made him the most influential American theatre critic of his generation. When Winter sent him a book of his poems, Wilkie admitted he was 'an incorrigible heretic in the matter of modern poetry . . . I positively decline to let the poet preach to me or puzzle me.' He remained an old-fashioned romantic, wanting verse 'to express passions and sentiment in language which is essentially intelligible as well as essentially noble and musical'. He added that his favourite poets were Byron, Scott and the little-read George Crabbe.

Another American visitor was the temperamental actress Rose Eytinge, a friend of Charles Reade. Wilkie met her on only one occasion, because his 'never sufficiently-to-be-damned-and-blasted rheumatic gout' was again affecting his eyes. She could not hide her disappointment when, as she reported in her memoirs, she found that, unlike the 'big, portentous, heavy' male characters in his fiction, Wilkie was modest, mild-mannered 'and almost the smallest [man] I ever met, who was not positively a dwarf. His hands and feet were almost dwarfed, and as he sat perched up on a rather high chair at his writing-table, with his grizzled beard flowing over his breast, and his low, soft voice flowing out in silvery accents, his head surmounted with a quaintly shaped skull-cap, he looked rather like a wizard who had fallen under the ban of his fairy godmother, who in anger had deprived him of his legs.'

On hearing from her that Wilkie was suffering from gout when she met him, Reade informed her 'and there seemed to be a sort of gusto, a sense of satisfaction in his tone: "Ah! Wilkie has been drinking champagne! He will do it, though he knows it's poison to him. The very moment he gets a bit better, off he will trot to the club and have a good 'tuck-in' of lobster and champagne, and so gets another attack."' Eytinge was amused at this 'gloating over the weakness of his literary brother', particularly as Reade was prone to dyspepsia if he gorged himself, 'with the inevitable result of reducing him to repentance, abstemiousness, and bad temper'.

Although Wilkie's doctors often restricted his movements, they seldom saw fit to advise on his diet (or, if they did, he tended to ignore them). Frank Beard, in fact, shared his taste for gourmandising. Once, when Wilkie visited him in Welbeck Street, they cooked a Don Pedro pie, a meat-heavy meal Wilkie had enjoyed on his travels. The recipe required large amounts of garlic, perhaps rather too much, because Frank's son Nathaniel and the rest of the Beard family could not stomach the strongly flavoured dish, which was eaten only by the two chefs. According to Nathaniel, both men subsequently took to their beds and were ill for days.

As soon as he felt well enough, Wilkie dragged himself down to Ramsgate, where his amanuensis, Harriet Graves, helped him complete *The Haunted Hotel*. The finished product, published by Chatto & Windus in October 1878, was dedicated to Sebastian

Schlesinger and his wife Berthe, in gratitude for the safe haven
they had provided him in Boston a few years earlier.

Back in London, Wilkie polished off a couple of inconsequential tales for the Christmas market – 'The Mystery of Marmaduke',
a £50 commission from Bentley's *Temple Bar*, with a similar sum
from *Spirit of the Times* in New York, and 'A Shocking Story',
which netted a more modest £31 10s from *Belgravia*, though
Wilkie had to chase up payment with the stern admonition that
Chatto's 'financial partner', Windus, had got it 'on unusually cheap
terms, and that I expect him to pay for it punctually'.

In the autumn of 1878, Wilkie finally turned his attention to
the novel he had been putting off. Envisaged as a trilogy, which
indicated its importance to him, *The Fallen Leaves* was another
spin-off from his few hours at Wallingford four years earlier. It
told the disjointed story of Amelius Goldenheart, a self-
proclaimed Primitive Christian Socialist, and four women, each
in her way a fallen member of her sex.

Amelius has been forced into exile from his religious community
in Illinois because of an unauthorised liaison with an older woman.
Coming to London, he has a letter of introduction to a loathsome
businessman, John Farnaby, whose beautiful niece, Regina Mildmay,
he becomes infatuated with. Farnaby had earlier ruthlessly seduced
Emma, the young unmarried daughter of his employer, so that he
could have a child with her (out of wedlock), force her into marriage
and thus inherit her father's thriving stationer's business. He then
despatched the inconvenient illegitimate girl to a baby-farmer.
Sixteen years on, Mrs Farnaby is trapped in a loveless marriage,
which she interprets as punishment for the 'sin' she committed in
allowing her daughter to be given up, and she asks Amelius to help
her find her long-lost child.

Having begun to lose interest in the boringly conventional Regina, Amelius is walking in a rough area of Lambeth, south of Waterloo Bridge, where he hears a girl, clearly a prostitute, call out, 'Are you good-natured, sir?' He sees her as delicate, frail and beautiful: 'robed in pure white, with her gentle blue eyes raised to heaven, a painter might have shown her on his canvas as a saint or an angel.' It does not take much acquaintance with Wilkie's work to predict that this waif turns out to Mrs Farnaby's lost daughter, whom the pitying Amelius sets up in 'a pretty bachelor cottage in the neighbourhood of the Regent's Park'. Before long he is in love with her, moves in, and marries her.

Along the way Amelius and Sally chance on a wedding, which allows Wilkie to indulge in a bravura attack on traditional marriage as a mode of commerce: 'The bride was a tall buxom girl, splendidly dressed: she performed her part in the ceremony with the most unruffled composure. The bridegroom exhibited an instructive spectacle of aged Nature, sustained by Art. His hair, his complexion, his teeth, his breast, his shoulders, and his legs, showed what the wig-maker, the valet, the dentist, the tailor, and the hosier can do for a rich old man, who wishes to present a juvenile appearance while he is buying a young wife. No less than three clergymen were present, conducting the sale. The demeanour of the rich congregation was worthy of the glorious bygone days of the Golden Calf.'

When one guest describes the scene as 'disgraceful', her young relation remonstrates with her, 'How can you talk so, grandmamma! He has twenty thousand a year – and that lucky girl will be mistress of the most splendid house in London.' But the old lady, a surrogate for Wilkie, persists, 'I don't care. It's not the less a disgrace to everybody concerned in it. There is many a poor friendless creature, driven by hunger to the streets, who has a better claim to our sympathy than that shameless girl, selling herself in the house of God!'

Wilkie was making his familiar case that women in degraded situations, the Carolines (as once was) of this world, are often morally superior to those in regular society, and that most marriages are no better than legalised prostitution. Once again he presented it in religious and allegorical terms (there is no escaping the significance of the name Goldenheart), but he couched it in an unusually strong political manner, portraying the horrors of life on the streets and betraying his leanings towards Christian Socialism of the type followed in communities such as Wallingford.

He had good professional reasons for tilting at capitalism. Following the demise of sensation fiction, the British public was demanding more down-to-earth reading material. His competitors were realists, such as the emerging Thomas Hardy and Emile Zola, whose 1877 novel *L'Assommoir*, about alcoholism and poverty in the suburbs of Paris, would be staged in London that summer as *Drink* (in a version by Charles Reade). Even the work of Mary Elizabeth Braddon had taken a naturalist turn with *Joshua Haggard's Daughter* in 1876. Although this was not Wilkie's natural inclination, he felt he now needed to address what a character in his book calls 'the people who have drawn blanks in the lottery of life – the people who have toiled hard after happiness, and have gathered nothing but disappointment and sorrow; the friendless and the lonely, the wounded and the lost'.

That does not explain the religious underpinnings. Here Wilkie may again have been encouraged by Holman Hunt, who had just returned from another extended stay in Jerusalem. But, as someone who regarded the life of Christ as exemplary, he was no less sincere for that. *The Fallen Leaves* was a very personal work, which he told Bentley 'excites and exhausts me in the writing – as no other story of mine as [sic] ever excited me'. He showed what it meant to him by dedicating it to

Caroline, which some commentators have seen as evidence that his mistress not only came from the streets but had once been a prostitute. However, she would never have allowed this to appear if it were really so.

Wilkie's composure was jolted when he learned that Ned Ward, the friend of his youth, had slit his throat on the morning of 10 January 1879, having been ill and depressed for some time. Ward's son Wriothesley discovered his father screaming, 'I was mad when I did it; the devil prompted me,' and had to hold him down until a doctor arrived. His injuries were initially not considered life-threatening, so on the 14th Wilkie wrote to Henrietta Ward, saying how sorry he was to hear that Ned was 'seriously ill' and bemoaning the fact that the Wards' now permanent residence in Windsor meant they had not seen each other for some time. The following day, Ned's continual writhing caused a deterioration in his condition and he died that evening. An inquest later concluded that he had committed suicide (still an illegal act) while temporarily insane. As had been the case with his mother eleven years earlier, Wilkie's health prevented him attending Ned's funeral.

Within a month Henrietta Ward was contemplating a book about her late husband and asked Wilkie if he possessed any of his letters. Wilkie replied that he had never received more than two or three lines from Ned and these he had given to autograph hunters. Old letters seemed to haunt him. Georgina Hogarth had recently asked his advice about publishing an edition of Dickens's correspondence. Eager to help, Wilkie called on Chatto to cost 2,000 copies of a two-volume work running to 400 pages. The quotation was £172 per volume, made up of £50 for composition, £45 for presswork, £60 for paper and around

£17 (or 2d per copy) for binding. Dickens's solicitor, Frederic Ouvry, later calculated that they could make £1,100 profit if the book sold at thirty shillings. Georgina considered the situation and, after fierce negotiation, *The Letters of Charles Dickens* was put out by Chapman and Hall in 1880.

When not keeping up with the schedule for serialising his novel in *The World*, Wilkie was occupied with his usual round of negotiations with foreign publishers. But for every Baron Tauchnitz, the scrupulous Leipzig-based publisher who had included Wilkie's work in his Collection of British and American Authors in Europe since the mid-1850s, there were others who took liberties with copyright. Wilkie was now forced to threaten legal action against a French writer who had put out a version of Dickens's unfinished *Edwin Drood*, claiming that it had been completed by Wilkie. However, when the writ reached the courts, it had to be withdrawn because the defendant had no money. Wilkie comforted himself with the thought that British authors were working closely together to fight cases of piracy, and an international agreement on copyright would soon follow.

By the end of June he had completed *The Fallen Leaves* (or at least the first part of it), though the book did not appear in volume form from Chatto & Windus until 1 July 1879. When, a week later, Harriet gave birth to her first child, a daughter called Doris Edith, Wilkie took this as an omen to go straight to Ramsgate, where he hoped to enjoy much of the next three months in the company of his extended family.

In the meantime, he had to endure a spate of unfavourable reviews of *The Fallen Leaves*. The *Sunday Times* mocked his attempt to rewrite the story of Christ: 'If . . . Mr Collins thinks he can accomplish, without being crucified, an attempt in which Godhead failed he is sanguine. His views about socialism and about women are as much unsuited to the world of today as to that of two thousand years ago.' The *Saturday Review* said, 'All his characters are forced and unnatural, and no less so are the incidents of his story. Everything, in fact, is so extravagant, so absurd, and so grossly improbable that a kind of low harmony is preserved throughout.' When such reactions were repeated, Wilkie cancelled the intended second 'series' of the novel and concentrated for the rest of the year on other projects.

His holiday mood did not improve when he received the not unexpected news of the death of his old friend Charles Fechter on 5 August. Kate Field later asked Wilkie to contribute to a memoir of the actor. He agreed, on condition that his words were printed in full since he felt there had already been too much speculation about Fechter's life. In the published *Recollections* of Charles Fechter, which he contributed to Field's book, he expanded on this, saying he might have included the actor's own words from his letters 'which I thought it right to preserve'. But, in a statement of his deep regard for privacy, though perhaps a curious admission for a writer with his track record of seeking to unearth the 'dead secrets' of his times, he felt, 'Even these are not only too personal to be present[ed] to the public, but they are, in many places, so expressed (unconsciously on his part, it is needless to say) as to be in danger of leading to erroneous impressions of him in the minds of strangers. This memorial portrait of Fechter would not be improved as a likeness by borrowing his own words.'

SIXTH EPOCH

19

GROWING IMMOBILITY

'WILKIE COLLINS ..., STILL lingered, not super-fluous, but not indispensable; like an historic edifice, respected, but unoccupied. Like many other fiction-mongers before and since, he had come to regard himself as a reformer, seer, and prophet; and if the people didn't give ear, as formerly, they and not the book were to blame.' The date of this pejorative judgement by Julian Hawthorne is not certain: it could have appeared any time between 1874 and 1881, when the American novelist and his wife were living in London.

Hawthorne was clearly unimpressed by Wilkie, perhaps seeing him as a rival for a market where mystery and the super-natural came together. He was unusually damning in his descrip-tion of Wilkie 'sitting in his plethoric, disorderly writing-room', a prime example of the 'hopelessly ramshackle' rather than 'raspingly tidy' kind of bachelor. 'Though the England of his prime had been a cricketing, athletic, outdoor England, Wilkie had ever slumped at his desk and breathed only indoor air. He was soft, plump, and pale, suffered from various ailments, his liver was wrong, his heart weak, his lungs faint, his stomach incompetent, he ate too much and the wrong things. He had a big head, a dingy complexion, was somewhat bald ... His air was of mild discomfort and fractiousness; he had a queer way of holding his hand, which was small, plump, and unclean, hanging up by the wrist, like a rabbit on its hind legs. He had strong opinions and prejudices, but his nature was obviously kind and lovable, and a humorous vein would occasionally be manifest. One felt that he was unfortunate and needed succour.'

As a writer and a seeker after the truth himself, Hawthorne showed a remarkable lack of sympathy. Wilkie, in his way, was sincerely groping for a philosophy in keeping with this latest stage in his life. As his novel *The Black Robe* would show, he remained averse to organised religion. And if he had problems with the Anglican Church, he had even more with Roman Catholicism. Nevertheless, influenced by Holman Hunt's gentle faith, by his own attraction to the Christian message, and by his new-found experience of fatherhood, he was still searching for sustenance from the smorgasbord of quasi-religions, such as Swedenborg-ism, spiritualism and Christian Socialism, which he mixed on his plate with his idiosyncratic synthesis of contemporary scientific research into the power of the mind.

Disappointed by the negative reaction to *The Fallen Leaves*, he still felt he would be vindicated when his story appeared in a cheap edition. He believed there would then be a clamour for a second volume dealing with Amelius and Sally's married life, which he pessimistically told a correspondent would be 'essentially' happy, 'but the outer influence of the world which surrounds the husband and wife – the world whose unchristian prejudices they have set at defiance – will slowly undermine their happiness, and will, I fear, make the close of the story a sad one.' Chatto put out a one-volume edition in 1880, but again it did not become the best-seller Wilkie had hoped for.

Instead, Wilkie worked on turning his 1858 play *The Red Vial* into a novel called *Jezebel's Daughter*. He had been advised more than two decades earlier that the story might be better written in chapters. And so it turned out. His sensationalist

hodgepodge for the theatre became on the printed page a measured plea for the humane treatment of lunatics – in this case, a
character called Jack Straw incarcerated in the Bethlehem
Hospital, or Bedlam – interlaced with an entertaining and well
researched exploration into the nefarious uses of poisons and
their antidotes. The story revolves around a widow, Madame
Fontaine, who uses the toxic remnants of her late husband's
medicine bag to try and secure her daughter's position in a
German trading house. In an introduction addressed to Antonio
Caccia, his Italian translator, Wilkie said that he had tried to
provide 'two interesting studies of humanity', the enfeebled
intellect of Jack Straw and the wickedness of Madame Fontaine,
whom he interprets as an interesting moral study, driven by the
over-riding instinct of maternal love. He also stressed the depth
of his research, which included visiting a morgue in Frankfurt.

As an indication of Wilkie's religious sympathies, Mrs
Wagner, the well-intentioned widow of the London partner of
the trading house, secures Jack Straw's release from Bedlam and
places him in a Quaker retreat in York. She and Madame
Fontaine provide contrasting examples of the determined woman
who so often featured in Wilkie's novels. Improbable events still
occur, such as Jack Straw's madness having been caused by a
poison provided by Madame Fontaine's late husband. Wilkie,
the eternal bachelor, cannot stop himself from concluding his
book with a blissful wedding. But *Jezebel's Daughter*, published
by Chatto at the end of March 1880, following serialisation in
Tillotson's newspapers, was a fine novel and showed that Wilkie
had lost none of his authorial touch.

Wilkie could now relax a bit. Having been overlooked for
Henry Irving's gala dinner to celebrate his hundredth performance of *The Merchant of Venice* at the Lyceum in February, he
accepted an invitation from the actor's secretary, Bram Stoker,
to see the play later in the month. Wilkie also found time to sit

for a portrait which Fred Lehmann had commissioned from his brother Rudolf. This showed him in a heavy overcoat with a thick fur collar, sporting a wispy white beard, looking alert but pensive, as if contemplating the spiritual dilemmas of his books.

Sorely troubled by his gout, he spent longer periods in Ramsgate, visiting it in March and April 1880, and again that summer and autumn. He was now so established in the town that, at one point, he rented two houses, installing Caroline and her immediate family in one (in Nelson Crescent) and Martha, or 'Mrs Dawson', and her children in the other (in Wellington Crescent on the other side of the harbour overlooking the railway terminus).

Maintaining good relations between his mistresses was not easy. Wilkie insisted on access to his children, wherever he was living, as was suggested in the census of 3 April 1881, when Martha's eldest daughter Marian (named as Marian Collins rather than Dawson), was staying at Gloucester Place, where the long-suffering Caroline Graves was still listed as the 'housekeeper'. Martha meanwhile remained in Taunton Place, with her other children Harriet and William, as well as her elder sister Alice, who looked after them all.

Two days after this poll Wilkie's new novel, *The Black Robe*, was published in three volumes by Chatto. This was a darker, more complex tale than *Jezebel's Daughter*, addressing another of his pet subjects, the marriage laws, again served up with lashings of religion. Reflecting his long-standing antipathy to Roman Catholicism, and particularly the Jesuits – a secretive, foreign force ideally suited to be cast as the villains of a sensational novel – the book tells of Lewis Romayne, a landowner wracked with guilt after killing a man in a duel. He returns to his Yorkshire home, Vange Abbey, which came into his family after being confiscated at the Reformation. There he is dogged by a Jesuit priest, Father Benwell, who preys on Romayne's vulnerability to wrest back control of the estate for his 'true' religion. As Romayne is split between the demands of love and Catholicism, the drama hangs on whether his wife's earlier marriage had been formalised in ecclesiastical as well as civil law. As in many of Wilkie's novels, the story focuses on the interpretation of wills. When the dying Romayne throws his will into a fire (thus denying Benwell's plans to repossess his property), he says he has done it for his 'wife and child' – a motive not too far from Wilkie's when he methodically changed his will every time Martha gave birth.

He enjoyed the controversy his book created, telling his American friend Jane Bigelow that he had received 'some tremendous letters from Roman Catholics' about it. 'They are all shocked that I should not know better than to doubt the Jesuits – the most harmless and innocent assembly of Gentlemen on the face of the earth.'

Over the summer he was unusually inactive, after submitting to a course of treatment for gout based on colchicum and calomel (otherwise known as mercury chloride, a poison used as a laxative). Rather than his preferred dry champagne, he was reduced to the 'nastiest drink' possible, weak brandy and water, which left him 'filled with morbid longings to destroy' himself 'by getting drunk on the excellent port in the solemn coffee-room at the Athenaeum'. Once the inflammation subsided he felt extremely weak: 'my knees tremble on the stairs, and my back aches after half an hour's walking – no, tottering – on the sunny side of the street. I am told to "drive out" – but I won't. An "airing in a carriage" is (to me) such a depressing proceeding that I am ready to burst out crying when I only think of it.' Consequently, he was forced to turn down an invitation to meet the visiting Russian author Ivan Turgenev. 'I don't remember whether Dante's Hell includes among its tortures Gout in the Eyes,' he told William Ralston, Turgenev's translator and promoter.

He still managed to put in long hours contacting publishers
and translators abroad. His anger at continuing literary piracy
in the United States led him to compose a pamphlet,
'Considerations on the Copyright Question', which was printed
there by Alfred Smith Barnes's *International Review*, though his
demand that nothing should be cut led the editors to add a note
stating that, while they supported his plea for an international
copyright treaty, they 'disclaim all responsibility for the language
adopted by him in his argument'. His strong views led to a
temporary breakdown in his relations with Harper and Brothers,
whom he had singled out for criticism. Through his contacts
on this issue, he met Alexander (A.P.) Watt, a tough-minded
Scotsman with a track record in publishing, who had set up as
London's first full-time literary agent. Feeling weighed down
by unnecessary paperwork, Wilkie invited Watt to visit and
immediately appointed him his business representative. Watt
helped him negotiate the intricacies of an ever-changing market
place, where the falling circulations and revenues of traditional
outlets, including *Belgravia*, required writers to seek simulta-
neous, often lowly-paid, publication in provincial newspapers,
such as those run by Tillotson in the north-west. This so-called
'belt and braces' approach to serialisation called for a considerable exchange of letters about fees and dates of publication. Watt
also responded to requests, such as that from Sir Ellis Ashmead-
Bartlett, a rich Conservative MP, who had asked Wilkie for a 'good
story for a paper in which I am interested'. This was *England*, the
first Conservative penny weekly, which he kept going at his own
expense. With a nod to Britain's changing demographics, Ashmead-
Bartlett added, 'It is principally for the masses and therefore the
more sensational the more effective.'

A more esoteric diatribe penned by Wilkie addressed
the topic of air pollution in theatres. 'The Air and the Audience'
started in playful manner, complimenting a New York playhouse

for having introduced a form of air conditioning ('ozoned air') that maintained a constant temperature in its auditorium. Wilkie reasonably suggested that it was in the 'pecuniary interests of a manager to consult the health and comfort of his audience', though he feared this was not the case in Britain, where, to take one example, only a couple of theatres had introduced electric light, while the others 'persist in poisoning us with gas'. At this point, his tone changed dramatically as he inveighed against contaminated air, which threatened people's health because it contained 'minute particles . . . "given off" by us and by our perspiring fellow creatures'. Worse still, and here he showed that he had been influenced by contemporary theories of degeneration, 'if there happen to be any playgoers of consumptive tendency present, their particles may be actually charged with diseases, and may sow the seeds that result in the future on which . . . we had better not dwell.'

Wilkie's basic thesis echoed that of the impresario Richard D'Oyly Carte, whose Savoy Theatre became the first public building in the world to introduce electric lighting (at a performance of the Gilbert and Sullivan operetta *H.M.S. Pinafore* in October 1881). Twelve hundred of Joseph Swan's newly patented incandescent light bulbs helped illuminate the event. D'Oyly Carte was quoted, 'The greatest drawbacks to the enjoyment of the theatrical performances are, undoubtedly, the foul air and heat which pervade all theatres. As everyone knows, each gasburner consumes as much oxygen as many people, and causes great heat beside.' Wilkie was in touch with D'Oyly Carte at the time, though he had declined an invitation to the Savoy's opening as he was going to Ramsgate.

In this latest article Wilkie let slip that he had altered his opinion about English theatre: he now referred to 'loathsome burlesques and idiotic adaptations from the French', while praising such 'original English plays' as *Masks and Faces* by his friend Charles Reade, along with the works of Tom Taylor, the comedies of T.W. Robertson, and *Our Boys* by Henry James Byron, which had enjoyed 'the longest "run" on record' (four years at the Vaudeville in 1875). However, this was dated fare by the 1880s, when the artistic world was being challenged by social realists such as Ibsen on the one hand and aesthetes including Oscar Wilde on the other.

Wilkie's changed perspective might have had something to do with his friend Ted Pigott's appointment as Britain's official theatre censor. This was amusing, given that Pigott had accompanied him to so many small theatres and dives in London and Paris over the previous thirty years. But Pigott was now respectable. His correspondence with Wilkie, once so prolific, had petered, or been weeded, out. As poacher turned gamekeeper, Pigott took his official duties seriously, seeing himself as not only an arbiter of plays but a guardian of public morals, such as taking a stand against any form of prostitution in playhouses. And he revelled in the public relations side of the job. Having defended his role to the Parliamentary Committee on Censorship in 1882, he would state the following year, 'What is sometimes rather invidiously called "censorship" is nothing, in effect, but the friendly and perfectly disinterested action of an adviser who has the permanent interests of the stage at heart.' This paternalistic approach would result a decade later in his rejecting Oscar Wilde's play *Salome* as 'a miracle of imprudence . . . half-biblical, half-pornographic'. George Bernard Shaw later dismissed him as a hypocritical mediocrity.

Wilkie was now working on a new novel, *Heart and Science*, whose subtitle 'A Story of the Present Time' signalled its contemporary relevance. It addressed the debate on vivisection, which had been raging since the mid-1870s when a doctor performed an operation on a howling dog at a conference of the British Medical Association. The ensuing controversy led to a licensing system for medical experiments using live animals, but not before several anti-vivisection societies, including the Victoria Street Society (VSS), headed by Wilkie's feminist friend Frances Power Cobbe, had sprung up and garnered support from personalities such as Lewis Carroll, Thomas Carlyle and Robert Browning.

Vivisection received a renewed airing in August 1881 when the International Medical Congress in London declared that animal experimentation was 'indispensable' to the future of medicine. Cobbe's VSS brought an action against Professor David Ferrier, an Edinburgh-trained neurologist, for performing vivisection on monkeys without the required licence. (The matter of his post-mortem experiments on patients from the West Riding lunatic asylum was overlooked.) The case collapsed through lack of evidence, but Cobbe attended and wrote passionately about it.

Wilkie's love of animals, together with his interest in a gentle Christian Socialist-cum-Quaker philosophy, made him sympathetic to the anti-vivisectionist cause. However, he did not want to write a mere manifesto, as he had done on ventilation in theatres. He was tired of the persistent criticism that his novels were driven by the demands of plot rather than character (a line Anthony Trollope took in his autobiography published posthumously in October 1883). So, as Wilkie wrote in his preface to *Heart and Science*, he was determined that qualities of character and humour should feature strongly in the book.

The result was a complex love story involving a young surgeon with the improbable name of Ovid Vere (the 'heart' of the title), overlaid with the machinations of Dr Nathan Benjulia, a specialist in nervous diseases, who experiments on animals in the interests of science. Benjulia is not wholly bad, but becomes corrupted by his work, which he is convinced is 'all for knowledge'. As Wilkie points out in his preface, 'You are purposely left in ignorance of the hideous secrets of Vivisection. The outside of the laboratory is a necessary object in my landscape – but I never once open the door and invite you to look in. I trace, in one of my characters, the result of the habitual practice of cruelty . . . in fatally deteriorating the nature of man – and I leave the picture to speak for itself.'

Throughout 1882, Wilkie scoured specialist literature, corresponded with experts such as the Queen's honorary physician, Surgeon General Charles Alexander Gordon, and interviewed avowed activists, including Frances Power Cobbe. He told Frederick Lehmann, 'Some critic said "The Woman In White" was "written in blood and vitriol". This book is being written in blood and dynamite.' Despite his strong commitment to the cause (he described vivisectionists as 'wretches'), he found the work more demanding than usual. He shed light on his intensely cerebral process of creativity when he told William Winter that the book 'so mercilessly excited me that I went on writing week after week without a day's interval of rest. Rest was impossible. I made a desperate effort, rushed to the sea, went sailing and fishing, and was writing my book all the time, <u>in my head</u> (as the children say). The one wise course to take was to go back to my desk, and empty my head – and then rest.' Luckily, he had a remedy: an armchair, a cigar 'and a hundred and fiftieth reading of the glorious Walter Scott (King, Emperor, President, and God Almighty of novelists) – there is the regimen that is doing me good!' Scott was now one of his three acknowledged 'kings of fiction', along with Fenimore Cooper and Balzac. (Significantly, perhaps, he did not include Dickens.)

Wilkie's robust taste in literature stood oddly with his increasingly eccentric behaviour in other areas of his life. 'Yesterday, being out for a little walk, and wearing a <u>paletot with a hood</u>

for travelling,' he informed Nina Lehmann, 'I heard a woman remark as I went by, "To think of a man wearing such a coat as that – at <u>his</u> time of life!"' A paletot was a close-fitting coat with a hood, but the point was that it was usually worn by women. Hearing this pricked Wilkie's vanity, and he went on to ask Nina, 'The question that arises is – Shall I dye my beard?' Such quirkiness extended to other aspects, such as food. Wybert Reeve noted, 'His diet was singular. At dinner he would sometimes take some bread soaked in meat-gravy only. In the night he was fond of cold soup and champagne. For exercise he often walked quickly up and down-stairs so many times by the aid of the banisters.'

Heart and Science was published in three volumes by Chatto in April 1883, after being serialised in various newspapers and in *Belgravia*. The response was positive; it was only later that Wilkie was seen as a polemical writer, as lightly pilloried in Swinburne's posthumous put-down:

> What brought good Wilkie's genius nigh perdition?
> Some demon whispered – 'Wilkie! have a mission'.

Wilkie proudly informed William Winter how Benjulia now 'matched' Fosco as a popular demon, while he described the novel to his most recent French translator, Count Robert du Pontavice de Heussey as 'a great advance' on *The Black Robe*. In this case, he had an added motive since Heussey had been trying to find a publisher for *The Black Robe* in France, without success, probably because the subject matter was controversial in a Catholic country. Wilkie suggested that if *Heart and Science* were to jump the queue, Heussey might subsequently find it easier to place his earlier effort.

While writing *Heart and Science*, Wilkie was also working on a play, *Rank and Riches*, which took him longer than expected and was not staged until June 1883. (He may have been trying too hard to write the sort of 'original English play' he had advocated in 'The Air and the Audience'). Despite a distinguished cast, which included Alice Lingard, George Alexander, Myra Holme (Mrs Pinero) and Charles Hawtrey, *Rank and Riches* folded after just six nights at the Adelphi Theatre. Hawtrey recalled how the producer Edgar Bruce had earlier talked up the show and told him rather fancifully that no dramatic offering by Wilkie had ever failed before. Wilkie had seen Lingard in *Camille* at the Gaiety in April and was greatly taken by her, though he found the play the 'very worst adaptation' of Dumas's *La Dame aux Camélias*. But neither his words nor her acting could do anything to save *Rank and Riches*, an unfocused story that rambled over topics such as bigamy and embezzlement. *The Times* referred to the 'outrageous improbability of the characters' and the 'want of dramatic purpose'. The management hurriedly brought in Lingard's *Camille* as a replacement, while Wilkie blamed the notoriously volatile 'Adelphi audience' for the failure. He had to take consolation from the continuing success in the provinces of Ada Cavendish's production of *The New Magdalen*, which would find its way back to London for a revival at the Novelty Theatre in January the following year.

The cast of *Rank and Riches* included Pigott's nephew Jim. One of the sons of the ill-fated Henry Smyth Pigott, he was now forging a career in the theatre, where Wilkie tried to help him. Towards the end of the decade, J.W. Pigott, his stage name, finally enjoyed some success with his comedy *The Bookmaker*, which toured Britain and crossed the Atlantic. He later acted with Lillie Langtry's company.

After this theatrical setback, Wilkie escaped for the summer to Ramsgate, where he hired a steam yacht called *Phyllis*. He described it to Pigott as 'a capital little vessel . . . Two reefs in the mainsail, and the top mast on deck, and <u>such</u> a sea off the Foreland!' Since Harriet Bartley had just given birth to her third daughter, he invited her to stay. 'Come – the sooner the better – and bring <u>all</u> the children. Good heavens! don't I like Dah, and the quiet little curlyhead? I wish <u>I</u> was a baby again – with nothing to do but suck and sleep.' (Dah was Doris, now four, while the curlyhead was either Cecile, who was two, or the newborn Evelyn.)

Wilkie confided to Harriet, 'Don't tell anybody – I <u>am quite mad</u> over my new book. It is at the present writing half a dozen books, with four or five hundred characters – and full of immoral situations.' He managed to cut down this behemoth to manageable proportions, but it was a wrong move, because *I Say No* failed to engage. Ostensibly the story was promising, as it followed an orphaned schoolgirl, Emily Brown, in her gradual discovery of the circumstances surrounding her father's gruesome murder. But Emily and her schoolfriends had none of the spark of Magdalen Vanstone or Marian Halcombe.

As usual, Wilkie worked as fast as his disabilities allowed. At one stage he misquoted Pope that 'the life of a writer is a warfare on earth.' (He should have said 'the life of a wit'.) By the following June of 1884, he had completed his task and the novel was published by Chatto that October, after being serialised in a syndicate of newspapers put together (such was the changing nature of publishing) by Kelly's, best known for its Post Office directories. Wilkie was able to retire to Ramsgate, where Pigott joined him in his family yacht and took him out to sea.

Wilkie returned to London feeling 'infinitely the better for' his 'thorough salting', but within a short time the awful cycle began again. As he launched into a new novel, *The Evil Genius*, he looked in the mirror and saw a red streak in his left eye, which three days later turned the colour of a cooked lobster. He took to the third person to explain to an American correspondent how 'the Gout-Fiend had got him' and 'bored holes in his eye with a red-hot needle. Calomel and colchicum knocked him down, and said (through the medium of the doctor) "Wilkie, it's all for your good". Laudanum – divine Laudanum – was his only friend.' His condition improved but he remained weak and half blind and needed to cover his eyes.

As his spiralling bill at his chemist (Corbyn and Company in New Bond Street) attests, laudanum was more of a necessity than a friend. His experiment with morphine had ended (partly as a result of the passage of the Poisons and Pharmacy Act of 1868), but proprietary brands of laudanum were still widely available and he was able to down a tincture that the surgeon Sir William Ferguson said would be enough to kill a dozen people. When he was out, he carried a hip flask of the drug. An actor friend recalled seeing 'Collins drink a wineglassful of laudanum at one swallow without affecting him in the least,' and he was manifestly right to conclude, 'Life would have been almost unbearable to him without it.'

With the help of this medicinal crutch, Wilkie was generally able to cope. Sometimes, as with *The Moonstone*, the drug enhanced his writing, but the effects now began to show in less benign ways. When he went up the stairs, he was confronted by ghosts who, he imagined, wanted to push him down. When he tried to sleep, he often saw a 'shapeless monster, with eyes of fire and big green fangs'. The writer Alethea Hayter later suggested that Wilkie's youthful ability to paint a scene in words deteriorated as he grew older and more addicted to opium. He no longer saw what he was describing, but conjured it up from his narcotised dreams in an intellectual rather than a visual manner.

Not that he lost confidence in opium's therapeutic qualities. When his friend Charles Kent was unable to sleep, Wilkie arranged for Corbyn to supply him with laudanum, and when that did not work (he explained that the drug sometimes acted as a stimulant rather than a sedative), he advised Kent to consult Beard for a professional opinion.

During 1885, he was beset by another problem – a pain in his chest, which was diagnosed as angina. This required him to add further 'devilish drugs' to his regime: sal volatile (smelling salts), a stimulant; chloroform, a depressant; and amyl nitrite, a specific muscle relaxant. All of these worked on his heart, though he asked friends not to mention it in case of newspaper publicity. At around the same time, he was also prescribed white arsenic as an additional cure for gout.

Wilkie admitted that this intoxicating brew inspired him to write 'The Ghost's Touch', which he called a ghost story but which was more of a psychological thriller with strong supernatural undertones. At its core was the question of whether the 'invisible presence' felt by its female protagonist was a supernatural revelation or an indication of madness. The story had a matrimonial subplot relating to a man marrying his dead brother's widow. This made reference to legal restrictions that, as Holman Hunt had found to his cost, prevented a man from marrying his deceased wife's sister.

'The Ghost's Touch', which appeared in Tillotson's newspapers in the autumn of 1885, was the latest and one of the most accomplished in a series of stories Wilkie had written over the previous few years, usually for the Christmas numbers of *Belgravia* and similar magazines. These stories played with his most enduring themes, such as love, marriage, detection and the supernatural. One of the earliest, 'Who Killed Zebedee?', offered an interesting variation on the detective story, taking the reader through a police investigation into a murder, before the detective involved confesses on his deathbed that he had concealed crucial evidence because he was in love with the perpetrator and wanted to save her from the gallows. This romantic policeman is Roman Catholic, which shows that Wilkie was not always prejudiced in matters of religion.

Having decided on collecting his stories, he was uncertain what to call his compilation. An inspirational meander around the streets left him with a list of twenty titles, which he whittled down to three – *Drawing-Room Stories*, *Little Novels* and *Mrs Zant and the Ghost; and Other Stories*. He preferred the last, but it proved too long, so he settled for *Little Novels*, though he dented his fading feminist credentials with his comment to Chatto, 'And if it should turn out that some damnable female writer has already got this title, let us stick to it nevertheless.' Like many authors of his sex, Wilkie was put out to find that a new generation of women were following in the steps of Miss Braddon and Mrs Wood and selling more copies than he did.

As well as these stories, Wilkie kept up his output of novels. *The Evil Genius*, his offering for 1885, provided another light trot over the hurdles of marriage and the inconsistent laws that governed it. Originally titled (with some irony) *Home! Sweet Home!*, it has an attractive governess, Sydney Westerfield, falling in love with the father of her charge, Kitty Linley. When she tries to leave her employers' household, Kitty is upset, becomes ill and demands her return. Matters are not improved when her mother seeks a divorce under Scottish law. However, they become unredeemably contrived when the Linley parents get back together and remarry.

The story has biographical implications since, before marrying a wayward aristocrat, Sydney's mother had worked as a barmaid in a public house. Wilkie takes up the cudgels on behalf of Martha Rudd when someone asks, 'By what right does Mr Westerfield's family dare to suppose that a barmaid may not be a perfectly virtuous woman?' In a sense, Kitty's mother also takes after Caroline Graves in making her bid for freedom when her husband (or partner in Wilkie's case) finds another woman. She then regrets the separation and returns to the status quo.

The novel was serialised in Tillotson's newspapers from October 1885 to May 1886, before being published by Chatto in September 1886. Although serious in intent, the book's light-hearted elements were more suited to the theatre, so that, even at this stage in his career, Wilkie felt the need to produce his own dramatic version, which was given a run-through at the Vaudeville Theatre at the end of October.

Although agreeably ensconced in Ramsgate for most of the time, he was not happy with 'this most accursed Irish business' (a racheting up of the debate over Home Rule), which caused a delay in the book's publication. Ireland was one of the few political issues that exercised him. This was a legacy of his family's Irish origins and Protestantism. While he was generally unsympathetic to gestures of imperial aggrandisement (and the following year would describe Queen Victoria's golden jubilee as simply 'idiotic'), he remained an unreconstructed Unionist, implacably opposed to any demonstrations of Irish nationalism. He also retained a romantic sense that the world of books was more important than politics, as was clear in his complaint to his friend Charles Kent, apropos the situation in Ireland: 'Nobody seems to know whether there is to be another general election – or a Civil War – and your old Literature hides her diminished head.'

He remained occupied with 'the Irish business', which would feature at the centre of his last novel, *Blind Love* (originally titled *The Lord Harry*). In the meantime, he worked on *The Guilty River*, looking once more at the psychological effects of disability, and on *The Legacy of Cain*, which took up much of his time in 1887.

The spectre of his young daughters again appeared in the latter work, the story of two girls who grow up together, though

one, Eunice, is adopted and the daughter of a murderess. As in
Armadale, an underlying theme is the influence of one generation on another: is it inevitable that the innocent young 'tigress'
Eunice will revert to the evil ways of her mother? (In his own
girls' case, the question preying on his mind seems to have been
whether they would be able to overcome the disadvantages of
their illegitimate birth.) *The Legacy of Cain* offers a contemporary
variation on the old 'nature versus nurture' debate, except that
Wilkie's views on heredity were now influenced by post-
Darwinian thinking on eugenics. Although often dismissed as
one of his later didactic novels, the story is a more nuanced
exploration of the pretensions of biological determinism, which
is given short shrift as a scientific theory since it is the other,
supposedly good daughter who goes to the bad and attempts to
poison her former lover with digitalis. The book was serialised
in Tillotson's papers in the first half of 1888 and published by
Chatto in November.

Wilkie appreciated a welcome interruption to his unremitting
round of hard work and poor health through his relationships
with two very different members of the opposite sex. One was
Mary Anderson, a glamorous American actress who had come
to London in 1883 to further her career. After being introduced
by Winter, the theatre critic, she and Wilkie became firm friends.
He showed his old Stagedoor Johnny spirit in the gushing fan
letter he wrote after seeing her in *Pygmalion and Galatea* by
W.S. Gilbert, another Chatto author who was creating successful
light musicals with Sir Arthur Sullivan. Wilkie invited himself
to tea so he could tell her 'of the strong impression that your
acting produced on me'.

A year later he proposed writing a play for her, provided he could find an interesting American theme that was not related to war. He sent her a draft of the first act, but she was not impressed and returned it. Nevertheless, she enjoyed his company and soaked up his stories of Dickens and other authors.

Wilkie's other female friend was very different – not a woman at all, but a twelve-year-old girl called Anne or 'Nannie' Wynne, with whom he carried on a strange, affectionate correspondence, as if they were a married couple and he was jealous of her admirers. She was the daughter of Emily Le Poer Wynne, the Irish-born widow of a senior civil servant in India, who was now living in Delamere Gardens, Maida Vale. Wilkie seems to have been inroduced to the family by Pigott.

It was odd that, having stuck out against marriage for sixty years, Wilkie should now call a pre-pubescent girl 'Mrs Collins'. She became 'my darling' and 'carissima sposa mia' (my dearest wife), from whom he looked forward to a 'conjugal embrace'. From a twenty-first-century perspective, such forms of address are suspect, though there was no suggestion of impropriety. Wilkie took trouble to include Nannie's mother in his exchanges. Taking his cue from Holman Hunt, he had a romantic idea, to which Lewis Carroll also subscribed, that young girls personified the spirit of innocence. Nannie acted as a substitute for his elder daughters, Marian and Harriet, who were now teenagers and safely ensconced at the Maria Grey School in Fitzroy Square. Nannie also provided a non-judgemental sounding board for Wilkie, who could prattle on about his 'excellent friends Opium and Quinine' and his need to sniff 'Amyl', which he protested 'is not the Christian name of another wife. It is only a glass capsule.'

His sexual preferences were made clear in an exchange with Napoleon Sarony in March 1887. In thanking his New York friend for the gift of photographs of some of his mildly erotic drawings, Wilkie said, apropos one of the images, 'I too think the back view of a finely-formed woman the loveliest view – and her hips and her bottom the most precious parts of that view. The line of beauty in those quarters enchants me, when it is not overladen by fat.' He confirmed that his ideal was the *Venus Callipyge* (the latter word meaning 'beautiful buttocks'), which he had almost certainly seen in Naples. He claimed he had spent his whole life searching for a woman like her.

As it happened, A.P. Watt, the man he called his 'good genius', had been sent a better, tinted version of this drawing, which showed a woman looking over her shoulder as she steps into a bath. He gave it to Wilkie, who compared his 'draped darling' to a chalk drawing by an old master. He exhibited it prominently beside his desk, allowing him to present the slightly inferior version (the gift from Sarony) to Frank Beard. Wilkie showed his gratitude to the photographer by ordering new copies of his own portrait taken in New York, telling Sarony it was still much in demand.

One effect of Wilkie's general immobility was that Caroline consolidated her position as the woman, both gatekeeper and housekeeper, at the centre of his life. Her sense of herself had strengthened since she was also the respected grandmother of a growing family, to whom Wilkie took pleasure in acting as honorary grandfather. There was no disguising his excitement in Ramsgate in July 1886 when, as he told Beard, 'The Bartleys are within two doors of us and the children are in and out a dozen times a day.'

Meanwhile, Martha got on with bringing up Wilkie's three children. She sometimes suggested she would rather have a more binding relationship, as when she insisted that Wilkie maintain the outward signs of respectability on a visit to Ramsgate. As he reported to Sebastian Schlesinger in August 1888, 'Wilkie Collins . . . has disappeared from this mortal sphere of action, and is replaced by William Dawson 27 Wellington Crescent Ramsgate.' He explained that he was staying at the Kent seaside with his '"morganatic family", and must travel (like the Royal Personages) under an alias – or not be admitted into the respectable house now occupied by my children and their mother. So . . . address W. Dawson Esq. for the next fortnight.' The idea that Wilkie should go by an assumed name in a town where he was well known was ridiculous. Perhaps such proprieties were required by the landlady, but it is more likely an indication of Martha's insecurity that she requested this petty deception.

Her peace of mind was not helped by the fact that the Graveses now commanded the purse strings in Wilkie's household. This was largely because Harry Bartley was not only his solicitor but, since Charles Ward's death in 1883, his main financial confidant.

Without Ward at his side, some of Wilkie's old insecurities about money returned, and he might have wished he was still earning the extravagant amounts he had enjoyed in the 1860s. Throughout much of the mid-1880s, his income hovered around the £2,000 mark, though in 1887 it dropped to £1,350. This was still an appreciable amount: £2,000 in 1884 was the equivalent of £163,000 in today's money.

Having tended to spurn his wider family, Wilkie was now happy to renew contact with his cousins. He liked the way Marion Gray used to bring him fresh eggs from her landlord's chickens. Having once worked as a photographer's assistant, she now lived on her own, following the deaths of her mother and father, Catherine and John (the latter still in Thun). Wilkie occasionally gave Marion Gray financial help, which she may have passed to her elder brother William, an artist, who was an inmate in the Wiltshire County Lunatic Asylum in Devizes.

Another Gray brother, Charles, had recently died in South Africa, where, under the name Charles Lascelles, he had pioneered opera in Pietermaritzburg. Another brother, Alexander, continued to live in San Francisco, where Wilkie might have visited him in 1874. Writing to him there, Wilkie gave a concise summary of his situation, 'As for me, I gave up, what is called "Society" some years since, in the interests of my health . . . I live in retirement (with a few old friends still left) – devoted to my art.'

Following the deaths of both Ward brothers, and of Charles Reade, Wilkie could count those 'few old friends' on the fingers of one hand. He was still close to Ted Pigott, with whom he occasionally ventured to the theatre. Having spent so many years trying to avoid permanent entanglement with the female sex, they now acted like a pair of old women. 'Be very careful about <u>draughts</u> on the railway tomorrow,' Wilkie counselled Pigott. But he showed excessive concern when he carried on, albeit with a hint of irony, 'I need not remind you to sit with your "back to the horses". And don't forget that the "joiners' work" is more carefully done in the first class carriages than in the second – and that the small unheeded currents of air, <u>sneaking</u> through window frames are capable of finding their way to weak bronchial tubes.'

Otherwise, Wilkie's most constant companions were the ever-hospitable Lehmanns. At lunch at their house in Berkeley Square in December 1887, he was introduced to Horace Pym, a book-loving solicitor, who told him about an elaborate insurance fraud carried out a few years earlier by a German adventurer called Scheurer (who inevitably passed himself off as Baron von Scheurer). This was the story which, wrapped up with topical details of the Irish Land League, Wilkie used for the basic plot of his final novel, *Blind Love*.

Since Frederick Lehmann was still often away, Wilkie continued his playful relationship with Nina. 'That's me, Padrona

– that's me,' he wrote to her at one stage. And then, unsure if this was correct, he added, 'Good God! is "<u>me</u>" grammar? Ought it to be "I"? My poor father paid ninety pounds a year for my education – and I give you my sacred word of honour I am not sure whether it is "me" or "I".'

This was a typically unaffected admission from a man who, though no longer at the summit of his profession, was still much admired. He had been vice president of the Society of Authors since its inauguration (with the novelist Walter Besant as general secretary) in 1884. Although visibly decrepit, he acted as a steward at a dinner given by the Society at London's Criterion Restaurant four years later in honour of visiting American authors who had helped lobby their government on copyright. There had been considerable progress over this matter, and an international agreement on copyright law (the Berne Convention) was signed in 1886. But there was still work to do: the United States did not recognise payment of copyright fees to foreign authors until the passage of the Chace Act of 1891, and it did not formally join the Berne Convention until 1988, more than a century after its inauguration.

Among the other guests at the Criterion was a young writer, Oscar Wilde, who edited a magazine called *The Woman's World*. A decade earlier, as an Oxford undergraduate, he had been given the nickname 'Fosco' because of his flamboyance. He and Wilkie had recently met through the novelist Ouida. But literary and social tastes were changing and Wilkie made no effort to keep up. Conversely, Wilde was no great fan of his, and advised Elizabeth Robins, a young American actress, not to appear in a proposed production of *Man and Wife* since 'the English public finds it tedious'.

Also present at the dinner was the stout Manchester-born Frances Hodgson Burnett, whose children's novel *Little Lord Fauntleroy* Wilkie had enjoyed. He skittishly asked Andrew

Chatto, who had given him the book, whether she would have known that 'her charming little boy' had 'the name of the last man hanged for forgery in England', the subject of Wilkie's story for *Household Words* three decades earlier. Hodgson Burnett had recently contributed a footnote to copyright law by taking legal action against E.V. Seebohm's unauthorised theatrical production of *Little Lord Fauntleroy* and preventing it from taking place.

Wilkie made it clear that he had no intention of writing his memoirs. Too many were being published, he said, and 'it will soon become a distinction not to have written one's autobiography.' However, he did relent to produce a light-hearted piece, 'Reminiscences of a Story-teller', for his rich young friend Harry Quilter, who had started a new periodical, the *Universal Review*. Quilter had studied at the bar before branching into art criticism, where his attacks on aestheticism infuriated Whistler, particularly after he purchased the artist's former home in Tite Street and refurbished it according to his own conservative taste.

Under his small publishing imprint, the Universal Review Library, Quilter had just produced *Is Marriage a Failure?*, which followed up on the intense debate about matrimony that had led 27,000 people to write to the *Daily Telegraph* on the subject. In his book, Quilter noted Wilkie's various written references on the subject, suggesting it had been a topic of mutual discussion between the two of them.

For his article, Wilkie recalled an episode in a railway carriage with a clergyman and his two daughters. When the parson went to sleep, one of the girls whipped out a book and blushed when Wilkie caught sight of a cheap edition of *The New Magdalen*. When her sister asked if it was interesting, she replied, 'It's perfectly dreadful.' When her father awoke, 'The New Magdalen instantly disappeared, and the young person caught me looking at her cheek. It reddened a little again. Alas for my art! . . . it was stuff concealed from Papa, stuff which raised the famous Blush, stuff registered on the Expurgatory Index of the national cant.'

Wilkie was happier to pen occasional pieces that were literary rather than autobiographical in subject matter, among them 'Books Necessary for a Liberal Education', which appeared in the *Pall Mall Gazette* in February 1886. The Liberal-oriented *Gazette* had been yet another venture of George Smith of Smith, Elder and the *Cornhill*, until he had passed over ownership to his son-in-law at the start of the decade. This allowed him to concentrate on a new project, the *Dictionary of National Biography*, for which Wilkie provided an entry on his brother Charley in 1887. Smith could afford this expensive indulgence since he had added to his fortune as the importer of the popular Apollinaris mineral water from Germany.

The *Pall Mall Gazette* was edited by the crusading journalist W.T. Stead, who had recently been jailed for purchasing an underage girl as part of his campaign against child prostitution. This was the sort of issue that Wilkie, in earlier days, might have written about. But now he was happy to write a gentle piece, making clear that he had little sympathy with proscriptive lists. 'I pick up the literature that happens to fall in my way, and live upon it as well as I can – like the sparrows who are picking up the crumbs outside my window while I write.' He then quoted Johnson, 'I would not advise a rigid adherence to a particular plan of study. I myself have never persisted in any plan for two days together. A man ought to read just as inclination leads him; for what he reads as a task will do him little good.' Wilkie added that these words (from Boswell's *Life*, which he regarded as 'the greatest biographical work that has ever been written') had consoled him when he had first read them while floundering at school.

He also expressed difficulty in understanding what was meant by a liberal education, saying that he supported 'any system of education the direct tendency of which is to make us better Christians'. Some of his readers might have been startled at this claim, but it was evident from his output over the past decade that he regarded simple, non-dogmatic Christianity as the best form of society. He went on to mention favourite authors such as Goldsmith (whose *The Vicar of Wakefield* he thought particularly fitting), Byron, Scott, Dickens, Balzac and Fenimore Cooper. He also said he 'never got any good out of a book unless the book interested me in the first instance'. By that criterion, he admitted he had cast aside works by Ben Jonson, Samuel Richardson and Edmund Burke.

His agent Alexander Watt tried to keep him apprised of new authors, such as Rider Haggard. However, Wilkie refused to be overwhelmed by *King Solomon's Mines*, describing it in early 1888 as 'a very clever book – of its kind'. He was more impressed when Watt told him that, while on holiday in Scotland, he had visited Walter Scott's home at Abbotsford. Wilkie was madly envious and claimed he had just been reading *A Legend of Montrose* for the hundredth time.

20

HANGING ON

WILKIE HAD KNOWN for some time that he would have to move from Gloucester Place, the house that in retrospect was most associated with his life. Much to his annoyance, his landlord, Lord Portman, had been demanding the sum of £1,200 to renew his lease. Wilkie thought this sum excessive and that the noble lord was quite rich enough anyway. Since there was little he could do, he was forced to look for somewhere else to live.

He found what he wanted at 82 Wimpole Street, less than a mile eastward across Marylebone, his favourite piece of real estate. A dentist called Joseph Walker wanted to let the upper floors of the house he used for his consulting rooms. Since the move took longer than expected, Wilkie experienced an uncomfortable hiatus in February 1888 when he was left in Gloucester Place without carpets and curtains. However, he told a visitor, the diminutive Manx author Hall Caine, that he was 'still possessed of a table and two chairs – pen and ink – cigars – and brandy and water' – no doubt the items he thought essential for a writer's existence (and clearly in strong doses since he had earlier denounced weak brandy and water). Caine, later a huge best-seller, was beginning to enjoy success as a novelist with *The Deemster* and wanted advice about dramatising his work. Wilkie, always happy to help fellow writers, was intrigued by a man who had lived with his wife since she was thirteen, marrying her when she was seventeen in a secret ceremony in Edinburgh.

After several false starts, Wilkie transferred to Wimpole Street in March that year, but family morale was low following the death of Harriet's fourth child, two-month-old Violet Clara, from whooping cough. He gave Harriet his usual matter-of-fact counsel, 'I cannot honestly suggest topics of "religious consolation" . . . Time is the only consoler.'

The new house was a haven of peace compared with Gloucester Place. 'There is no mews at the back of this house', he explained to Tillotson. 'In other words, no organs, no crashing carriage-wheels, no noisy children, no hideous Salvation Army celebrations, nothing in short but the silent storehouses of the tradesmen in Wigmore Street. My irritable nerves consider themselves to be in The Garden of Eden.'

That did not mean his move was noise-free. He left a vivid picture of the commotion caused by removal men, builders and family. "If you please, sir, I don't think the looking glass will fit in above the bookcase in this house," suggested one of the workmen. "Your father's lovely little picture can't go above the chimney-piece, the heat will spoil it," said another voice, clearly Caroline's. "Take down the picture in the next room," Wilkie replied, "and try it there." "But that is the portrait of your grandmother." "Damn my grandmother." At the day's end Caroline piped up, "I say, Wilkie! when you told Marian and Harriet that they might help to put the books in their places, did you know that [*Les Amours du chevalier de*] *Faublas* and Casanova's *Memoirs* were left out on the drawing-room table?'" At least this reference to two mildly erotic works in Wilkie's library showed that the move was a joint family effort and his two eldest daughters by Martha Rudd were involved.

After settling in and starting work on *The Lord Harry*, as *Blind Love* was still called, Wilkie had an abrupt intimation of his mortality when he was involved in one of the more unexpected phenomena of his age, a potentially fatal traffic accident. At the start of 1889, he was returning from dinner with Sebastian Schlesinger in Wilton Place, when suddenly his four-wheel cab hit another vehicle and he was thrown out of the door. Although covered in glass, he suffered no damage to his face, eyes or hands. He only admitted to feeling a bit shaken the following day.

Schlesinger had recently moved to London as the European agent for the controversial Philadelphia and Reading Railroad Company. One reason was the break-down of his marriage to his beautiful first wife, Berthe, who had sat for Millais in 1876. He was being hounded for a financial settlement and regarded Wilkie as a man to consult on this sort of matter.

Unaccustomed though he was to the role of marital counsellor, Wilkie advised his friend to act tough and avoid contacting her again, except to tell her that he was prepared to pay her a yearly allowance, on a quarterly basis. 'You will very likely receive a penitent letter – perhaps a "heart-rending" letter. Don't answer! . . . I have had between 40 and 50 years' experience of women of all sorts and sizes.' His response once again showed that he had lost some of his earlier sympathy for married women in potential financial predicaments.

Wilkie enjoyed Sebastian's company and enjoyed trading mildly suggestive comments with him. In March, he mentioned a constitutional drive he had been taking under 'a cloudless sky' with a pretty woman (presumably a nurse). However, he was 'dumb to the utterance of Love' since he had a mouth abscess, which required hot laudanum and water. In their communications, Wilkie revealed more about Caroline's nature to Schlesinger than to anyone else – as when a box of game birds, a present from Sebastian, had failed to turn up at Wimpole Street. Wilkie suggested that Caroline would be the right person to chase this up, as she was 'a woman who is not to be trifled with – who will insist and persevere – and take advantage of the "privileges of her sex", and bother the authorities till they will wish they had never been born.'

Wilkie's main task was completing the serial version of *The Lord Harry* for John Dicks, the publisher of *Bow Bells*, a new penny periodical. At the same time he was discussing a similar commission with the *Illustrated London News*, and, although he claimed to have several ideas in mind, including a sequel to *The Moonstone*, nothing had been finalised. In March 1889, he suddenly found he was falling behind with his serial for Dicks and felt unable to complete it in the required time.

At this juncture, Watt came into his own as an agent. Since Dicks had yet to find any other publisher willing to share the risk of serialising *The Lord Harry*, he was happy to forgo his rights, which were passed to the *Illustrated London News*. This was a double victory for Wilkie: he no longer had to worry about thinking up a new idea for the *Illustrated London News*, which nevertheless was happy to pay him the money he would have received from Dicks. Wilkie was greatly relieved and ladled out compliments to Watt, telling him he was 'a born diplomatist' whose name was now united with that of Talleyrand in his mind.

Failing health made Wilkie unusually worried about keeping his bank balance topped up. The copyrights of his lifetime's work were his main asset, and he had been in contact with Chatto about selling or leasing them. A few months earlier he had agreed to a minimal sum (£250) for a seven-year lease on several of his lesser novels. He now hoped to obtain £2,500 for an outright sale of all his copyrights. When Chatto offered only £1,800, plus

£500 for the book version of *The Lord Harry*, Wilkie was grudgingly forced to accept. There was no escaping that this was a
significant drop from the amounts he used to command.

For a short period in June, when it was particularly hot in
London, Wilkie travelled to Ramsgate. On 30 June, ten days
after his return, he suffered a stroke while reading the radical
Sunday broadsheet *Reynolds's Newspaper*. His left side was para-
lysed and for a while it seemed that his brain was affected. 'It
is a terrible shock – to see such a wonderful genius struck down
in an instant,' Harriet Bartley told Mary Elizabeth Braddon,
asking her not to mention this development to anyone 'as we
hope it is not generally known'.

For a while Wilkie was seen only by Caroline and his medical
attendants – Frank Beard, Dr Samuel Fenwick (a Harley Street
specialist) and a nurse. In August he rallied slightly, enabling
Harriet to go to Brighton with her children, and Wilkie's daughter
Marian took over secretarial duties. A few select people were
allowed to visit, among them Pigott's friend George Redford,
who recalled Wilkie grasping his hand 'with all his old warmth'
and saying, '"You see, I'm all right – feel my arm" – but I had
hard work to hide my eyes lest he should see what I really
dreaded.' Wilkie even prevailed on Caroline to allow him to
smoke a cigar with Redford, who had witnessed his original will
twenty years earlier.

Sustained work was now out of the question. On 17 August,
Beard told Watt that 'Wilkie's absolutely incapable of finishing
the present number of his work within the next three or four
weeks.' A couple of days later Watt called at Wimpole Street to
pick up the 'Black Book' in which Wilkie had jotted down his
notes for *Blind Love*. There was a suggestion that Hall Caine
might complete it, but he was away and the task fell to Walter
Besant.

Wilkie hung on precariously for another month. On 21

September he managed to pencil a note to Beard, 'I am <u>dying</u> old friend. They are driving me mad by <u>forbidding the</u> hy— [which probably meant the hypodermic needle]. Come for God's sake. I am too wretched to write.' Beard made his way to Wimpole Street and administered what was required. Two days later it was all over: on the morning of 23rd September, Wilkie was dead.

Those around him were heartbroken. Harriet Bartley, who had remained close to her 'god-father' and cared for him through many ups and downs for almost thirty years, wrote to Wilkie's friend Frank Archer the next day, 'My news is so sad. I coudnt [*sic*] write to you before it has all been so miserable. Our dear one left us at 10.35 yesterday morning. We are so sad. He died so peacefully & so quietly – and his face is beautiful with such a calm expression. Poor dear Wilkie.'

The day after, Nina Lehmann informed her son Rudolph, 'And so our poor dear genial delightful matchless old Wilkie has gone. It made me very sad but he could never have enjoyed life again even if he had recovered . . . Wilkie was almost the very last link left that bound us to the glory of departed days. Dickens, Lytton, Houghton, Wilkie, Charlie [*sic*] Collins, poor old Chorley – it seems like a former life, not on this earth at all . . .'

21

LEGACY

DESPITE OVERCAST CONDITIONS on the morning of Friday 27 September, a crowd gathered outside 82 Wimpole Street, eager to see Wilkie begin his journey to his final resting place in Kensal Green cemetery. Bona fide mourners were received at the door of the house by Caroline, Harriet and Harry Bartley, before disappearing to the back room where Wilkie was laid out. At around 10.30, his coffin was solemnly placed in a glass-panelled hearse covered in wreaths, including what the *Standard* described as 'a handsome cross of white crysanthemums from Mrs Dawson and family'. A quarter of an hour later the horse-drawn vehicle pulled away, followed by more than a dozen carriages transporting family members and friends, including Pigott, Lehmann, Watt, Chatto, Schlesinger and Beard.

The procession wound through north London to the cemetery, where it was met by the Reverend Edward Ker Gray, minister in charge of St George's Chapel in Albemarle Street. Possibly because of his connections with the stage, Ker Gray had been singled out to conduct the funeral service, which was ironic since his chapel had regularly clashed with the ecclesiastical authorities for not having a licence to perform marriages. Doubtless this local difficulty endeared him to Wilkie, several of whose theatrical friends were present.

The ambience at the graveside was subdued, since Wilkie had asked for a simple ceremony, costing no more than £25. However, the sun had begun to shine and it was unlikely that the dead man's strangely puritanical request that 'no scarves, hat bands or feathers shall be worn or used at my funeral' was fully adhered to. One mourner was reported to be Oscar Wilde, though this identification was the result of a confusion with Wilde's brother Willie, a journalist.

Martha and her children took no part in the official ceremony, though one newspaper did refer to Mrs Dawson and her children being present, 'but they were not among the chief mourners and kept out of view as much as possible'.

The obituaries lamented the loss of a great storyteller. Several echoed the *Penny Illustrated Paper*'s note that Wilkie 'was remarkable . . . for his independence of character, and always said precisely what he thought; and no mind was ever more entirely clear of cant and humbug.' According to Andrew Chatto in the *Pall Mall Gazette*, he 'was one of the kindest and most modest of men'. One or two friends, such as Edmund Yates, wrote lengthier appreciations, though Hall Caine's encomium in the *Globe* grated with Harriet, who thought he was cashing in with his 'personal recollections'. 'Mr Hall Caine and I are antipathetic,' she told Watt, uncompromisingly.

Harry Quilter, one of Wilkie's newer friends, embarked on an ill-fated attempt to raise money for a memorial to him in Westminster Abbey or St Paul's Cathedral. On 3 October, ten days after Wilkie's death, Quilter wrote to *The Times* soliciting subscriptions on behalf of a committee that he said included Andrew Chatto, Hall Caine and Ted Pigott. However, Pigott claimed to know nothing about this initiative, telling Edmund Yates that Wilkie's 'work was the only monument he cared for, and he was the last of men to claim the honour of a medallion in the crypt'. Although the *Daily Telegraph* came out firmly against the proposal, arguing sniffily that 'the mere fact that it is found necessary to "agitate" for the admission of a memorial . . . affords the strongest possible presumption that the proper place for such a memorial is elsewhere', Quilter persisted and over £300 was raised, including five guineas from Henry James. Neither place of worship showed any interest, and Quilter later revealed that the dean of St Paul's had told him that '"other considerations than Mr Wilkie Collins's literary excellence" had to be taken into account.' This no doubt meant that Wilkie's domestic arrangements (which had become open knowledge after his will was proved on 11 November) had stymied the idea. Quilter subsequently arranged for the money to be used to buy books for a Wilkie Collins Memorial Library at the People's Palace in Mile End Road.

The Palace was a large cultural centre for the inhabitants of the East End, first mooted by Walter Besant in his novel *All Sorts and Conditions of Men* in 1882, and opened five years later, incorporating a library run exclusively by women. Besant, whose contribution to *Blind Love* started shortly after Wilkie's death, retained close links with the institution and almost certainly assisted in the setting up of the Wilkie Collins Memorial Library, which was generously supported by some of his old publishers, such as Bentley and Sampson Low. However, when in 1911 all the books in the main People's Palace had to be moved to the local Mile End public library, the Wilkie Collins section, which was housed in its own room, does not appear to have made the transition. No one now knows what happened to it.

Since Wilkie had already written forty-eight chapters of *Blind Love*, Besant had only sixteen more to complete – a task he found surprisingly easy because Wilkie had typically planned the framework of his novel with great precision. As Besant wrote in the preface, 'I found that these were not merely notes such as I expected – simple indications of the plot and the development of events, but an actual detailed scenario, in which every incident, however trivial, was carefully laid down: there were also fragments of dialogue inserted at those places where dialogue was wanted to emphasise the situation and make it real.' Serialisation in the *Illustrated London News* was completed on 28 December, and publication of the three-volume book by Chatto & Windus followed in January.

Meanwhile, as soon as Wilkie was buried, it became a matter of urgency to clear and vacate his house. Since Caroline could not afford to run the place, she moved a short distance to Newman Street. The auction of the contents of Wimpole Street on 24 October proved a low-key affair. According to the *St James's Gazette*, 'The day was gloomy, the house was gloomy, and the occasion was gloomy.' The paper was put off by the spectacle of people traipsing through Wilkie's house eyeing 'bundles of odds and ends which only a dustman would have thought worth the carriage'. These included bed linen, mattresses and pots and pans. Even the main item on sale, the '4ft. 6 in. mahogany table, on castors with four drawers in frame, top lined with leather', elicited little enthusiastic response. Previously the property of his father, this was where Wilkie had written all his books. But now, with its ink stains and scuffed leather, it was knocked down to £10. The writing slope, which Wilkie placed on this desk, in emulation of Dickens, realised only £3 5s. More interesting was a folding version, with a compartment for writing materials, which looked like a miniature gun case and which he used when travelling.

A few days later Wilkie's will was proved. He had taken particular care to ensure that his affairs were in order and that there should be no grounds for friction within his extended family after his death. He had frequently rewritten his will, adding a codicil as recently as 18 July. Aside from small bequests totalling £490 to servants and relations, plus a further £1,000 kept back to pay life annuities of £20 to his cousin Marion Gray and to his one surviving aunt Mrs Dyke (the 'aunt Christy' of his childhood), the remainder of his estate was divided equally between Caroline and her daughter, and Martha and her (and Wilkie's) three children. The resulting document was remarkable because it provided his first public acknowledgement of his children and his two families.

The proceeds were initially valued at £10,831 11s 3d. But after further sales of his library (at Messrs Puttick and Simpson), paintings (at Christie's) and manuscripts (at Sotheby's) during the first half of 1890, his estate was revalued at £11,414 16s 1d in April 1892. This was the equivalent of just over £1 million in 2013.

Recalling the plight of Laura Fairlie in *The Woman in White*, who was inveigled into signing over her fortune to her husband, Wilkie tried to be as fair as possible, stipulating that his daughters' (and their daughters') inheritances should be for their 'sole and separate use free and independent of any husband' and that none of them should 'have the power to deprive herself of the benefit thereof in anticipation'. In other words, their money could not be used by any husband as a charge on his debts – a fate that had befallen Laura Fairlie.

This was all well and good, but Wilkie had overlooked a couple of his own unwritten rules about the proper treatment of women in matters of inheritance. Despite his apparent fairness in apportioning his money and property, he laid down that his son, William, would receive his share of the estate in full at the age of twenty-one, but his daughters Marian and Harriet would only be entitled to the income from their equal shares. Moreover, Wilkie put oversight of these matters in the hands of four male trustees, Harry Bartley, Frederick Lehmann, Sebastian Schlesinger and Frank Beard. And he specified that Bartley or any further trustee who was both a relation and a lawyer could charge the estate for his professional services. It was odd that someone once so sceptical about the law should now put so much faith in its workings.

After the death of Lehmann in 1891 and Beard two years

later, Harry Bartley became by default responsible for the financial side of the estate. At the start of the decade, he appeared to have all the trappings of a prosperous Victorian solicitor, after moving a few hundred yards to a more substantial house on the Finchley Road, where he lived with his wife, three daughters and four servants.

This domestic solidarity was mirrored on the professional front in Somerset Street, Portman Square, where Harry had been joined by his younger brother Richard in running the family firm. However, the Bartleys were still snared in litigation over their property interests. This may have contributed in March 1892 to the suicide of the Reverend Henry Powell, the clergyman who had presided over his nephew Harry's marriage to Harriet. He shot himself in mysterious circumstances while in temporary charge of a parish in Bedfordshire. Two bottles of laudanum were found beside him. His death only exacerbated the disputes in the Bartley family, leading to the dissolution of the partnership between the two brothers in May 1893.

By the following year Harry was beginning to suffer financially. He had bought Millais's affectionate portrait of Wilkie at the posthumous Christie's auction. But in August 1894 he was forced to write to the National Portrait Gallery, offering it for sale at £100. After liaising with the artist, the Gallery was prepared to pay £52 10s, a mere two guineas more than Bartley had bid for it four years earlier. Harry's financial difficulties were in retrospect evident from the brusque manner in which be demanded payment and when, five days later, this had not appeared, he wrote again asking, 'When may I expect a cheque?'

The exact date when Harry began siphoning off money from Wilkie's estate is not clear. However, after he began being regularly absent from home, it emerged that he was seeing another woman. In 1895 he decamped to Reading where in May that year he was forced to sue for bankruptcy. This disgrace was too much for his ever prim mother-in-law Caroline, who died the following month. Its burden also told on Harry who, just over two years later, himself succumbed to cancer and died in Guildford, aged just forty-four.

Harriet simply had to get used to living in reduced circumstances. She moved to Kilburn Priory, close to the Bartleys in Upper Hamilton Terrace, and, for a while, her mother-in-law supported her with an allowance. But when old Mrs Bartley died in 1900, she left Harriet a mere £50, with the abrupt prescription that this would 'give her a reasonable time for making arrangements for herself and her children that may become necessary'.

By then Doris, the eldest of this brood, had left home and was pursuing a career in the theatre. Making the most of her blue eyes and golden hair – legacies from her grandmother – she joined the Gaiety Girls, a troupe of dancing girls (originally started by Wilkie's friend, John Hollingshead, in homage to Paris and the can-can) which had been reinvented and gained some respectability as a musical comedy turn. She was entertaining her mother in her theatrical digs in Richmond in February 1905 when, to her consternation, her mother dropped dead at the premature age of fifty-four. Doris's three sisters then tried to follow her on to the boards, but with less success.

Around this time Joseph Clow, a forgotten figure from the past, returned to England from Australia. After working as a mining engineer, he had raised a family (two sons and two daughters) in Bairnsdale, Victoria, with a woman called Ellen Watson. At some stage his sons (Charles and Hector) were fostered out to the Hollow family, who were vague relations of Ellen's and had a history of taking in children. Following the death of Caroline Graves, the woman who was still legally his wife, in England in 1895, Clow was at last free to marry again. He did this in June 1902, after Ellen Watson had passed away in Melbourne the previous year. His second wife was Louisa

Maguire, who three years earlier had obtained a messy divorce from a violent and abusive husband. However, she had four children, and the mixture does not seem to have worked, because, by 1911, Clow had returned to England with his son Charles. Although Charles died soon afterwards, his father, Joseph Charles Clow, the man who married Caroline Graves, survived in Willesden until 1927.

Without even in-laws to lend support, Martha Rudd (or Dawson, as she still preferred to call herself) soldiered on as best she could at Taunton Place, with her three children. At least she was used to being out of the limelight. She was initially cushioned by proceeds from Wilkie's will, which helped pay her daughters' fees at the Maria Grey School. But after Harry Bartley's bankruptcy this source of funds dried up. Martha was forced to move steadily further out of London, first to Kilburn, then to Willesden, and finally by 1911 to Southend, where she, Marian and Harriet lived modestly in a house half a mile in from the seafront. Her son Charles fought with distinction in the Boer War and then, after marrying, flourished briefly as an up-market motor mechanic. But he too died young on the eve of the First World War. By then, his sisters, Wilkie's daughters, had long reconciled themselves to a life of obscurity. Marian Dawson had over the years been employed as a governess and her sister Harriet as a mother's help, but, although Martha described herself as a widow, they, even more than Caroline Graves, were both acutely aware of the stigma of illegitimacy. As she approached her death in 1919, Martha opened up slightly and used to tell the world unrealistically that she could have married Wilkie at any time.

Wilkie Collins has never been easy to pigeonhole. But this is what makes him so appealing more than a century after his death.

He was certainly not a typical self-righteous Victorian male. If there was a model, he was the exception who proved the rule. His whole life was carried on in a curious struggle between the forces of illumination and obfuscation. While he strove publicly for the advancement of knowledge, writing obsessively about the unearthing of secrets, his inner self remained shrouded in mystery, which was all the more difficult to fathom because he himself appeared so down-to-earth. As Nathaniel Beard, the son of his doctor, observed, 'He was the least *posé* public man I ever met. He would tell amusing anecdotes, and make very pertinent remarks, but never talked "for effect".'

Yet this undemonstrative character was a best-selling author who scandalised his readers with his carefully crafted imaginings. As he pushed back the boundaries of literary taste, he managed to live privately and unostentatiously with two women in two separate households. Only towards the end of his life did his most unexpected secret begin to emerge – that one of his enduring principles had been a deep-felt Christian ethic that set him against any organised religion.

As Beard suggested, Wilkie was seldom pretentious. His affectations did not stretch much beyond a liking for flamboyant clothes and a taste for laudanum and fine cigars. He had little time for convention, whether it involved dressing up for dinner or putting his name to a marriage register. His early immersion in European culture contributed to his general lack of inhibition and his attachment to cosmopolitan families such as the Lehmanns.

As a friend he was attentive and supportive – qualities that endeared him to people as wide-ranging as Dickens, Charles Fechter and Nina Lehmann, who, after receiving a 'charming' letter from Wilkie, wrote to her husband, 'Ah me! yes, steady friendship that continues for nearly twenty years, always the same, always kind, always earnest, always interested, always true, always loving and faithful – *that* is worthy the name of friendship indeed.

I value my Wilkie and I love him dearly.' His capacity for affectionate relationships with women helped him gain insights into the minds, aspirations and frustrations of the opposite sex.

Behind his bluff exterior, he was a gentle, often emotional man, rarely troubled by ambition, except in his chosen profession as a writer. As was clear from *Man and Wife*, he did not like competitive sports. In geo-political terms, he was a pacifist, who opposed the Crimean War, and he had no interest in the swagger of Queen Victoria's golden jubilee celebrations. His lack of enthusiasm for imperial adventures was one of the few things that set him apart from Dickens.

Wilkie's cerebral side took over when he was writing his novels and guided him through the hard grind of his intricate plots. When this aspect of his personality was in the ascendant, he was often disposed, as his children noted, to live 'in his head'. This tendency was compounded, certainly in his later years, by his opium consumption, which anaesthetised him against his immediate surroundings and made him oblivious to all but the task of completing his work. At such times, his proto-feminist principles were forgotten and he kept his two women in their economically and socially disadvantaged positions, ignoring any desire they might have had for matrimony and respectability.

The combination of Wilkie's opium intake and his chronic illnesses contributed to a coarsening in his later fiction, which lacked the verve of his earlier work. Although he wrote many interesting novels during his last fifteen years, they were often vehicles for his ideas rather than his creative imagination.

His heyday as a novelist occurred between the publication of *Basil* in 1852 and *Man and Wife* in 1870. During this period he helped develop the sensation genre as a potent and irreverent guide to the hidden side of Victorian existence, highlighting its hypocrisies in a manner that was often more informative and entertaining than Dickens's. The criticism that his books relied too much on plot was overplayed, the literary equivalent of the brickbats hurled at the Pre-Raphaelites for their excessive detail. Wilkie may have planned his stories carefully, but his manu-scripts attest to the spontaneity and intensity of his writing. Along the way, he created a host of memorable characters, from the feckless Basil and the lively Magdalen Vanstone, through the villainous Count Fosco and the redoubtable Marian Halcombe, to the honourable Sir Patrick Lundie. *The Moonstone* stands out as one of the most sophisticated novels of the nine-teenth century.

After his death, Wilkie's reputation suffered a downturn, the nadir coming when the library collection established in his name in the East End of London was transferred to a new site and lost. The revival began quietly, with T.S. Eliot leading the way with his piece on Wilkie and Dickens in the *Times Literary Supplement* in 1927. At around the same time, Dorothy Sayers started work on a biography of Wilkie. Thirty years later she was forced to retire from the project, having been defeated by her inability to make any headway into the story of Wilkie's two women, Caroline and Martha.

This problem became less imposing as a result of the forensic biographies written in 1989 by William Clarke, the husband of one of the last direct descendants of Martha Rudd, and in 1991 by Catherine Peters. These two books coincided with renewed interest in Wilkie among academics, who discovered that he offered an illuminating and often unusual entrée into the period. He wrote about people at the margins of nineteenth-century society – the dispossessed, the disabled and the mad; he offered interesting observations on science and psychology; and he was sympathetic to women, whom he regarded as victims of a patri-archal legal system. All these topics tallied with fields of study that were finding their way onto university syllabuses.

Helped by new, well-annotated editions from Oxford, Penguin

and other publishers, the general public began to rediscover and enjoy Wilkie's books. His stories proved exciting and readable – a welcome antidote to some of the crimped literature that was fashionable in the late twentieth century. And the more Wilkie was studied, the more he came to be regarded as an innovative writer playing with fictional forms, using multiple narrators, and even dabbling with alternative consciousness – themes that came together in his masterpiece *The Moonstone*. By the late twentieth-century, his influence could be seen in a range of unabashed populist authors, such as Sarah Waters and Susan Hill.

It is an irony typical of Wilkie that his expansive novels are returning to fashion at a time when people's attention spans have been reduced by exposure to electronic media. It is also a testament to his sheer page-turning readability. In this context, his own colourful life – with its vertiginous changes of fortune, passed in close proximity to the literary and artistic establishments of his day – is a fitting and most engaging reflection of the complexities of the Victorian age he inhabited.

NOTES

Abbreviations for Names and Publications

WC – Wilkie Collins
WmC – William Collins
HC – Harriet Collins
CAC – Charles Allston Collins
KC – Katey Collins (née Dickens)
CD – Charles Dickens
CW – Charles Ward
FL – Frederick Lehmann
NL – Nina Lehmann
DW – David Wilkie
EP – Edward (Smyth) Pigott
WHH – William Holman Hunt

HW — *Household Words*
P. – Pilgrim edition of Dickens's *Letters* (see Bibliography)
RP – Reserved Photocopy (in BL)
ODNB – *Oxford Dictionary of National Biography*

Abbreviations for Libraries and Other Sources of Letters

BL – British Library
NYPL – New York Public Library
NAL – National Art Library
NPG – National Portrait Gallery
Mitchell – Mitchell Library, Glasgow

Berg – Berg Collection, NYPL

Princeton – Firestone Memorial Library, Princeton University, NJ

Houghton – Houghton Library, Harvard University

Texas – Harry Ransom Center, University of Texas at Austin

Huntington – Huntington Library, San Marino, California

Fales – Fales Library, New York University

Folger – Folger Shakespeare Library, Washington DC

Harrowby – Harrowby Manuscripts Trust, Sandon, Staffordshire

Manx – Manx National Heritage, Archives and Public Library, Douglas, Isle of Man

Bolton – Bolton Central Library, Bolton, Lancashire

Lewis – Paul Lewis Collection, UK

Hanes – Susan Hanes, USA

Rosenbach – Rosenbach Museum and Library, Philadelphia, Pa.

Maine – Maine Historical Society, USA

Clarke – Faith Clarke Collection, UK

Canterbury – Canterbury Christ Church University, Kent, UK

Illinois – University of Illinois at Urbana-Champaign, Ill.

Pembroke – Pembroke College, Cambridge, UK

I have tried, as far as possible, to give the names of the libraries and other institutions where the various letters can be consulted. As far as Wilkie Collins is concerned, his correspondence is also gathered in the four volumes of the *Collected Letters*, edited by William Baker, Andrew Gasson, Graham Law and Paul Lewis (see Bibliography).

In referencing books, I have used a shortened title if the full title of the book can be found in the Bibliography.

Given the wide range of texts, I have not provided references for quotations from Wilkie Collins's own fictional works. A list of these can be found on page 467. Apart from the original editions, Chatto and Windus, Wilkie's publisher towards the end of his life, put out a variety of comprehensive editions, including the New Illustrated Library and the Piccadilly Novels. Many of Wilkie's books are still in print. I recommend the well-annotated versions from Oxford and Penguin.

xii　'Nothing in this world is hidden for ever.': Wilkie Collins, *No Name*, First Scene, Chapter 4

1　For a version of his physical appearance and domestic set up, see Yates, 'Celebrities at Home', reprinted from *The World*, 26 December 1877

1　'his tiny delicate hands': Nathaniel Beard referred to Wilkie's 'pretty little hands and feet, very like a woman's' in 'Some Recollections of Yesterday', *Temple Bar*, July 1894

3　'those most mysterious of mysteries': Henry James, *Nation*, 9 November 1865, pp.593–5

3　'the first and greatest of English detective novels': T.S. Eliot, 'Wilkie Collins and Dickens', *Times Literary Supplement*, 4 August 1927. T.S. Eliot also referred to *The Moonstone* as 'the first, the longest and the best of Modern English detective novels' in his introduction to the book, published by OUP in 1928

7　'the Regent's Park': the definitive article would later be lost, for this and the New and Marylebone Roads

9　'lucrative appointment': WmC to Washington Allston, 4 November 1818, quoted WC, *Memoirs*

9　'Shandean profusion': WC, *Memoirs*

11　'his painting *Disposal of a Favourite Lamb*': for details of WmC's paintings, see appendix to WC, *Memoirs*

11　'simple yet impressive': WC, *Memoirs*

11　'an unpublished memoir': now at the Harry Ransom Center, University of Texas at Austin

14　'honourably shrunk': WC, *Memoirs*

14　'to abstain from any compliance': resolution made on

Sunday, September 29th, 1816 in St Clement's Church at
Hastings, see WC, *Memoirs*

14   'opposite to each other by the fireside': Wright (ed.),
      Correspondence of Washington Allston

15   'the most beautiful Fancy-figure I ever saw': quoted
      Holmes, *Coleridge*

15   'poetical associations': WC, *Memoirs*

16   'helping William gain election': WC, *Memoirs*

16   'Sommerset [sic] House': Washington Allston to WmC,
      18 May 1821, quoted Wright (ed.), *Correspondence of
      Washington Allston*

18   'sighing for years': Cunningham, *Life of Sir David Wilkie*

20   'Edward Bulwer Lytton conjured up': Flanders, *The
      Invention of Murder*, p.43. This book provides much of the
      background on the Thurtell case

20   'When Wilkie Collins and his friend': see Wilkie Collins
      and Charles Dickens, *The Lazy Tour of Two Idle Apprentices*

22   'He sees': WC, *Memoirs*

22   'simply a gentleman, mild and pleasing': article by 'A Lady',
      Dublin Literary Gazette, 15 May 1830

22   'whatever of poetry and imagination': *Men and Women*,
      Vol.III, No.36, Saturday 5 February 1887, pp.281–2

23   'nest of portrait painters': quoted Taylor, *Life of Benjamin
      Haydon*

24   'Your godson grows a strapping fellow': WmC to David
      Wilkie, April 17 1828, WC, *Memoirs*

25   'No one attempted to approach': WC, *Memoirs*

26   'I could go on': WmC to HC, 2 October 1828, quoted
      WC, *Memoirs*

27   'Here he first met': see WC, *Memoirs*. Irving's celebrity status
      was lampooned in Hazlitt's 'The Spirit of the Age', 1825

29   'Mr Dodsworth continues his sermons': WmC to HC,
      17 October 1831, quoted WC, *Memoirs*

29   'to Mr Dodsworth's, heard an excellent sermon': WmC to
      HC, 2 September 1833, Morgan. For background on
      William Dodsworth see his 'Autobiographical Memoir' in
      *From Reformation to the Permissive Society: a miscellany in
      celebration of the 400th anniversary of Lambeth Palace
      Library*, edited by Melanie Barber and Stephen Taylor with
      Gabriel Sewell, Woodbridge: Boydell Press, 2010

29   'The worthy Academician': Story, *Linnell*

30   'Go on praying': letter of 4 October 1835 from Weston
      House, near Chipping Norton, quoted WC, *Memoirs*

30   'At home very poorly': HC diary, 22 November 1835,
      NAL

30   'by the blessing of God': WmC to HC, 17 October 1831,
      Morgan

31   'says you may with much chance of benefit': WmC to HC,
      2 September 1833, Morgan

31   'a popular educative series for youth': William would have
      approved of Taylor's preface to his book on Bunyan, which
      warned parents against expecting their children to read 'all
      the many hours a wet Sabbath presents', lest they 'make
      that day hated, which ought to be loved': http://tarquin-
      tarsbookcase.blogspot.com/2009/10/before-fodors-there-
      was-reverend-isaac.html

31   'the society of Christians': written 26 May 1834, see WC,
      Memoirs

34   'quite out of his element': WC to Richard Dana Jr, 17
      June 1850, Texas

34   as he told David Wilkie: 14 January 1837, WC, *Memoirs*

35   'sang, chiefly in Italian': Mrs E.M. Ward, *Reminiscences*,
      p.34

35   'a very sincere kind of man': Edward M. Ward to his father
      Charles, 8 April 1838, quoted Dafforne, *Life and Works*

36   'fallen in love with a woman': see Ernst Freiherr von

Wolzogen, *Wilkie Collins: Ein biographisch-kritischer*, Versuch, 1885

36   'gave us . . . in a carriage one day': CD to Georgina Hogarth, 25 November 1853, Berg, P. v7, p.210

37   'Willy very tiresome all day': HC diary, 24 July 1837, NAL

37   'in disgrace again': HC diary, 6 October 1837, NAL

39   'After a short stay with the Carpenters': see DW to Miss Wilkie, 19 August 1838, Cunningham, *The Life of Sir David Wilkie*

40   'all in the highest spirits': DW to Miss Wilkie, 19 August 1838, Cunningham, *The Life of Sir David Wilkie*

42   'Cole published a 136 page pamphlet': London, Hatchard's, 1834

42   'assumes a more than papal infallibility': *Atheneaum*, No. 363, pp.740–1, 11 October 1834

44   'nothing new here': WC to HC, 14 October 1840, Morgan

44   'show-off manner': WC to HC, 22 November 1839 and 14 October 1840, Morgan

44   '£90 a year': WC to Emanuel Deutsch, 20 November 1872, BL

45   'The oldest of the boys': 'Reminiscences of a Story Teller', *Universal Review*, 15 June 1888, p.183

45   'French frog': Yates, 'Celebrities at Home', pp.145–56

46   'passion for pastry': *Universal Review*, 15 June 1888

46   'another of the principal's arguments': see *A Manual of Practical Observations on our Public Schools*, published by Seeley, Burnside and Seeley, 1847

46   'If it had been Collins': WC to William Winter, 3 September 1881, Berg

48   '85 Oxford Terrace': now 167 Sussex Gardens

48   'begged his mother': WC to HC, 14 October 1840, Morgan

50   'two alarmist pamphlets': 'Anarchy and Order. Facts for the consideration of all classes in the community, more

especially for the mechanic, artisan, &c.' and 'London, its Danger and Safety; suggestions for its present and future protection, etc.', both published by Staunton and Sons, 9 Strand, in the revolutionary year of 1848

50   'The Prison and the School': published by Staunton and Sons

51   'an hour or two in the day': *Men and Women*, 5 February 1887

52   'Don't say a word': WmC to HC, 10 August 1841, Morgan

52   'Master at the great house': WmC to HC, 10 September 1841, Morgan

52   'but as I find': ibid.

53   'If it were not for the Academy': Pope (ed.), *Haydon Diary*, v5, 15 June 1841

53   'most amiable of men': ibid., 5 October 1843

53   'Rizzio's blood: WC to HC, 13 June 1842, Pembroke

54   'one knee on the ground': WC, *Memoirs*

54   'as deeply and brilliantly blue': WC, *Memoirs*

55   'Every sentence that fell': WC to HC, 24 August 1842, Morgan

56   'A woman is wanted in the house': WC to HC, 1842/3, Morgan

56   'In 1841 Joseph published': *A Winter in the Azores*, John van Voorst, London, 1841, 2 vols

57   'In an anonymously published book': *Evening Thoughts by A Physician*, John van Voorst, London, 1850

58   'confirmed a few months later': 13 May 1844

59   'Mrs C to be embraced': WC to HC, 13 January 1844, Pembroke

61   '(I) don't take much interest in Matrimony': WC to HC, 21 September 1844, Morgan

63   'worst Suffolk street': WC to HC, 16 September 1845, Morgan

63   'Considering that he is a lamb': ibid

63   '"The Evil One" (whom you mention'): ibid

63   'the actual difference between imprisonment': WC to HC,
      30 September 1845, Morgan

64   'not published until 1999': by Princeton University Press

64   'old tea-bags': WC to unknown n.d. (1841–5?) Folder 179,
      box 1, Mortlake Collection, Eberly Family Special
      Collections Library, Pennsylvania State University

65   'their seven-month-old daughter': Margaret Ward, born 1
      December 1845

66   'But, at fifteen': Henrietta Ward, born on 1 June 1832 at
      6 Newman St.

67   'made us all shiver': Ward, *Reminiscences*, p.43

67   'He impressed great caution and secrecy': Ward, *Memories
      of Ninety Years*. Much of the detail comes from this source

69   'Samuel Carter Hall': 1800–89. In his native Ireland this
      great networker had known Daniel Maclise, as well as the
      poet Thomas Moore, whose poem, *Lalla Rookh*, inspired
      one of the epigrams in Wilkie's *Volpurno*

70   'Although favourably reviewed in The Observer':
      31 December 1848

70   'After reading it on a Boxing Day train': *The Diary of Henry
      Crabb Robinson: An Abridgement*, edited by Derek Hudson,
      OUP, 1967

71   'follow my father's profession', WC to Richard Dana Jr.,
      12 January 1849, Princeton

72   'exceedingly good': WC to HC, 2 August 1847, Morgan

73   'The disappointments we have met with': WC to Miss
      Clarkson, [5/12 June] 1849, Morgan

74   'Frith painted a scene directly from *The Good Natur'd
      Man*': WC reminded Ned Ward of this on 1 April 1862
      when he had been writing *No Name*: 'I read "The Good
      Natured Man", and "The Rivals" again – while I was

writing it – and saw you once more in "Croaker" as plainly as I see this paper. I have been engaged in far more elaborate private theatrical work, since that time – but the real enjoyment was at the T. R. Blandford Square.'

75   'Still needing a publisher': see letters to Bentley starting 30 August 1849, Berg, with many others from Bentley Archives, University of Illinois

77   'cursed confused chirping': WC to CW, 19 March 1850, private

78   'Need we remind a painter's son': *Athenaeum*, 16 March 1850

78   'The anonymous reviewer in the Spectator': *Spectator*, 11 March 1850

78   'his future would be devoted to writing books.': Alexander Gray, *Reminiscences of Rambles Around the World*. Unpublished memoir, 1898?, property of Donald Whitton

79   'deep red': WC to HC, 14 August 1850, Morgan

80   'and fifty other succulent dishes': WC to CW, 15 August 1850, private

80   'busily engaged': Ward's comment was quoted in WC to HC, 14 August 1850, Morgan

82   'I think *you* told *me*': CD to Augustus Egg, 8 March 1851, P. v6, p.310

88   'Frank Stone using his position as art correspondent': see http://www.victorianweb.org/art/illustration/fstone/contreras1.html

89   'mean, odious, repulsive, and revolting': 'Old Lamps for New Ones', *Household Words*, 12, 15 June 1850, 12–14

90   'all escaped revolutionists': Hunt, *Pre-Raphaelitism*. WC recreated this environment for Count Fosco in *The Moonstone*

91   'disgrac(ing) their walls': *Times*, 3 May 1851

91   'Mr Collins was the superior in refinement': WC in *Bentley's Miscellany*, XXIX No. 174, June 1851, pp.617–27

92   'A Plea for Sunday Reform': *The Leader*, 27 September 1851

93   'playing his favourite game of leapfrog': R. H. Horne,
      'Mr Nightingale's Diary', *The Gentleman's Magazine*, May
      1871

93   'What a night!', WC To EP, 22 November 1851, Huntington

94   'One of these "Brothers" happens': WC to Richard Bentley,
      28 November 1851, Illinois

94   'forbade from using his 'brains': WC to EP, 22 December
      1851, Huntington

96   'his articles for The Leader': over the months January to
      March 1853, Wilkie wrote six articles for *The Leader*,
      described collectively as 'Magnetic Evenings At Home'.
      After G.H. Lewes wrote a rejoinder, Wilkie penned a
      final piece defending his sympathetic approach to animal
      magnetism

96   'having hired a local upholsterer': WC to EP, 19 February
      1852, Huntington

96   'I am neither a Protestant': WC to EP, 6 February 1852,
      Huntington

97   'The Monktons of Wincot Abbey': first published *Fraser's
      Magazine*, November–December 1855. This was later
      published in book form in *The Queen of Hearts* (1859) as
      'Brother Griffith's Story of Mad Monkton'

98   '(The Traveller's Story of) a Terribly Strange Bed': HW,
      24 April 1852, later gathered in *After Dark*, 1856

98   'helped an unidentified friend': 'The Midnight Mass: An
      Episode in the History of the Reign of the Terror', *Bentley's
      Miscellany*, June 1852, pp.629–38

98   'George Eliot's employer': Eliot was assistant editor of
      John Chapman's *Westminster Review*. Whether or not they
      had an affair is still debated. See Ashton, *142 Strand*

99   'John Millais reported to Mrs Combe': quoted in Ellis,
      Wilkie Collins, le Fanu and Others

99   'I am glad to hear that you could travel': WC to HC,
      7 July 1852, Morgan

100   'French dishes that would make you turn pale': WC to
      HC, 13 February 1852, Pembroke

100   'the cleverest and the most agreeable woman': WC to HC,
      1 September 1852, Morgan

101   'Miss Chambers has sent me a very sharp letter': WC to
      Nina Chambers, 27 March 1852, Princeton

101   'From there she described the Guild's performance': Nina
      Chambers to FL, 28 August 1852, Princeton

101   'The amateurs did not lose for Wilkie Collins': *New York
      Daily Times*, 27 July 1852

102   'You have no idea how good Tenniel, Topham and Collins
      have been': CD to John Forster, 4? September 1852, quoted
      Forster, *Charles Dickens*, P. v6, p.753

102   'hitherto interminable book': WC to EP, 16 September
      1852, Huntington

107   'a tale of criminality, almost revolting': *Athenaeum*,
      4 December 1852

107   'been vehemently objected to as immoral(!)': WC to F.O.
      Ward, 5 March 1853, John Rylands Library, University of
      Manchester

109   'not strong enough yet': WC to EP, 25 June 1853, Huntington

109   'Observe the hour above written': WC to HC, 7 July 1853,
      Morgan

110   'Mr Coleridge, do not cry': quoted Winter, *Old Friends*

111   'her personal memoir': this is in the Harry Ransom Center,
      University of Texas at Austin. The date, 25 April 1853,
      neatly written out in her hand.

113   'the most delightful unselfish kind hearted creature': quoted
      Fagence Cooper, *The Model Wife*

113   'jest with the old lady': John E. Millais to WHH,
      25 October 1852, BL, RP 565

115 'still a virgin at the age of thirty': Marsh, *Rossetti*, p.199

115 'Hunt rented a room in a 'maison de convenance': this
     was Woodbine Villa, 7 Alpha Place, St John's Wood, resi-
     dence of Mrs Ford

116 'I am very sorry indeed to hear so bad': CD to WC, 30
     June 1953, Berg, P. v7, p.108

117 'really, and not conventionally': WC to HC, 1 September
     1853, Morgan

117 'at half the sacred': WC to CAC, 12 August 1853, Morgan

117 'say I wish him long life': ibid.

118 'the only real difficulty': WC to George Bentley, 17 August
     1853, Berg

119 'an accomplished man — but effeminate and mildly selfish':
     Bulwer Lytton to CD, House et al. (ed.s), *Letters of Charles
     Dickens*, P. v2, p.110n

120 'Verdi's last and noisiest production': WC to CW,
     31 October 1853, Morgan

121 'Wilkie, with his inbred': a decade after Wilkie's death, the
     Cornhill Magazine (November 1899) printed the following,
     under the initials W.H.: 'I cannot leave this subject without
     recalling an anecdote Wilkie Collins once told me. At the
     time when the excitement against the Papal aggression was
     at its height, a Catholic friend offered to take him to one
     of Cardinal Wiseman's receptions. Wilkie Collins accepted
     eagerly, and a few days later found himself ascending the
     stairs of the Cardinal's modest house in York Place. He soon
     noticed that the men in front of him, as they arrived near
     their host, bent their knee and kissed his episcopal ring. As
     a good Protestant Wilkie Collins could not do likewise; 'so
     it ended in our shaking hands and having a most pleasant
     talk after the crowd had passed.' It is not known who W.H.
     was. Possibly it was a Shakespearean reference

122 'excruciatingly jealous of': CD to Emile de la Rue, 23

October 1857, Berg, P. v8, p.472, quoted Tomalin, *Charles Dickens*, p.253

122 'because my present course of life': WC to HC, 16 October 1853, Morgan

123 'his habit of whistling opera hits': CD told his wife that Wilkie liked to whistle whole overtures, but never remembered them from start to finish. He had to ask Wilkie to lay off singing the Overture to Rossini's 'William Tell'. See CD to Catherine Dickens, BL, 27 November 1853, P. v7, p.215

123 'Imagine the procession – led by Collins': CD to Catherine Dickens, BL, 27 November 1853, P. v7, p.215

124 'occasionally expands a code of morals': CD to Catherine Dickens, BL, 21 November 1853, P v.7, p.204

125 For background on whiskers in the mid-nineteenth century I am indebted to the article 'From Squalid Impropriety to Manly Respectability: The Revival of Beards, Moustaches and Martial Values in the 1850s in England' by Susan Walton in *Nineteenth Century Contexts*, vol. 30, No 3, September 2008, and to Paul Lewis for drawing it to my attention

126 'Why Shave?': HW, 27 August 1853

126 'My sentiments on the subject': WC to CW, 16 March 1854, Huntington

126 'expressing support for John Bright': WC to George Bentley, 24 January 1855, BL

126 'If this war continues': WC to Richard Bentley, 12 July 1854, Illinois

127 'go to Thebes & Memphis': CAC to WHH, BL, RP 565

127 'not so much because she had been denied': see Fagence Cooper, *The Model Wife*. WC would refer cynically the following year to the French way of describing childbirth

as 'the Sublime Fact of Maternity'(to E.M. Ward, 13/20 March 1855, Texas)

131 'William Rossetti compared it': *Morning Post*, 13 July 1854

131 'far away the cleverest Novel': CD to Georgina Hogarth, 22 July 1854, Princeton, P. v7, p.376

132 'the candidates' book': my thanks to Marcus Risdell, archivist at the Garrick Club, for this information

133. 'Wilkie lent him support': WC to EP, (Tuesday) July 1854, Huntington

134 'the celebrated 1846 champagne': CD to WC, 12 July 1854, Morgan, P v7, p.366

135 'in the English way': WC to CAC, 7 September 1854, Morgan

135 'The Lawyer's Story of a Stolen Letter': published HW, December 1854, p.408 – later *After Dark*

136 'I am as poor as Job just now': WC to EP, 14 March 1855, Huntington

137 'he had felt he would explode': CD to Forster, 29? September 1854, quoted Forster, *Dickens* P. v7, p.428

137 'gorgeously-furnished drawing-room': WC to HC, 14 February 1855, Morgan

138 'strong medicine': CD to Regnier, 14 February 1855, Comedie Francaise, P. v7, p.537

138 'inspect the Hospital': CD to WC, 4 March 1855, Morgan, P v.7, p.554

138 'I am in the Doctor's hands again': WC to E.M Ward, 13/20 March 1855, Texas

138 'an amiably, corroded hermit': CD to WC, 4 April 1855, P v7, p.585, Morgan

139 'three scabrous articles in consecutive weeks': *The Leader* on 12, 19, 26 May 1855

140 'where Egg was now living': The Elms, Campden Hill

from *c.* 1853. This was a charity performance in aid of the Bournemouth Sanitorium for Consumption and Diseases of the Chest on 10 July 1855

140 'a regular old-style Melo Drama'; CD to Curtis Stanfield, v7, pp.624–5. See Bibliography for information on the edition edited by Andrew Gasson and Caroline Radcliffe

140 'Mrs Collins sat next to me': quoted Lehmann, *Ancestors and Friends*

142 'he 'half reside[d]'': Millais to Thomas Combe, 30 January 1855, quoted Millais, *Life and Letters*, p.245

142 'May he consummate successfully!: WC to EP, 3 July 1855, Huntington

143 'I cannot helping touting for matrimony': Millais to WHH from Annat Lodge, Saturday, n.y., BL, RP 565

143 'a new, quieter holiday house': 3 Albion Villas, Folkestone

143 'This place is full': WC to HC, 2 September 1855, Morgan

145 'tempting Providence': WC to EP, 4 September 1855, Huntington

147 'old complaint': CD to WC, 12 February 1856, Morgan, P. v8, p.53

148 'rheumatic pains': WC to HC, 11 March 1856, Morgan

148 'I like the situation of the house': WC to HC, 5 April 1856, Morgan

148 'rather proud': WC to HC, 19 March 1856, Morgan

149 'five consecutive editions': HW, 1–29 March 1856

150 'who has a good eye for pictures': CD to John Forster, 2? March 1856, extracts in Forster, *Dickens* P. v8, p.66

150 'the corrupt Institution to which you belong': WC to E.M. Ward, 18 March 1856, Texas

150 'old days': CD to Forster, 13 April 1856, extracts in Forster, *Dickens* P. v8, p.89

151 'our own National Argyll Rooms': CD to WC, 22 April 1856, Morgan, P. v8, p.96

151 'a distressingly pained account': see Charles A. Collins, 'Apology for his Art under a deep sense of high minded responsibility' (essay about the Electric Telegraph), dated 22 April 1856, 2 Percy St, Huntington

152 'Howland Street': Wilkie's arrival in Howland Street can be dated from a letter from CAC to WHH, dated 23 April 1856, which refers to him there. BL, RP 565

156 Caroline's birth: see register of births for Toddington Parish Church at Gloucestershire Archives, P335/IN1/4

158 'Caroline gave birth': Elizabeth Harriet Graves, b. 3 February 1851, GRO birth certificate

158 'Cumming Street': number 11 Cumming Street

158 'seedier Charlton Street': number 5 Charlton Street

159 'by John Guille Millais': *The Life and Letters of Sir John Everett Millais*, published in 1899

160 'The observation from Katey': see Storey, *Dickens and Daughter*, p.213

161 'very *decolleté* white silk gown': FL to NL, quoted Lehmann, *Ancestors and Friends*

161 'Ancient Mariner': CD to WC, 26 October 1856, Morgan, P. v8, p.214

162 'In his piece for *Household Words*': 'My London Lodgings', HW, 14 June 1856

162 'The Diary of Anne Rodway': HW, 19–26 July 1856

164 'personal pride and pleasure', CD to WC, 13 July 1856, Morgan, P. v8, p.162

164 'great merit, and real pathos': CD to Macready, 8 July 1856, Morgan, P. v8, p.157

164 'a £20 bonus': CD to Wills, 10 July 1856, Rosenbach, P. v8, p.159

166 'exceedingly quick to take my notions': CD to W.H.

Wills, 16 September 1856, Huntington, P. v8, p.188

167 'I am the Captain': CD to Burdett Coutts, 4 December 1856, Morgan, P. v8, p.231

167 'My Black Mirror': HW, 6 September 1856

167 'To Think, or Be Thought For': HW, 13 September 1856

168 'A Petition to the Novel-Writers': HW, 6 December 1856

168 'Bold Words by a Bachelor': HW, 13 December 1856

174 'exclusive exhibition of Pre-Raphaelite art': this was dominated by Rossetti – with Lizzie Siddall – cocking a snook at the Royal Academy

176 'a perfect hurricane': WC to HC, 10 August 1857, Pembroke

177 'Mrs Badgery': HW, 26 September 1857

178 'The Lazy Tour of Two Idle Apprentices': published in HW, starting 3 October 1857, and in the following four numbers

179 'A Sermon for Sepoys': HW, 27 February 1858

179 'Dr Livingstone in Africa': HW, 23 January 1858

179 'a moment's peace or content': CD to WC, 21 March 1858, Morgan, P v8, p.536

182 'Who is the Thief': *Atlantic Monthly*, April 1858

183 'recent trial of Madeline Smith': March 1857

183 'A Paradoxical Experience': HW, 13 November 1858

183 'proliferation of crinolines': HW, 13 February 1858

183 'to protest against poor service on trains and buses': HW, 6 February 1858

183 'the problem of female bores': 'A Shockingly Rude Article', HW, 28 August 1858

184 'in one piece': 'Dr Dulcamara MP', HW, 18 December 1858

185 'The Unknown Public': HW, 21 August 1858

186 'extreme suffering and anxiety': CAC to WHH, in 1855, Hunt Mss, Huntingdon Library, quoted ODNB

186 'caution Willie against committing himself': CAC to HC,
     19 November 1858, Morgan, MA 3153

186 'My term, at my own house': WC to Jane Ward, 1
     December 1858, Private

187 'Only eighteen months earlier': *Reynolds's Newspaper*, 7 June
     1857

188 'keeps you company and makes you your grog': WC to
     CW, 4 May 1859

189 'a small malady': CD to F C Beard, 25 June 1859, Dickens
     Museum, P v9, p.84

189 'no silver nitrate': CD to WC, 16 August 1859, Dartmouth
     College, P v9, p.106

190 'I have nothing particular to record': WC to CW, 19 July
     1859, Morgan

190 'Etude sur le roman anglais': Revue des Deux Mondes,
     1 November 1855

190 'a gentleman, an admirable English scholar': WC to Reade,
     31 March 1863, Morgan

191 'all drawn out': WC to James Lowe, 13 April 1858, Texas

191 'an *entirely new form of narrative*': WC to F.H. Underwood,
     12 August 1858, Houghton

191 'According to a note': see *The Woman in White: A chrono-
     logical study* by Andrew Gasson, Wilkie Collins Society, 2010

191 'I must stagger the public into attention': WC to Wills,
     15 August 1859, quoted Lehmann, *Memories of Half a
     Century*

191 'Edmund Yates later expanded on this': Yates, 'Celebrities
     at Home'. It is not entirely clear that Yates wrote this
     piece, which appeared in his magazine *Temple Bar* on
     28 December 1877, but it seems likely. It was later reprinted
     in his book *Celebrities at Home*, published in 1879

192 'name of names': CD to WC, 16 August 1859, Dartmouth
     College, P. v9, p.106

194 for more on Dr John Conolly and the 'lunacy panic' see http://www.erudit.org/revue/ravon/2008/v/n49/017855ar.html and Wise, *Inconvenient People*.

Barlow, *The Abode of Love* is illuminating on the Nottidge case and Agapemone

195 'he devised a form': *Medical Digest*, vol 1, 1865. See also letter from Dr Richard Neale, BMJ, 10 January 1885

195 'Pigott's brother in law': Edwin Fydell Fox, 1814–91

195 'inveighed against the abuses': see John Perceval, *A narrative of the treatment experienced by a gentleman, during a state of mental derangement*, London Effingham Wilson, 1840. See also Andrew Roberts's magnificent online work on the Lunacy Commission: http://studymore.org.uk/01.htm

197 'What Shall We Do With Our Old Maids?': *Fraser's Magazine*, November 1862

197 'Celibacy vs. Marriage': *Fraser's Magazine*, also 1862

197 'revealed secrets which must tend to modify immensely': quoted in Griffin, *The Politics of Genders in Victorian Britain*

197 'an evident understanding': see Mitchell, *Frances Power Cobbe*

200 'In civil life, I am neither daughter': see Sarah Wise, 'A Novel for Hysterical Times', *History Today*, August 2012. I am grateful to her for the insights both in this article and her book, *Inconvenient People*

200 'The two of them met': see 'Walter's Walk' by Paul Lewis, Wilkie Collins Society, 2010

200 'one of the two 'most dramatic' scenes in literature': quoted Sir Henry Dickens, *The Recollections of Sir Henry Dickens*, Heinemann, 1934

202 'all but insuperable... difficulties': WC to CW, 18 August 1859, Morgan

202 'two 'disagreeable' evangelical girls': CD to Mary and Kate Dickens, 2 September 1859, P. v9, p.115, quoted Georgina Hogarth and Mamie Dickens, *The Letters of Charles Dickens*

203   'charmed with the Butler': CD to WC, 16 September 1859, Morgan, P. v9, p.123

203   'commending Pigott's 'delicious tenor voice': George Eliot to Charles Lee Lewes, 7 October 1859, copy courtesy Jonathan Ouvry

203   'a sturdy uprightness about him': George Eliot, *Journals*, 10 November 1858

205   (she) must have seen My Person!': WC to CW, 14 August 1860, Pembroke

205   'continues to spin madly': WC to CW, 19 July 1859, Morgan

205   'a pattern wedding': WC to Mrs Procter, 23 July 1860, Princeton

206   'Lehmann, saw it differently': Frederick Lehmann's account of the wedding between Charley Collins and Katey Dickens appears in his son Rudolph Lehmann's *Memories of Half a Century*, pp.92–5

206   'departed for a honeymoon in France': CAC/KC to HC from Calais, 29 July [1860], Morgan

207   "Hooray!!!!! I have this instant written': WC to HC, 26 July 1860, Morgan

207   'Dickens's congratulations': CD to WC, 29 July 1860, Morgan, P. v9, p.276

208   'impression of Alice's brother Leslie': Ward, *Forty Years of Spy*

209   'Frederick Lehmann's son Rudolph': Lehmann, *Memories of Half a Century*

209   'Wilkie has finished his White Woman': CD to Frances Dickinson, 19 August 1860, Brotherton Library, Leeds, P. v9, p.287

209   'Wilkie had a bank account': His first deposit was a sum of £300 on 23 August 1860

209   'agreed a new two year contract': see WC to CD, 7 August 1860, Johns Hopkins

210 'keen to lay in some Chateau Lafite': WC to CW, 11 July 1860, Morgan

210 'The Genoese cook really did wonders': WC to CW, 14 August 1860, Pembroke

210 'pay his respects to the Procters': this was on 30 July 1860

210 'Among the several other guests was Ricciotti Garibaldi': at the time, Ricciotti's father, Giuseppe Garibaldi, was much feted in Britain. He had recently moved decisively towards the unification of Italy, following the defeat of the Neapolitan army at the battle of Volturno

213 'he would sit down': Beard, 'Some Recollections'

213 'There would be seven in all': Andrew Gasson in 'The Woman in White: A Chronological Study', London, Wilkie Collins Society, 2010

214 'death of his brother Alfred': 27 July 1860

214 'set fire to them all': this mirrored the fire in *The Woman in White* in which Sir Percival Glyde sought to destroy the evidence of his illegitimacy; CD thus did away with any evidence about his relationship with, say, Nelly Ternan, which might compromise him. He did not realise that in the process he also laid himself open to all sorts of speculation. For an overview of Dickens's burning of his letters, see Paul Lewis's website: http://www.web40571. clarahost.co.uk/wilkie/Burning/burn.htm

214 'another block-buster': see Slater, *Charles Dickens*, p.486 ff

215 'soothing the dying moments': WC to HC, 12–15 September 1860, Morgan

215 'asked Charles Ward to intercede': WC to CW, 14 August 1860, Pembroke

216 'the latest, and by many degrees': Spectator, 33, 8 September 1860, p.864

216 'I see no reviews': WC to HC, 12–15 September, 1860
     Morgan

216 An interesting personal reaction to *The Woman in White*
     came from the sociologist Harriet Martineau in a letter
     to her friend, Samuel Lucas, the editor of the *Morning
     Star* who strongly supported the anti-slavery cause in the
     United States. She had read the book out of a sense of
     duty and 'found it simply a bore – at least till the latter
     part where the question of evidence constitutes the
     interest. There is to me no charm of character whatever
     (unless in Mrs Mitchelson the housekeeper), no moral
     interest, and the horrors are done by a mere chafing of
     the reader's memory and imagination. I can't conceive
     how it can be so popular. I don't believe I know anything
     about fiction writing.' 18 October 1862, Berg

217 'he regularly paid Harriet's school fees by cheque': Paul Lewis
     has calculated that he paid almost £100 before she left this
     school. See his 'Educating Elizabeth Harriet Graves': http://
     www.web40571.clarahost.co.uk/wilkie/Educating_EHG.pdf
     Also published as a supplement to the newsletter of the
     Wilkie Collins Society, 2010

218 'I am going abroad next week (probably)': WC to HC,
     3 October 1860, Pembroke

219 A Cruise Upon Wheels: *The Chronicle of Some Autumn
     Wanderings among the Deserted Post-roads of France.*
     Routledge, 1862

219 'disfigure Wilkie's cap in that way": CAC and KC to HC,
     3 December 1860, Morgan

219 'Young Leslie Ward': see Ward, *Forty Years of Spy*

220 'offering a feeble excuse': WC to Charles Mudie,
     18 December 1860, Illinois

220 'Written by the respected critic E.S. Dallas': *The Times*,
     30 October 1860

221 'a journal of misfortunes': WC to EP, 31 January 1853, Huntington

221 'He has died at Melbourne': WC to HC, 12–15 September 1860, Morgan

221 'A Message from the Sea': by CD, WC et al. Christmas Number, *All the Year Round*, 13 December 1860

222 'as he had already written to Wilkie': CD to WC, 24 October 1860, Morgan, P v9, pp.329–31

222 'I am in earnest when I tell you': KC to HC from Paris, 20 December 1860, Morgan

222 'Charley took up the matter of the move': CAC to HC from Brussels, 30 December 1860, Morgan

223 'Dickens wrote to *The Times*': *The Times*, 8 January 1861

223 'We never speak of the (female) skeleton': CD to Esther Nash, 5 March 1861, Princeton, P. v9, p.388

224 'building up the scaffolding of a new book': WC to HC, 24 May 1861, Morgan. This was a phrase he repeated WC to CR, 4 June 1861

225 'a pasted-in photograph': photograph by Cundall, Downes & Co, 168 New Bond St

225 'if I live & keep my brains': WC to HC, 31 July 1861, Morgan.

225 'On 31 October 1860 he had written to Thackeray': George Smith to Thackeray, Alpin (ed.), *Correspondence Thackeray family*, vol. 1, B173

226 'old enemy whose name is Liver': WC to EM Ward, 27 June 1861, Texas

226 'he and Caroline went to Whitby': see letter to George Gregson, 7 August 1861. They arrived at the Royal Hotel on 6 August 1861

228 'with strong interest and great admiration': CD to WC, 24 January 1862, Morgan, P. v10, p.20

229 'the slashing battle (still undecided)': WC to F.C. Beard, 30 June 1862, Princeton

229 'participated with Dickens's friend Dr John Elliotson': see *Standard*, 2 May 1854

230 'some wonderful Turkish baths': WC to HC, 12 December 1861, Morgan

230 'Is there any hope': WC to F.C. Beard, 10 October 1862, Princeton

230 'If you should want help': CD to WC, 14 October 1862, Morgan, P. v10, p.142

231 'You will be almost as glad as I am': WC to F.C. Beard, 24 December 1862, Princeton

232 'We are threatened with a new variety of the sensation novel': review of *The Castleford Case* by Frances Browne, *Spectator*, 28 December 1861

234 'His effects are produced': Margaret Oliphant, 'Sensation Novels', *Blackwood's Magazine*, 91, May 1862, pp.564–84

235 'a very fleshly and unlovely record of femininity': Margaret Oliphant, 'Novels', *Blackwood's Magazine* 102, September 1867, p.259, quoted Gilbert, *A Companion to Sensation Fiction*

235 'Henry Chorley, took this approach': quoted Gilbert, *Companion to Sensation Fiction*

235 'I always say that I owe Lady Audley's Secret': 'Miss Braddon at Home', *London Society*, January 1888

236 'a simple poultice of cabbage leaves': WC to HC, 16 January 1863, Morgan

237 'up all last night with the "palpitations"': WC to F. C Beard, 5 February 1863, Princeton

237 'still too weak to leave her bed': WC to CW, 15 January 1863, Morgan

238 'Henry Chorley set the tone': *Athenaeum*, 3 January 1863

238 'Alexander Smith': *North British Review*, February 1863

238 'Margaret Oliphant provided the textbook version': *Blackwood's Magazine*, August 1863

239 'Ladies who take in boarders': WC to HC, 21 April 1863, Morgan

239 'Dr Caplin's Electro-Chemical Bath': the bath had been developed by Jean Francois Isidore Caplin, a medical entrepreneur who over the years had developed a variety of ingenious patent cures, including an improved corset and a gymnastic apparatus designed to cure curvature of the spine. Lately he had concentrated on his electrical baths, leaving the corset business to his Canadian-born wife, Roxey Ann, who also ran an 'anatomical museum' for ladies only, though medical gentleman were able to visit on Friday afternoons if they showed their cards

240 'hateful railway travelling': WC to HC, 19 March 1863, Morgan

240 'required to drink a glass': WC to CAC, 22 April 1863, Morgan

241 'the off-putting sulphurous smell of Aachen': WC to HC, 21 May and 2 June 1863, Morgan

241 'every third shop': WC to CW, 29 August 1863, Morgan

242 'The two Carolines suffered sea-martyrdom': WC to CW, 4 November 1863, Morgan. To confuse matters, Harriet/Carrie was often known as Lizzie in the family circle

243 'gray hairs springing fast': WC to HC, 8 January 1864, Morgan

244 'at the request of Charles Fechter': CD was continuing to look after his son-in-law. CAC wrote a further story – 'Mrs Lirriper's Legacy' – for the 1864 Christmas annual. WC did 'No Thoroughfare' for the Christmas 1867 number

244 'Charley kept his brother informed': see CAC to WC, 17 February 1864, Berg

245 'there is one price for the Pope's gold': WC to CW, 14 January 1864, Morgan

245   'he told her not to worry': WC to HC, 8 January 1864, Morgan

245   'How like cats women are!': WC to CW, 14 January 1864, Morgan

247   'he had completed three parts': WC to HC, 19 and 26 July 1864, Morgan

250   'difficulties in reconciling necessary chemical facts': WC to HC, March 26 1866, Morgan

251   'keep all this a profound Secret': WC to EP, 24 September 1864, Huntington

251   'exciting (him)self with "Society"': WC to HC, 18 December 1864, Pembroke

252   'nothing but pianos': WC to HC, 26 July 1864, Morgan

252   'in the right direction': CAC to HC, 29 January 1865, Morgan

252   'my book is as entirely off my mind': WC to HC, 27 February 1865, Morgan

252   'over head and ears': WC to HC, 8 March 1865, Pembroke

253   'election to the Club's general committee': he was elected to the General Committee at the Annual General Meeting on 27 April 1863. He was originally elected to the Club on 3 June 1854

253   'I leave the little puddle': WC to George Russell, 6 June 1864, noted at Woolley and Wallis auctioneer Salisbury, Wiltshire

253   'informed another correspondent': WC to John Edmund Reade, 11 June 1865

254   'Charley enjoyed working in Dickens's new Swiss chalet': CAC to HC, 3 June 1865, Morgan

254   'Katey was the only member': Tomalin, *Charles Dickens*, p.332

254   'I want the sea badly' WC to HC, 1 July 1865, Morgan

255   'C. & the child have come back': WC to CW, 17 August 1865, Harrowby

255 'I roam the empty streets': WC to HC, 17 August 1865, Pembroke

256 'a fortifying compound of drugs': WC to HC, 6 February 1866, Pembroke

256 'I am half sorry too to have parted': WC to HC, 22 April 1866, Pembroke

260 'only to let Mrs Graves know it': WC to Charles Reade, 12 October 1866, Private. This letter was published in December 2011 by the Wilkie Collins Society in the seventh Addenda and Corrigenda to the *Collected Letters*

260 'Martha Rudd': born 10 January 1845

262 'as droll as ever': HC to WHH, 24 July, n.y. (1866), Princeton

262 'In the wake of Wilkie's death': New York World, 29 September 1889

263 'not until 20 April 1868': this first payment of £4.17s was made on 20 April 1868. The 1871 census shows Martha Dawson at 33 Bolsover St, with her daughter Marian, RG 10 154

263 'a lively pretty little creature, piquante & clever': Hudson (ed.), *Munby*

266 'the latest offering': Taylor's 'Our American Cousin' was playing when Lincoln was assassinated in 1865

266 'Dickens's old friend, Francois Regnier': adopting the style of Carlyle, CD referred to Regnier in a letter of 13 March 1867 as 'a deft and shifty little man, brisk and sudden, of a most ingenious carpentering facility, and not without constructive qualities of a higher than the Beaver sort'

267 'A woman has got in the way': WC to NL from Milan, 26 October 1866, Princeton

267 'in the language of cats': WC to NL, 9 December 1866, Lewis

268 'counselled Nina to wrap up well': WC to NL, 26 October
      1866, Princeton

268 'Royal commands will not make a successful piece': *Daily
      News*, 29 October 1866

269 'Is my tail put down?': WC to NL, 9 December 1866,
      Lewis

269 "lively' two volume novel': WC to HC, 6 Jan 1867,
      Pembroke

270 'I have got my name and my brains': ibid.

270 'Successful play-writing': WC to HC, 26 February 1867,
      Morgan

270 'breakfasted on 'eggs and black butter": WC to HC,
      26 February 1867, Morgan

271 'a very curious story': CD to Wills, 30 June 1867,
      Huntington, P. vii, p.385

272 '90 Gloucester Place': now renumbered 65

273 'The Female Detective by Andrew Forrester': Andrew
      Forrester was a pseudonym for J.R. Ware, who had written
      on the Road murder in 1862. See J.R. Ware, 'The Road
      Murder. Analysis of This Persistent Mystery, 1862. Now
      Re-Printed, with Farther [sic] Remarks, by J.R. Ware',
      London, W. Oliver, 1865

274 'James Fitzjames Stephen argued': 'Detectives in Fiction
      and Real Life', *Saturday Review* 17, 1864, pp.712–13

275 'Wilkie's friend G.H. Lewes now argued, 'When a man
      avers that he has 'seen a ghost", quoted Smajic,
      Ghost-seers

275 'As John Stuart Mill': *A System of Logic*, 1843

275 'With inference begins error.': G.H. Lewes, *Problems of Life
      and Mind*, first series 1875, quoted Smajic, *Ghost-seers*

281 'Had written to Lady Constance': WC to Miss Lennox,
      15 September 1866, Lewis

282 'Before long a Scottish terrier called Tommy': Tommy

featured in the short story 'My Lady's Money' in 1878. See letter to A. P. Watt, 7 September 1885, Pembroke, on his anguish at Tommy's death

282 'large and rather dingy': Caine, *My Story*, 1908. Keen still to furnish his house, he acquired a portrait of his grandmother from 'Coosey' – his cousin, Margaret Ward, who was Charles Ward's daughter. She was happy to give it to him, but he insisted on buying her a new silk dress in recompense. See WC to HC, 11 October 1867, Morgan

284 'she was 'sinking'': WC to WHH, 18 January 1868, Huntington

284 'I am (luckily) obliged to work': WC to WHH, 28 January 1868, Huntington

286 'William Tinsley, the publisher, recorded': William Tinsley, *Random Recollections of an Old Publisher*, London, 1900, vol. I, pp.114–17

286 'lukewarm reviews of *The Moonstone*': Geraldine Jewsbury in the *Athenaeum*, 25 July 1868, and unsigned in the *Spectator*, 25 July 1868

287 'seemed on the point of death': CD to J.T. Fields, 7 July 1868, Huntington, P. v12, pp.148–150

288 'kindest remembrances': WC to Joseph Stringfield, 16 August 1866, Princeton

288 'asked Benham for advice': WC to Ebenezer Benham, 2 June 1868, Mitchell

288 'Kennet Paper Making Company': see *London Gazette*, 7 August 1868

289 'wearisome beyond endurance': CD to W.H. Wills, 26 July 1868, Huntington, P. v12, p.159

289 'It is a part of the bump': CD to Wills, 17 July 1868, Huntington, P. v12, p.153. CD mentioned his son's bankruptcy to Mr and Mrs J T Fields on 30 October 1868. He

also said, 'Wilkie always has the gout – and is always chronically injured by the public.'

292   'trail round four chemists': see Lehmann, *An Artist's Reminiscences*

293   'Let me communicate another point of interest': CD to W.H. Wills, 25 October 1868, Huntington, P. VI2, p.210

293   'Wilkie's affairs defy all prediction': CD to Georgina Hogarth, 29 October 1868, Dickens Museum, P. VI2, p.211

294   'Wilkie had a mistress Caroline': Mrs Storey's diary records of meeting with Kate Perugini née Dickens, 27 May 1928, Charles Dickens Museum

296   'spend time at Woodlands in Muswell Hill': Wilkie was often there at the same time as the critic Henry Chorley, who seemed to have difficulty remembering where he was, and would give orders to the Lehmanns' man-servant, Martin, as if he was his own. Once, when going to bed, he asked Martin to make sure that Wilkie had the wine he desired. Another time, when Fred Lehmann was absent, he became perturbed when Wilkie lit a cigar. He told Wilkie that he really could not allow smoking in the living room, which caused Wilkie to respond angrily that this was Fred's house, not Chorley's; he had always been allowed to smoke when Fred was at home, and 'he should certainly smoke now he was away.' Princeton Lehmann Family papers, box 123

296   'She has done all sorts of dreadful things': WC to NL, 4 January 1869, Princeton

296   'Herr Schumann's music, Madame Schumann's playing': WC to Elizabeth Benzon, 26 February 1869, Private

296   'My doctor is trying to break me of the habit': ibid.

297   'All art constantly aspires': Walter Pater, *Studies in the History of the Renaissance*, 1873

298   'too similar to Dion Boucicault's The Octoroon': *Daily News*, 30 March 1869

299 Wilkie had given him a cheque for £100': 3 March 1869

299 'Thank you, from the bottom of my heart': WC to FL, 24 April 1869, Princeton

299 'I am not the charming person': WC to Belinfante Brothers, 10 November 1869, Unknown

300 'a new will': George Redford acted as witness, and Henry Bullar as executor. Although Wilkie no longer had much direct contact with the art world, he was still enough in touch with his roots to contribute £15 2s (over £1,000 in 2012 terms) to the Slade Fund which had been set up to supplement the substantial legacy given by the recently deceased solicitor Felix Slade to finance three art lectureships at Oxford, Cambridge and University College, London, where the Slade School of Art would be operational by 1871

304 'a crusading journalist (and prominent freemason)': Wilkie was not a mason – though Pigott, Frith and Yates were

304 'I suspended an immortal work of fiction': WC to FL, 25 October 1869, Princeton

305 'Readers who object to expletives': WC to Cassell, Petter and Galpin, 25 September 1869, Texas

306 'Dickens's last laboured effort': marginalia in a copy of Forster's *Life of Dickens*. See Collins, *Dickens: Interviews and Recollections*

306 'fourteen people had attended the funeral': see Slater, *The Great Charles Dickens Scandal*, p.108

307 'stands in some need': WC to Georgina Hogarth, 20 July 1870, Charles Dickens Museum

307 'as in the *Saturday Review*': 9 July 1870

307 'Mrs Oliphant in *Blackwood's Magazine*': November 1870

308 'he regarded this approach as offensive': WC to Augustin Daly, 4 March 1871, Houghton

308 'never hitherto paid sixpence': WC to Hunter Rose, 12 August 1871, Texas

308 'heartily on the German side': WC to Emil Lehmann, 7 August 1870, Princeton

309 'one civilising influence': ibid.

310 The 1871 census for Marylebone Cavendish Square, district 9, p.40, shows that twenty-seven-year-old Alice Rudd was the cook in the household of John H. Davis, physician, at 24 Harley Street

311 'As he complained to Harper and Brothers': WC to Harper Brothers, 13 January 1872, Maine

313 Birth of Harriet Dawson, 14 May 1871

314 'he consulted his new solicitor Tindell': WC to William Tindell, 16 April 1871, Mitchell

314 'how 'drunk' he was with 'this fine air'': WC to William Tindell, 15 August 1871, Mitchell

314 'his medical regime had been extended': see WC to F.C. Beard, 9 September 1871, Princeton

314 'a new stock of Moselle': WC to Reade, 20 October 1871, Private

316 'enlisted his friend W.H. Hooper': see *Life and Letters of Frederick Walker ARA* by John George Marks, London, Macmillian, 1891. Walker wrote to Hooper on 6 September 1871, Wilkie's letter was written around the 11th September

316 'My story is not addressed': WC to Arthur Locker, Unknown, September–November 1871

317 'pressed by so many proposals': WC to Cassell, Petter, & Galpin, 30 October 1871, Texas

317 'took up an offer from George Bentley': Richard Bentley, born in 1794, died in 1871. George Bentley (1828–95) had a son, also called Richard (1854–1936), who joined the firm.

317 'Whatever may be said against the vanity of existence': *Nation*, 7 March 1872

317 'Sunday reading': *Athenaeum*, 17 February 1872

318 'a puritanical reaction was setting in': see *The Fallen Angel: Chastity, Class and Women's Reading 1835–1880* by Sally Mitchell, Bowling Green Press, 1981

318 'going away soon to get a little rest': WC to John Hollingshead, 27 January 1872, Huntington

318 'positively resolved not to saddle': WC to C.S. Carter, 27 February 1872, Private

321 'short, moderately thick-set': Reeve, *From Life*

324 'the same sweet fellow as ever': WC to FL, 15 August 1872, Susan Hanes

325 'The principle [*sic*] female character': ibid.

326 'a flat denial of the right of property': WC to Hunter Rose, 13 July 1872, Princeton

326 'his elder daughter Marian broke her leg': see WC to William Tindell, 18 June 1872, Mitchell

327 'horrible sore on his leg': WC to FL, 15 August 1872, Private

327 'something which feels like liquid velvet': ibid.

327 'I am comfortably established': WC to Tindell, 27 September 1872, Mitchell

328 'with great effect and nervous force': Bancroft, *Recollections*, p.167

329 'the services of my friends were not required': WC to Wybert Reeve, 23 February 1873

329 'Two of Britain's most illustrious surgeons': *Birmingham Daily Post*, 12 April 1873

329 'life's idle business has ended for me': WC to WHH, 11 May 1873, Huntington

330 'Nothing would incude me to modify the title': WC to George Bentley, 18 March 1873, Berg

331 'that fanatical old fool Mudie': WC to George Bentley, 20 May 1873, Berg

331 'one of the most signal triumphs': *Sunday Times*, 25 May 1873

331 'the Speculator' WC to William F Tindell, 21 July 1873, Mitchell

332 'His turn was not a great success': *Pall Mall Gazette*, 30 June 1873

332 'I have heard he is to read': Georgina Hogarth to Annie Fields, 30 August 1873, Huntington

332 'The least I can do': WC to Squire Bancroft, 17 July 1873

333 'his last payment of £25': this was on 20 January 1873 – see Wilkie Collins's bank account at Coutts

333 'They spent £100': see Clarke, *Secret Life*

333 'He asked Tindell to advise': WC to William Tindell, 18 July 1873, Mitchell

334 'only the prospect of composing a new Christmas story': with the help of input in the United States, this turned out to be 'The Dead Alive' or 'John Jago's Ghost'

336 'You will find friends here wherever you go': WC in 'Wilkie Collins's Recollections of Charles Fechter', contributed to K. Field, *Charles Albert Fechter*

336 'He never sent me sixpence.': WC, 'Considerations on the Copyright Question', *International Review*, New York, June 1880

336 'not quite what is suggested by his portraits': *Boston Commonwealth*, 1 November 1873

336 'a stylish suit': quoted Reeve Recollections of Wilkie Collins. Another version of this story has it that his clothes were gnawed by rats on board the *Algeria*. He had a cheap new suit rustled up in New York and was later complimented for being well-dressed. See Walford, *Memories of Victorian London*

336 'his second night in New York': 27 September 1873

338 'Collins enjoyed his dinner': journal of John Bigelow, quoted Hanes, *Wilkie Collins's American Tour*, 1873–4

338 'his creepy 1855 story The Ostler': originally in Holly Tree Inn, Christmas Number of HW, 1855

338 'no actor': *Troy Daily Press*, 9 October 1873

338 'unquestionably a failure': *Syracuse Daily Courier*, 13 October 1873

339 'nervous prostration and a severe cold': letter sent by Charles Brelsford to newpapers, quoted Hanes, *Wilkie Collins's American Tour*, pp.34–5

339 'greatly preferred Baltimore': WC to Jane Bigelow, 2 January 1882, NYPL

340 'opened a recruiting office for prostitutes': *New York Daily Graphic*, 11 November 1873

341 'Some of the audience went to sleep': *New York Herald*, 11 November 1873

341 'getting on famously': WC to Frank Archer, 6 January 1874, Private

342 'going "out West"': WC to FL, 2 January 1874, Princeton

343 'landscapes 'as flat, as monotonous"': from 'John Jago's Ghost'

343 'I feel the "sleeping car"': WC to Sebastian Schlesinger, 17 January 1874, Houghton

343 'after two days and a night's.': *Men and Women – A Weekly Biographical and Social Journal*, vol.III No.36., Saturday 5 February, 1887, pp.281–2

344 'N.B. You remember our name': WC to William Tindell, 27 January 1874, Mitchell

344 'Don't tell anybody': WC to Jane Bigelow, 17 January 1874, NYPL

344 'the cream of New England's intelligentsia': this dinner took place on 16 February 1874

345 'a religious community at Wallingford in Connecticut': this trip was arranged by Boston publisher William F. Gill

345 'Mr Collins thought our system of communism': quoted Hanes, *Wilkie Collins's American Tour*, p.87

346 'A kinder, warmer-hearted set of people': Walford, *Memories of Victorian London*

347 'Wilkie had earned £2,500': Hanes, *Wilkie Collins's American Tour*, p.91. He packaged a selection of his readings from America in *The Frozen Deep, and Other Stories*, Richard Bentley, 1874. The English version was dedicated to Wendell Holmes

347 'My native climate has already': WC to Isabelle Frith, 2 April 1874, NAL

351 'a thirty page booklet': this is available in the National Archives

351 'written another story, A Fatal Fortune': Sarah Wise in *Inconvenient People*, p.200, says 'A Fatal Fortune' is based on the true case of a mis-certified, eccentric very rich young man, Old Etonian Oxford graduate, James Tovey-Tennent, who wished to marry against his family's wishes See also *The Times*, 27 April 8 and 9 May 1867

352 'a huge explosion on a barge': also badly affected was Hepworth Dixon's house in 6 St James's Terrace

352 'a Christmas Box': WC to William Tindell, 29 December 1874, Mitchell

352 'there is really no news here': WC to Jane Bigelow, 31 December 1874, NYPL

354 'My own impression': WC to George Smith, 23 October 1871, Berg

355 'He seems to have a good chance': WC to Sebastian Schlesinger, 30 December 1876, Houghton

356 'to allow Wilkie to vent his spleen': *The World*, 20 April 1875

356 'Anything less literary': *Observer*, 28 March 1875

356 'If a man has the misfortune': *Pall Mall Gazette*, 4 June 1875

356 'For literary ingenuity': quoted John Coleman, *Charles Reade As I Knew Him*, London, Treherne & Company, 1903

356 'Reade's mistress Mrs Seymour': when Mrs Seymour died in September 1879, Wilkie showed his unusual admiration for her in a letter to Reade in which he stated how much he 'appreciated her fine qualities as an artist,' and he 'sincerely admired and prized her bright true and generous nature as a woman.' WC to Charles Reade, 29 September 1879, Private

356 'For literary ingenuity': quoted Coleman, *Charles Reade*

357 'the idlest man living': WC to George Bentley, 27 March 1875, Berg

357 'wandering about the Eastern coast': WC to George Bentley, 12 September 1875, Berg

358 'got an idea of another new story': ibid.

359 'There was leavening too': in the book, Swedenborg was the mentor of Mary's mother. The 1875/76 annual report of the Swedenborg Society noted that *The Two Destinies* 'evidently show(ed) that the doctrine of Swedenborg . . . is finding its way into popular literature, however imperfectly'

360 'work, walk, visit': WC to FL, 26 April 1876, Princeton

360 'wandering about the south coast': WC to Frank Archer, 26 July 1876, Private

361 'an amazingly silly book': *Saturday Review*, 20 January 1877

361 'I am indeed sorry': WC to Henry P Bartley, 17 October 1876, Princeton

363 'a little rest and change': WC to Augustin Daly, 22 September 1877, Houghton

363 'a trip to Venice': this was the high spot of the journey, where he was bowled over by the 'feast of magnificent colour' in the galleries. WC to WHH, 24 July 1886. Wilkie and Caroline's progress can be charted by the cheques he cashed with various correspondent banks and agencies en route, including £100 with S & A Blumenthal in Venice

on 23 November, £50 with P Perrero in Genoa on 6 December, £100 with Nigra Freres in Turin on 7 December. See WC's bank accounts, Coutts

363 'her former mother in law': Mary Ann Graves died on 8 May 1877

364 'a Christmas profile of Wilkie': *The World*, 26 December 1877

364 'put forward various alternatives': WC to Augustin Daly, 25 September 1877, Houghton

364 'the greatness of Napoleon': WC's admiration for Napoleon had caused him to compare Count Fosco to the French Emperor. 'He is a most remarkable likeness, on a large scale, of the great Napoleon. His features have Napoleon's magnificent regularity—his expression recalls the grandly calm, immovable power of the Great Soldier's face.' (*The Woman in White*)

365 'all sorts of impediments': WC to NL, 28 December 1877, Princeton

365 'I am (say) half alive': WC to James Payn, 13 February 1878, Texas

365 'he gave Harriet a wedding gift of £50': see WC's bank accounts, Coutts

365 'a couple of fibs': Henry was born on 9 December 1854, Harriet on 3 February 1851

366 'an extravagant wedding dinner': my thanks to Jeanette Iredale for a copy of the menu

367 'an incorrigible heretic': WC to William Winter, 5 August 1878. Winter was a friend of Augustin Daly, who came to London in a short-lived attempt to revive his theatrical career. Wilkie helped out with local contacts such as Trollope. He also gave him the manuscript of *Iolani*, his first as yet unpublished novel. This was the version which was later sold at auction in New York and which did not

appear in book form until 1999. Daly soon returned to New York where he regained his position as the city's leading theatre manager

367 'never sufficiently-to be-damned-and-blasted-rheumatic gout': WC to William A. Seaver, 6 August 1878, Princeton

367 'unlike the 'big, portentous, heavy' male characters': Eytinge, *The Memoirs of Rose Eytinge*

368 'cooked a Don Pedro pie': Beard, 'Some Recollections'

369 'Wilkie had to chase up payment': WC to Chatto & Windus, 30 December 1878, Princeton

371 'excites and exhausts me': WC to George Bentley, 24 March 1879, Berg

372 'I was mad when I did it': *Standard*, 18 January 1879. For funeral, *Daily News*, 22 January 1879

372 'Wilkie called on Chatto to cost 2000 copies': WC to Andrew Chatto, 21 October 1878, Princeton

373 'mocked his attempt to rewrite': *Sunday Times*, 27 July 1879

373 'All his characters are forced and unnatural': *Saturday Review*, 2 August 1879

374 'He agreed, on condition': WC to James R. Osgood, 18 January 1882

374 'In the published *Recollections*': 'Wilkie Collins's Recollections of Charles Fechter' in K. Field, *Fechter*

399 'Wilkie Collins . . . still lingered': Hawthorne, *Shapes That Pass*

379 'He also stressed the depth of his research': this included reading deeply on poisoners, such as the multiple murderer Anna Maria Zwanziger – as featured in Lady Duff Gordon's 1856 translation of von Feuerbach's *Narrative of Remarkable Criminal Trials*

381 'some tremendous letters from Roman Catholics': WC to Jane Bigelow, 6 September 1881, NYPL

381 'reduced to the 'nastiest drink'': WC to Charles Kent,
     8 January 1882, Princeton

381 'my knees tremble on the stairs': WC to NL, 22 June
     1881, Princeton

381 'I don't remember whether Dante's Hell': WC to William
     Ralston, 20 October 1881, Baylor University

382 'Considerations on the Copyright Question': *International
     Review*, New York, June 1880 and in a pamphlet published
     by Trubner &. Co. that year

382 'Ashmed-Bartlett added': letter to WC, 20 December 1881,
     Watt collection, Berg

383 'The Air and the Audience': written 1881, first published
     1885 by C. Allen Thorndike Rice, publisher and editor in
     chief of the North American Review. Republished as 'The
     Use of Gas in Theatres' in the *Mask*, October 1924, and
     WCSJ, 6 (1986), pp.19–26

383 'declined an invitation to the Savoy's opening': WC to
     Richard D'Oyly Carte, 8 October 1881

384 'What is sometimes rather invidiously called 'censorship':
     quoted Shellard and Nicholson, *The Lord Chamberlain Regrets*

386 'Some critic said "The Woman In White"': WC to FL,
     5 July 1882, Princeton

386 'so mercilessly excited me': WC to William Winter,
     14 January 1883, Princeton

386 'kings of fiction': WC to Paul Hamilton Hayne, 3 May
     1884, Syracuse University

386 'Yesterday, being out for a little walk': WC to NL, 1 March
     1883, Texas

387 'His diet was singular': Reeve, *From Life*

387 'after being serialised in various newspapers': the copy for
     serialisation was set up by the *Liverpool Post* and distributed
     to other outlets

387 'Swinburne's posthumous put-down': A.C. Swinburne,

'Wilkie Collins', *Fortnightly Review*, 1 November 1889, pp.589–99

387 'Benjulia now 'matched' Fosco': WC to William Winter, 3 July 1883, Princeton

387 "a great advance' on The Black Robe': WC to Count Robert de Heussey, 3 November 1882, Princeton

388 'Hawtrey recalled': Charles Hawtrey, *The Truth at Last*, edited by Somerset Maugham, London, Thornton Butterworth, 1924

388 'outrageous improbability of the characters': *The Times*, 11 June 1883

388 'notoriously volatile 'Adelphi audience'': WC to Winter, 3 July 1883, Princeton

388 'a capital little vessel': Wilkie to EP, 1 August 1883

389 'Come – the sooner the better': WC to Harriet Bartley, 11 July 1883, Princeton

389 'misquoted Pope': WC to EP, 1 August 1883, Huntington

389 'thorough salting': WC to William Winter, 5 October 1884, Clarke Collection

389 'turned the colour of a cooked lobster': WC to Paul Hamilton Hayne, 28 January 1885, Private

390 'enough to kill a dozen people': Bancroft, *Empty Chairs*

390 'Collins drink a wineglassful of laudanum': *New York World*, 29 September 1889

390 'in an intellectual rather than visual manner': see Hayter, *Opium and the Romantic Imagination*

390 'Charles Kent was unable to sleep': WC to Charles Kent, 8 August 1884, Fales and 17 August 1884, Princeton

390 'not that he lost confidence': when his friend Pigott was laid low with a cough, Wilkie told him, 'If you could only take opium!': WC to EP, 20 Nov? 1885, Huntington

391 'devilish drugs': WC to Nannie Wynne, 27 November 1885, Private

392   'And if it should turn out': WC to Chatto, 23 March 1887,
       Princeton

392   'The Evil Genius': was dedicated to WHH

393   'would describe Queen Victoria's golden jubilee': WC to
       Mrs Wynne, 25 June 1887, Private

393   'Nobody seems to know': WC to Charles Kent, 11 May
       1886, Texas

394   'the strong impression that your acting': WC to Mary
       Anderson, 6 April 1884, Private

395   'looked forward to a 'conjugal embrace": WC to Nannie
       Wynne, 19 March 1886, Private

395   'excellent friends Opium and Quinine': WC to Nannie
       Wynne, 1 June 1887, Private

395   'not the Christian name of another wife': WC to Nannie
       Wynne, 23 December 1886, Private. Nannie's mother died
       in Monte Carlo in 1898. In 1904 Nannie herself married
       Sir Alexander Lawrence, 4th Baronet and grandson of Lord
       Lawrence, the former Viceroy of India

395   'an exchange with Napoleon Sarony': WC to Napoleon
       Sarony, 19 March 1887, Folger

396   'his 'good genius': WC to A. P. Watt, 6 February 1888,
       Pembroke

396   'The Bartleys are within two doors': WC to Frank Beard,
       26 July 1886, Princeton

397   'Wilkie Collins... has disappeared': WC to Sebastian
       Schlesinger, 26 August 1888, Houghton

397   'Wellington Crescent': this was the parade where Nina
       Lehmann had gone on holidays as a child – and again in
       the 1860s

398   'As for me, I gave up': WC to Alexander Gray, 26 May
       1888, Donald Whitton

398   'Be very careful about draughts': WC to EP, 19 March
       1886, Huntington

398 'That's me, Padrona': WC to to Nina Lehmann, 2 February 1887, Princeton

399 'he acted as a steward': on 25 July, 1888

399 'had recently met at the house': see Eileen Bigland, *Ouida – the Passionate Victorian*, London, Jarrolds, 1950

399 'the English public finds it tedious': quoted in Richard Ellman, *Oscar Wilde*, London, Hamish Hamilton, 1987

400 'her charming little boy': WC to Andrew Chatto, 26 April 1888, Princeton

400 'It will soon become a distinction': WC to Edward Bok, 15 January 1889, Private

400 'Reminiscences of a Story-teller': *Universal Register*, 15 June 1888, p.183

401 'I pick up the literature': 'Books Necessary for a Liberal Education', *Pall Mall Gazette*, 11 February 1886

402 'a very clever book – of its kind': WC to Sebastian Schlesinger, 3 January 1888, Houghton

402 'reading *A Legend of Montrose*': WC to A P Watt, 4 August 1885, Pembroke

403 'still possessed of a table': WC to Hall Caine, 5 February 1888, Manx

404 'I cannot honestly suggest topics': WC to Harriet Bartley, 14 March 1888, Princeton

404 'There is no mews': WC to Tillotson, 30 May 1888, Bolton

404 'If you please, sir': WC to Harry Quilter, 11 April 1888, Huntington

405 'You will very likely receive': WC to Sebastain Schlesinger, 2 May 1889, Houghton.

405 'dumb to the utterance of Love': WC to Sebastian Schlesinger, 27 March 1889, Houghton

406 'a woman who is not to be trifled with': WC to Sebastian Schlesinger, 9 January 1889, Houghton

406   'born diplomatist': WC to A.P. Watt, 7th March 1889, Pembroke

407   'grudgingly forced to accept': WC to Andrew Chatto, 27th March 1889, Reading

407   'It is a terrible shock': Harriet Bartley to Mary Elizabeth Braddon, July 21 1889, Canterbury

407   'with all his old warmth': George Redford to Harriet Bartley, 23 September 1889, Princeton

407   'the task fell to Walter Besant': this was confirmed by Marian, his eldest daughter by Martha, who was acting as his temporary secretary, in a letter to Watt, 26 August 1889

408   'forbidding the hy----': WC to F.C. Beard, 21 September 1889 Princeton. Although this probably meant the hypodermic needle, it could also have referred to hyoscine, which is used as an antimuscarinic or sedative

408   'My news is so sad': Harriet Bartley to Frank Archer, 24 September 1889, Lewis

408   'And so our poor dear genial': NL to Rudolph Lehmann, 25 September 1889, Princeton

409   'several of whose theatrical friends': *Morning Post*, 28 September 1889

410   'a confusion with Wilde's brother Willie': *Sunday Times*, 29 September 1889. Oscar Wilde's presence was denied by Edmund Yates in the pages of *The World*

410   'one newspaper did refer to Mrs Dawson': *New York World*, 29 September 1889

410   'remarkable . . . for his independence of character': *Penny Illustrated Paper*, 19 October 1889

410   'one the kindest': *Pall Mall Gazette*, 24 September 1889

410   'Mr Hall Caine and I are antipathetic': Harriet Bartley to A.P. Watt, 4 October 1889, Berg

410 'the only monument he cared for': see 'The Wilkie Collins Memorial Library' by Andrew Gasson, Wilkie Collins Society, 2004

411 'the mere fact that it is found necessary to "agitate"': *Daily Telegraph*, 5 October 1889

411 '"other considerations"': *The Times*, 26 March 1890

412 'The day was gloomy': *Sydney Morning Herald*, 13 December 1889, quoting *St James's Gazette*

412 'Wilkie's will was proved': 11 November 1889

414 'When may I expect a cheque?': Henry Bartley to George Sharf, Director, National Portrait Gallery, 6 September 1894, NPG

415 'Caroline who died the following month': 14 June 1895. She was buried beside Wilkie in Kensal Green

415 For details of Clow and the Hollow family, see *The Hollow Log*, issue 41, December 2012, p.4 or http://freepages. genealogy.rootsweb.ancestry.com/~chollow/news%2041. pdf

416 'a messy divorce': *The Argus*, 11 August 1899. Joseph Clow married Louisa Maguire in Melbourne on 27 June 1902

416 'survived in Willesden until 1927': although his son predeceased him, his daughter-in-law Ethel lived for a further four decades, before dying in Suffolk in 1969

417 'least posé': Beard, 'Some Recollections'

I have calculated modern equivalents of Victorian monetary values using the site http://www.measuringworth.com/ppoweruk/

BIBLIOGRAPHY

BOOKS BY WILKIE COLLINS

Memoirs of the Life of William Collins, Esq., R. A., 2 vols, London, Longman, Brown, Green and Longman, 1848

Antonina; or, The Fall of Rome, 3 vols, London, Richard Bentley, 1850

Rambles Beyond Railways; or, Notes in Cornwall Taken A-Foot, 1 vol., London, Richard Bentley, 1851

Mr Wray's Cash-Box; or, the Mask and the Mystery, 1 vol., London, Richard Bentley, 1851

Basil: A Story of Modern Life, 3 vols, London, Richard Bentley, 1852

Hide and Seek , 3 vols, London, Richard Bentley, 1854

After Dark, 2 vols, London, Smith, Elder and Company, 1856

The Dead Secret, 2 vols, London, Bradbury & Evans, 1857

The Queen of Hearts, 3 vols, London, Hurst and Blackett, 1859

The Woman in White, 3 vols, London, Sampson Low, Son, & Co., 1860

No Name, 3 vols, London, Sampson Low, Son, & Co., 1862

My Miscellanies, 2 vols, London, Sampson Low, Son, & Co., 1863

Armadale, 2 vols, London, Smith, Elder and Co., 1866

The Moonstone: A Romance, 3 vols, London, Tinsley Brothers, 1868

Man and Wife, 3 vols, London, F. S. Ellis, 1870

Poor Miss Finch: A Novel, 3 vols, London, Richard Bentley and Son, 1872

Miss or Mrs? And Other Stories in Outline, 1 vol., London, Richard Bentley and Son, 1873

The New Magdalen, 2 vols, London, Richard Bentley and Son, 1873

The Frozen Deep and Other Stories, 2 vols, London, Richard Bentley and Son, 1874

The Law and the Lady, 3 vols, London, Chatto and Windus, 1875

The Two Destinies: A Romance, 2 vols, London, Chatto and Windus, 1876

A Rogue's Life: From His Birth to His Marriage, 1 Vol., London, Richard Bentley and Son, 1879

The Fallen Leaves, 3 vols, London, Chatto and Windus, 1879

The Haunted Hotel: A Mystery of Modern Venice to which is added My Lady's Money, 2 vols, London, Chatto and Windus, 1879

Jezebel's Daughter, 3 vols, London, Chatto & Windus, 1880

The Black Robe, 3 vols, London, Chatto & Windus, 1881

Heart and Science: A Story of the Present Time, 3 vols, London, Chatto & Windus, 1883

I Say No, 3 vols, London, Chatto & Windus, 1884

The Evil Genius: A Domestic Story, 3 vols, London, Chatto & Windus, 1886

The Guilty River, 1 vol., Bristol, J. W. Arrowsmith, 1886

Little Novels, 3 vols, London, Chatto and Windus, 1887

The Legacy of Cain, 3 vols, London, Chatto & Windus, 1888

Blind Love, 3 vols, completed by Walter Besant after Collins's death. London, Chatto & Windus, 1890

The Lazy Tour of Two Idle Apprentices, 1 vol. (with Charles Dickens), London, Chapman and Hall, 1890

Iolani, or Tahiti as it was. A Romance. Princeton, Princeton University Press, 1999

KEY COLLECTIONS

Baker, William, Andrew Gasson, Graham Law and Paul Lewis (eds): *The Public Face of Wilkie Collins: The Collected Letters*, 4 vols, London, Pickering & Chatto, 2005. (In addition there are seven booklets of Addenda and Corrigenda, published by the Wilkie Collins Society.)

Baker, William and William M. Clarke (eds): *The Letters of Wilkie Collins*, Basingstoke, Macmillan Press, 1999

House, Madeline, Graham Storey, Kathleen Tillotson et al. (eds): *The Letters of Charles Dickens*, Pilgrim edition, 12 vols, Oxford Clarendon Press, 1965–2002

Thompson, Julian: *Wilkie Collins: The Complete Shorter Fiction*, London, Robinson, 1995

SELECTED REFERENCE WORKS

Ackroyd, Peter: *Wilkie Collins*, London, Chatto & Windus, 2012

Alpin, John (ed.): *The Correspondence and Journals of the Thackeray Family*, London, Pickering and Chatto, 2011

Anderson, Mary: *A Few Memories*, London, Osgood, McIlvaine & Co, 1896

Andres, Sophia: *The Pre-Raphaelite Art of the Victorian Novel*, Columbus, Ohio, Ohio State University Press, 2005

Antrobus Edmund E.: *The Prison and the School*, London, Staunton & Sons, 1853

Antrobus Edmund E.: *Anarchy and Order*, London, Staunton & Sons, 1848

Archer, Frank: *An Actor's Notebooks*, London, Sampson Low, Marston, Searle & Rivington, 1882

Ashley, Robert: *Wilkie Collins*, Arthur Barker, 1952

Ashton, Rosemary: *142 Strand*, London, Jonathan Cape, 2007

Ashton, Rosemary: *G.H. Lewes: A Life*, Oxford, OUP, 1991

Baker, Michael: *The Rise of the Victorian Actor*, London, Croom Helm, 1978

Baker, William: *A Wilkie Collins Chronology*, Basingstoke, Palgrave Macmillan, 2007

Baker, William: *Wilkie Collins' Library: A Reconstruction*, Westwood, Ct., Greenwood Press, 2002

Bancroft, Sir Squire and Lady Marie Effie: *The Bancrofts: Recollections of Sixty Years*, London, John Murray, 1909

Bancroft, Squire: *Empty Chairs*, London, John Murray, 1925

Barlow, Kate: *The Abode of Love*, Edinburgh, Mainstream, 2006

Beard, Nathaniel: 'Some Recollections of Yesterday', Temple Bar, July 1894

Beaton, Richard: 'The World is Hard on Women'; *Women and Marriage in the novels of Wilkie Collins*, thesis for Doctorate of Philosophy at University of Wales, 1987

Bonham-Carter, Victor: *Authors by Profession* (2 vols), Society of Authors, 1978

Bronkhurst, Judith: *William Holman Hunt: A Catalogue Raisonée*, New Haven and London, Yale University Press, 2006

Caine, Hall: *My Story*, London, William Heinemann, 1908

Carnell, Jennifer: *The Literary Lives of Mary Elizabeth Braddon*, Hastings, Sensation Press, 2000

Clarke, Alison Thora: 'The Other Twin: A Study of the Plays of Wilkie Collins', PhD thesis, King's College London, July 2005

Clarke, William: *Rambles around Marylebone*, Wilkie Collins Society, 1974

Clarke, William: *The Secret Life of Wilkie Collins*, London, Allison & Busby, 1988

Cohen, Deborah: *Family Secrets*, London, Viking, 2013

Collins Philip: *Dickens Interviews and Recollections*, London, Macmillan, 1981

Collins, William: *Memoirs of a Picture, containing the adventures of many conspicuous characters... including a genuine biographical sketch of the late George Morland etc.*, London, H.D. Symonds etc., 1805

Cross, Nigel: *The Common Writer*, Cambridge, Cambridge University Press, 1985

Cunningham, Allan: *The Life of Sir David Wilkie*, John Murray, 1843

Dafforne, James: *The Life and Works of Edward Matthew Ward R.A.*, London, Virtue & Co, 1879

Daly, Nicolas: *Sensation and Modernity in the 1860s*, Cambridge, Cambridge University Press, 2009

Davenport, Rowland Ashley: *Albury Apostles*, Birdlip, Gloucestershire, United Writers, 1970

Davis, Nuel Pharr: *The Life of Wilkie Collins*, Urbana, University of Illinois Press, 1956

De Fonblanque, Margaret: 'Edward and Henrietta Ward: Painters and Partners', University of Buckingham, M.A. thesis, 2006

Dixon, William Hepworth: *New America*, London, Hurst and Blackett, 1867

Dixon, William Hepworth: *Spiritual Wives*, London, Hurst and Blackett, 1868

Dormandy, Thomas: *Opium*, London, Yale University Press, 2012

Drummond, Andrew Landale: *Irving and his Circle*, London, J. Clarke & Co, 1937

Ellis, S.M.: *Wilkie Collins, Le Fanu, and Others*, London, Constable, 1931

Eytinge, Rose: *The Memories of Rose Eytinge*, New York, Frederick A. Stokes Co., 1905

Fagence Cooper, Suzanne: *The Model Wife*, London, Duckworth, Overlook, 2010

Field, K[ate]: *Charles Albert Fechter*, Boston, James R. Osgood, 1882

Finn, Margot, Michael Lobban and Jenny Bourne Taylor (eds): *Legitimacy and illegitimacy in 19th-century law, literature and history*, Basingstoke, Palgrave Macmillan, 2010

Flanders, Judith: *The Invention of Murder*, London, HarperPress, 2011

Fleming, G.H.: *John Everett Millais*, Constable, 1998

Forster, John: *The Life of Charles Dickens*, 3 vols, London, Cecil Palmer, 1872–4

Gasson, Andrew: *Wilkie Collins: An Illustrated Guide*, Oxford, Oxford University Press, 1998

Gasson, Andrew and Radcliffe, Caroline (eds): *Wilkie Collins: The Lighthouse*, London, Francis Boutle and Wilkie Collins Society, 2013

Gilbert, Pamela K.: *A Companion to Sensation Fiction*, Oxford, Blackwell, 2011

Griffin, Ben: *The Politics of Genders in Victorian Britain: Masculinity, Political Culture and the Struggle for Women's Rights*, Cambridge, CUP, 2012

Hanes, Susan R.: *Wilkie Collins's American Tour, 1873–4*, London, Pickering and Chatto, 2008

Hawksley, Lucinda: *Katey*, London, Doubleday, 2006

Hawthorne, Julian: *Shapes That Pass – Memories of Old Days*, Boston, Houghton Mifflin, 1928

Hayter, Alethea: *Opium and the Romantic Imagination*, London, Faber, 1971

Higgins, David: *The Winterton Story*, King's Lynn, Phoenix Publications, 2009

Hogarth, Georgina and Mamie Dickens: *The Letters of Charles Dickens. Edited by his sister-in-law and his eldest daughter*, London, Chapman Hall, 1880

Holmes, Richard: *Coleridge: Early Visions*, London, Hodder and Stoughton, 1989, and *Coleridge Darker Reflections*, HarperCollins, 1998

Hoppen, Theodore: *The Mid-Victorian Generation*, Oxford, Clarendon Press, 1998

Hudson, Derek (ed.): *Munby, man of two worlds: the life and diaries of Arthur J. Munby, 1828–1910*, London, John Murray, 1972

Hunt, W. Holman: *Pre-Raphaelitism and the Pre-Raphaelite Brotherhood*, London, Macmillan, 1905

Huxley, Leonard: *The House of Smith, Elder*, London, William Clowes, 1923

Klimaszewski, Melisa: *Brief Lives: Wilkie Collins*, London, Hesperus Press, 2011

Law, Graham and Maunder, Andrew: *Wilkie Collins: A Literary Life*, Basingstoke, Palgrave Macmillan, 2008

Lehmann, John: *Ancestors and Friends*, London, Eyre & Spottiswoode, 1962

Lehmann, R.C.: *Memories of Half a Century*, London, Smith, Elder, 1908

Lehmann, Rudolf: *An Artist's Reminiscences*, London, Smith, Elder, 1894

Lehmann, Rudolph (ed.): *Familiar Letters NL to FL 1864–1867*, Privately published, 1892

Lewes, George Henry: *The Letters of George Henry Lewes*, (ed. William Baker), Victoria B.C., English Literary Studies, University of Victoria, 1995–9

Lonoff, Sue: *Wilkie Collins and his Victorian Readers*, New York, AMS Press, 1982

Lycett, Andrew: *Conan Doyle: The Man Who Created Sherlock Holmes*, London, Weidenfeld & Nicolson, 2007

Maas, Jeremy: *The Victorian Art World in Photographs*, London, Barrie & Jenkins, 1984

Mangham, Andrew (ed.): *Wilkie Collins; Interdisciplinary Essays*, Newcastle, Cambridge Scholars, 2007

Marsh, Jan: *Dante Gabriel Rossetti: Painter and Poet*, London, Weidenfeld & Nicolson, 1999

Marsh, Jan: *The Pre-Raphaelites: Their Lives in Letters and Diaries*, London, Collins & Brown, 1996

Mayhew, Henry: *London Labour and the London Poor*, a selected edition by Robert Douglas Fairhurst, Oxford, Oxford University Press, 2010

McCorristine, Shane: *Spectres of the Self: thinking about ghosts and ghost-seeing in England, 1750–1920*, Cambridge, Cambridge University Press, 2010

Millais, John Guille: *The Life and Letters of Sir John Everett Millais*, London, Methuen, 1899

Miller, D.A.: *The Novel and the Police*, Berkeley, University of California Press, 1988

Mitchell, Sally: *Frances Power Cobbe: Victorian Feminist, Journalist, Reformer*, Charlottesville and London, University of Virginia Press, 2004

O'Gorman, Francis (ed.): *The Cambridge Companion to Victorian Culture*, Cambridge, Cambridge University Press, 2010

Page, Norman ed.: *Wilkie Collins: The Critical Heritage*, London, Routledge, 1974

Peters, Catherine: *The King of Inventors: A Life of Wilkie Collins*, London, Secker & Warburg, 1991

Pope, William Bissell (ed.): *The Diary of Benjamin Robert Haydon*, Cambridge, Massachussets, Harvard University Press, 1963

Pykett, Lyn: *Wilkie Collins*, Oxford, OUP, 2005

Quilter, Harry: *Opinions on Men, Women & Things*, London, Swan Sonnenschein, 1909

Quilter, Harry: *Preferences in Life, Literature and Art*, London, Swan Sonnenschein, 1892

Rance, Nicholas: *Wilkie Collins and Other Sensation Novelists*, Basingstoke, Macmillian 1991

Reeve, Wybert: *From Life*, Melbourne, George Robertson, 1891

Reeve, Wybert: 'Recollections of Wilkie Collins', Chambers's Journal, 9 June 1906, pp.458–61

Robinson, Kenneth: *Wilkie Collins: A Biography*, London, Bodley Head, 1951

Robson, John M.: *Marriage or Celibacy? The Daily Telegraph on a Victorian Dilemma*, Toronto, University of Toronto Press, 1995

Russell, Lady Constance: *Swallowfield and its Owners*, London, Longmans Green, 1901

Sayers, Dorothy: *Wilkie Collins: A Critical and Biographical Study*, edited by E.R. Gregory, Toledo, Ohio, Friends of the University Library, 1977

Scott, J.D.: *Vickers, A History*, London, Weidenfeld & Nicolson, 1962

Shellard, Dominic and Steve Nicholson with Miriam Handley: *The Lord Chamberlain Regrets: A History of British Theatre Censorship*, London British Library, 2004

Showalter, Elaine: *The Female Malady*, London, Virago, 1987

Shpayer-Makov, Haia: *The Ascent of the Detective*, Oxford, OUP, 2011

Slater, Michael: *Charles Dickens*, New Haven and London, Yale University Press, 2009

Slater, Michael: *The Great Charles Dickens Scandal*, New Haven and London Yale, University Press, 2012

Smajic, Srdjan: *Ghost-Seers, Detectives and Spiritualists*, Cambridge, Cambridge University Press, 2010

Storey, Gladys: *Dickens and Daughter*, London, Frederick Muller, 1939

Story, Alfred T.: *The Life of John Linnell*, London, Richard Bentley, 1892

Summerscale, Kate: *The Suspicions of Mr Whicher*, London, Bloomsbury, 2008

Sutherland, John: *Victorian Fiction: Writers, Publishers and Readers*, London, Macmillan Press, 1995

Sutherland, John: *Victorian Novelists and Publishers*, London, Athlone Press, 1976

Sweet, Matthew: *Inventing the Victorians*, London, Faber and Faber, 2001

Taylor, Jenny Bourne: *In the Secret Theatre of Home*, London, Routledge, 1988

Taylor, Jenny Bourne ed.: *The Cambridge Companion to Wilkie Collins*, Cambridge, Cambridge University Press, 2006

Taylor, Tom: *The Life of Benjamin Haydon*, London, Longman, Brown, Green and Longmans, 1853

Thirlwell, Angela: *Into the Frame*, London, Chatto and Windus, 2010

Tomalin, Clare: *The Invisible Woman*, London, Viking, 1990

Tomalin, Clare: *Charles Dickens A Life*, London, Viking, 2011

Tromans, Nicholas: *David Wilkie*, London, Dulwich Picture Gallery, 2002

Walford, Lucy Bethia, *Memories of Victorian London*, London, Edward Arnold, 1912

Walton, Susan: 'From Squlaid Impropriety to Manly Respectablity', *Nineteenth-Century Contexts* v30, no. 3, September 2008, pp.229–45

Ward, Leslie: *Forty Years of Spy*, London: Chatto and Windus, 1915

Ward, Mrs E.M.: *Mrs E.M. Ward's Reminiscences*, (ed. Elliott O'Donnell) London, Sir Isaac Pitman, 1911

Ward, Mrs E.M.: *Memories of Ninety Years*, London, Hutchinson, 1924

Whitton, Donald C.: *The Grays of Salisbury*, San Francisco, 1976

Williams, Merryn: *Effie – A Victorian Scandal*, Book Guild, 2010

Winter, William: *Old Friends*, New York, Moffat, Yard & Company, 1905

Wise, Sarah: *Inconvenient People*, London, Bodley Head, 2012

Wright, Natalia (ed.): *The Correspondence of Washington Allston*, Kentucky, The University Press, 1993

Yates, Edmund: *Celebrities At Home*, London, The World, 1879

In addition there are several small, but useful, publications from the Wilkie Collins Society, some of which are referred to in the Notes section.

ACKNOWLEDGEMENTS

I AM GREATLY indebted to Faith Clarke, Wilkie Collins's great-granddaughter for her support and encouragement, and for her kind permission to quote from Wilkie Collins's works and letters. I would also like to thank her late husband, William Clarke, who himself wrote a fine biography of Wilkie Collins and who pointed me on my way at the start of my own efforts.

In the field of Wilkie Collins studies, there are two additional people who a) know more about the author than anyone else and b) are incredibly generous with their time and resources. I am extremely grateful to Andrew Gasson and Paul Lewis for the help and guidance they have freely given me at every juncture. I could not have written my book without them. They both run excellent websites http://www.wilkie-collins.info/ and http://www.paullewis.co.uk/ There are many acts of kindness that they showed, but I would particularly like to thank Andrew and Paul for granting me access to an invaluable asset: an electronic edition of the *Collected Letters* of Wilkie Collins which they compiled with their fellow editors William Baker and Graham Law (see Bibliography).

Two other members of Wilkie's wider family were also unfailingly helpful: Donald Whitton in California and Jeanette Iredale in Australia. They have both helped with documents, photographs and ideas.

I would like to thank the people who read various versions

of my text and assisted me with their comments: Katrin Williams, Charlotte Rogers, Sam Hudson, Nigel Cross and Angela Richardson (as well as Paul Lewis and Andrew Gasson). Sue Greenhill's love and support have kept me going throughout.

Various people have kindly provided me with material from their archives. I am grateful in this context to Susan Hanes, Margaret de Fonblanque, Michael de Navarro and Guy Philipps (Lord Milford).

Any biographer benefits from the input of experts and other interested people at all stages. Among those who have given me excellent information and advice have been Mary Lovell, Judith Flanders, David Higgins, John Pym, Tish Seligman, Nigel Pope, Penny Smyth-Pigott, Kate Barlow, Jane Root, Catherine Wynne, John Pym, William Baker, The Rev. Aidan Platten, Richard Vowles, Richard Lawrence, Paul Spencer-Longhurst, Jonathan Ouvry, Colin Davies and Mary Ellen Lane.

As before, in moments of crisis, Andrew Holmes has generously offered me the benefit of his unrivalled computer knowledge.

This book has involved me spending a great deal of time in libraries and archives. My thanks to various institutions and libraries which have helped me along the way: Bodleian Library (Colin Harris), National Library of Scotland (Rachel Beattie, Donald McClay), British Library (Jamie Andrews), Mitchell Library, Glasgow (Enda Ryan), Huntington Library (Gayle Richardson, Jacqueline Dugas), Morgan Library (Inge Dupont, Carolyn Vega and Maria Molestina), Harry Ransom Center (Molly Schwarzberg, Pat Fox and W. Roger Louis), Firestone Library at Princeton University (Gabriel Swift), University of Toledo (Barbara L. Floyd), University of Cape Town (Tanya Barden and Lesley Hart), Pennsylvania State University Eberly Family Special Collections Library (Sandra Stelts), King's School Canterbury (Peter Henderson), Getty Research Institute

(Jeanette Clough), Canterbury Christ Church University (Carolyn Oulton, Gabrielle Malcolm, Kathy Chaney, Andrew Hudson), Coutts Bank (Tracey Earl), Royal Academy (Mark Pomeroy), Tate Gallery (Adrian Glew), Lincoln's Inn (Jo Hutchings, Guy Holborn), Yale University (Tim Young), Southampton City Council (Joanne Smith, Penny Rudkin), Portsmouth History Centre (Dr John Stedman), London Library (Helen O'Neill), Garrick Club (Marcus Risdell), Charles Dickens Museum (Fiona Jenkins), Pembroke College Cambridge (Patricia Aske), Royal Academy (Mark Pomeroy), Gloucestershire Archives (Paul Evans), Wellcome Library, National Portrait Gallery, the National Art Library and the National Archives.

I would like to thank the Society of Authors for making me a grant through the Authors' Foundation, which enabled me to carry out research in some American university libraries.

Two additional websites that have been useful are Andrew Roberts's magnificent online work on the Lunacy Commission, http://studymore.org.uk/01.htm and the Victorian Web, http://www.victorianweb.org/

Working with my editor Sarah Rigby has been both a pleasure and a privilege. My thanks are due too to Jocasta Hamilton, Philippa Cotton and the rest of the team at Hutchinson and Random House. In addition I am very grateful to Jamie Whyte for his map and to Douglas Matthews for compiling an excellent index.

For further information, please refer to my website, www.andrewlycett.co.uk

INDEX

Works by Wilkie Collins (WC) appear directly under title; works by others under the author's name